The
WILD RANTING
OF A
MAD WOMAN

The
WILD RANTING
OF A
MAD WOMAN

By Rose Bush

Strategic Book Group
Durham, Connecticut

Strategic Book Group
P. O. Box 333
Durham, CT 06422
http://www.strategicbookclub.com

ISBN: 978-1-60976-311-4

Book Design by Julius Kiskis

Printed in the United States of America
18 17 16 15 14 13 12 11 10   1 2 3 4 5

Dedication

"I dedicate this book to all the teachers I have met on my
journey through life, to all those I have yet to meet and to the most
loving and eccentric life scholar ever to bless my life:
David Bradford, my Father."

In gratitude,
Rose Bush

Contents

Preface..ix

1. The Bit Where I Rant About Labels 1

2. The Bit Where I   Rant About Visulation 41

3. The Bit Where I Rant About Truth 55

4. The Bit Where I Rant About Parents and Children 80

5. The Bit Where I   Rant About Relationships 167

6. The Bit Where I Rant About Sex..236

7. The Bit Where I   Rant About Religion.......................................258

8. The Bit Where I   Rant About Food.. 357

9. Cease Ranting 429

The reason I have written this book

A few weeks ago, I was asked by an organisation I have worked with for over five years, to be a tutor for a young Asian girls' group. The topic they wished me to focus on, over a four-week period, was 'confidence.' I agreed and decided what kind of format would give these young women the best guidance. While I was thinking about it, I remembered being their age, early teens, and in that mixed up place, where every time I felt powerful inside myself, somehow the authority would be removed, and yet desiring, almost passionately, to *feel* powerful, liberated and free.

There was a 'rule book' that meant everything and everyone had their place and, if anyone or anything stepped outside the limits, their life would be ruined and their family devastated. Life was a constant round of 'self-talk,' chatting to myself about which words to allow out of my mouth, rehearsing imagined arguments with my 'elders and betters,' where I was victorious and they understood how capable I really was. Sometimes I would stand in front of a mirror and practice different 'faces,' occasionally pleading for mercy and other times, being authoritative and strong. I never followed my self-talk through, or performed the rehearsed arguments.

As I thought about my teenage years, I reflected deeply on how much I had grown since those times. Looking back at my own development made me aware of how the outcome could have been so different, if I had known then, what I know now.

So, after much consideration, the format was clear. I would take the young women on an introspective journey and give them some of the knowledge that it has taken me my whole lifetime to experience. I would open their eyes to visualisation, dreams and goals, the way we use language, and the power of their subconscious minds. It would clarify how they see the world consciously, and build skills to change their personal histories and learn from their journeys.

The first week, seven students arrived and, along with two older 'assistants,' we began our expedition. Slowly, slowly the ice started to melt and a real sense of friendship, sisterhood and interest began to develop. To emphasise certain points, I would reflect on my own life experiences to provide a clearer understanding of my meaning. By the end of the first session I felt elated and energised. The second week proved even more empowering than the first, and the group really got involved in all we were discussing.

One of the young women had been biting her fingernails for years and, the previous week, I had given her some tips on how to break the habit. When I asked to see her nails, she smiled proudly saying that she had only bitten them a couple of times over the week. It was wonderful to see her smile and to acknowledge that she was in control of her life, that she had taken the power to break this habit. Amazing!

When it was time for the second session to end, a couple of the young women said how they loved the group and wanted more sessions and one begged me to sort it out. I told them that it was they who had to ask, as it was their group and, that if they managed to get an agreement from the centre, then I would be more than happy to continue.

I was feeling so thrilled, so joyous and so inspired that this group of young teenagers really wanted to take control of their emotions, power and ultimately, their existence on this planet; to live *their* lives. Even the assistants were getting involved and participating in the tasks. One even asked if I could hypnotise her, and we agreed to meet up after the following week's session. I was so happy about the whole thing and couldn't wait until Wednesday, when the group would meet again.

On Friday, I got a call from the Centre Manager who had set up the group, asking if we could meet either that day or Monday. When

I asked her what it was about, she replied that it was to do with the group at the centre. I agreed to meet her at my home on Monday and thought to myself that maybe the young women had managed to get their voices heard, and that extra sessions were going to be agreed. It gave me a real buzz all weekend and I kept thinking of all the things we could experience over the extra sessions.

On Monday I was really looking forward to the meeting, I just kept smiling. I sang songs and felt really wonderful. The meeting didn't go as well as I had expected, in fact, the very reverse happened. The Centre Manager informed me that the girls had really enjoyed the group and wanted extra sessions, and that the staff at the centre were really happy about that, but the thing was, their *parents* weren't happy. Two of the mothers had said their daughters would not be returning; a few days later another did the same. Their mothers did not like some of the words I had used during the sessions and even though the assistants had tried to defend me, saying how the words were used in context, it didn't matter. The course was cancelled.

The irony of the whole thing is that the centre is meant to be a women's empowerment centre! So, this book is for all those young women who want to understand how to take control of *their* lives and for all those others out there who *know* that there is much more to life than this!

The Bit Where I Rant About...
Labels

For years, I haven't really understood exactly what a 'label' is. I use to think that it was something attached to something else, like a tag on a carton of strawberries, which tells you that this box contains strawberries. And that is strange really, because when I look at the strawberries I already know what they are, yet I still read the tag!

Why is that?

Some of you may say that the tag is there to give us more information about the strawberries, like whether they are organic or not and where they come from, and, for the most part that would be a true assumption to make. But in reading that they are organic, what does that tell us? Well, your guess is as good as mine! It should mean a whole list of things, but most of us don't know what the hell those things are. And what difference does it make what country they were grown in?

Why are we given that information and once we are informed, is there a significant message behind it? For example, if the fruit is grown in Scotland does this mean it is preferable to those grown in Canada, or the other way round? I mean Canada is a pretty big place and I am sure that there are some wonderful strawberry fields there, and some fairly disgusting ones too, and the same goes for Scotland. So what exactly is the point in telling me where they are from?

Some of you might say that if the strawberries are from Canada, then they may not be as fresh as those from Scotland, but neither you nor I have any knowledge of when the fruit was harvested, or whether

1

it has been chilled to keep it 'fresher,' or injected with a substance to lengthen its shelf life. So, why have the information on the label? More importantly, what difference does knowing where it's from actually make to the taste? Personally, I think the best way to judge that, is to eat it!

Labels contain all kinds of hidden messages, some of which we can see and some we can't and we all interpret them differently, which is kind of amazing really, yet we all have a basic idea of what the other person means, when he or she is describing something.

*   *   *

Have you ever noticed how reading a tag on something leads to another label, and then another? For example, if I went out to buy a pair of jeans and saw some that I really liked, tried them on and they were a little tight, I might look at the label and if it said 'size 14,' I would suddenly find my mind bombarded by other kind of labels that I might attach to 'size 14.' If these thoughts are negative, such as "I can't believe I'm *too fat* for a 14," or "I have never been this *huge* before" then the chances are, that no matter how much I liked them, I would not purchase the next size up. If, however, the comments were positive, like "Wow, I'll soon be *slim* enough for a size 14," or, "Fantastic, I'm *looking really good*," then it's likely that I would buy them. The person who felt negative about the jeans will probably let it eat away at them for the next few hours, feeling self-conscious about their size and depriving themselves of coffee and cakes with friends. The ones who felt positive will continue to feel great, and most probably strut about with new-found confidence. So, we need to be aware of exactly what else labels are *telling* us, as often there is much hidden within an apparently simple tag.

It is so easy for us to hide behind the labels that society and our families stick all over us, and also the ones we cover ourselves with, which deflect responsibility for our lives onto other individuals, or events, or moments in history.

When we store information about our experiences, we do so in a way that best suits ourselves, so that when we are relating our experiences to others, they will come at it from as close to our own remembered reality as possible. And to emphasise the emotions or feelings we wish to evoke in the listener, we will check out that they understand *our* experiences by getting them to look at parallels in *their own* understanding. We use phrases like "Do you know what I mean?" and "How do you think I felt when I heard that?" It is almost as if we have to acknowledge that we are not alone with our feelings and emotions, and if that is true, then the way we react, or act, in a certain situation, is in the same manner as another person may have done. It gives our behaviour some kind of validation or justification.

Labels can be confusing and disturbing! And the weird thing is, they don't need to be, we just rarely use labels in a positive way. To emphasise this point, test yourself out.

Think about a friend or colleague that you get on well with. Jot down a few thoughts about them, either in your mind (if you are good at visualisation), or on a piece of paper, if it is easier. Now, as you write down, or visualise, your thoughts, pay particular attention to how you are feeling emotionally. I also want you to become aware of colour, just let it drift into your mind. Focus on how that colour makes you feel. Now, just drift with those feelings and emotions.

Do you have a smile on your face? Are you 'hugging' yourself? What are you saying with your body language? My guess is that you will be feeling warm and content. Now clear the thoughts from your mind by thinking of something totally different. What are you going to wear tomorrow? When are you next going on holiday?

Now I want you to think about someone you don't really like, maybe someone who makes you feel down, just by being in the same room. Again, bring them into your mind's eye and jot down some thoughts about them. What are you feeling emotionally and physically as you think about them? What colour comes to mind? Focus on how that colour makes you feel. Now, just let yourself drift with those feelings and emotions. What are you saying this time with your body language?

Now clear the thoughts from your mind by thinking of the last person you gave a gift to. Why did you give it to them and who will be the next person you give a gift to?

Now, the chances are that when you thought about the person you don't like much, your emotions and feelings were stronger and you probably wrote more negative comments about them, than the positive comments you wrote about the person you like.

It is the same when we apply labels to ourselves. If I asked you to stand naked in front of a full-length mirror, would you be happy to do it? And of those of you who agreed, stripped naked, and actually did it, how many of you would fold your arms across your body, or drape them in front of your 'naughty/dirty/sexual' bits? Well, I am not going to ask you to do it right now, but I hope that by the end of this book, you have the self-belief to do it for real. For now, we are just going to visualise doing it. So, I want you to think about being in a safe, secluded room all by yourself. In front of you is a full length, Victorian-style mirror, which has three faces to enable you to see yourself from all angles.

I want you to visualise removing your clothing and placing it on a matching chaise longue, which is on your right. As you remove each item of clothing, I want you to stand in front of the mirror and take a good look at yourself. What words come into your mind with each layer of clothing you remove? What colours drift into your mind?

Continue to do this until you have removed all of your clothing and are standing naked. Now take a good look at your body language.

How many of you saw yourself as perfect? Chances are that most of us will see ourselves as being too thin, too fat, too short, too tall, too spotty, too wrinkled, too plain or just too damn ugly.

Once we begin to apply these labels, we begin to believe them and start to act like the label. So, like the majority of us who look at ourselves and see faults, the hidden power of the tag will kick in, and we will actually *believe* that we are less than perfect.

Why is that? And how does it make you feel inside? Uncomfortable maybe, not good enough or possibly wishing you had been born someone else, living your life through their supposedly perfect body? What, or who is it that we measure ourselves against? And, as virtually all of us do this, then aren't we making the rest of mankind feel bad too and, if that's the case, why do we continue to do it?

No one on this earth should ever feel inadequate or insecure or less than anyone else, yet in our own deluded sense of reality, by comparing ourselves to those who we believe, for whatever reason, are better than us, we are continuing with the illusion. You are perfect just the way you are and, right now, this is just the way you should be. Yet in this moment you have so many choices and opportunities to direct your life the way you want it to go. It is no good to point the finger of blame at other people, you are the way you think yourself to be, but the trouble is that we often confuse that with the way we have already been labelled by society.

*   *   *

Where do we get the information that informs our opinions and beliefs about who the beautiful people are? Well, I guess it starts when we are not yet old enough to speak. We are told stories about beautiful princesses and handsome knights and, somehow, we are made to feel inadequate next to them, not instantly, but over time. Not only are they extraordinarily striking, they are also kind-hearted, valiant, courageous, and loved by one and all. Now, as a child you may well believe that you, too, hold matching characteristics. I mean when I was young, I could see myself as Snow White…Well, for a short while anyway, until I realised that when I sang, the animals didn't land on my perfectly formed fingers, or carry my dirty dishes out to the kitchen and wash them. Then, little by little, you realise that you have very little in common at all, yet she, for the briefest of moments, is who you believe that you could be.

*   *   *

So, what happens next? Well, once you get over the shock of realising that you are never going to be a beautiful princess or valiant knight, you begin to measure yourself against the other mere mortals that inhabit your world. Sometimes siblings or school friends or maybe the children of neighbours, or cousins, or whoever happens to walk down your street, and the outcome is always the same – you lose. Even if the other person, in your perception, is not as good as you, you have still lost because you are perpetuating the myth. You have become enmeshed in a game full of losers, which takes your time, money, self-esteem and confidence, and gives you but a moment of glory along the way, rather than a lifetime of happiness.

Throughout our lives we are taught to compete, even those who say they are not competitive are forced to engage and it is all done with labels. How can you escape from this dilemma that robs you of so much? Well, you can begin by saying "I'm not playing any more," that is as good a place as any. Start to learn exactly how you are programmed so that you can change the software within yourself.

We are all magnificent human beings and I believe we are made up of three very distinct parts. The first part is the 'humanbot.' This is the physical part of our being that is present to experience this existence through a physical five-sense reality. Some humanbots will have access to more than five senses, and some to less, but for the most part the majority of humanbots have access at this point in time to five senses.

At birth, a humanbot has no idea that it is a separate being or babybot, it has no concept of an identity; it just *is*. Yet it will learn its identity through the rest of society and value itself accordingly. Sometimes, before it is even born, it will be allotted a gender label and shortly after birth it will have a little tag tied to its cot, informing the world of its gender, family name, weight, length, head circumference, and what milk it is drinking. From that point on, the labels will come thick and fast.

This will continue for the rest of the humanbot's life, until it is a living, walking, talking personification of all the labels that are plastered all over it. Before it even realises that it will never be the beautiful princess or courageous knight, it will have begun to identify with most of the tags and so our humanbot now forms a personality, one that is constantly reinforced by the way the rest of society communicates with it, and vice versa.

However, like all good fairy tales, help is at hand. We all have a fairy godmother (FG) nestling inside us. We are aware that she exists as we often have conversations (even if we are led to believe that those who talk to themselves are mad). FG is benevolent and always wants to make our desires come true and she has access to all the data that we have stored in our humanbot. FG can access this information in zillionths of a second, sometimes before we have even had a thought. FG has no concept of time, of what is the past or present, or of the words 'want' and 'don't want.' FG takes all of our experiences of life and all of the labels and stores them as 'movies' in databanks and she will use the same to give you exactly what you wish for.

So, if you think to yourself, "I don't want to be late for work", FG will hear you wish "late for work" and will zoom back through your memory banks and find ways to make you late for work because she wants to make you happy. If, however, you say to yourself (FG = your inner self) "I want to get to work with time to spare," FG will grant your wish by providing you with the data to achieve that, as she 'hears' the command "get to work with time to spare." It is all quite simple really; you just need to understand *how* to communicate with FG.

There is also another part to your amazing self and that is the wisdom and wonder of all that is. Every single one of us is part of this magnificent whole and everything we do has an effect on it, no matter how insignificant we think our actions might be. So, this means that even though we perceive ourselves to be separate, we are in fact whole. Isn't that amazing! You and me and the whole world are really one being, so that when you attempt to hurt another humanbot all you are really doing is hurting yourself. You might not notice it right away; you may believe that you don't actually observe it at all, but "the truth will out," eventually.

Have you ever had one of those 'guilty' moments when you have remembered something that you have done or said to another person, and you feel a wave of revulsion at your words or actions? Or have you felt angry about the way someone has treated you, yet it was all right for you to behave in exactly the same manner to another individual, only moments before?

We throw labels around like there is no tomorrow, calling people all kinds of names, yet we get upset when someone bats one back. The sad thing here is that most of the labels we throw out are negative and, even though we intend for them to 'hurt' someone else, as we will find out, that is only possible if they *allow themselves* to get hurt. So, who does end up on the receiving end of the negativity? Surprisingly, it's you. In generating the disapproval within yourself, you are creating a whole series of physiological changes that occur inside your own body and can have instantaneous effects in some cases, and long-term consequences in most cases.

Even something as simple as driving to town has become fraught these days, like some kind of manic competition between you and the rest of the world. Imagine you are in your car driving to wherever and the rush hour traffic is, ironically, moving at its usual snail's pace. You knew that you should have left earlier but you misplaced your keys, causing you to spend another twenty minutes searching before finding them in your pocket. You remember thinking to yourself the previous evening, "I mustn't lose my keys," and don't quite understand how it is that whenever you say this, you can never find them, even though you put them somewhere safe in an attempt to avoid this situation.

Due to the search for the keys, you did not have time for your breakfast and so, with a rumbling tummy and your mind drifting to images of tea and toast, you jump into the car. Now, FG knows that you *want* to be late for whatever appointment you have, as you repeatedly thought "I mustn't *be late*…I mustn't *be late.*" So, intent on making your wish come true, FG will distract you with images of wonderful food, so that you forget your mobile, which you realise just as you are about to drive off. So, it's back to the house with all the locking and unlocking of doors and then, hurriedly, back to the car.

You join the slow moving traffic and become irritated by the driver in front who leaves a gap of at least two car lengths between his car and the one in front of him, and for some reason this really begins to frustrate you, and you begin to tap your fingers on the steering wheel in agitation. Then he lets someone pull in front of him from a side junction and you raise your hands in disbelief at his total thoughtlessness. Doesn't he realise you are late?

When you approach the traffic lights, they turn amber and he brakes, which makes your blood boil because, in your mind, if he had just put his foot down maybe both of you would have got through. As the lights turn green the road ahead is blocked by traffic feeding in from the opposite direction. This makes you even madder, as they should have stopped at the lights and not blocked up the junction, so you slam your hands on the steering wheel and begin to swear.

Finally, the traffic starts to move but not before the guy in front allows yet another car to slip in ahead of him and this, for you, is the final straw so you swerve out, almost hitting a motorcyclist that, in your anger, you didn't notice, and pull up almost level with the driver in front.

You look at him with daggers and then mouth an expletive before attempting to overtake and pull in front of him. Sadly, this doesn't work and you have now blocked the lane of oncoming cars and they are all pretty pissed off at you, many honking their horns or shouting abuse. One driver is particularly vocal, screaming that "you shouldn't be allowed on the road," and you become so incensed that the anger is directed at you, rather than the guy in front who, after all, is the cause of all the chaos. So then you exchange some non-verbal communication, like sticking up a single finger, and follow it through with other comments like, "Hey, asshole, next year ask Santa for some driving lessons, you moron."

By the time you get to where you are meant to be going, you are stressed to the max and start your working day by justifying to yourself and others about what a dreadful journey you had and how the world is full of idiots who don't understand basic road courtesy. The thing is, FG has achieved her objective and you are well and truly late, not to mention hungry and upset. It doesn't occur to you to look within yourself to see exactly *why* you were late, or to understand that the responsibility lies solely with how you communicate with FG, meaning, *yourself.*

So, unaware that you yourself are to blame for arriving late, you struggle for justification that it was, in fact, someone else's fault. Within a few minutes you will have found a co-conspirator who will utter words such as, "Oh, I know, I know… a similar thing happened to me the other day. People are just so rude these days."

And the lesson that you have learnt is that you just keep on throwing out negativity and blaming everyone else in the world for *your* stress and trauma. The sad thing is that at some point, during all the name calling and labelling that took place during your journey, some of those labels will have attached themselves to you and you may quietly question your driving abilities, or whether you acted reasonably, or not. It may just be a fleeting thought, but the fact that it raised its head, albeit very slightly, means that on some level the insults and labels join the thousands of other negative statements about you, that are stored within.

Now, think about the way you live each day and the things that you say to yourself and the negative labels that others attach to you. Even though we are focussing on your life, I want you to really direct your attention to the way that *you* communicate with others. How often do you speak to people in a positive manner and genuinely mean what you are saying? You need to be honest here and think about members of your family, your partner, colleagues and friends.

For one day each week, I would like you to begin to have a positive labelling day. I want you to start the positive labelling day the moment you open your eyes and begin to wake up. Before you say a single word to anyone, I want you to tell yourself that today is going to be a wonderful day and that you are going to achieve everything that you set out to do. To reinforce this message, I would like you to say at least three positive affirmations to yourself. These could be anything so long as the words *are* positive. Here are some ideas:

- I am strong and confident
- I am looking forward to all the beneficial challenges of the day
- I am a positive influence in my place of work

* * *

Whatever you decide to say is up to you; just make sure that you say the words clearly and with total belief. Give your body a good start with a refreshing shower, drink some pure water and provide your body with some nourishment that is good for it. Don't feed yourself shit food, because if you do, then that's all you are going to get from it... shit. No other benefit.

Plan ahead, so that you are taking control of the day, rather than the day taking control of you. If your time cannot be organised for some reason, then take as much control as you can by planning lunch breaks, or coffee breaks ahead of time, and actually use them to relax and recharge your batteries.

Before you leave for work, take one minute to visualise something that makes you think of tranquility or peace. You may want to focus on a meadow full of wild flowers, or a waterfall, or even an isolated beach. I personally always focus on a beautiful yellow rose. Once you have the image in your mind, make it brighter, clearer and sharper. Enhance the colours and add any sounds or smells that make the image more real. Now, at any time during the day when you need to change your state of mind, for example, if you are beginning to feel stressed, or tired, just bring up the image and focus on it for at least one minute. If you find visualising difficult, then put a picture of the object, person or place in your pocket, or on your mobile, and use that instead.

Again, it could be a snapshot of a particular holiday that fills you with happy memories, or an inspiring poem or even a page from a magazine that brings positive thoughts to mind. If any negative thoughts, or labels, rear their ugly heads, don't allow them to take shape in your mind. Take control by bringing your particular 'peace and tranquility' image into your mind. I want you to think about the way *you* label people and on one day of the week, decide that you are not going to throw negative labels at anyone, and that means everyone, including the asshole that tries to cut you up!

At the end of the day, I want you to take a couple of moments to sit quietly even if this means going into the bathroom and locking the door, and review the positive aspects of the day and congratulate yourself on remaining in control. Finally, thank your FG for bringing all the resources you needed to make it work.

Thanking ourselves is something that we don't do enough. If you smile, rather than call someone a moron, then thank yourself for it. If you allow someone to go ahead of you on a busy road and you smile at him or her, rather than mutter an expletive, thank yourself. If you hold a door open for someone, rather than rushing through and letting it close in their face, thank yourself. If you got through all of your tasks, rather than procrastinating, thank yourself. There is one other thing that you should do and that is to forgive yourself for any indiscretions.

With time, you will realise that these positive days earn you two different kinds of respect; respect from others and most important of all, self-respect. Once you start to really respect yourself it won't be long before everyone else starts to follow suit.

Now, while we are on the subject of labels, I want you to really begin to understand the power that labels hold over each and every one of us. The other day I was presenting a training course at a respected organisation, based in London. At the end of the course each student has to complete a monitoring and evaluation form. These forms are totally amazing and ask such personal information, in the form of 'tick boxes,' all for the benefit of their funder. The questions ask for your ethnic origin and list a whole series of potential ethnic origins, as well as a box named 'other.' They say (whoever 'they' may be), that they need this information to ensure equality of opportunity, which appears quite laudable: however, the thing is they are not inclusive; they are, in fact, exclusive. If they were inclusive, then every single person would have a box that they could tick and there would be no need for the box marked 'other.' And do you know what, one day the 'others' will take over the world. The more of these forms I see, the more I notice that people are actually scanning the sheet, looking for where they fit in, and when they can't find it, they ask me, in a state of confusion, what they should do, and I tell them to tick 'other.'

What is the real reason that we require such a vast amount of statistical information? Well, I don't know what the party line might be on this one, but I do have my own thoughts, which I would like you to consider. The 'powers that be' that run and organise this world, our world, need to compartmentalise us, and they require *us* to slot *ourselves* into our little boxes. This way they achieve two major objectives. The first is that we accept labelling as part and parcel of life and no longer question the amount of labels that are applied to us, and that we apply to ourselves. The other is, if you tag yourself as coming from, say, an area of great deprivation, in some way you will actually start to believe that you are deprived and that there is nothing that you can do about it, it's just the way it is. Bullshit.

At one point in my life I was labelled a 'teenage mum' and this tag had a whole host of other labels attached to it, some obvious and some more covert. So, in accepting the label of 'teenage mum', I was also signing up, albeit unwittingly, to a whole host of other assumptions about being a 'teenage mum.' The obvious ones were that because I was a 'teenage mum,' I wouldn't be able to cope. My parenting skills would not be developed, that I would yearn for nightclubs and my youth, and live on benefits for the rest of my life. This meant, for me at least, that a social worker was allocated to me for no other reason than the age at which I conceived my child. This, in turn, meant that rather than be allowed to take control of my situation, and that of my child, I had to be guided by a 'qualified' social worker, who would constantly assess my parenting skills and who had the power to decide where I would live, who I would live with, and how I would spend my time. The crazy thing about this situation is that you are a parent who is still being treated like a child and who is then told to "grow up and act like an adult" by the same person who is making all your decisions for you.

I remember very well an experience I had with a social worker when I was 19 years old and had just moved to my parents' house in Northern Ireland. I had two children: Faye, aged two and James, six months, and had been involved in an extremely destructive and abusive marriage, which eventually I had to escape from, and I relocated to my parents' home at the height of the 'troubles' in Northern Ireland.

The relationship had left me seriously underweight and I had real difficulty relating what had taken place during the marriage. Once I arrived at my parents' home, because of the ages of my children, I was allocated a health visitor who took it upon herself to refer me to social services and the psychology department of the local hospital. The labelling had begun in earnest. Even though I did not want their involvement, I felt totally threatened by the power that this social worker had to remove my children from my care. The fact that I was living in a very supportive environment, with a mother who worked as a midwife and had experience of raising six children of her own, and a father, who by this time was one of Her Majesty's Inspectors and a brilliant role model, didn't seem to make any difference to the situation, or the labels that had already been attached.

At the time, my two younger sisters still lived in the family home and, as both were in their teens, they were quite happy to offer their support by taking my children out for walks, or allowing me to enjoy a quiet bath by myself, or time to read a book.

My son, who I was still breastfeeding, was quite active, and rarely slept for more than a couple of hours at any one time and, as the months passed and he began to eat more solid food, having the breast milk just for comfort rather than need, his behaviour became quite challenging to say the least. Getting James to sleep in his cot was the greatest of struggles and some nights it took me hours to get him into a deep enough sleep to be able to leave the room.

My health visitor decided that James should be referred for allergy testing, to eliminate the possibility of food being the reason for his 'behavioural problems', as they had now become labelled. So, even though I had no wish to take my son to the hospital and have his arms impregnated with various doses of who knows what, the health visitor told me that I would be failing in my duty as his mother, not to attend the appointment that *she* had made on *our* behalf.

Throughout our conversation she referred to the fact that I was a teenage mum (even though at this stage I was 20 years old – it appears that the label sticks with you for life!) and that if I didn't act like a responsible mother, then she may not be able to prevent other measures being taken to ensure my children were raised appropriately. So, I attended the appointment with my son, who at the time was just over a year old, and watched as they pricked his arms and introduced all kinds of 'samples' into his body. James was really quite fractious and screamed throughout his ordeal, which, in turn, upset me, and I was informed that if I couldn't calm him down, then it might be better if I waited outside rather than fuel his mood! At no point during the whole procedure did I feel included in the decision-making process for the care and health of my own child.

My parents' home was a large semi-detached house, with four double bedrooms, a study, dining room, morning room, breakfast kitchen, conservatory and secure rear garden, and it was two minutes walk from the beach. Due to their postal address, my children were in the catchment area of one of the best primary schools in Northern Ireland and Faye, my daughter, was at the top of her class. When Faye returned home from school, there was always someone who would listen to her spellings, or help her with her reading, and her best friend Lee lived close by. Our happy times with my family were soon to be disrupted, again due to labelling and presumptions made by those, that in our ignorance and fear for reprisals, we hold up as 'professional.'

One day, I was extremely tired, as James had not slept the previous night. I think I slept for around two hours. I knew that my social worker was due to visit and, as was the custom at the time, I left the door 'on the latch' and lay on the sofa while my children played with some of their toys on the living room floor. I don't know if you have ever had the experience I am about to describe, but as I lay there, desperately trying to keep my eyes open and answer their constant questions, I jolted awake, as I realised that for a brief moment I had fallen asleep.

I got up and made us all some drinks and cut some banana for the children and then lay down on the sofa again. My eyes were so heavy and it felt like a steel strap was tightening around my skull. I lay back on the sofa and shut my eyes while the kids ate their banana, muttering answers to their constant questions, when I heard the front door open and then close. I got to my feet and walked towards the living room door, only to have it pushed open into my path by my social worker, who had let herself into the house. I was not happy about this and told her that she should have rung the bell, after all this was my parents' house and their privacy, at least, should be respected.

My social worker paid no attention to what I was saying and told me that she had looked through the window and seen me sleeping, leaving my children unattended and at risk of harm. I pointed out to her that my drink was still hot and that my kids were actually still eating the banana that I had cut for them, but she wouldn't listen. She informed me that I was showing signs of 'not being able to cope' and that living with my parents was not benefiting my children's development, or my own.

Apparently, this was a cause for concern amongst health visitors and social workers, especially with regard to 'teenage mums' and 'single parent families' (both labels now applied, with all their own hidden labels of course!). I tried to explain to her about James's sleepless night and that I just felt exhausted and I asked her how she had coped when her own children had sleepless nights, to which she replied that she had no children of her own, as she and her husband were not ready for the responsibility of children yet! Hey, but stick your flipping judgmental nose into the rearing of my kids, why don't you.

For about the twentieth time, I had the responsibilities of

motherhood lectured to me along with the heavy threat of removal if I did not take the role seriously. She told me that notes would be made on my file. This probably meant that a whole new list of labels would be added to my case. Within two weeks my social worker came to visit again and told me that in the interests of the children, I was to be re-housed in temporary accommodation in the centre of town.

The accommodation was a rather 'institutional' flat, owned by Barnados Charity, and had six sets of bunk beds crammed into two tiny bedrooms. There were basic amenities, such as hot water and a cooker, but that was it. The whole flat reeked of an institution and I hated it, as did my children. I was informed that I had no choice in the matter, as my parenting abilities were being called into question.

It now became even harder to settle James at bedtime and most nights he slept with me, as his stamina always seemed to beat my own. There was no feeling of 'home' to this place and I became very depressed. At my parents' house there was always someone around to talk to, but here I was totally alone. I even began to wonder if I had done the right thing in leaving the children's father, as it appeared that even though he used a great deal of violence against me, neither the police, health nor social professions gave two shits about that, or had threatened to take my children into care.

When Faye needed to go to school, it now meant a 15 minute walk, with no direct bus route (even if I could have afforded it) and as part of the route was along the coast road, often, especially during the colder months, we would end up freezing, and as the flat had no central heating, James and I would go back to bed to get warm when we returned from dropping Faye off. This, of course, only made both of our sleeping habits worse.

The social worker could not understand why I was feeling depressed, as there were lots of women who would be happy to have such a flat, to which I replied, rather childishly, that she could give it to them then and let me go back to my parents. This only reinforced her beliefs in all of my labels.

To sort out my depression, my social worker made an appointment for a referral to psychological services as a matter of urgency. In the meantime, my doctor prescribed anti-depressants, which made me feel like I didn't give a damn about anything. I didn't even want to leave the flat to go to the library, which, as I had no TV or radio, was my only form of entertainment.

I have to add a bit here about the labels bestowed upon me by the psychologist, who contributed in quite a major way, by influencing my second disastrous marriage. The psychologist was a fairly young guy, maybe around 28, and was quite hip in a '70s kind of way. He always seemed to want to talk about my sexual history, which I didn't. Many things had happened to me, not just during my marriage, which were to my mind quite disgusting and I certainly didn't want to discuss them with a man not that much older than myself.

He asked me constantly about my intention to get involved in a physical relationship again and I, in turn, constantly told him that I had no interest in men; in fact I preferred my life without them in it. He then inferred that I was in danger of becoming a 'man hater' and that I should not blame the whole of mankind for the behaviour of a few. This was not what I was saying; it was what he was interpreting as what I was saying. In my head I wanted to just tell him to fuck off, but when you feel powerless, you just say what 'they' want to hear and hope 'they' will get bored and discharge you.

A few months later, I went to the local pub with two of my brothers while my parents had the children. While I was in the pub an older man, in his forties, kept looking across at me and eventually plucked up the courage to ask if he could buy me a drink. My brothers were playing darts at the time, so were away from the table. Although the guy seemed pleasant enough, the last thing I wanted was to get chatted up by someone old enough to be my father, so I gently tried to put him off. He smiled and just said he would try again next time I came in.

My parents were happy that I had been out and enjoyed myself, so agreed to look after the kids every other Friday, so that I could go out with my sisters and brothers. The following week in the local pub, the same guy approached me again and, once more, I told him I wasn't interested; I had just come out for a quiet drink with my brothers. This time he stood chatting to me for a while, telling me that he was a merchant seaman home on leave and that he would be going back to sea soon and would like to get to know me better before he left, adding that maybe we could write to each other.

On my next visit to the psychologist, when he started on my sex life and hatred for all things male, I made the monumental mistake of telling him about the guy in the bar. Suddenly, he became very interested and asked me why I refused to meet with him. I said that I just wasn't interested and then he started going on about paranoia and isolating myself from the norms of society. So, the next time I went out with my brothers and the guy asked me to meet him, I agreed, as much to shut him up, as well as the psychologist.

The guy's name was Fergus and he was single, having never married. We agreed to meet four days later and it stressed me out so much that I felt nauseous just thinking about it. All too soon the day of my date arrived and I just knew I wouldn't be able to go through with it, even though my sisters walked me to within 50 feet of the place we were to meet. I diverted my route and sat watching the sea for half an hour before returning home.

The psychologist was very concerned about my behaviour and even went as far as to suggest that maybe he should refer me on to a more appropriate department. I couldn't believe it. On the one hand, the fact that I was labelled a 'teenage' mother gave some people the impression that this meant I was a right old tart and that anyone could have me, and here was the psychologist inferring that I was frigid, cold and incapable of exchanging affection with anyone. I wished they would get their labels sorted out! I decided the lesser of two evils would be to meet Fergus, who I knew would be gong back to sea soon, rather than let myself be examined by yet some other 'professional' label sticker. I did meet Fergus and our story is tragic and painful. So much misery and confusion awaited all of us: Fergus, Faye, James, my baby Rebecca, and me. We will return to this story further on in the book.

You see, the amazing thing about labels is that once you acquire one, they kind of breed, so soon you don't know *whom* you are any more; you just know *what* you are.

There are many other labels that I would like us to discuss and I will highlight them as this book develops, however I will conclude with the last set of labels that hypnotise and categorise us... designer and merchandising labels.

OK, it's time for you to reflect on your own behaviour again. Look at everything you buy – clothes, cars, technical equipment, holidays, food and other consumables and ask yourself why do you purchase them?

I have honestly seen some fairly shitty trainers over the years, but you know what, it doesn't matter how ridiculous the design, if they have the label 'Nike' or 'Adidas,' people will comment on how stylish they are. If the trainer had the label 'Rogers' then, when asked for their opinion, people might say, "I don't know, mate, never heard of them myself and I mean the design is a bit naff", but add the label 'Nike' to the same trainers and suddenly it becomes, "Yeah, man, they're cool, I love Nike trainers." It would be interesting to remove all insignia from dozens of pairs of trainers and just get people to wear them for the particular tasks they are designed for and see which came out on top.

Don't walk around in a trance being brainwashed into what you should and shouldn't buy. This whole planet, so full of creativity and wonder, is being hijacked by a few multi-nationals that are taking away our choices and telling us what to wear, what to eat, where to live, what to sit on and what colours we should paint our walls this season. It is all a con and you need to break free.

How long will it be before Tesco becomes your local shop where you buy everything? In supporting these huge, impersonal, restricted outlets we are killing the development of diverse products and innovation, just so we can all slowly start to merge into the same consumer market, controlled by the same small group of individuals. Small, unique enterprises are being squeezed out of business by these huge 'labels' and no matter what town you go to in this country, there is little that makes them unique any more, they are all full of labels such as Marks and Spencer, Faith, Tesco, Pizza Hut, McDonalds, Boots and so on. We are left with so little choice, and the choice is increasingly restricted.

Safeway, one of the big supermarket chains, has already sold out to the competition and it won't be long before Morrison's, which bought out Safeway will, in turn, be taken over by one of the remaining three supermarket giants: Tesco, Asda or Sainsbury's. Eventually, and I don't actually think it will be that long, all will be under one label and your choice will be gone.

A few years ago, I lived in a lovely village called Bradby, and I often spent time with my neighbours, socialising in the evening. My neighbour's name was Ray and he was a great wine connoisseur who loved one particular wine label above all. One evening we decided to perform a blind wine tasting, which resulted in Ray placing his own particular, favourite label in third place, second going to a bottle of red wine that was under half the price of his beloved label, and first going to one priced in between the two. Ray admitted that the cheaper wine was really rather pleasant, but added that it didn't look as good in his wine rack!!

So, think about what you are doing every time you decide to purchase something and ask yourself why you are buying that particular label. We are all being hypnotised on a daily basis by people who want no more from us that our hard-earned cash.

We are captivated by phrases that we actually believe mean something, when all they really mean is lack of choice, huge profits and reinforcement of their product. The phrases they use to market these products make us want to belong either to a pack or a flock, maybe. We follow them like sheep muttering, "Well, it says on the advert that this is the best a man can get," or we repeat their advertising slogans "Don't you owe it to yourself to have the best." Well, I guess I do then. I'll have six, please and here is my money to help increase your profits so that you can generate enough money to buy out the competition.

Competition actually translates into the variety of choices available to us, the consumers. Instead of just buying into the hypnotic sales bullshit, we should maybe ask ourselves, "Who says this is the best a man can get?" We are so easy to manipulate and with the manipulation comes the removal of power for us to choose and we are all actively buying into these restrictions of our future freedoms.

Our children are also being subjected to hard-nosed sales pitches and are now beginning to value their parents *love* for them, based on the products that their parents *purchase* for them. Children, some only weeks old, are fixed to screens that throw labels at them from every angle, and the marketing gurus don't give a shit that small, innocent minds are being hypnotised in the same way that they do with adults.

When there is a toy advert for the latest technology doll who can feed, cry, shit and even suck her thumb, the advertising companies make sure that the little girl lucky enough to have the doll in the advertisement, (normally blue-eyed with long blonde hair, neatly styled in two perfectly identical pigtails) is playing in an immaculate garden, complete with fantastic playhouse, with her matching friend. Their mother is ever present, with her perfectly made-up face, in stylish clothing, looking so happy and proud that her daughter has this new doll that can do everything except masturbate itself. Not a blade of grass is out of place in advertising land. All the colours are bright and sharp and the girls keep opening their eyes wide, in amazement, at what the new doll can do. Now, for many little girls, this means that in their minds, not only do they get the amazing, shitting doll, but also they may even get the 'model' mother, perfect designer garden and bright and amazing home life.

And what of the little boys? Well, they can have a battery operated 'Rolls Royce' type imitation car that eats electricity, doesn't even fit in the fucking house, and has to be dragged home by an exhausted parent, accompanied by the screaming child who can't be bothered to walk, and who only came out because he could drive the car the four miles it took for the battery to exhaust itself. You can't let your son go out on his own to play with his toy because it cost you an arm and a leg to buy it on your credit card, and you can't get insurance for 'Rolls Royces' in your area. So, it means, that whenever little one wants to play, you have to play too.

This is probably a slightly different picture to the one advertising the heap of crap on the TV! No happy father is standing in your back garden, unlike the advertiser's, which looks as if Capability Brown designed it, smiling at 'his boy' as he navigates the magnolia bushes. Oh, no. In fact, in your reality, dad only visits once a week and that involves a trip to McDonalds, and there is no way he's dragging that bloody thing back from there. So, the beautiful 'Rolls Royce,' that offered so much hope to you, the parent, as the perfect gift, suddenly becomes 'that fucking car' as people jump over it to access the kitchen, or trip over the battery charging lead, or drag it another couple of miles home.

What are we doing? Why are we doing it? Why are we allowing this to happen and not saying, "Do you know what, I'm not buying into that shit any more?"

In my time, I have worked with many parents who always tell me how much they adore children, yet for the sake of this year's "must buy toy" many children suffer bullying, isolation, ridicule and actually believe that they are unloved by their parents because "all the other kids have got it," and if you really loved your kids, surely you would want them to be able to play with all the other kids whose parents love them enough to buy them the "must have" toy?

Throughout this book, labels play a significant part in understanding life, as we know it, or the reality we create for ourselves. Labels also played a really important role in Jack's life, so now I am going to tell you his story.

Once, not so very long ago, a vagrant, or tramp as they are also labelled, was pushing his wooden trolley, in which he had all of life's necessities, through a busy town centre.

He was around 70 years old and had long grey hair, which had twisted itself into silvery braids that hung down his back, matched by a long beard that draped almost like curtains about his face. His coat was long and heavy, the colour quite indistinguishable, and was secured by a length of blue twine about his waist. On his feet he wore work boots that had been discarded by another and, in place of laces, were held with string secured through the top two ringlets. He didn't shuffle, as one might expect, but walked with a purpose that, should anyone even notice, left him or her pondering what that purpose might be.

As he pushed his small wooden cart ahead of him, he would look this way and that, at passers by who gave him a wide berth, or at children pointing him out whilst tugging at their mother's arm, commenting excitedly, "Mummy look, look mummy... it's a trampy-man... look!" until the mother would admonish the child saying, "Don't point Thomas, it's rude." It never really concerned him how people would react and he liked to think of himself as the 'invisibly visible man.'

On this particular cold November day, he was making his way towards a local charity shop where he was hoping to secure some 'new' books to read and, as he had visited this shop before, he hoped that the friendly 'volunteer,' a young woman called Mary, would be there.

Even though he knew her name, he chose to call her Merry, because that's how he felt in her company. Merry was different to most of the other shop volunteers who would often 'shoo' him out of the shop just in case he 'upset' the paying customers. If Merry was there, she would tell him to sit in the back and pull up a chair for him amidst the piles of clothes, ornaments, books and shoes and she would make him a "nice cup of tea." Often, she would give him a biscuit and, while he dunked it in the hot sweet liquid, she would sort through some "bits and pieces" for him.

Merry didn't really know anything about him, yet she felt safe in his company and knew that he would always go on his way after he had finished his drink, in spite of what the shop manager said about not encouraging tramps to "hang around the shop."

He was looking forward to seeing her cheerful grin and just being in her presence and, as he thought of her, her image came into his head, making him smile. As he arrived at the charity shop, he peered through the glass of the window, moving his head from side to side, trying to see past the displays of clothes and ornaments, carefully chosen to tempt customers in. As he peered, he was suddenly disturbed as the shop door opened and an annoyed looking woman motioned angrily with her hands for him to move away, saying, "If you don't mind, can you stop blocking the window so the customers can see the goods… you shouldn't peer in through the glass like that, it's not polite… now be on your way, before I call the police." He was about to ask her if Merry was working but, before he got the chance, she had shut the shop door with a bang.

"Oh well," he thought to himself, "Maybe next time," and he took hold of his cart and walked behind the shop fronts to a back alleyway where the bins were stored to see if he could find any goodies.

A few doors down from the charity shop there was a greengrocers and the old man noticed that one of the bins was brimming with discarded fruit, so he began to select some of the less damaged apples and oranges and store them in his trolley. A man, using the passage as a short-cut, walked past, spitting at the ground at the side of the old man before muttering, "Dirty, filthy vagabond" and continuing on his way. Moments later, the owner of the greengrocers came to deposit some more rubbish and catching the old man rummaging through the bin, threw one of the tomatoes at him that he was about to discard saying, "Oy… get out of my bin… go on, sod off… bloody tramp."

Without a word, he took hold of his trolley and went on his way, deciding to walk the couple of miles to a park, where he knew he could sit for a while, without concerning too many people.

As he strolled along the main street that led out of the town, he was unaware of two cars a little further down the street, both containing drivers who were shouting abuse at each other. Nor was he aware that one of the drivers was going to overtake the other, giving him the finger as he did so, to show that "ignorant git" what for. Neither of the drivers noticed that the old man was halfway across the busy road, so totally engrossed were they in their own drama, so neither could give any warning to alert him, until the inevitable happened and he was thrown into the air, landing with a bang on the kerb, hit by the overtaking and still angry driver. Neither of the cars stopped, they just sped off, not wanting to get caught up in a road rage incident.

The old man struggled to regain his senses in the gutter at the side of the road, noticing that his trolley had smashed on its side close to him and its contents were strewn all over the pavement. No one rushed to help him and as the first couple of people passed him by, the drama of what had taken place was lost and he was now only seen as a *drunken* tramp lying in the gutter.

He tried to get to his feet and realised that his foot was incredibly painful and try as he might, he couldn't stand, so instead he dragged himself up on to the edge of the kerb. As he held his hand outstretched to passers-by in a request for help, some would make a tutting sound, or utter the word "disgusting" and one even threw him a pound coin, yet not one would help him to his feet.

He reached out his hand and grabbed the handle of his now buckled cart and used it to pull himself up. Once standing, he attempted to support his weight on his legs and felt a pain shoot up from his ankle. He looked about him, trying to find a bench or place to sit, so that he could give his injured foot a chance to heal. As he was looking about, he became aware of a car pulling up next to him, before seeing a young man, maybe in his late twenties, dashing to his side calling breathlessly, "Are you all right? I witnessed what happened and went after them to get their licence plates... but are you OK?"

The old man explained that his foot was hurting quite badly and he was a little shaken but so grateful for the kindness the young man had showed in returning. The young man had already notified the emergency services and within a few moments of his return the distant wails of sirens could be heard.

The old man was taken to the hospital where he was assessed and diagnosed with a broken ankle and a severe cut which required stitching. It was decided that it would be necessary for him to stay in hospital for at least a week, or, until they were satisfied that there would be no further complications.

During his stay he noticed that many of the nurses did not want to spend time chatting to him as they did the other patients and the few that did wanted to shave his beard or cut his long grey hair to "tidy him up a bit," but he refused to allow it, saying he was happy the way he was.

One day, as he was safely hidden behind the curtains that surrounded his bed, he heard a voice call out, "Knock, knock, can I come in?" There was something about the voice that was familiar to him and when he responded, "Yes, do come in", he was totally surprised to see the familiar face of Merry smiling at him and she, in turn, was amazed to recognise him.

For a moment they both stood with their mouths open in total shock at recognising the other, before Merry spoke, "Oh my goodness, it's you," and then, approaching the bed, she asked, "What on earth has happened to you?"

He looked at Merry and said, "Oh... I have broken my ankle... nothing to worry about" and then smiled and quickly asked, "Why are you here?"

Merry explained that she no longer worked at the charity shop; she had a part-time job in an office and, as she enjoyed voluntary work, had chosen to become a hospital visitor, as there was more flexibility than there had been at the shop.

The old man indicated that she should pull up a chair, like she had previously so often invited him to do, and share tea and biscuits. He listened as she chatted to him about her job and before she left she told him that she would visit again, but not in her role, rather, she would be visiting as a friend.

After a few days the old man noticed that his back had become painful and although he had suffered from twinges every now and then in the past, this pain was hard to ignore. He had also begun to feel a little weaker than normal and was not so interested in his food, leaving much of it on his plate to the annoyance of some of the nurses who would mutter, "You would think a tramp like him would be thankful for some hot food in his stomach... ungrateful so-and-so."

The physicians ordered a series of tests and were sad to inform the old man that he had cancer and that they would need to start therapy

as soon as possible in order to prevent further spread of the illness, and
that once it started he would be required to move into a local hostel so
that his treatments could continue. It was stressed that unless he did
this he would be beyond the help of the hospital and may not have
long left to live.

The old man thought about the position he found himself in and
decided that he did not want to be imprisoned in a hospital or hostel
and made up his mind that as soon as his ankle was healed, he would
leave and continue with his familiar lifestyle, against the insistence of
his consultant, who actually found the old man to be "unexpectedly
civilized," really.

When Merry came to visit a couple of days later, the old man asked
if she would be kind enough to do a couple of things for him, which
she readily agreed to, noticing that he had lost weight and did not seem
as strong as he once had. He handed her a couple of envelopes and
asked her to keep them safe and that maybe, sometime in the future,
she might be asked to post them for him. Merry looked at the buff
hand-written labels, secured them in her bag, then pulled her chair up
close beside his bed and spoke, "Do you realise that I know almost
nothing about you?"

His face, now grey with the pain and medication, lifted and he gazed
into her gentle eyes and said, "Maybe it's best that way, Merry."

She smiled in return and said, "Yes… maybe," and never raised
the issue again.

As the old man's ankle became stronger, his body grew weaker and
he realised that maybe he would never again be able to walk across the
fields and countryside, stopping off in familiar towns to gather bits and
bobs discarded by others; he may never see the sunrise on a beautiful,
spring morning or feel the cold snowflakes awaken him in winter. He
felt sad and the thoughts made tears drop from his eyes and dampen
the white sheet of the hospital bed.

As he grew weaker and weaker, he looked forward more and more
to Merry's visits and one day, when she arrived, he told her that he
wanted to tell her a story. This was the story of Jack and once she was

comfortable he began.

Once, a long time ago now, there was a man called Jack. He was a very strong, confident man born around the late 1920s. He had been fortunate, as he was too young to fight for his country during the war, but old enough to make a lot of money during the post war boom. He was a man of few friends, as he spent his time working, as hard as he could, to increase the turnover of his business, and the friends that he had once enjoyed leisure time with, found him always too busy making money to join their outings. Jack's father, John, had died during the war. He had no brothers or sisters and his mother could not hear her husband's name spoken without lamenting her loss. Jack found it easier to be out of the family home and put all his energy into making money to provide everything his heartbroken mother could ever wish for, but what she wished for could never be bought with money, and a few years later she died.

Jack now focused all his attention on his business. His hard work paid off and soon he had built up his company into a multi-million pound enterprise. In order to secure deals he would entertain his customers before returning home to his empty house and working out the worth of his labour. As his business had grown, so had his circle of friends, many of whom were self-made men, like him. The thing was that when the boom turned on its side, friends became competitors, and it was difficult to know whom to trust.

Many went under, losing everything they had worked so hard for and Jack thanked his lucky stars that his business was secure. During this period he was often invited out for meals, or to clubs or parties, but he soon realised that rather than for his company, it was for what he was, a millionaire. Always, at some point during the social intercourse, the word 'money' would rear its ugly head and Jack would feel a surge of anger and then disappointment, at being invited to attend, for no other reason than that he was seen as successful and rich.

One day, he was invited to a private gathering at a new casino that an old competitor of his had channelled his remaining money into, and Jack decided to go. He rarely spent time relaxing and looked forward to meeting his old friend who had rather gallantly risked his remaining cash in this new venture. Jack was greeted by his old adversary, Richard, and welcomed to join the crowd of happy, chatting guests. He was also given £100 in complimentary chips and invited to enjoy a little gamble.

Jack met some old familiar faces that, once recognising him, made their way across, eagerly extending their hands shouting, "Well, I'll be… how are you, Jack? Still making millions, you old so and so?"

Jack would smile and engage in polite conversation until it diverted the way it always would, into how he could maybe invest a little something here, or loan a bit of money there and soon he tired of the whole event and wished that he had listened to his head and not gone at all.

He was about to leave when Richard came towards him with a tray of sumptuous food and beckoned him to share it with him at a nearby table. Jack had always respected Richard, even when they were competitors, and decided to spend fifteen minutes with him before making his excuses to leave. They caught up on old times and Richard asked if Jack was seeing anyone yet, to which he replied that he never managed to find the time for women and that when he had, they had always been the sisters, aunties, cousins and even once the mother of colleagues whose businesses were, surprisingly, about to fold. Richard sympathised with his predicament and said that he, too, had been in that situation a few years ago and, with a smile, added that hopefully he would be again soon. Jack laughed and then pondered for a moment and said, "Well… there is one woman who I kind of like…" Richard encouraged him to continue: "Hey, come on Jack, tell me more."

Jack told him about Claire, who was one of the cleaners who worked in the executive suites at his company and, as Jack usually worked late, he had often found himself chatting to her. She was in her late twenties maybe, divorced with two children and had always been a faithful worker and Jack and she had often enjoyed a laugh over a cup of tea. Richard rocked back on his chair with laughter saying, "Hold on a moment… let me just check that I've got this right…" He paused and then lent his arms on the table, looking Jack right in the eyes before continuing, "So, she's a cleaner... a *cleaner*, Jack, *and* she is divorced. Doesn't that raise some questions, like, why would another guy divorce her if she was worth hanging on to? Then she has two kids... Jack, listen to yourself, mate...,these are the words of a desperate man. If you really fancy a bit of a tussle with her, drop her a £20 note, then move on. You need a woman who matches your status, not some second-hand reject who cleans out the executive toilet."

Richard gave Jack a friendly punch on the arm before adding, "Jack, you are one in a million and you deserve nothing less, come on let's raise a glass to the fairer sex, 'cos all work and no play makes Jack a really dull, not to mention desperate, boy."

They never discussed money, rather they reminisced about days gone by and Jack relaxed, enjoying Richard's company. Before Jack was about to leave, Richard asked him to join him at the roulette table and chance his luck with the £100 chip, clapping him on the back and ordering a waitress to bring him a glass of the best cognac.

While they were seated at the roulette table, Jack noticed an attractive young woman dressed in a gold satin gown that played with the lights in her glossy blonde, fashionably cut hair. Richard followed his friend's gaze and gave him a slight nudge, saying, "There are perks to running a casino, eh?" Jack smiled in response before Richard added with a nudge, "and I bet she doesn't smell of bleach, either." As Jack placed his bet, she momentarily caught his eye and gave him a polite smile before becoming engaged in conversation with an older woman seated beside her. Jack did not win any money that night and decided to bid his old friend goodbye; he called for his chauffeur to bring the car.

Richard and Jack met up quite often after that and sometimes Richard would accompany Jack on board his yacht where they would fish and smoke cigars. It was after one such trip that Jack realised that Richard was his closest friend and that the two of them shared many interests in common, often playing a round of golf or dining together in the finest restaurants. Richard never expected Jack to pay, and vice versa, and he realised that this made his company such great value.

One day, Jack arrived at the casino to meet Richard, as they had exclusive tickets for a premier boxing match and were travelling together. Richard said he had a few things to deal with and invited Jack to have a cognac while he waited. Richard was about to call over the waitress when he prodded Jack and said, "Hey, maybe you should go and get it yourself from the bar. Look who's there!"

Jack looked over to where Richard was indicating and recognised the familiar blonde bob of the beauty that had caught his eyes a few weeks earlier. Richard gave Jack a cheeky wink, telling him jokingly, "You've got fifteen minutes to make an impression."

Jack approached the bar and sat on a chrome high stool and gazed at the woman, who was ordering a drink, and after a few moments she turned to face him, as if aware that he was watching her. He thought she was stunning and indicated to the barman that he would pay for the lady's drink. She raised the now filled glass and acknowledged his attention, thanking him with a smile.

During the boxing match, Jack could think of nothing else but the image of her and asked Richard if he knew anything about her. Richard said that she usually visited the casino once a week, normally on a Friday evening and that she was always immaculately turned out. She usually came with an older woman, who he thought might be her aunt, but apart from that he knew little more.

From that point on, Jack attended the casino every Friday and, at first, he would just smile an acknowledgement until he built up the courage to actually sit next to her at the roulette table. From there it was easy. They began to talk and once he was sure that she was not married, he asked her to accompany him to the theatre, followed by a meal at 'Sparrows,' a top-notch restaurant where he always managed to secure the best table.

Her name was Melanie and apparently she knew absolutely nothing about Jack; in fact she told him with slight embarrassment that she had never even heard his name. Within a short space of time he was hooked and met with her two or three times a week. She was always happy to see him and never asked about his wealth; he liked that. Richard encouraged his friend saying that beautiful women were hard to find, but beautiful *and* engaging women were a real rarity and he should make sure that she didn't slip through his fingers.

And so it was that Jack proposed to Melanie and Richard was their best man. The couple had what appeared to be a happy life with a penthouse apartment in the best part of the city, a country residence with land and stables and a villa in the South of France. Jack thought that his life was almost perfect; the only thing missing now was a child, although he thought better than to mention such a thing so soon after marriage.

Melanie was easy to be with and never seemed to complain about Jack's frequent business trips that took him away from home for days at a time and he would return with the most expensive gifts and have fresh flowers sent for her every day while he was away.

One evening, after he had returned from a weeklong trip, Jack and Melanie sat out on the balcony of their apartment and watched the city lights shimmering below, as they ate their meal. Jack looked lovingly into Melanie's eyes and told her that she was the most precious of all jewels and that he would like to think that one day maybe they could think about starting a family. Melanie took his hand in hers and said, "Maybe we already have, Jack."

He was stunned at first and then jumped for joy at the wonderful news. This was the best evening of his entire life. When he broke the news to Richard he clapped him on the back so enthusiastically that Jack nearly dropped his drink that had been raised in a toast to the joyous occasion.

Jack took Melanie to buy the best of everything and said that when the child was born they would move to their country residence and he would take a couple of months off just to be with her, to care for her and make sure that both she and their child had everything they could ever wish for. Jack was so excited that on his next trip away from home he ordered a hand-built pram from an exclusive supplier and had it delivered to their country home as a surprise for when they moved there, to make ready for the birth.

A few weeks later, Jack was to attend a business meeting that would mean he would be away from home for 10 days and Melanie, as usual, never complained. She told Jack that she might spend some time at their country retreat and return to the city before he was due back. Jack agreed that it was a good idea and kissed her farewell, arranging to meet up with her at the apartment at the end of his trip.

Jack had only been gone for two days when the CEO of the company he was cementing a deal with, caught a virus and apologetically had to reschedule the meeting for later in the year. Jack rang his home apartment and, when there was no response, realised that Melanie had probably gone to their country home as discussed. He was about to call her to let her know he was on his way when he thought better of it, and decided instead, to surprise her.

When he arrived at the secluded entrance to the estate he looked up the long drive and noticed that, rather than one car, there were two. It was a beautiful sunny afternoon and he guessed that maybe Melanie had invited her aunt to keep her company and that they would probably be enjoying the sun out by the pool.

Rather than go straight out the back, he decided to deposit his cases in the hallway and grab a cognac before joining them. He walked through the house into the kitchen, where there was a huge open fireplace, which made it appear so homely when lit during the winter months. As he raised his glass to take a drink, he thought he heard raised voices. At first he did not realise where the sounds were coming from and then he understood that they were coming down the chimney from the room above, their bedroom.

He stood quietly and listened and heard Melanie almost screaming, "But I don't want him to think he's the father... you are!" Then a male voice, "Just give it another couple of months will you... he will have to pay loads more for a child he *thinks* is his."

Melanie's voice grew louder: "I can't do this to him any more... I don't want him to touch me, either and I don't understand how you can stand the thought of him screwing me with your baby growing inside me."

* * *

"Mel baby, listen honey, the casino needs a huge injection of capital right now, otherwise the banks will take everything... Come on, honey bun, we've put so much effort into this, don't drop at the last hurdle."

"Why didn't you just ask him for money? I didn't mind so much before, but now I'm pregnant it's different."

"Ask *him* for money? Now there's a joke. Look, just let's stick with the plan and you, me and the baby will all be together soon."

Jack didn't have to go upstairs to confront them. There was little point. In that moment his world fell apart and he poured himself a final drink before walking back through the hallway, passing the open door of the lounge where stood the hand-built pram, so recently delivered.

Jack and Melanie divorced. She had the villa in France and the city apartment. She also received a one-off award of nearly three million pounds. Jack sold his company to the highest bidder, realising a rather tidy sum, and put all the money in offshore accounts.

Before he had met up with Melanie, he had found Claire attractive and funny, but realised that they came from different worlds. It made their relationship quite easy really, and she had been the one he turned to when he needed guidance about what changes to expect in Melanie during her pregnancy. So, Jack went to see Claire and told her that he was going away, far away and that he had a proposition for her, if she was interested. He said that he had a large country residence, with a pool, stables and plenty of farmland and that he wanted her to live there as payment for taking care of the property. He would not put the house in her name, as should she ever marry, she may lose it through divorce, but that she was free to move in any future partner and raise her children out of the bustle of the city. He would continue to pay all the bills on the house through his bank account and he would set up an amount of money that could be used for any repairs, all of which he would organise with a solicitor. Claire was overwhelmed by his offer and accepted but not before asking where he was going. Jack replied that he was in search of something, something that appears elusive to most people.

Jack never saw Richard, Melanie or Claire again.

The old man paused, as he had throughout the telling of the tale, before closing his eyes and falling into a sleep. Merry wondered what had prompted him to tell her such a story, and then, for the first time ever, kissed him gently on his forehead and quietly left him to rest.

A few days later the hospital contacted her to say that the old man was extremely poorly and it might be in her best interests to visit before the week was out.

As she was packing her bag ready to visit the old man, she noticed the two envelopes he had given her previously. The first was addressed to a Miss Claire Burrage and the second to a firm of solicitors in London.

Merry decided to act on an impulse and moments later she was dialling a telephone number given by Directory Enquiries. A woman with a gentle voice answered and asked to whom she was speaking. Merry explained that she had been visiting an old man called John in the hospital and relayed the story of how she knew him, his accident and subsequent illness with cancer. Claire was very polite, but insisted that she did not know anyone called John and there must be a mistake. Merry couldn't let the opportunity pass her by, not now while she had Claire on the phone, so she asked if she knew a man called Jack. At once the older lady's voice broke and began to quiver as she asked urgently, "You know Jack? Where is he... how is he?"

Merry explained that she had no idea but that the old man had told her a story about this man called Jack and so she had thought that maybe Claire might have been some relation to John as he apparently knew so much about her. Claire was intrigued, but had no knowledge of John at all. Merry did not mention the envelope as there appeared little point and anyway she had promised the old man that she would only send it for delivery as and when he instructed. Before she ended the call, Merry gave the old lady her name and telephone number and said that if she had any further thoughts to contact her, and with that she apologised for troubling her and replaced the receiver, more than a little confused.

The next day Merry went to visit the old man again, who was now in a very sorry state. His breathing was shallow and his long beard appeared to emphasise the thinness of his face. She watched him for a while as he slept and then rose to leave, not wanting to wake him. He needed his rest but as she quietly left some fruit on his locker, he opened his weary eyes, which wrinkled at the corners with his smile at seeing her. He told her to take a seat, and as she insisted that she should leave him to sleep, he reached out and gently took hold of her wrist and repeated his request. Merry did not argue. She had grown so fond of this lovely old man and imagined the sadness he must have surely felt, being alone to face death with no family member beside him.

The old man looked at her and said that she had always made him feel happy, and she had no idea how important that was to him. Merry took the opportunity to ask him about the story he had told her the previous day. She asked him if he knew who Jack was and he was silent for a while before breathing out a shallow sigh and stating, "I never knew Jack… I don't think anyone really knew him."

Just at that moment Merry was aware of quiet footsteps approaching the bed and assumed that it would be the nurse bringing his medication, but she saw something in the old man's eyes that made her turn, and there, standing just inside the door was a woman in her sixties. Her soft grey hair was twisted into a single long plait that hung over her shoulder and her soft brown eyes were brimming with tears.

"Jack!" she cried, "Jack, oh Jack, where have you been all these years?" He struggled to pull himself up in the bed, his own eyes spilling with tears, "Claire, is that you Claire? How did you find me, how did you know I was here?" Claire ran the few short steps to the bed, took hold of the old man's hand and kissed it again and again and the old man stroked her silver head as she did so. Merry pulled up another chair for the woman, who thanked her, and then began to admonish the old man: "Why did you never come back, Jack?"

"What did I have to come back to? I needed to disappear in order to find myself... too many people knew of me... yet I never knew myself..."

"I knew you, Jack, I knew you as the kindest, most lovely human being on the planet. You were always so kind to me, even though I was just a cleaner, you would share a cup of tea and a smile, not like most of the other haughty so and so's who worked for you."

She held his hand and kissed it repeatedly while the old man spoke, "And I thought you to be the most lovely girl in the world, so easy to talk to, always a smile for me. No matter how bad my day had been, I knew that you would always give me something to laugh about. I have thought about you so much on my travels, Claire, you have always been in my thoughts... you must know that?"

Claire let her head dip and the old man gently raised it with a finger, saying, "It is so, so good to see you again."

"You too, Jack... but when did you get back to England? I thought that you had made a new life for yourself abroad somewhere?"

The old man sighed deeply and raised his eyes to the ceiling, "I never left the country, Claire... I left Jack. I was a very rich man and with riches can come all kinds of problems. Inside, I wasn't rich at all, I was a pauper. I thought I had everything, but in reality, I had nothing. People who smiled to my face, sneered behind my back... My life was so empty... and then I met Melanie." he took in a short breath and his voice wavered as he continued, "For the briefest of moments I believed I was the most fortunate man in the world... a beautiful wife, a child on the way and the best friend a man could ever wish for... the briefest of moments."

He turned his head to the side, releasing tears that spilled silently onto the white, starched pillowslip, and then he continued, "When you wear the label of a millionaire it appears you are fair game for everyone. That day, after I left the house, I swore I would never go back there, but after the divorce, she came to take all her belongings and once she had gone I looked about the empty rooms and saw the pram... the pram that I had built dreams around... and something inside me woke up. I couldn't leave it there for you, so I took it with me. Once everything was sorted out and you had moved into the house, I put my most treasured memories in the pram and began to walk… I had no idea where I was going, yet it didn't really matter… I just kept walking. I was in search of something most people never find in their lives. People wear their labels like badges and then wonder why people trick them or use and abuse them… I just kept walking." He sighed and smiled before closing his eyes and drifting into a quiet sleep. Claire kissed him gently on his lips and whispered quietly, "But I would never have done those things, Jack… I have always loved *you*, the man beneath the label."

The two women decided to leave the old man to rest and went and had a coffee together and Claire asked Merry what the prognosis was for his recovery. Merry repeated what the consultant had said and added sadly, "I don't think there is much time left. Maybe a week, maybe less."

"Well, he won't spend his last days in this place… he is coming home," and with a determined air she went in search of the doctor to arrange his transfer to the home she had poured her love into for so many years, awaiting his return.

Merry walked back to the old man's room and noticed him stirring from his sleep. She gently pushed open the door and walked in to stand next to his bed before enquiring, "John… what did Jack go in search of that was so elusive?" The old man smiled and patted the bed for her to sit close to him.

"Jack went in search of truth and John found it. The happiest years of my life were spent as John, at first pushing my pram and then as the years passed, the pram, along with my unhappy memories, decayed and fell apart. I became known as a tramp, yet for the first time in my life people treated me with honesty. No one tried to impress me. Those who gave to me did so with an open, full and selfless heart… the rest just passed me by, just grateful that they weren't in my rather shoddy shoes. I have met some of the most wonderfully honest people on Earth as John, yet as Jack I met the most devious and twisted. I have slept under stars and have survived on whatever God and those blessed by God have given me. No one has asked John to come for a dip in their solar-heated swimming pool, but many would have asked Jack, just to try to prove something to him. I have had the best thirty or more years a man could ask for… freedom and honesty… and who knows, maybe if I had lived Jack's lost life I would have died years ago from heart disease or a stroke. Instead, I met wonderful people like you who didn't care who I might have been. You accepted me and allowed me to *be*… and for that, my sweet Merry, I will always be grateful." He squeezed her hand gently before letting it slip through his fingers.

Merry visited John and Claire a couple of times over the next month in their home in the countryside before getting the tearful phone call to say that John had passed away peacefully in his sleep. A few months after the funeral, Merry was called to the solicitor's office that was on the envelope she duly posted, and told that John had left her £1,000,000 in his will. He had also left her a note, which said:

My Dearest Merry,
You will probably never realise how much joy and happiness you brought to my life. You never once made me feel like a tramp, you always made me feel like a human being. I hope that the money will bring you joy, and a way to guarantee this, is to spend it supporting those who have none. In doing this, the wealth you already have in your heart will grow beyond measure. Thank you so much.
John

The Bit Where I Rant About...
Visualisation

I love spending time visualising, thinking about how I want my life to pan out and talking to my FG about giving me the resources to make it happen. Now, there may be some of you out there who say they cannot visualise, so I want to ask you to do something. First of all, I want you to think about the home that you grew up in. It doesn't matter if it was the first home you can remember, or the one you are still living in right now, I just want you to think about it. Now I want you to take me on a grand tour of the house, starting with the street, lane, close or wherever it is located.

OK, now I want you to open the door and describe what you can see. What does the wallpaper look like, or is it painted, and if so, what colour is it? Where are the stairs, if there are any, and what about the kitchen? Are there any smells associated with the house and if so, what are they? Take a good, long look around and see what you can remember.

OK, done that? Let's carry on then. Now, I would like you to think about the kind of house that you would love to live in. Where would it be located? What kind of frontage would it have? What would the living room look like and would you have a real fire or some other form of heating? How many bedrooms would it have and what would yours look like? Would it have a garden and if so how would it be laid out? Would you have friends come and visit and if so, how would you socialise in your future home? Now, really start to focus on yourself moving around your future home. Notice how you look, what you are wearing and how you are feeling in this future home.

Ok, now if you are able to do that, then you are able to visualise, and this will be an important technique to utilise when you decide to take responsibility for *your* life.

Even though some people say they can't visualise, we do it all the time, and don't even realise we are doing it. An example of this is getting from point A to point B. If we could not visualise, then every time we made the journey from point A to point B we would have to take written direction, such as using autoroute, or some form of satellite navigation. Once we have travelled the route once or twice, we begin to visualise it as we start our journey. We remember visual images of the route from our previous journeys and then start to advance, or fast forward the images, so that we can visualise when to exit junctions or roundabouts so we know approximately how much further we have to go to reach our destination.

Think about a journey that you make regularly. Now, *how* are you thinking about it? Imagine that a friend is asking you for directions from the local hospital to your home, how do you explain it to them?

Let's imagine that you are going out for a meal at your favourite eating establishment. First of all, where is it and where would you like to sit to eat your meal? Now, what is it that you are going to order? How will it look when it is presented to you? Can you smell the food? Can you *taste* the food?

When you buy someone special a gift, do you think about *why* you have chosen that particular gift? Of course you do. Think about it now: buying someone special a gift. Now think about what you would buy them and why you would buy that particular gift.

Next, I want you to think about how you would give them the gift. Where would you be and who else would be there? How will they react when they open the gift?

Now, imagine a picture of Elvis Presley. That's enough. Quickly erase the image from your mind and replace it with a picture of a giraffe eating leaves from a tall tree. We visualise things all of the time. It is how we understand what all the 'labels' mean. For example, the label 'giraffe' = tall animal, long neck, little horn type things, huge brown eyes with long eyelashes, reaching its twitching lips to a lone tree, somewhere in a dry country. We don't visualise the letters GIRAFFE unless we want to spell the word, and even then the chances are that you will get a flash of an image of a giraffe before you spell it.

We also use our other four senses to visualise and we will talk about those, but for now I want us to focus on the incredible, creative, seeing mind that we have. You can create any pictures in your mind that you want to, which is pretty amazing really. I can visualise you reading this book and I haven't even got through the first half of it, in fact it is still being formed in my mind at this 'exact moment,' yet I can visualise you reading it. How amazing is that? At my exact moment, you have not even heard of my book, yet at this 'exact moment' you are reading it, the very person that I had visualised reading it.

Visualisation is incredibly important in our lives, yet we pay very little attention to what we are storing in our minds and how we are visualising our own futures. Sometimes visualisation can bring forth unhelpful emotions, when what we really need to do is utilise our emotions effectively.

An example of this, for me, would be thinking about a visit to the dentist. Even now, as I put a visual to the label 'dentist,' I can see him as clearly as if he was standing in front of me. I can see his pale blue jacket with cream piping, which is trendily buttoned to the side, with the top button left open. Dangling around his neck is a matching facemask and, accessorised to the max, he wears latex gloves, the colour matching the piping detail on his jacket. He is standing slightly to the rear of his high tech dental chair and smiling at me to sit down. The room smells like no other place on earth, it is just 'dentist smell.' Everything has sparkles shining off surfaces, like something off a TV quiz show, or a motor exhibition. There is no life in the room, just clinically cold surfaces. A smiling, beautiful assistant stands perfectly, near a work surface, and I try to think what she might be there for. I now visualise myself laying back in the chair and being moved, electronically, by the now invisible dentist. I am aware of the 'dentist smell' invading my lungs, and I start to feel like I am out of control.

I don't want to be here.

He asks me to open my mouth as he pushes his latex clad finger into the side of my cheek, pressing down on my lower jaw to ease my mouth further open. Instinct is telling me to just bite his finger and run off.

Then I see them. The pick and mirror. Moments later, I see a huge needle and hear the nightmare sound of the drill.

So, imagine for one moment that I have a dental appointment in a couple of days' time and I am not looking forward to it; what would be the best thing for me to visualise? If I bring to mind the images, smells, tastes, feelings and sounds that I have just outlined, what kind of emotions am I going to evoke? Well, I can tell you that writing about the dentist in that particular way has made me feel so glad that I don't have an appointment in the next couple of days. But, if I did, what then?

For a start I would be feeling nauseous already, even with a couple of days to go. Images would pop into my mind over that time period that would seriously make me consider cancelling my appointment. As the day of the visit dawned, I would realise on opening my eyes that the dreaded time had arrived. I would be imagining it with every step I took, no matter how many. By the time I finally arrive at the dentist's, my nerves would be all over the place, my stomach in knots, my heart would be beating out of my chest, and I would be feeling totally out of control of *all* my senses. In short, I would be having a 'panic attack.' All this without even sitting in his chair; by just walking through the door of the dental surgery! This is the power of visualisation.

Now, there is a reason why this happens and, in my case, it is a conflict between two different parts of 'me.' Your FG will always be benevolent; in other words, FG will grant your wishes for you, to create what it is that you want.

I tell myself repeatedly that I hate going to the dentist and my stored images of 'dentist' are very negative, so the message I am sending FG is that I hate to visit the dentist, as doing so gives me a panic attack and makes me feel out of control. I reinforce these images every time I think of the label 'dentist,' so when I make an appointment to attend, my FG wants to be benevolent and spare me the panic attack and feeling of being out of control, so brings up lots of visuals and smells, tastes, and feelings to remind me that I hate the dentist. In this way FG will remind me that it might be best for me to avoid going.

Now, all human behaviour is purposeful, so we have to identify the reason why I made an appointment for the dentist. I made the appointment because I have hole in one of my teeth. I know that I need to have it filled before it gets any worse and causes me pain and a course of antibiotics. This is another part of my huge, incredible FG, who has noticed me probing the hole in my tooth and understands that without care and attention, the hole could become infected. This part of my FG is also acting in a benevolent manner and is putting images into my head, so that I react and make an appointment. Both parts of FG are trying to grant my wish, kind of a "You will go to the dentist," "Oh no, you won't," "Oh yes, you will." The part that will succeed will be the part that has the best visuals.

So what could I do to make sure I attend my appointment?

Well, I could start by replacing the visuals to the label 'dentist' with new ones, or, whenever I think of the word dentist, I replace the images, smells, sounds and tastes with a picture of a warm summer meadow, with the aromas of fragrant flowers blowing on a gentle breeze and tasting the sweetness of fresh strawberries. If every time I thought of the label 'dentist' I did this, it wouldn't be long before the old images were removed, unless *specifically* recalled. I would then continue to visualise, this time focusing my attention on myself with a healthy, smiling mouth, thanking the dentist for his attention. And finally, I would imagine me cleaning, or running my tongue over my teeth and feeling happy that the hole was gone.

I want you to think of a situation of your own now where your visuals are evoking unhelpful emotions. Let the visuals run their course and then acknowledge the support of FG and say that these visuals are no longer helpful to you any more and that you wish to replace them.

The reason that you should run them for one last time is that you need to pay special attention to exactly what emotions they evoke, so that you can bring in replacement visuals that take in all the senses that the label brings with it. Next, you should think up replacement visuals to record over the originals, making sure that all the senses are satisfied. Before you re-record, you need to make sure that by changing the visuals you are not going to make your situation worse, either for yourself or anyone else. Once you are clear that it is OK to make the changes, think of the label again and, as soon as the old visuals start to appear, push them away with the new ones that you have created. Do it a few times to make sure FG understands your commands. Then think of the benefits you will gain, like I did with the clean, smiling teeth.

When you visualise, changes can happen, amazing changes that can be directed by you. Just think of the differences that you could make in your life, to your health and stress levels. Yet people continue to do the same old thing and get the same old responses and even if they are aware that what they are doing is not of any benefit to them, they just keep on doing it. Well, you don't have to any more, you can actually start to take a little more control and responsibility for the way you experience this life, instead of giving all your power away to a tiny group of individuals who are attempting, and in some cases are *actually* succeeding, to create your reality for you.

I want you to take a few minutes to just focus on this planet that you are experiencing, living and contributing to. Think of the world and what do you see? Do you see what you experience, or do you see the world as the media portrays it? When you think of the planet, do you see tsunamis, war, starvation, hatred, fighting, pain, and destruction? If you do, how have *you* experienced that portrayal of reality, and where have the visuals come from?

If we can experience our reality through the eyes, ears and emotions of another, then whose reality is it? Whose visuals are we decoding and storing on our own personal hard drive?

If you give away control of your information and labelling systems, then you are not experiencing your own life and reality, you are experiencing someone else's, second hand.

Now, I want you to think of this planet as *experienced* by you.

How many wars have you experienced? How much starvation? The chances are that the answer will be zilch, or at most, a little. However, knowing this to be true, how many hours of tsunamis, death, war, pain, starvation and destruction do we visualise every day of our lives? Have you personally experienced it, or have you *experienced* someone else's *reality* of it?

Really, you have to think about this, as this is the key to taking responsibility for *your* life and living it the way *you* want to experience it. Whose experiences base your reality for living? So, let's just stick with this for a moment, as it is very important. Imagine that you want to go on holiday, somewhere special that you have never been to before. You decide to ask some friends and colleagues for some ideas about where to go.

First of all, you ask friend 'A' who comments, "Oh, if I were you, I would go to New York. You'll have a brilliant time. So much to see, loads of shops, friendly people, really smart hotels, out of this world, and excellent service. Yes, I would say go to New York."

Next you meet friend 'B' and you tell them that you are thinking of taking a holiday in New York and are shocked by their response. "Oh don't go there, oh dear me, no. A friend of mine went there and had the most awful time. The hotel was full to bursting with some kind of convention, where everyone wore stupid hats and she said the noise was unbelievable. Then, when they went shopping their money was stolen and the police didn't give a damn – too busy out shooting people, I suppose. Anyway, she said that everywhere she looked she could see poverty, not like they show you on the TV, oh no, she said it was worse than you could even begin to imagine. She said the people were "in your face" and brash, and that everything was too big, too loud, and too American, really. If I were you, I would go somewhere like New Zealand."

Now, something happens inside your mind and body, or your physiology, when you hear other people's visuals. When you listened to friend 'A's interpretation of New York, maybe that type of shopping holiday appealed to you. Maybe you got a visual impression of what the hotel looked like. Possibly you may have imagined yourself in your hotel room, being waited on hand and foot. And as you created those visuals, along with them would have come emotions, feelings, smells, sounds and a 'state of mind.' As friend 'A' continued to speak, maybe you would have started to feel a smile pull at the corners of your mouth, then your eyes might open wide indicting that you want more information and, as you hear more, you create yet more visuals that wrap around your whole sense of self. You may start to feel warmth spread over your being. You may begin to feel excited at the thought of being there, and you may want to rush to the nearest computer and book your hotel and flights, whatever, you want to experience this kind of holiday.

Ok, so now you talk to friend 'B,' and remember, as you begin to talk about New York, the visuals you now create are all extremely positive. So, when friend 'B' starts to recount her 'second hand' visuals of New York, what do you think begins to happen to the ones *you* have created? They start to change; your visuals start to become overwhelmed by someone else's second-hand 'reality' of New York. In other words, they begin to control your perception of how something is in your version of reality. So, as you continue to listen to friend 'B,' maybe the smile that spreads across your face when you mention the label 'New York,' slowly starts to disappear, maybe your wide eyes begin to narrow and your brow furrow as your visual of the fantastic hotel is suddenly invaded by a herd of loud 'Americans' wearing bulls' horns and getting louder and drunker by the moment. Maybe you see yourself on a shopping trip and getting knocked to the 'sidewalk' as the cops chase a shoplifter down the street, guns at the ready. Maybe your body starts to droop a little, as you think of the new visuals that you are recording for the label 'New York.' You are now in a different state of mind and it shows within, and without, your whole being.

What we need to get our heads around is this; language, as in verbal or written communication, is not the way we record information. We record it through our five senses and relive it, even if we have never experienced it, through our five senses. Isn't that amazing!

What is even more amazing is how we can generate our five sense visuals 'just like that,' by applying five-sense information to each of the labels we store within our being. It follows, then, that every label we have stored on our own personal hard drives will have a level of each of those five senses attached to it. We experience the 'label' by the way it is expressed through our five sense visuals, and will continue to do so, until a time comes when we re-record the five sense visuals to that particular label. This means that we can make those 'labels' into whatever we want to experience them as, until we rewrite the hard drive. Wonderful, eh?

When I began to understand all of this, it was as if blinkers were being removed from my eyes. It meant that I could experience reality in the way I want to experience reality. I decided to experiment with it a little, and then I began to experiment with it a lot.

Let me explain one of my experiments.

As you might have guessed, I do not particularly like going to the dentist. So, I started to focus on my visuals attached to the label 'dentist' and separate them out a little. The smell was a part of my five-sense visual, so I focused on the smell sense of the label 'dentist' to see what emotions it evoked and how strong they were. Did the smell alone create all of the emotional and physiological factors that made me experience the label 'dentist? I realised that although the smell was a factor, it was not a major factor, more like a finishing touch. Then I thought about 'taste' and realised that although I did not enjoy the taste of latex-clad fingers, taste was not the sense that had the greatest impact. Now I focused on sound and imagined the drill whizzing away and noticed that this specific sound does have a more profound impact, but I also realised that I can hear other kinds of drills and not automatically experience the label 'dentist.' Basically, as I continued with my exploration, I realised that it is the visual aspect of the five sense label, that has the most intense reaction to my physiology and just bringing up the 'movie still' of the label 'dentist' made my whole being react.

I understood that it was 'seeing' the surgery that hauled in all the other five-sense visuals. So what does this mean? Well, it means that you can trace back in your own labelling filing cabinet and find out where, when, how and for what benevolent reason you stored the five sense code for the label 'dentist,' and in my case, focusing specifically on sight.

This is what I did.

I thought back to the first time I can recall going to the dentist, which was when I was around seven years old. There may have been earlier occasions, which I cannot recall, so to me, the significant time was the visit when I was around this age. When I bring that visit to mind I can clearly see my parents, three brothers, two sisters and myself sitting in the waiting room. My father is very anxious and is not behaving as he usually does. He is normally always smiling and making people happy, but now he is looking around as if searching for a demon that he knows is there, but can't locate. My mother is agitated, probably because she has a struggling infant in her arms and five other young children to keep her eyes on and, of course, she wants us all to behave and not cause her any embarrassment in the waiting room.

My eldest brother is poking the next brother in line and using his finger like a drill to burrow into his cheek, laughing and saying, "You're gonna have the driiiilll, you're gonna have the driiiillll." Mum is telling him to be quiet and stop acting so stupid. I go over to my father and ask him why we have to be here and instead of his usual warm and approachable response, he just tells me to go and sit down. Suddenly, the sound of a high-speed drill whizzes through the waiting room and every single person in that room reacts to the sound. It brings with it a wave of energy that catapults itself into the minds of every person there, releasing each individual's corresponding energy, which can now be felt as an atmosphere that invades every being in that waiting area. My two-year-old sister starts to cry and says she doesn't like it, even though she does not really understand what *it* is that she doesn't like; she just doesn't like 'it.' My three brothers and my father are called through and leave the waiting area. My father looks terrified and my mother tells him not to be a baby and smiles reassuringly.

This is not normal. This is not how my family behaves. What is going on? And because I don't understand, I become confused and then I feel scared. Moments later, my mother, sisters and I are called through, but when we enter the treatment room, my dad and brothers are not there. I don't understand and feel my stomach turning over and over, wanting to ask my mum questions, but I can't, because she is in conversation with the dentist. I look around the room and the first thing I notice is the huge black chair, which looks as if it could swallow you right up. Next to it is a high black and chrome stool and then a high table that has lots of tools and instruments on it. Above the chair is an enormous chrome lighting unit, suspended from the ceiling with gigantic, bending, metal arms. Standing at the side of the room is a pretty young woman who is looking at her nails, apparently disinterested in the proceedings.

The dentist speaks, "Which of you is Rose, then?"

I slowly raise my hand and try to say 'me' but my tongue is stuck to the roof of my mouth. He asks me to climb onto the chair, and I want to just run away and find my dad and brothers, but I can't. My parents told me to always respect my elders and do as I am told, so I step towards the monstrosity of a chair. My mum urges me to hurry up, as "we don't want to be here all day, you know." I don't want to be here for a single second, but I know I have to do as I'm told.

Once I am in the chair, it is 'pumped up' somehow and I can feel myself rising up higher. Then it tips back and I am lying staring up at the ceiling feeling completely and totally vulnerable and out of control. Next, the dentist pulls at the lighting unit, which drops in front of my face, bright and harsh, adding to my confusion. Then he instructs me to relax and open my mouth. As I tip my head further back, in a vain attempt to make eye contact with him, I catch sight only of his hairy hands, which are holding two instruments above my head. I want to do what he says, and make my mum proud, but I need to understand what he is going to do to me, so I ask him. He tells me that he just wants to "take a little look to make sure my teeth are doing alright" and repeats his command for me to open my mouth. I ask him what those things in his hands are for if he just wants to have a look, and he shows me the mirror and says that it is just a little mirror that will enable him to see properly.

So, I open my mouth slightly and he takes the opportunity to push his finger into the inside of my cheek. It tastes horrible, like cigarettes and I can feel myself becoming more and more fearful. He starts to call out numbers to his assistant and appears to be tapping my teeth with the mirror then, quite suddenly, I feel a sharp pain in my mouth and move my head in an attempt to free myself, but the dentist is far stronger than me, and tells me to "open up." I notice that the instrument I can now see in his hands is not a mirror but a sharp hook and he wants me to open my mouth. Not on your life. I can't understand why my mother is letting this man hurt me, and try to speak to her, but as I open my mouth to speak his fingers are again inside it, along with the hook. Now he tells me, something along the lines of "just be brave, this isn't going to hurt, you have a little hole in one of your teeth and I need to see how big it is," as he forces my jaws apart.

Once more he scrapes and pokes at the tiny hole causing shooting pains that bring tears to my eyes. Finally, he stops and tells me to swill my mouth out with some pink water, which he holds out to me in a small glass. I hold the glass in my hand and look to my mother for confirmation and she nods at me to do as I'm told. The pink liquid invades the hole in my tooth and again I feel a sensation that I don't like. I am feeling very tearful and want to run away, but I have no idea where, or who, I could run to. The dentist starts to adjust the chair and then tells me to hop off. I carefully climb off the chair and wipe the tears from my eyes. Mum gives me a cuddle and then tells me to sit down next to her and wait while the dentist checks out my sister's teeth. I didn't want to sit there and watch my sister being tortured; I just wanted to get out of that room, as far away from that man as possible.

Once I had relived my first experience of the label 'dentist', things began to make sense to me. The way I stored my five-sense experience of the label 'dentist' is how I still experience it today. So from there I wanted to find the key that would enable me to re-record the label 'dentist.' If I could do this, then maybe, I would never have to experience the whole five sense emotional and physiological expression of that label.

The key was the visual impression, what I see in my mind's eye, and what that evokes in my being. The image of the surgery makes me feel vulnerable and out of control and that, in turn, awakens all kind of negative monsters within. I start to panic and send out messages to my FG that I don't like to go to the dentist. FG wants to makes my wishes come true, so develops the negative visuals to persuade me not to go, which in turn bring all of the physiological effects and it all becomes like a vicious cycle, repeated again and again in an attempt by FG to stop me attending the appointment that I have no wish to attend.

An event, such as a visit to the dentist, which lasts at most half an hour, actually eats into whole days of my existence by generating feelings of vulnerability, fear, panic and a sense of being 'out of control,' which are all contained within my recording of the label 'dentist.'

This is the key, and I can now use the key, to take control of my reality.

How can I do this? Well, one way would be to contact various dental surgeries until I found one dentist who understood my issues and who would take the time to talk to me about the procedures and techniques he used. I would be able to inform him of my fears, and we could develop ways of making me feel safe and in control of the situation. I could then develop an image, such as the flower filled meadow that I focused on whenever I felt my physiology responding to the label 'dentist,' so that I give FG the message that I need to change the imagery. I could also visualise a future visit to the dental surgery in a totally different way, almost like producing my own home-movie of the event, where I am completely relaxed and in control.

Some people believe that they cannot do this alone and for them there is always the option of visiting a Neuro Linguistic Programming (NLP) practitioner, who will be more than happy to go though some techniques with you. The important point to remember is that you have all the resources within your own being to change your perception and response to the labels stored on your hard drive.

There is something quite magical about visualisation and the people who organise this world understand just how magical it is and constantly use hypnotic imagery to keep us part of the flock. Don't see things how *you* see them, see them how *we* want you to see them, because if you do that, then *we* have total control over your sense of reality.

Visualisation can free you so from so many prisons, which are only prisons in your own map of the world. I mean, not everyone is terrified of going to the dentist. How can that be, surely I am not the only person who feels the way I do? Well actually yes, I am the only person who feels the way *I* do. No one else on this planet will experience reality the way that I do and that is the way that it should be, otherwise the world would be populated by millions of Rose Bush's, and that would be extremely boring and monotonous, especially for me! So, why do so many of us believe that we see things the same way? Mass marketing and hypnotic suggestion is the answer.

We are bombarded throughout our waking lives, and for some our sleeping lives as well, by images (visuals) that are constantly telling us how we should be labelling every single damn thing. We live in a world of 24 hour TV, world wide web, education, radio, magazines, newspapers, advertising and marketing campaigns, groups, and a system of categorisation and stereotypes that generate propaganda for us to digest second by second. To stop us from collectively saying, "Hang on, we don't agree with what 'they' say, we think it is like this," the powers that be split us into different groups, ethnic origins, religions, collectives, genders, social classes, educational abilities, right down to the football teams we support and our star signs.

* * *

Then they make us focus on the differences between us; rather than unite in the similarities, which would of course, make us stronger. Mahatma Ghandi is quoted as saying that "even in a minority of one, the truth is still the truth," and David Icke has written, "the truth shall set you free." So, the question now becomes "what is the truth?"

The Bit Where I Rant About...
Truth

et's just take a deeper look at the question, "what is the truth?" In my copy of Chambers Twentieth Century Dictionary, the explanation is given thus: *'truth, trooth, n. faithfulness: constancy: veracity: agreement with reality: accuracy of adjustment or conformity.'*

So 'truth' is a noun, a naming word or label, and faithfulness is an adjective, which describes belief in or about something. So, the truth could be described as an agreed belief about reality, or an adjustment or conforming to an agreed belief about reality. Reality means "that which is real and not imagined" and real is defined as, "actually existing: not counterfeit or assumed" and the definition of assumed is, "appropriated, usurped: pretended: taken as the basis of an argument," and finally, the definition of usurped is, "forced possession, without right, or unjustly: assumed (the authority, place etc., of someone or something else; taken possession of (the mind): supplanted."

What does all of this mean in my map of the world? It means that the truth is a belief; therefore truth is my own natural judgment or a persuasion of the truth of anything. In other words, the truth exists for each of us as something that is real, or actually exists, which cannot be possessed by force, or assumed by any authority. WOW! When I actually got my head around that, it nearly blew my mind.

Finally, I understand that the only truth that I have to accept is *my* truth and that no one on this earth can take that away from me. So, everything that I have been *told to believe my whole life*, even when I knew the beliefs were wrong (in my reality), I could rightly have walked away from, as I didn't want to join the agreement, and belief cannot be possessed by force. What a revelation!

When you join this up to visualisation techniques, it becomes apparent that you can see yourself as anything on this earth that you want to be *and* you can actually believe it to be the truth. And if you believe it, then no one can tell you that it isn't true. So when I ask people to visualise themselves in a particular way and to believe that they really are that way, if they believe enough, it will become truth.

This is the magic of visualisation. It enables us to become other 'people.' Sometimes, people have characteristic traits that we wish we possessed, but don't believe we have, for example confidence. So, if it is possible for us to believe that we don't have confidence, and then we prove the truth by having no confidence, therefore, it must follow that if we believe that we do have confidence, we can prove the truth by being confident. This means that the boundaries have been removed, they do not exist, and we can be whoever we believe ourselves to be, and no one on this planet can make us believe otherwise. It's in your control.

Using visualisation, especially before you go to sleep, can enable you to *see* what you want, feel it, smell it, taste it and hear it. If you can visualise whatever 'it' is, then it is possible to make 'it' happen. For example, many of the labels that have been 'attached' to me for years have only applied and had any kind of meaning, because *I* believed them to be true. And because I believed them to be true, this is how I perceived myself to be in reality. I did not think I had a choice.

If I can recognise 'confidence' in another person, then I must accept an understanding of what 'confidence' is in my reality, and if I can do that then I can believe that I have confidence because it exists in my reality.

It makes you realise that belief is power beyond measure, as it can never be taken away from you, as long as it *exists* in your reality. This gives you infinite choices and possibilities. You do not have to *be* the 'label' that someone else attaches to you; you do not even have to believe the 'labels' that you *have* agreed to as truth, for years, maybe even lifetimes, you are free to live your own truth.

One of the ways that understanding all of this can be useful is to go back to times in our past, when we have accepted a belief that we now understand was not useful to us… and change the outcome. This means that instead of looking back at our lives, reliving the story again and again and reinforcing the belief, we can rewrite history with us *not* agreeing to the belief.

If we use 'confidence' as an example, it would mean that if, as a child, I believed that I was not confident, as that was how it was agreed by others, making comments such as, "oh no, Rose is not confident at all," or school reports stating, "Rose shows no confidence in front of her peers," then every time I look back at my past, I am buying *into* the belief and dragging it with me as baggage into my present.

We do this all of the time when we say things like, "Oh no, I've never been a confident person, everyone says it, no, I'm the quiet type, wouldn't say 'boo' to a goose." We become other people's beliefs of what we are, rather than creating our own truth. As I said earlier, when I was younger, I believed in respect for my elders and to do as I was told, by my 'elders and betters.' I did not know that I had any kind of choice in the matter; it was just the way it was.

One day when I was nine years old, I went out to play with two of my friends, who used to come and stay with their grandmother, who lived across the road from me. They were sisters, Marion was eight and Jessica, six years old. At the end of the street was open countryside, which people were free to roam, field after field after field. It was such an amazing space and many children spent their after-school hours, weekends and holidays playing in the fields. Whenever Marion and Jessica came to stay at their grandmother's house, we would always go off over the fields on some kind of adventure or other. The fields were interlinked with various 'lanes' and 'walks,' where there were a few houses dotted here and there. One of the lanes was called Staircase Lane and hidden away, amongst the trees and brambles, was a distant house that was said to be haunted. We would often sit on exposed tree roots, which reached about eight feet up from the ground, and see if we could spot any ghosts or spooky goings-on.

One Saturday, late afternoon, the three of us were sitting high upon the tree roots when an old man I saw everyday walked down the lane, stopped and then called up to me. I said hello back to him but I didn't want to clamber down to speak to him as I was enjoying the company of my friends. I knew him from the bus stop I passed every day on my way to school, and at first he just used to say hello. Over time, he would give me a sweet until finally he would walk up to the school gates with me and from there, I assumed, catch his bus.

The reason he began talking to me was that one morning, as I was walking to school, I started to cry. He was alone at the bus stop and asked me if I was all right. Not wanting to appear rude, I told him that I would be OK. He reached into his pocket and gave me his handkerchief and told me to wipe my eyes and then he gave my cheek a pinch and said, "Can't see a pretty little thing like you upset, can we?" I recall that I gave him back his handkerchief and carried on my journey, actually feeling slightly better for being called a "pretty little thing."

The next morning he was at the bus stop again and we waved at each other and then he stuck his thumb in the air and gave me a wink. It carried on like this for maybe a week, with nothing more than a passing wave or shouted "hello." After the weekend, he was there again, waiting at the bus stop, only this time he beckoned me over when we exchanged waves. I walked and stood in front of him and he said, "How's my pretty young thing today?"

"I'm fine, thank you. How are you?" He wore a trilby hat and he tilted it back when I answered and said, "Pretty *and* well mannered! I think that deserves a treat," and with that he pulled a couple of boiled sweets from his pocket and offered them to me. I shook my head and said, "No, thank you" But he insisted and said, "Come on, take them, I'm not a stranger now. Why I could practically be your uncle we see each other so often" and he pushed the sweets into my hand.

Looking back can bring all kinds of memories surging forward, guilt in this case, as I can remember looking forward to seeing him. He was always so nice and kind and made me feel good about myself.

Anyway, this is how it remained for the rest of the week. I would go and say hello to him and he would say lovely things to me and then give me two boiled sweets to suck on my way to school.

On the following Monday, when I went to say hello, he held out his hand and said, "Come on, how about your 'uncle' walking you to the school gates, instead of always walking alone?" It was a statement, rather than a suggestion, and he took my hand in his and started to chat to me about all sorts of things. He now knew my name and said that, "A rose by any other name would smell as sweet, and you are by far the prettiest rose I have ever seen."

One morning, he asked me why I had been crying the first day we met and I explained to him that I hadn't lived in Coventry for long and that I hadn't made any real friends yet. I also told him about how I was bullied at school by some of the other girls and that they called me horrible names. I spoke about Marion and Jessica and explained that they often came to stay at their grandmother's, and that I really liked them both. He reminded me of a granddad and I felt special because he was my secret 'uncle' that I didn't have to share with anyone else. No one ever took any notice of us walking up to school together and I am sure we did not look out of place, or arouse suspicion in anyone, not that I was aware at this point in time that there was anything, for anyone, to feel suspicious about.

Now you may be wondering, what on earth my mother was doing allowing me to walk to school on my own. Well, actually she didn't. I was supposed to walk up with my three brothers, but they usually ran on ahead, with the eldest carrying on to secondary school. I never liked walking with them, as I didn't get along with my eldest brother at all. I didn't like school either, so getting there quickly just meant longer in the playground where the 'bullies' would use me as the 'butt' of their jokes. Most days, I used to try and get the whole way to school without treading on any cracks in the pavement, convincing myself that if I managed to do so, then it meant that I wouldn't get bullied, and besides, my brothers didn't have time for my nonsense. They wanted to get to school to spend time playing marbles or conkers before assembly. To me, it wasn't nonsense, when you are being bullied at school, you will do anything to escape the torment, no matter how painful it might be to you, or stupid it may appear to others.

The first morning that we walked to school together, my secret 'uncle' had a surprise for me. He told me to put my hand in his coat pocket and see what I would find there, so I did as I was told and, to my surprise, pulled out a Mars bar. I was shocked, and grateful, as chocolate bars were a treat; on Fridays my father would arrive home with a brown paper bag containing six different chocolate bars; one for each child. The two bars that always got 'baggsied' first were the Mars bar and the Marathon, which my elder brothers always claimed. I would usually take the Turkish Delight, which I loved, even though I would have preferred the ones selected by my brothers. So, to have a whole Mars bar to myself was great, and it wasn't even Friday.

On Thursday morning, my secret uncle was not there and I hoped that nothing had happened to him, and after waiting for five minutes, I walked to school alone, taking care not to step on any cracks in the pavement, something that I didn't do when he was there walking beside me. The journey felt empty without him to chat away; he would divert my thoughts from the bullies. Now my mind focused on how to avoid being noticed and therefore picked on.

By Friday, he was back and I felt so happy to see him waiting for me. I almost ran to be by his side and he ruffled my hair and called me his "pretty little one." I told him that Marion and Jessica would be coming to their grandmother's for the weekend and that it would be great to see them. He asked what we intended to do, so I told him all about the haunted house and tree roots on Staircase Lane. He said that he knew of the place and that he had heard that the house was definitely haunted, and that we should not venture into the grounds, just to be on the safe side. Before I said goodbye, I searched his pockets and was repaid by another Mars bar. He told me not to tell anyone about the chocolate, or "they might all want one!"

The weekend was spent running over the fields, feeding the horses, jumping the brook, making daisy chains and eating home made jam 'doorsteps' (thick chunks of white bread with a slither of strawberry jam in the middle). Eventually we ended up at Staircase Lane, about a mile into the fields, and started to talk about 'spooky' things. We were all sitting right at the top of the exposed roots, where the tree trunks meet the field, dangling our mud splattered legs over the edge. It was late afternoon and it must have been around the end of June; the sun was still bright in the sky. Horses were shaking their manes and tails and standing beneath the shade of a tree, resting their hooves. It was a lovely day and I wished we could stay there forever.

Every so often, people, enjoying an afternoon stroll, would pass down the lane and on a couple of occasions, girls out on ponies would turn into the stables a little further along. In front of the stables was a farmhouse that was guarded not just by dogs, but geese as well and people said that the geese were worse at attacking strangers than the dogs. Every time someone passed by the farm entrance you could hear the dogs bark, and this would alert the geese, who would come spitting up the driveway and scare the passers by half out of their wits. It also meant that we could hear when anyone was approaching from the right, and we could clearly see down the lane to the left. That's how we knew someone was coming, but I really didn't expect it to be him.

I didn't want to talk to him really, as I was with my friends and knew it would soon be time to head back home, which would take at least 45 minutes. Also, I didn't want my friends to know about my secret 'uncle', as it meant it wouldn't be a secret any more, so instead of making my way down the tree roots, I acknowledged him from where I was. He indicated for me to come down, but I shook my head and said I wanted to stay with my friends. He shook his head back and said, "And there was me thinking that you were a well-mannered girl, tch, fancy saying no to your uncle." Marion nudged me and indicated that I should go down and then reinforced it by saying, "He is your uncle, after all."

I can vividly remembering feeling angry with him for letting our secret out of the bag, wanting to shout at him that he had spoilt everything by telling my friends, but I didn't. Instead, I stayed put and swung my legs, as I looked everywhere but at him. He didn't move though and once more spoke, "Rose I think you should come down now." Then checking his watch, he continued, "It's half past four, what time are you supposed to be home?" Before I could reply, Marion exclaimed, "I have to be back at grandma's at five… come on, let's go." With that she stood up, brushed the dry dirt off her skirt and pulled Jessica to her feet.

Secret 'uncle' smiled and told us to come down and he would escort us back. I don't know why, but I really didn't want him to walk with us, I just wanted him to go away. He must have seen my hesitancy because he said, "It will be getting dark soon and it is really not safe for you to be walking through fields on your own. Come down, and I will make sure you get back safely, oh and I might have something special hidden away in my pockets, but only if you come down."

I still didn't want to go, but now Marion was worried about not getting back safely and so I agreed and clambered down the tree roots, closely followed by the two sisters. When I got onto the lane, he took hold of my right arm and pulled me close to him and then breathed into my hair, "Don't say 'no' to me ever again, do you understand?" He then shook my arm loose. What he did to me didn't hurt, but it made me feel scared and I wanted to run away and never see him again, he had ruined everything. Secret 'uncle' ruffled Jessica's hair and then put his arm on her shoulder and looking at me, he directed his comments to her, "You are such a pretty little girl and your hair is beautiful. I've got something for such a pretty girl…" He paused and looked directly at Jessica. "Put your hand in my coat pocket and see what you can find." Jessica pulled out two boiled sweets and secret 'uncle' feigned surprise at the booty Jessica had secured. "My word," he smiled. "Pretty and clever." He then told us that we should make a move before our parents became worried.

We walked up Staircase Lane and turned into Church Walk before leaving the lanes and making our way into one of the fields. Secret 'uncle' wasn't talking to me, he had Marion on one side and Jessica on the other and was holding each of their hands. I lagged behind feeling fed up and wished as hard as I could wish, that he would disappear.

Ahead of us was a five-bar gate that we had to climb over and Marion ran on ahead and started to clamber up the slats of wood while Jessica was pointing at the barbed wire to the side of the gate, which she would normally choose as her entry to the next field. Secret 'uncle' called back to me to get a move on and again put his arm around Jessica's shoulder and pulled her body in close to his own. They didn't start to climb the gate until I got there and when I told Jessica to go through the barbed wire, he told her not to, saying, "Why should she have to miss out on the climbing just because she's the smallest." He gave her a squeeze and asked her if she wanted to climb.

Jessica nodded enthusiastically. Marion, who was by now on the other side of the gate, told her that she was too little to climb, that she might fall and hurt herself. Secret 'uncle' told us that he would make sure she didn't hurt herself and with that, Jessica began to climb up the gate. Marion offered words of encouragement from the other side and secret 'uncle', who was standing to Jessica's left, was supporting her, with his right arm about her waist. He then turned his head to look me straight in the eyes and as Jessica lifted her right leg up on to the next slat, he moved his right hand under her short cotton skirt and put his hand inside her knickers. Jessica turned her head sharply and he quickly urged her on, smiling and said, "Keep going there's a good girl, you're a natural climber." He then turned to me and said, "Come on, Rose, or are you waiting for me to help you, too?" I didn't know what to do. I wanted to shout at him then to run away, but the words never left my mouth, instead I just stood there looking at him.

As Jessica got to the top he had his hand on her backside and then slid his hand up the inside of her bare thigh in the pretence of helping her to swing her leg over the top bar. All the time he was watching me, almost daring me to say something, but I couldn't. Everything felt strange and confused. So many thoughts were whirring through my mind, yet it felt as if time was standing still.

With Jessica straddling the top of the gate, he told her to wait while he climbed over himself, to assist her down the other side. He called me and told me to get over first and to stop being a 'mardy pants,' and for some reason, I did as I was told. As I dropped down the other side of the gate, I looked up at Jessica waiting to be assisted; something had changed in her face. She looked really scared, so I told secret 'uncle' that I would help her and lifted my arms up towards her, but he swiped them out of the way and put his own hands out, telling her to swing her leg over. She was now sitting nervously on top of the gate with his hands on her bare knees. He then slid his hands upwards over her little naked legs, before changing his direction and securing his arms around her waist.

So much was going on in my head, but it was almost as if I couldn't separate the thoughts, or make any sense of them, all I knew was that this did not feel right; it was making my skin crawl. He continued to hold her around the waist and then told her to jump towards him. Jessica looked terrified and Marion, who was not aware of what was going on, laughed at her sister, telling her not to be a 'scardey cat.' So, Jessica leant forward and he lifted her into his body telling her to open her legs and wrap them around him to "make sure you don't fall and hurt yourself." Jessica did as she was told and once her legs were wrapped around his waist, he turned to face me and lifted her short skirt with his fingers and then put both of his hands inside her knickers. As he did this, he smiled at me, and I wanted so much to look away and pretend that I was not seeing, whatever it was I was seeing, but I couldn't. He then gently set Jessica onto her feet and pulled her close to his side with his arm resting on her shoulder, telling her what a brave little girl she was.

Confusion was now being replaced by fear and suddenly, like a bolt of lightning shooting through my body, I understood that this was what grown ups meant when they talked about bad men; secret 'uncle' was a bad man. I also became aware that we were still half an hour from home, stuck with him, with no one around to help us. I felt a huge lump rise from my stomach and lodge itself in my throat, and I knew that if I didn't control myself, I would burst into tears and that might make him angry, which I knew was the last thing I wanted to do.

I walked ahead briskly and Marion came after me, telling me to slow down and then asked me what was wrong with me. I didn't know what to do, whether to tell her, or to keep her in ignorance, so I just muttered something about wanting to get home. As all of this was happening, thoughts were racing and colliding with each other in my mind. This was my fault, all my fault. My parents would kill me. I had taken sweets from him. We had gone to Staircase Lane and we weren't meant to go there. They would never let me play in the fields again. My friends, the only real friends I had, would probably not be allowed to play with me any more. What if he kills us all? I felt sick.

Secret 'uncle' shouted angrily for us to wait and instantly I obeyed him, stopping dead in my tracks. When he reached us he put his arm around my waist and squeezed my flesh and then whispered in my ear, "We are not going home yet. I want you to all come over there with me, so tell your friends we are going to play a game, OK?" and he squeezed my skin hard between his fingers.

The area he had indicated towards was at the far edge of the field. It was a sectioned off corner, surrounded by hedgerow that almost separated it from the rest of the field. I looked across at Jessica, who looked so empty, nothing showing on her face, just blank. I knew I had to do something so I told him I wanted to talk to him on his own. He smiled and let go of Jessica, telling her to be a good girl and not to move and she stood there like a zombie and Marion, oblivious to everything, happily played, performing clumsy cartwheels in the lush grass. We stood a few feet from Jessica and he looked directly at me and said, "Well, what do you want to talk about?"

He didn't look kind any more, he looked really scary and it took all my courage to speak. "Please don't hurt my friends, please, let them go. They have a sad life, please don't hurt them." He reached out and took my hand in his and then said, "If I let them go, what fun will that be for me?" I lowered my head and muttered, almost under my breath, "Are you a bad man?"

He laughed, "Yes, I guess that is just what I am." He lifted my chin so that I was looking into his face before continuing, "In fact, I am a wizard, do you know what a wizard is?" I slowly nodded. "Good, then you will know that I am very powerful and can do all kinds of magic and spells, do you understand, Rose? All kinds."

Again, I nodded.

"So, what are you saying to me, my sweet little thing?"

Quietly I spoke, "Let them go and I will come with you, please let them go."

He now pulled my head into his chest and stroked the back of my hair. "Such a brave little thing, aren't you? Are you scared, Rose? Are you scared of your 'uncle'?"

I nodded my head into his chest. Still holding me he continued, "If I let them go, you better do as you are told, otherwise 'uncle' will be angry and I don't want 'uncle' to get angry with you. If you disobey, uncle will hurt you, do you understand?"

Once more I nodded my acknowledgement.

"OK then, 'uncle' will let them go, but you tell them to go home and not say anything to anyone, if they do, it will make 'uncle' very angry."

With that he pushed me away from him and told me to go and talk to them both.

I approached Marion and told her to go home without me and I whispered quietly that my 'uncle' was really a wizard and that if they told anyone about him, then he would put a spell on us all. They had to go home and not even speak to my family, just say that I had stayed behind to feed the horses, if anyone should ask. Marion was totally shocked and said that we should just run away while he wasn't looking, but I told her to just go, he would only catch one of us and it would make him angry. Jessica now came and stood by Marion and said softly, "I want to go home, Marion".

Secret 'uncle' now approached and said, "So, are you two going to go then?"

They nodded.

"Good, then off you go and remember 'uncle' will know if you say anything and 'uncle' will come and find you and make you sorry, do you understand?"

Marion looked at me pleadingly, almost begging me with her eyes to make a run for it, but I knew that he would catch one of us, and that the one he caught would probably be Jessica. This was my fault, not hers; she was just a little girl. I shook my head and then walked and stood next to secret 'uncle' and, as he put his arm around my shoulders, he shouted, "Shoo," which made both sisters turn on their heels and run.

Now before I progress any further with this, I want to give you, the reader, some options. As you are probably aware, I was sexually abused, and for the first time ever I am writing about it, and I am writing it as I remember it. For those of you who are bothered by 'profanities' or swear words then be warned, the next section contains quite a few. I would also like to add my thoughts on the use of swear words. If we did not label them as such, then there would be nothing to get *upset* about. If we made full use of all the words in our language and did not attach *special significance* to a select group, then no one would ever be offended and it would have made my ordeal easier to bear, because I could have recounted the words to adults without the fear that I was saying something bad. Calling specific words 'swear words' gives those words power.

I would also like to point out that anyone who has been abused and whom the next section might affect, can miss it out totally and turn to page 75.

So, now I will continue.

"Good girl, Rose, now let's go and sit down somewhere quiet."

He escorted me and was talking, but nothing he said registered with me, I just kept thinking that I was going to die. When we got to the secluded corner of the field he took off his coat and spread it on the grass and then looked at his watch. He then lowered himself down onto the coat and patted it, indicating that I was to sit down next to him. I did as I was told. He then started to stroke my hair and tell me how pretty I was, and how he would like to see all the other pretty parts of me adding, "Would you like that, would you like uncle to look at all your pretty parts?"

I said nothing. He held himself up and said, "Where are your manners, Rose? Speak when you're spoken to. Now answer the question. Tell me how much you want your uncle to see your pretty bits and don't get me angry. Just do as you're told and you will be OK, understand?"

I nodded, which seemed to make him really angry as he took my shoulders in his hands and started to shake me saying, "Fucking speak, you little bitch, ask uncle nicely to look at your pretty bits, or I'll have to hurt you, now speak."

Now I was really scared and knew I had to say something, so I said all I could think of to say, "I don't know what you want me to say."

He mimicked my voice, "I don't know what to say," then added forcefully, "What you mean is, I don't know what to say 'uncle', get it, 'uncle'."

I nodded my head frantically, not knowing what to do. His mood changed and he lay down, supporting his head in his hand, "Are you a good girl, Rose?"

I nodded.

"I didn't hear you. I said are you a good little girl, Rose?"

"Yes" I replied quietly.

"Good, then everything will be OK."

He sat up and then told me to look at him before continuing, "I want you to tell me that you want your 'uncle' to look at your pretty fucking bits and I want you to say please like a good girl. Now say it."

My heart was beating so hard in my chest that I felt like I was suffocating and my mouth was so dry that it was hard to speak. I just wanted whatever was going to happen, to be over, even if I was going to die, I just wanted it to be over. He lent towards me and said in a quiet, slow voice, "Cat got your tongue?" He was slowly nodding his head, so I nodded with him. "Well, if you aren't going to speak to me, there is no need for you to have a tongue in your head, is there?" and with that he put his hand into his trouser pocket as if looking for something, then in a matter of fact kind of tone said, "Last chance. Repeat after me, 'I want you to fuck me, uncle'. Repeat."

I tried to speak but my voice was so quiet I could hardly hear it myself, "I… want you to… me uncle."

"Didn't hear you and sit up straight there, facing me, so that I can see your face. Go on hurry up, there isn't much time left."

I moved to where he had indicated and he told me to cross my legs and he lifted my dress so that it lay on my lap. "Now, tell uncle what you want him to do, there's a good girl."

He smiled and shifted his position so that he could lower his head and look between my crossed legs. I thought I would vomit; my stomach was churning and making all kinds of noises that sounded so loud in the quiet field. He put his hand inside his trousers and started fidgeting around and then reached out a finger and prodded me, "Say the word 'fuck', Rose, say it and you can keep your tongue."

In a small, terrified voice I said the word "fuck" and thought that a bolt would open from the sky and God would send me to hell.

"Again, louder."

"Fuck"

"Louder"

"FUCK"

He had a strange look on his face which made me feel even more scared, "OK, sweetheart, now 'uncle' wants you to open your legs wide, so that 'uncle' can see all those pretty little things you hide away, and pull your panties to one side. If *you* don't do it, 'uncle' is going to rip off your panties and make you eat them. Do it."

With total shame I did as he asked and not satisfied with my position, he moved my legs until he was.

"That's better, now 'uncle' wants you to open those lips and let 'uncle' have a real good look, 'cos we know that's what you want 'uncle' to do."

I didn't understand what he meant, so I opened my mouth wide, thinking this must be what he wanted. I was so scared thinking that he was going to cut my tongue out, but instead he smiled and pointed between my legs, "Those lips, either you do it or uncle does it."

The lump in my throat felt as if it was as big as an apple and I felt sure that if I didn't get away soon I would die from lack of breath. I did as he asked and my chest started to take in short breaths in a silent cry.

He undid his trousers and took hold of his penis in his hand and said, "Uncle wants you to enjoy this, and you will if you do just what 'uncle' asks. I know you want 'uncle' to touch you, but 'uncle' can't, so you touch yourself and 'uncle' will touch himself and we will both have a nice time, OK? So, rub your finger up and down your fanny and 'uncle' will watch and play with his cock. Do it, and talk to your 'uncle.' Tell him how much you love him, how you love his big cock, tell him you want him to fuck you."

"I love you uncle, I love you uncle…"

He reached and took my hand and then put one of my fingers in his mouth, licked it, leaving it wet, before putting it back and telling me to rub myself again. His hand was moving up and down on his penis and he then spat on it and started to rub again.

"Rose, say what 'uncle' told you or 'uncle' is going to shove this in your fucking arse."

"I love you 'uncle.' Fuck me 'uncle.' I love you 'uncle.'"

As I spluttered the words, I noticed his breathing had changed and after a quick glance at his watch he said, "Good girl, it feels nice what you are doing, huh? 'Uncle' loves watching you play with yourself."

He shifted his position and continued, "Now, I want you to come closer because 'uncle' wants you to look at his magic wand, come on."

He pulled at my arm, until I was right next to him then he told me to open my mouth, and that if I did anything bad, he would chop me into small pieces and throw me into the brook so no one would ever find me. Not content with my position, he manoeuvred me so that I was lying on my side, head by his lap, with my upper leg bent and my lower leg straight and then lifted my skirt and told me to pull my knickers across and open my lips. I did as I was told. Then he moved himself slightly so that he could put his penis into my mouth. My neck was bent in an awkward way and my mouth was totally dry, so he took it out and told me to lie down on his coat on my back. He lifted my legs so that they were apart, and then told me to open my lips again and he just kept watching and masturbating, then he said, "Put your head back and open your mouth."

Again, I did as I was told and he moved so that he was straddling my chest and taking his weight on one hand, he spat on his penis and then shoved it hard into my mouth. I closed my eyes and he ordered me to open them saying, "See how nice that is, put your hands down and play with yourself, 'uncle' wants you to enjoy it."

I did as I was told. He was looking really strange now and his breathing was hard and when he spoke it was in small, breathless sentences. "Uncle wants… to fuck you, 'uncle'… wants to come in your mouth first… then we can go for a walk, or we can go to the seaside… oh, my God."

He stopped moving for a moment and looked at me, almost choking on his penis. "In a minute 'uncle' is going to shoot something into your mouth and you have to swallow it, because if you don't, 'uncle' is going to be really angry, OK, good girl, it won't take long." And with that he started moving in and out of my mouth faster and faster until he ejaculated.

I started choking and couldn't breathe and after what seemed like an eternity, he got off me and fell to the side, pushing his penis into his trousers as he did so. I started spluttering and spitting, trying to get the horrible slime out of my mouth and he lent across and grabbed my hair and said, "Uncle told you to swallow. Do it, swallow all of it."

It was the final straw and I felt tears burst from my eyes and fall down my cheeks. He let out a big sigh and pulled himself into a sitting position, "What are you crying for? 'Uncle' didn't hurt you, 'uncle' didn't even touch you, did he? Stop crying. Did 'uncle' touch you?"

I shook my head.

"No, 'uncle' didn't touch you. You played with yourself and sucked 'uncle's' cock at the same time 'cos you enjoyed it, didn't you?"

I nodded my head and he knelt in front of me and said, "Listen, I have a friend who has a caravan by the seaside. How about going there? No more getting bullied at school, No one would ever hurt you again. 'Uncle' would look after you."

He checked his watch again and said, "Come on, let's go before it gets too late."

"I don't want to go, I just want to go home, please 'uncle', can I go home?"

I was sobbing now.

"Shh there, you can't go home sweetheart, because you might tell someone about what *you* did, and they would be really angry with you and send you away because they would think you were a bad girl, but 'uncle' loves you and knows that you are a good girl."

He started to brush off his shoulders as if nothing had happened and then started to brush me down. He pulled down my skirt and spoke menacingly, "You look like a little whore lying like that showing me everything, sit up and wipe your eyes then let's go. Good girls don't do that."

He looked deep into my eyes and said, "Come on, up you get, you understand that you have to come with 'uncle' now. 'Uncle' will look after you. You know your mum and dad don't want you any more because you're a dirty little bitch."

* * *

He took my head in my hands asking, "What are you?"

"A dirty little bitch."

"That's right, now why would your mum and dad want a dirty little bitch in their nice clean home, eh? And you are a whore. Do you know what a whore is?"

I shook my head and he continued in a strange, almost friendly voice, "*You* are a whore. A dirty whore who says the word "fuck." A whore is someone who opens her legs, begging men to fuck her. *You* wanted 'uncle' to fuck you, didn't you, so that makes you a dirty whore. What are you?"

"A dirty whore."

"That's right, a foul-mouthed, dirty whore. What do you think your dad would do to you if he knew you showed men your fanny and played with yourself, so that they could see? I bet you show all the boys at school your fanny. I bet you show the teachers, too. Is that why you get bullied, because they know you show your fanny to everyone? Let 'uncle' tell you what your dad would do if he knew what a dirty little whore you were. He would beat you and then throw you out in the street like the dirty little whore you are. Now, 'uncle' will make sure that daddy never finds out. And 'uncle' knows that because you are a dirty whore that you want him to watch you play with your fanny and he doesn't mind. So, what do you want to do, get thrown out on the street, or let 'uncle' take care of you?"

I wiped my eyes, realising that what he said was right; I couldn't go home now. Maybe he would look after me and I wouldn't have to be sent away.

At that moment, the remote sound of voices broke my train of thought. In the distance I could see Marion and Jessica trying to find a spot to cross the brook. They were waving their arms and shouting my name. I turned to look at secret 'uncle,' who had his arms on his hips and was shaking his head, "What the hell do they want?"

"I don't know"

They had now crossed the brook and secret 'uncle' seemed to be getting agitated, "Who have they got with them?" he asked, straining his eyes to check it out.

"No one, 'uncle.'"

He turned to look at me and said, "Uncle has to go; they may have told someone." He bent down so that his eyes were level with mine and said, "But before I do, I have to tell you something."

He lifted his head to check out where the sisters were, "That stuff that you swallowed was magic, now, if you tell a single soul what happened today, 'uncle' will know, and then 'uncle' will say some magic words and it will turn into poison and kill you slowly and horribly, do you understand?"

I nervously nodded in agreement.

Then he continued hurriedly, "And listen, you played with yourself, *you* swallowed 'uncle's' stuff. 'Uncle' never did anything, and that means that you are the one who is bad, not 'uncle.' Do you understand? No one will believe a word you say, and if you say anything anyway, 'uncle' will know and you will be dead. OK, now go."

He pushed me in the chest and when I didn't move he pushed me again, "Go on, fuck off."

"Please don't make me die," I whimpered.

"Fuck off and keep your mouth shut then. Go on, go."

I could see the sisters getting closer and closer and their voices getting louder and louder, but inside, somewhere deep inside, I didn't want to go. If I stayed with 'uncle', he would make sure I didn't die.

"I don't want to go 'uncle'. What if something happens to me?"

He shook his head and turned once more to check on the sisters progress, "Look, I don't want you. It's no wonder you're bullied. You're a stupid, ugly little whore who wants to be fucked. Why would I want a disgusting, filthy, little smelly bitch like you?"

He bent down, picked up his coat, shook and put it on, then reached in the pocket and smiled, "Here," he laughed, "it's for you, worth every penny, now fuck off and remember what I said."

He threw the squashed Mars bar at my feet. I just looked at where it landed and felt so disgusting and dirty that I hated and despised myself. The sisters were only feet away and shouting excitedly, "Rose, Rose, your brothers are coming. We met them on the way home and told them that you were with your 'uncle.' Your brothers are coming."

Secret 'uncle' just gave a little snort and gathered himself together. He began to walk off rather briskly, shouting over his shoulder for me to remember what he had said.

I turned and ran towards the girls, not once looking back.

Now, although I didn't have a watch, I guess that the whole episode alone with him lasted; realistically, under half an hour; yet it seemed like a lifetime to me. The thing is, it could have lasted a lifetime, because for years, I allowed that event to take control of my life. It had a devastating effect on who I *believed* myself to be. I didn't really know who I was any more.

Many years later, I gained courage to go and rescue that part of me, which was still trapped in my past. Although I didn't realise what I was doing at the time I did it, I was using a technique similar to one used in NLP called Changing Personal History. I realised that I could not let the memories and the words (labels) from the past, continue to have power in my present. I was a parent myself by this time, so I took the children to nursery and school and spent the day alone thinking of all that had happened.

This time I didn't just focus on the words; I focused on everything, the whole thing from start to finish. Then I closed my eyes and wrapped my arms around myself, telling the younger child, still trapped in the torment within me, that I was sorry that I had left her there for so long, and that everything was going to be OK now. I forgave myself completely and it was such a relief. Then I just rocked back and forth for a few minutes, enjoying the feeling of completeness.

I then stood up and visualised the event in my mind's eye and as he spoke, I allowed the younger Rose to say what she would say now, as if she was still there.

It was amazing. I shouted, "You are not my uncle and yes, I say the words 'fuck' and 'bollocks' and 'cunt'. I am not a whore and never have been a whore. You, on the other hand, are a disgusting old slime ball who has to trick children for cheap thrills because you are so weak and pathetic. Bend over and let me shove this Mars bar up your arse."

I said much more than that, but to include it all would take too many pages. The important thing is that I allowed my younger self to take control of the situation and realise that he could *never* hurt her again. After about an hour of shouting, screaming and crying I was finished and to my total surprise I burst out laughing, shouting, "Yes."

Now, I don't think about it any more and this is the first time that I have ever told anyone exactly what happened all those years ago, and do you know what, it didn't hurt a bit. The amazing thing is that if something doesn't feel right, to you *individually* as a belief, then you have to have the courage to be *different* and to stand by what it is that you actually believe. It is no good just going along with a belief because everybody else does; you need to understand *what it is* that you are agreeing to believe in. This is really important for parents to understand, when they are downloading their own personal beliefs into their children's minds. Explain what you mean, then let them ask questions, then give the child the choice to believe it or not.

* * *

Just because someone is older, does not mean that they are wiser. We have to give children the confidence to take a different road, which maybe doesn't match our own. We have to let them know that they are loved, no matter what happens to them on life's journey. We must encourage them to ask questions; phrases like "because I said so", are not good enough. And we should answer their questions honestly and in a way that affords options and personal choice.

Child molesters are not stupid. They know what parents say to their children, and they manipulate the children with that knowledge. As parents, we need to clearly think through how we equip our children with as many resources as possible to make informed choices and decisions and to enable them to explore this world, their planet, safely.

So, let's look at some of those 'labels' that have been attached to us for years and ask ourselves:

a) Do you believe the 'label' to be true?
b) Are you happy with the belief?
c) Do you want to believe it?

If you answered 'no' to those questions, then for you it is easy. Just remove the label. If it was a confidence issue, then the next time someone mentions your supposed lack of confidence, surprise him or her. Say in an assertive voice, "Actually, you are totally wrong. I am a confident person."

If you draft out a kind of one or two sentence script, and practise repeating it, then the first time you actually say it to someone, you *will* totally surprise them.

Think out the different remarks that you would like to say and start to believe them yourself. Be who *you* believe yourself to be, who you want to be and your FG will do everything to make it happen.

There are other beliefs that we need to look at and question. Like, do you believe everything you read in the newspapers? If you answered 'no' then good on you! If you answered 'yes', then how do you decide what you will believe and what you won't? And if it is a case of believing some articles and disbelieving others, then what is the point of them? Surely they should just write what is *truth* and leave the bullshit out, and as they don't, then why read the newspapers at all? The media lies, even in the midst of truth, the media lies.

For many years, I was an avid newspaper and TV news fanatic. I wanted to get Sky installed, just so that I had 24-hour access to world news. When Princess Diana was killed, I watched the unfolding news for days, wanting to get the full story. When 9-11 happened, I didn't move from in front of the TV screen for weeks. When Afghanistan was invaded, I constantly had the radio or TV tuned in. Why? Because I wanted to know the *truth* and in my innocence and naivety, I thought that truth was exactly what the newsreaders were giving us. The truth, the whole truth and nothing but the truth. I thought that they were giving me the information to make informed choices. If they said Bin Laden did it, then it must be true, and let's get him and make him answer for his crimes.

In fact, I was quite proud of my knowledge of current affairs and prone to showing off just how well *informed* I was. If I didn't watch at least one news program in a day, I felt like I was missing an arm. I needed to know what was going on; I needed to follow the plot, like others follow soap operas. I actually *believed* that I knew what was happening in the world and I thought I had quite an unnerving accuracy in predicting the various world leaders' next moves. I was not anti anything and believed I had an open mind, watching Middle Eastern as well as Western channels and often, criticising Western leaders for their bullying tactics.

How wrong could I be?

Just as it doesn't take a genius to work out the plots of a soap opera, it doesn't take one to follow the world soap opera, in fact the script for that gets leaked quite often, just like they do in the soaps. All for a purpose – to keep us hanging on tenterhooks, wondering if they will invade Iran. What if Syria gets involved in the Lebanon conflict? Will Harry meet Sally?"

That is exactly what they want. I use to watch *Eastenders* every time it was broadcast and my eldest daughter, Faye, use to say, "Oooo, you have to watch '*Enders* on Friday, Mum. Grant is coming back and guess what he's going to do this time?" Faye would read up on the various 'leaks' and then bait me with the tidbit, and sure enough I would wait expectantly for the next thrilling installment. Sad, eh? Then one day I watched a so-called 'conspiracy theory' film on the Internet, which showed footage of 9-11 from various different perspectives and my belief started to waver. I spoke to friends about it, who commented that there was no way on this earth that President Bush or his government would actually blow up his own people (isn't that what he's doing, sending them to die in manipulated wars?).

Others said that all these types of conspiracy downloads were shot with high tech equipment so that they could cut and paste anything they wanted people to see (a bit like the high tech equipment the media has then?), and advised me to take it with a 'pinch of salt' (remember that saying for later in the book), but the nagging feeling didn't go away. I had to know what really happened. I started to look for clues so that I could understand, because if it was true and Bush, or someone or something above him, did order 9-11 then the world I inhabited had suddenly become a very scary place.

One day, a friend said to me that if I was into all of that *alternative* kind of stuff, I should read some of David Icke's thoughts. Now, I'd heard of David Icke through Anne, one of the volunteers on the project I managed, so I spoke with her and she was full of him, singing his praises and saying not to get put off by all the propaganda that's been written about him. Still, I didn't read any of his work because media advertising had performed its magic and I actually thought he sounded a bit weird myself, all that stuff about reptiles (not so weird any more!).

In fact, it took me five years to read one of his books and even then, I only picked it up and flicked through it, because it literally fell off the shelf and dropped at my feet (synchronicity). I bought it and I read the book in a single sitting; I just couldn't put it down. Since then I have read many of his books and have his 2006 DVD from his session in London. If you want to know what I believe 'truth' is, you should watch the DVD. It's actually three DVD's, and again, I had to watch them one after the other, and then watched them again with my partner. David Icke is amazing and the research he has done to get his version of 'truth' out there is incredible.

These days, I don't watch TV at all, and I don't read newspapers either.

The thing is if I don't keep up with the bullshit, life smells a whole lot sweeter. I don't worry about whatever disaster is heading our way; if it happens, it happens. I don't start conversations any more with the words, "So, what do you think of the situation in Gaza?" Instead, I say something positive like, "You are looking so relaxed." I focus my attention on the positive I can bring to the world rather than wasting my time 'buying' into the negatives.

Belief is your 'truth.' Find out what yours is and spread the word.

The Bit Where I Rant About...
Parents and Children

Most of us will experience either being a parent or, being cared for by a parent, at some point in our lives. I accept that not all of us will and that some people may spend their entire lives being 'cared for' by the system and/or never having a child of their own.

Most of us think that we are good parents, or forgive our own parents for any mistakes they made in our own growing up, maybe not even being fully aware of what those 'mistakes' were. I am a parent and I am ashamed of the way I have raised my children, not through lack of care or love, but through ignorance and I have now forgiven myself. The greatest gift a parent can give their child is independence, not only in body, but in mind and spirit as well, and on those counts, I made a hash of it.

With my oldest two, *they* were experiencing the entire trauma that I was, even though I believed I was protecting them. My other two children had a more stable upbringing, without any of the trauma the others had suffered and I did try to be the perfect mother, enduring a rather loveless relationship with their father for over twenty years, in the *belief* that I was giving them the best option of a secure childhood. I remember one particular evening, many years ago. My youngest daughter Hannah was around 14 years old and, after school, I would often take the girls out to exercise our two dogs around the village lanes and footpaths.

On this particular evening, I think it was just me and Hannah who went out and, as we walked down the footpath throwing the ball for the dogs to chase, Hannah said, "Guess what? At school today we were asked to remember our first memory and then tell the class what it was. Do you know what? Everyone's first memory, apart from mine, was of something horrible. When the teacher heard mine, she asked if I could remember anything negative and I said I didn't have a single bad memory about growing up."

I was so happy when she told me that, so happy. Little did Hannah, or I know, that within two years her castle walls were going to collapse around her feet, and that the effect on her would be enormous, but that is her story to tell, not mine.

As a teenage mum, no one could ever have prepared me for motherhood and, if they had tried, I wouldn't have believed them. I was one of six kids; I saw my mum and dad managing, so why did people think I couldn't do what they did? I also thought that I wanted so much to 'love' and had so much love to give, that my baby would be happy, bonny and never cry.

My parents moved to Northern Ireland just months before my baby was born. Luckily, my mother was visiting me in England the night Faye was delivered but, sadly, had to return to Ireland the next day. On the day Faye was born, I promised to love her forever and to give her as much as I could to ensure she had a happy life. The problem with making this kind of promise was that I didn't know *how* to ensure she experienced a happy life. I only had my own *perception* of reality.

Babies are like little sponges, they absorb everything and are very intuitive, picking up on energies and trying to make sense of their world and we, the adults, provide so much of the information they need. And we feed them such conflicting information, expecting them to make sense of parents who say one thing and then do another. How many of you believed in the 'tooth fairy' when you were little? How many of you have told your children about the 'tooth fairy'? How many of you have told your children that it is wrong to tell lies? How many of you have told them about the 'tooth fairy' *and* told them not to tell lies?

How many of you have told them that it's rude to interrupt and then told them to send their friend home "right now" even though they are in the middle of doing something? How many of you have told the children to turn off the television and listen to what you are saying and then told them to "hang on until this program has finished" when they have something that they view as important to tell you? How many of you have told your children to play "nicely" and then shouted at them to "go away" when then tell you and daddy to stop being horrible to each other, when you are having a major disagreement? How many of you tell them to eat their food whilst not eating yourself?

What are we doing? How are they meant to make sense of that, and more to the point, how do we make sense of it? We are doing so much harm to our children, not just with what we say, but how we say it. We are so busy that most of us don't monitor them, leaving them to their own devices with computers or Playstations as their only company. We also send them to school at a younger age so that the 'powers that be' can corrupt and brainwash them, towing the party line, turning them into *citizens,* or even worse, cannon fodder to fight in political soap operas. We even clean their teeth with poisons and fill their tummies with crap.

Is this what being a parent is all about?

About ten years ago, I was a project manager for a wonderful organisation called Home Start, which offered support to parents with at least one child under the age of five years. It was an excellent scheme that linked volunteers with families to offer 1-2-1 support and friendship, delivered in the family's own home. My role was to interview potential volunteers, train the suitable ones and link them to a family considered, in my opinion, to be a good match.

Part of the process, for referred families, was to fill in a questionnaire, which asked the parent to self-assess how they were feeling, by scoring themselves against specific emotions. The idea was that the parent would repeat this self-assessment at intervals of three months. What amazed me about this process was the amount of parents, mainly women, who scored themselves 'highly' as depressed and isolated. Most of the scores were in excess of seven, out of a maximum score of 10. In all my time with the scheme, less than 10% did not rate themselves as depressed, and only 20% did not feel they were isolated, on their first self-assessment. The parents were also asked to inform us if they were taking any prescribed medication, and I am horrified to report that over 80% of the parents our project supported, were on prescribed antidepressants.

Now I have been on antidepressants a few times in my life and, in my opinion as a user of this type of medication, they never remove the cause of the depression they just mask it. One prescribed drug that I was on made me totally zombified. I couldn't perform simple tasks like remembering what I went to the shops to buy, or where I was actually meant to be going. I felt as if my mind was wrapped in cotton wool, and I was so tired that I would just turn on the TV and watch the same channel for hours at a time, regardless of what programmes came on.

Once, I forgot to collect my children from school and then burst into tears because I didn't know what I should do about it, as my ability to make decisions had been affected. On more than one occasion, when I felt totally unconnected with who I *believed* myself to be, I thought it would be easier for everyone if I just bought a bottle of vodka and swallowed all the medication. I am sad to say that one day, in total desperation, that is exactly what I did.

Antidepressants *make you believe* that you are depressed. The good news about Home Start was that after three months of joining the project, the parents' scores had always improved, with them making comments like "my volunteer is a life-saver, I look forward to her visit so much, and it makes my week." Although this was something to be happy about, it also makes one aware of the opposite. It is really sad, really, really sad, and is a reflection of the absolute isolation many parents feel. It is incredible to think, that a volunteer, visiting for a couple of hours, one day a week, could be considered to be a 'life saver.' So many parents are *convinced* that the volunteer literally saved their lives! What kind of value does this mean *we*, represented by our elected (if you can believe that they really are) government, put on the health and wellbeing of parents, women in particular, and on the future health and wellbeing of our country?

Many of the referred parents eventually became volunteers themselves, and I have many happy memories of my time at Home Start, watching parents who were medicated out of their heads, transform in so many wonderful and magnificent ways, free of prescribed drugs. One of the referred mothers is now a qualified midwife, another, a social worker, and many have gone to college or became volunteers. I am jubilant to be able to say, that when I eventually left the organisation one of the first parents to join the project, stepped into my role as Scheme Manager.

How many parents out there do not have an organisation like Home Start to make a difference to their week? Home Start supports thousands of parents every year and the really sad fact is, that they *all* have at least one child under the age of 5 years. How many parents do you know, maybe you are one yourself, who view their lives as isolating and depressing? This means that thousands of young, brilliant, amazing human beings are being raised by at least one parent who *feels* depressed and isolated. Now just think about this for one minute, if the *parent* feels like that, imagine what the *child* must be experiencing. When a parent is feeling isolated, worthless or depressed they often *feel* unable to perform the role of 'perfect parent.' Many of them deal with their children in a similar way:

- Sitting the child in front of the same video (the child's favourite e.g. Tweenies, Bob the Builder) for as long as they possible can.
- Let them get all their toys out and watch them trash the house with them, then shove them all back, ready for the next day.
- Go out somewhere, anywhere, just to get out, usually McDonalds.
- Leave them to it, whatever 'it' might be, and watch daytime TV.
- Cry themselves, in the hope the child will stop crying.
- Go outside every half an hour, just to get away from it all.

- Go into town and walk around for hours, looking in the shops at things they either don't want, can't afford or, in most cases, both.
- Spend most of the day in Internet 'chat rooms,' their back to the kids, shouting at them over their shoulder to 'play nicely' interspersed with "I'll get it in a minute for you, poppet," while being chatted up by total strangers, just to *feel* good about themselves for a short while.
- Buy loads of 'stuff' from catalogues to take their mind off 'it' and to give themselves something to look forward to, especially if it's next day delivery.
- Get some excitement by playing online gambling, even though they are running up huge credit card debts.
- Go to a 'mums and tots' or 'parents and babes' group once a week for two hours and feel majorly stressed that their child can't socially interact, in other words, she wants all the toys, bites and throws tantrums, while sitting with the other mums, extolling the virtues of nappies and baby formula.
- Eat.
- Spend most of the day shouting and feeling exhausted.
- Cry, then eat, and then cry some more.
- Pop a double dose of prescribed medication and drift through the day not noticing anything too much.
- Smoke a cigarette every 10 minutes.
- Drink alcohol.
- Take some class A drugs.
- Don't cope at all.

* * *

Now, before any parents out there start ranting that they don't do *any* of the above and are quite good parents, I should point out that I am basing these comments, on the coping mechanisms that *I* am aware of and that have been mentioned to me *repeatedly*, by hundreds of parents who do use them. On a personal level, I have done *all* of the above, apart from online gambling and class A drugs, which I didn't know how to get hold of. Actually, thinking about it, I probably did the class A drugs as well, prescribed by my GP. Gosh, just think, all those years I wanted them, and *believed* I couldn't get hold of them, and they were just a prescription away! Oh, and the other thing I would like to say to those parents who *do not* use any of the coping mechanisms outlined is this, 'quite good' is *nowhere near* good enough!

Imagine if you were to go for brain surgery. Would you be feeling positive about the outcome of surgery, if the medical team that performed the operation were 'quite good'? No, I didn't think so. So, why do you think your child should be content with 'quite good'? And for those of you, including myself, who have 'survived' parenthood in any of the ways bullet pointed above, would you like the same surgery performed by staff who 'coped' in any of those ways identified, during your operation?

I am constantly amazed that I survived – am still surviving – parenthood. It is without a shadow of doubt, the most stressful, isolating, tortuous, unrewarding, undervalued, soul destroying 'job' I have ever had to do, and when I see young parents dragging children through 'cloned' shopping centres, my heart goes out to all of them. And when I hear a friend or family member celebrating the fact that they are pregnant, why do I think "oh no, poor you," instead of "wow, great news, lucky you"?

The thing is, parenthood should, and could, be a wondrous experience that everyone *should* celebrate (everybody on the planet, actually), because it is bringing a whole new being, with endless possibilities, into our three-dimensional reality. We have to demand new methods of supporting parents, as eventually, we shall reap what we sow, and I for one, want to reap abundance, happiness and blissful joy.

If you are a parent, think about how you cope, or what *represents* 'quite good' in your reality. If you were to employ a childminder or babysitter, would you accept 'quite good'? In fact, why not get a sheet of paper and imagine that you are looking to employ someone to care for your baby (if you haven't got one (either pen, paper, or baby) then use your imagination and visualise it). You require this person to work between the hours of 8.00am-6.00pm, five days a week. In fact, make two lists. On the first list put 'must haves' and on the other 'must nots' (for this to work, you need to be quite visual in your thoughts and imagine it is for real). If you feel you are just 'coping', you may put a single word in the 'must haves,' which might be 'alive', as I know there have been times in my life when I would have given my child to a total stranger, just for five minutes peace. In fact, I did do it; I sent them to nursery and then school for the majority of their childhood!

When you have done this, ask yourself what needs to change to make being a parent all that it *should* be? Maybe one of the things that *should* happen, is that *our* money which the government spends on *our* behalf, should be invested into parenting rather than being spent in its billions, to bomb, murder, maim, terrify and obliterate parents and children in other parts of the world. If enough people say the same thing for long enough, change will happen, but apathy, the antithesis of change is contagious. The choice is ours, or rather yours, and with choice comes responsibility. It is *your* responsibility, not theirs, or his, or hers. It is yours.

To give a quote that has been quoted endlessly, 'a journey of a thousand miles begins with the first step' and it is *you* that has to take that step. To take that first step involves a little visualisation, so if you want to give it a try, get ready, and if not, I will meet up with you at the beginning of the following paragraph. Now, I want you to imagine yourself as being totally dependent on another human being's support, for your survival. I personally imagine that I am paralysed, and in need of complete support for *all* my bodily functions. Now visualise the 'carer' who is going to live with you and *be* that support. Ask yourself the following questions:

- What would they look like?
- What characteristics would they display?
- What standards would you expect them to attain?
- How would you like them to talk to you?
- How would you like them to respond to your demands?

- How would they stimulate you mentally?
- How would they stimulate you emotionally?
- How would you expect them to deal with your physical needs?
- How would you ensure that they took breaks to take care of their own needs?
- What kinds of things would you do together during the day?
- What would you expect them to feed you, or give you to drink?
- How would they make sure you socialised and felt entertained?
- What 'labels' would you not want them to attach to you?
- What would you like them to think about their 'job'?
- How would they settle you for the night, remember that you are dependent, which could make you feel frightened?

* * *

If it were *you* who needed almost complete support from a fellow human being, you would soon voice your concerns if the carer did not live up to your expectations. You would complain, or replace them with someone more appropriate, someone who understood your needs. If we hear of care homes that mistreat the people they are employed to care *for*, we become outraged and call for them to close down; we force the change.

Probably, one of the most important steps to making change happen is to open your eyes so that you can *see* what needs to be modified. Too many of us walk around with our heads stuck in boxes, that only have one transparent side. We have restricted our awareness of so much that exists around us, like a racehorse in blinkers. We block out images that we don't want to see. We turn the volume down on noises and sounds we don't want to hear, and the box prevents us from *feeling* the world we inhabit. Take the box off your head and feel, experience, participate, see, hear, smell and taste this reality. When you go out somewhere, anywhere, focus on where you are and what is going on around you. Focus on it all, as, in being selective, you are still in the box. Go somewhere just to experience being there, and then experience *all* of it.

One of the things I love to do is 'people watch.' I will go and sit somewhere for an hour, just to experience *being* there. I do not take a book or a friend, or a dog; I just take me. Then I centre myself into the energy of the place, so for example, the other day I went to experience '*being*' in the town centre. I sat on a bench that formed part of a surround, to a huge planter, filled with spring flowers, on a surprisingly warm April morning. To centre myself, I clear my mind by closing my eyes and focusing on a yellow rose, and then I take a few deep breaths, before opening my eyes.

I took a good look around, not just at the people, but the buildings, the sky, the ground, and the space I was occupying. Then I made myself aware of the sounds: music, voices, birds, breeze, traffic, distant helicopter, dogs, personal music systems, opening and closing doors, whistles, security systems, alarms, distant sirens, things being dropped, paper, discarded rubbish scraping on the paving, cans being kicked, crying, laughter, rustling, mutterings, mumblings, shouting, and secret whisperings. I am amazed at what I can hear when I really listen. I also breathed in the air and tried to identify the different scents and aromas: perfumes and aftershaves, flowers, body odour, various foods and drinks, alcohol, cigarettes, cigars, chewing gum, deodorant, babies, dogs, exhaust fumes, and garlic. I repeated this process for all my senses and then just sat back and experienced it.

Some of the visuals that stayed with me from that experience are listed below:

• A woman, maybe in her 70's, walking hunched over, hardly lifting her feet. Her eyes are fixed on the pavement in front of her and every few steps she straightens a little, to check out her path. No one gives her eye contact or smiles at her, they just move out of her path, and this reminds me of the way people sidestep a barrier, like a waste bin, to avoid bumping into it. It takes her a full half an hour to disappear from my field of vision and she reminds me, in some way, of a tortoise. If she were a tortoise though, she would have benefited from some attention. My perception was that she was 'invisible' to almost everyone. I wonder who she is and what she has experienced in her life. I wonder whether she was taken out on 'Mother's Day' and if she was, did her child enjoy being with her, or did they see it as an unavoidable consequence of having a mother?

• Two mothers chatting intently about their neighbour. Both have babies in pushchairs and a young boy, maybe six years old, is struggling to keep up with them. Every so often the women stop and go into a shop and then one will reappear and shout, "Come on, Callum, we haven't got all day," and he runs to join them inside the shop. Moments later, they emerge, engrossed in conversation, with Callum a few paces behind them.

I watch him as he checks where they are, and then stops to pick up something on the ground. He is looking around and his head moves in all directions, including upwards, unlike his mothers. He observes his own fingers and then sticks one of them up his nose before looking at what he has excavated. He scrapes the toe of his shoe along the ground for a while and then realises he has stood on a paving slab that 'wobbles' and stops to play. I am engrossed in Callum and, like him, only become aware of his mother's presence, when she shrieks at him, "Callum, get here noowwww!"

I momentarily glance at her and then focus my attention on Callum, who doesn't move. He looks directly ahead, in the direction of his mother who is advancing towards him, looking really annoyed. Now I can see both of them and switch my view from one to the other. His mother continues to march towards him and I notice that his bottom lip drops and he shuffles his feet quickly, to enjoy the last moments of the wobbling paving slab. Then she is there, one hand extended and with the other, she reaches out to grab his upper arm. Callum struggles, whimpering as his mother brings the extended hand across the back of his coat, in a half-hearted slap, shouting as she does so, "Why can't you *ever* just do as you're told, you little git?"

Callum is then dragged behind his mother, as she marches back up the shopping precinct, continuing to berate him. When she reaches her companion, she lets go of his hand roughly, and they all continue on their way, replaying the scene over and over again, until they leave my view.

• Outside one of the shops, a rather disheveled man sits on his coat holding out his hand to passers by. Most give him a sideways glance before continuing on their journey. One mother shouts at her child to "come away" when she ventures too close. A man, drinking from a plastic litre bottle, labelled 'White Lightning Cider,' sits down on the ground next to the disheveled man and offers him the bottle. His offer is refused and the disheveled man turns his head away and continues to try to gain the attention of the busy shoppers.

After about five minutes, the disheveled man starts to talk to the other man, and although I cannot hear their words, their body language says it all and eventually the man with the cider leaves, spitting on the ground as he goes. The disheveled man looks around 30 years old and his face is unshaven and dirty. I wonder at where he will sleep tonight, who his parents are, and why he chooses to exist in the way he does.

• A man comes to my attention, probably in his early forties. He is dressed in a suit that is bursting at the seams, in a fragile attempt to cover his overweight body. His suit jacket is open, exposing a shirt stretched over a stomach that looks as if it could produce a baby at any given moment. His shirt collar button is open with a tie strangling his neck. His trousers are secured under his belly, with a belt stretching beneath his girth to prevent slippage. His face is bright red and he is almost breathless as he passes by, talking to someone on his mobile, in an agitated voice, "Yes, I understand that, but that is not what we agreed…I'm not interested in what they *say* we agreed…just tell them we are not doing it…"

He disappears into a sandwich shop, and a few minutes later, reappears eating a Cornish-style pastry, while still talking on his mobile. I wonder how his blood pressure is and why he doesn't take two minutes to sit and eat his food and then continue with his call. I wonder if he is married and if so, what mood he will arrive home in. I wonder if he knows that his life doesn't have to be like this, if he doesn't want it to be.

•   Some pigeons flutter to the ground and start pecking around, clearing the pavement of dropped crusts, crumbs, chips and pastry flakes. They have an amazing way of avoiding feet, and dodge and hop from one place to another. One pigeon starts to flaunt himself in front of a female, who appears more interested in the discarded food, ignoring him puffing himself up and dropping his tail feathers behind in a fan. Moments later, a rival appears and challenges him, with his own display, which also appears to have no effect whatsoever on the female, but it does elicit a reaction from the other male. Both attempt to out perform the other and hardly notice when the female flies off to scan the ground for food, rather than courtship rituals, from a better advantage. Moments later, the males join her on the window ledge of a shop.

•   A man walks past with a woman at his side. She has her head down and is holding the hand of a little girl, who is maybe three years old. The man appears angry and every now and then, stops briefly to look directly at the woman, and after saying something, he carries on walking. When he stops, she stops and so does the little girl. When he speaks both of them lift their eyes to his, and when he begins to walk again, so do they. He stops a few feet away from me and I listen as he speaks, "I don't give a shit what they do. The point is, you are not doing that. I've had enough of it, I have. I told you what would happen and that's it, OK, end of story." And with that, they continue on. I wonder if the little girl realises that the comments are not intended for her.

•   An old man sits quite close to me and takes a paper bag out of his pocket and starts to throw breadcrumbs on the pavement. Soon, he is rewarded by the arrival of birds that gather in the space, so recently occupied by the man, woman and little girl. The birds make all kinds of calls and sounds as they feast on the crumbs and the old man smiles, talking to them as they eat. He only appears to see the birds and beams at their entertaining antics. I wonder how often he comes to this place to feed the birds, and if they recognise him as a reliable source of food.

•   A group of young girls approach and it is difficult to assess how old they are. They are all dressed in the same 'fashionable style' and they appear hyper and excited, all trying to speak at the same time. They are laughing and stop every now and then to gather in a little huddle, and then laugh some more, before moving on. I wonder if they realise how powerful they really are.

*   *   *

If you take time to connect with your senses, you can begin to understand what needs to happen to make changes, and if town planners took some time to observe how these shopping centres, or town precincts, were utilised, it would help them to design more positive, creative spaces that people will value. In most town centres, there is no place for children to play, explore or interact with other children. Most are devoid of grassy areas, where picnic tables and play equipment could be provided, so that mothers could shop and then reward their childrens' good behaviour by spending some time in the grassy space. Most food outlets are not child friendly, even though we are made to think they are because they offer child-sized portions, highchairs and the odd free gift, strategically placed in the box of crap that our children are about to eat.

We need to demand change and to make sure we get what we ask for, so that a visit to the town centre, or shopping mall, becomes an enjoyable experience for all of us, no matter what age. One day, our children will no longer depend on us; we will depend on them, for they will be the ones who become the designers, managers and creators of our physical world. We need to take responsibility for their growth and development, so that they make *being* in this world a wonderful experience for themselves, as well as for us.

Earlier, we talked about 'labels' and the impact they can have on us as individuals, Well, most of these labels take hold when we are children, and their impact can be amazing. Children are trying to find their place in the world and a huge amount of the information they need to find that place comes from us, as adults. We tell our children, by labelling them, how *we* define *their* place. How many people do you know who label their children? How often have you heard parents say things like this?

• "He's so independent. He doesn't let me do anything for him, do you Daniel?" The child's response is to *believe* the label that is constantly attached to him and he may struggle to perform tasks, becoming frustrated and aggressive, because he is *labelled* 'independent.' As he grows up, he may find himself unable to ask for support, because assistance does not *fit* with his label. Maybe he will keep his problems to himself and labour to find solutions and, if he can't achieve them, feel like a failure to whom he *believes* himself to be, saying things like "I don't know what's wrong with me. I should be able to deal with this."

Many grown men, who end up committing suicide, are so called 'self-made men.' People are shocked that they have taken their own lives passing comments such as, "He was always so strong. I don't understand why he never asked for help. He always appeared so totally in control of everything... if only we'd known." Well, here's the hard bit to swallow, you did know because you gave him the label in the first place.

• "She's such a shy little thing, aren't you Sarah? Most of the time, you wouldn't even know she was in the room." The child's response is to *believe* the label attached to them and sit quietly entertaining themselves, reinforcing the label in her own mind. When Sarah goes to nursery, the staff might voice concerns, as Sarah doesn't seem to want to join in with the others. You explain that it's just because she is shy, she's always been that way. As the years pass, it is harder for Sarah to join in, because of her shyness label, and when she does want to participate to gain social experience, she finds it incredibly difficult because she has no experience of being sociable. She conforms to the characteristics of 'shy,' which she *believes* herself to be.

As a teenager, Sarah is introduced to alcohol and finds that when she drinks, she sometimes *forgets* to act like her label, and as she actually *enjoys* the company of others and being 'social,' she binge drinks every weekend. So, Sarah is putting herself at risk each time she binges, just so she can forget the label that only actually *exists* in her own, and others, minds.

• "He is so strong, aren't you Charlie? He pulls himself up and supports his own weight, and sometimes when he holds my finger, I have to literally prise it free; he's such a strong little boy. He'll be picking me up before long, won't you Charlie?" The child's response is to believe the label, and the more it is applied to him, the more he *believes* it. So, as Charlie grows, he focuses his attention on being physically strong, encouraged by the parent of course, who will supply him with appropriate toys and reading materials to reinforce the label that she has unwittingly bestowed upon him. When Charlie reaches his teens, he will probably spend lots of time in the gym and participate in sports that allow him to display his strength. He will probably command 'respect' from his peers who never pick a fight with him, because of his physical strength. But what happens when Charlie realises he is not the strongest any more, or when no amount of weight training can keep him at the top? Maybe Charlie will become a tyrant at work, bullying others with his 'strong' position, or maybe he will show his 'strength' to those who are not as physically strong as him, such as his wife, children or mother, or maybe he will inject steroids to give him the advantage.

• "He's a real little terror, aren't you Jack? Always getting into trouble." The child's response is to 'fit' the label, and the chances are that a grown-up, somewhere, will buy him a t-shirt with the words 'Here comes trouble' emblazoned on the front, just so that everyone who meets him understands his label and reacts accordingly. His bedroom wallpaper will be 'Dennis the Menace' and his quilt will have a large picture of Dennis and Gnasher on it. When Jack goes to school he will *continue to behave as his label dictates* and cause trouble, because that is what he *believes* himself to be, a troublemaker.

When Jack is little, you might find his troublesome ways amusing, but what about when he's older and you are getting constant complaints about his behaviour? Jack is just being what you told him he was when he was younger, remember, when you use to laugh when he behaved as the label that you inadvertently gave him.

•   "She's a right little actress, aren't you India? Always being the drama queen." Little India's response is to become the drama queen, and when she is small it seems cute, but as she gets older it can become embarrassing, especially in supermarkets when she demands sweets or toys and throws herself on the floor when they are not forthcoming. Maybe India is sent to drama classes to channel her behaviour, but all it actually does is reinforce it. And when India is older and meets a partner, maybe, initially, he thinks her behaviour is cute, until her constant diva demands drive him away, and then India will throw herself on the floor and scream, "No-one understands me. I'm only temperamental because I am so artistic."

* * *

Think about some of the children you have contact with, or look back on your own childhood, and see what labelling is going on right under your nose, and how *you* are reinforcing it. Don't limit anyone or allow anyone to limit you; you are more than a label and you have the freedom to be whatever *you choose to be,* at any given moment.

We also dictate to children *how* they will react in certain situations and then take great pride in saying "I told you so" when they react as we predicted. I can remember having an injection once, when I was around 10 years old, and the nurse said to me, "This is going to hurt a little, but I will try to be quick, OK dear?"

Now, the moment she said the word 'hurt' it awakened a physiological response. I started to *believe* it would hurt and with the belief came a feeling of apprehension, which heightened my nervous system, so that I was screaming before she even put the needle into my arm. In fact, my fear of needles continued until fairly recently. We fill our children with all kinds of fears and phobias, just by telling them what reaction we *expect* them to give.

We also push our own likes and dislikes onto them, sometimes knowingly, other times unknowingly. An example of this is that until I was about 25 years old, I hated sprouts and beetroot, so these items were never found in my home, meaning that my children had never *experienced* the taste of either. Every year, on Christmas Day, sprouts were definitely not on the menu, and if we were invited to anyone else's home to eat a festive turkey dinner, when they offered us sprouts, I would say, "Oh no thanks, we don't like sprouts," usually with a picture of disgust on my face. No surprise then, when one year, a sprout was put on my son's plate in error, and he got upset, not wanting to eat anything on his plate that the sprout may have contaminated, yet he had never *experienced* the actual taste for himself.

When I was 25, I met a man who adored sprouts and one day his mother invited me for a family dinner at her home. I wanted to make a good impression, so when my dinner arrived; I was horrified to see a mound of sprouts. I whispered to my boyfriend that I didn't like sprouts and for him to take them off my plate before his mum came back into the dining room, but he just said, "They're lovely, at least try one."

I can remember cutting a sprout into quarters, and then heaping mashed potato and carrot on top, before wiping the fork around in gravy. I held the fork close to my mouth and with an expression bordering on fearful, slowly put the heaped forkful into my mouth. Do you know what? I actually liked it. That day, I finished up most of the sprouts on my plate and have been enjoying them ever since!

We do this all the time, and what it actually does is *limit* our children's experiences. An acquaintance of mine married a man who *believes* he has to eat the same food on the same night of the week, every week. At first she found this rather sweet, but after years of preparing Shepherd's Pie, carrots and peas on Monday, steak pie with chips and peas every Tuesday, then pork chop, mashed potato and cabbage for

Wednesday and so on, she became really frustrated with it all. The trouble was that she had two children who now also expected the same food on the same day of the week, so it was hard for her to break the routine, which had begun years ago with her partner's own mother. It impinged on many areas of their lives, including holidays, as he would only agree to go where he was guaranteed to be able to continue his eating routines. This meant that many foreign holidays were out of the question, and if they did travel abroad, they went self-catering, which meant little or no break for her from her usual routines.

We do the same thing with our likes, or what we would *like* our children to like. I have seen babies crawling along floors, exploring everything. They use two of their senses, taste and smell, that tend to be under-developed, and when they pick up a piece of discarded cabbage leaf from the floor to experiment with, we let out a shriek saying, "Oh no poppet, don't eat that, it's nasty, yeuk" and then we hand them a lollipop, exclaiming with a sweet smile, "Have this instead, bab. It's really tasty and nice."

Now the child reacts to 'pictures' and also has a good understanding of body language, so he takes in the 'picture' of a terrified, high-pitched, frightened mum, and links it to the image of the discarded cabbage leaf, and he records the image in his mind with the words "nasty, yeuk." The child will then link the taste and sight of the lollipop to an image of calm, relaxed and happy mum.

So, even if the poor child prefers to 'explore' the cabbage leaf, rather than 'exploring' the lollipop, the reaction he gets from his mum will always be the same, until the child has *learnt* to 'like' the lollipop and 'dislike' the cabbage leaf. As parents, we do need to keep our children safe, but we must remember that the greatest gift we can give them is independence, and that means allowing them to make their own choices independently, even if those choices are the polar opposite to our own. Children are being programmed by us to detach, rather than develop, two essential senses; we are actually weakening these senses to a point that even when something is burning right next to us, it takes a while for us to smell it. The same applies to the sense of taste.

When we download information to our minds, we want to record as much 'data' or visuals, as we can about the 'label.' Due to the way that information is being delivered, we rely more heavily on sight and sound, rather than touch, taste and smell. An obvious case in point is television. You can determine how much you yourself do this personally by experimenting with your five senses.

Go and pick a leaf off a tree and then bring it into the house. Now tell me what visuals/data you have stored on your hard drive, under the label 'leaf from garden.'

OK, now put the leaf to one side, out of sight. Clear your mind by thinking of a beautiful, tranquil alpine meadow, where a waterfall feeds a sparkling brook that tumbles down majestic mountains. Birds are flying in the pale blue sky, occasionally swooping through the grassy meadow that you are relaxing in. The sun is high in the sky, tempting small, fluffy, white clouds to spoil its view. From a far off field you hear the call of a goat, drifting on the alpine breeze, and as the wind gently sweeps across your body, you feel a gentle touch on your leg. You look to see what it is, and can't believe your eyes. It's the 'leaf from the garden.'

OK, so now tell me all the data you have stored on your hard drive under the label 'leaf from the garden.' Write it down somewhere and then turn it over.

Now, of course, I can't divulge what I am going to say right now, otherwise you might cheat (yourself, not me) and look at what I have to say *before* you do this little test, and what would be the point in that? So, to give you the opportunity to do it *without* cheating, I am going to carry on talking about those senses that we don't use as often as we should, and how if we did, we would get far more enjoyment and pleasure out of life.

Take sex as a prime example. Next time you get sexual with someone, arouse *all* of your senses. Try some of these different alternatives:

- Get into the bath together and wash each other. Feel their skin under the wet, soapy water. Feel its contours as you wash their body with your warm hands. Before you get out, drop some baby oil onto their skin and smooth it all over their body, including their toes, back of their knees and shoulders.

•   Turn off the bedroom lights after lighting one small candle and put it somewhere safe. Undress each other in the dim candlelight and really smell their body as you unwrap them. When you are both naked, hold each other close, still standing, and embrace in a silent dance. Do you 'hear' a tune in your mind?

•   At the 'quietest' part of the day, unplug your phones, alarms, music systems and go to the bedroom, and if possible, place a mirror strategically, so that the bed can be seen. Do not speak to each other. Do everything by 'gut' instinct. Do not form any words; just allow natural, bodily sounds. When you touch each other, listen to their body; *hear* how it responds to your body. Notice your reflections, as they move in and out of view, through the mirror. Listen to each other's heartbeat, feel the blood running through your veins, and feel how you are exploring the art of sex.

*   *   *

OK, so I hope that distracted you for a while, so now, before you try any of the sexual suggestions, let's clear our minds and turn our attention to your list.

So, what did 'leaf from the garden', or 'LG,' look like? Was the underside the same as the topside? What did the edges look like? Were there any fine hairs on it? How did the veins weave through LG? Was the colour a constant, or was it deeper in one place than the other? What colour were the veins? Was this the same for the underside? Did it have any marks or blemishes on it? How was its stem? Could you see where it had been detached from the tree or plant? Was the stem the same colour as the leaf?

What did LG feel like? Did the underside feel the same as the topside? What did the veins on LG feel like? Were the edges spiky, or smooth? Did it feel rough to the touch? Were there any bumps or blemishes on LG that you could feel? How old did it feel, or did it feel quite young? How do you tell the difference? How did the stem feel? Was the stem's tip wet or dry? Did it have a rough surface, or a smooth one? How light did it feel? Did you feel any energy coming from LG, or was LG dead? How did you tell the difference?

What did LG smell like? Was it the same aroma on both sides, or were there subtle differences? Did your own personal smell, from your hand, intermingle with the smell of LG, or were they separate? How did you tell the difference? Did the end of the stem smell of the plant, or of the leaf? What was the difference between both scents? What did your hand smell of? Was the smell of your hands natural or affected by perfume, or soap? Did the aroma from LG increase when you tasted him? Did the two senses combine? How did you separate one sense from the other?

What did LG sound like? Did you put LG to your ear? Did you listen as you touched LG with your finger? Did you touch LG against any other surface? What different kinds of sounds did LG make on each of the different surfaces? Did LG make a crunchy sound when you squeezed him, or was it more fluid? What does fluid sound like to you? How did you expect LG to sound? What did LG sound like when you ate him? What other labels can you compare the sound to?

What did LG taste like? Did it taste rough or smooth? Did it crunch when you bit it, or did it give gently with the pressure of your teeth? Did it crunch up easily or go into a mushy clump? Did the stem taste bitter or sweet? Was it easy to move around your mouth, or did it get stuck in your teeth? What would you say that LG most tasted like? What taste sensations happened when you moved LG around your mouth? Was LG hard to swallow, or did you spit it out? If you spat LG out, ask yourself why, but well done for at least using your sense of taste.

If you didn't even taste LG, not even a lick, then you need to start to bring this vitally important sense into your experience a bit more. Do it as often as you can, as taste brings important data to our labels;

to our experience of what the label means. I am not suggesting that you go out and start eating anything that could potentially harm you. I am saying use your mouth as another important method of storing data on labels.

All of us as adults want the best for our children, so our own FG who has already experienced the visuals of certain labels, will act in a benevolent manner, and remind us that we have experienced it so, as we want our children to experience the 'nice' things in life, making us believe ourselves to be helpful parents. We auto write our visuals/data onto their labels, often by using body language, as well as speech, to ensure they have some visuals to attach. This, the child will then store for future reference. How many times have you heard the words below, and how many times are you saying them to others, not just children?

- Oh, don't go and see that film. I went the other week and it was so boring, I nearly fell asleep. That lead role was pathetic. The only good bit was when his top came off, but even that was a disappointment. The soundtrack was lousy, too.
- Come on this roller coaster with me, please, you'll love it!
- I've just read a fantastic book. It was so good; you'll have to borrow it.
- Don't eat that, it's disgusting, yeuk!
- We are doing this for the benefit of mankind.
- Don't climb up there. You might fall.
- You're going too fast, slow down or you'll be sick.
- Her hair just looked nasty.
- I can't believe you just said that about her. She's not like that at all, she's really lovely.
- Calm down, you're acting hysterical and making a fool of yourself.
- You look lovely, honestly.
- I wouldn't do that if I were you.

*   *   *

Now, when we are being helpful and offering others our 'suggestions' of the visuals/data that we want them to attach to the 'label', we accompany the 'suggestion' with lots of other visuals/data. If we are adult and we have experienced the 'label' ourselves before, we make a choice as to whether we stick with our own visuals/data for that particular 'label' or overwrite it with the suggested one. This is how we make decisions and update our databases and it is also how hypnotism and hypnotherapy works. As you have experienced the visuals before for a particular 'label,' the hypnotist can insert different data onto that 'label,' but only if it is your choice for the hypnotist to do so.

So, to use the classic stage show hypnosis example, if you are hypnotised and the hypnotist suggests that when you hear the word 'dog,' you will start to 'bark.' The hypnotist has written over your label for dog, so instead of just bringing an image of a dog to mind, you will do as the new label suggests, and bark! You know what sound to make because you have heard a dog bark and have downloaded the auditory visuals on your database. Imagine if a hypnotist said, "And when you hear the word hippopotamus you will begin to sound like one." How many of us have auditory data for a hippo stored inside us?

I will give you an example from my own recent experience. I am so alive at the moment that I want to experience as much as possible, using as many different senses as possible. So, the other day my partner and I went out for an outing to Wicksteed Park, which is a local theme park. Now, I use to believe I had tremendous fear of heights, and over the years I have been addressing this in small steps. First I stood on a chair, and then progressed to a stool and finally I climbed to the top of a ladder. Due to my fear, I have never been on a fairground ride that leaves the ground apart from a caged children's Ferris wheel, and this ride had to be stopped after two cycles, because the attendant feared I was going to have a heart attack!

So, when my partner Mostafa suggested we go on the rollercoaster, my whole being was engulfed by the data I store for the 'label' rollercoaster. I began to feel panic just imagining it, my heart began to race, and I kept wiping my palms. Once I realised what I was doing, I replaced the image with a yellow rose and then, once I was calm, I focused my attention on where I had gathered my data from, as if I had never *experienced* the label 'rollercoaster.' It appeared to me that it was all linked to my fear of heights, which in turn stemmed from when I was a child, and got 'stuck' walking across a metal drainage pipe that was an unofficial bridge between two fields. My fear was not really of heights at all; my fear was of falling. Once I understood this, it made me think of all the data I had *not* stored on my database about the 'label' rollercoaster. My data was based on second-hand information, which I would have heard from other people, many of whom I selected further information from, as they reinforced my fear, giving me even more reasons *not* to experience a rollercoaster ride.

In other words, this process has happened again and again over the years:

• I have a fear of 'heights' so do not want to ride a rollercoaster.
• My children tell me I should because it is fun and I should not be scared.
• I choose to select the word 'scared' to focus on, which massively overrides the word 'fun.'
• I seek out other people, unwittingly, to support my fear and ask them what they have experienced (their data).
• They give me their data on rollercoaster rides: scary, terrifying, awful, made me feel sick, shaking, screaming etc, reinforcing the data I have already gathered.

* * *

So, the next time my children ask me to go on a rollercoaster ride, I retrieve my stored 'second- hand' data on roller coasters e.g. "I'm not going on the ride because a friend of mine said that when she went on it, she was actually sick while the ride was going and she couldn't move because of the force, and nearly choked to death on her own vomit and because everyone was screaming, no one knew how close to death she was." This friend also told me that the ride triggered her motion sickness. Now, the interesting thing about this is that even though their 'fear' is actually different to mine, their data gives me an excuse to increase my visuals for roller coasters, even though the 'fear' that they have expressed is not the same as mine. So, having established that my 'real fear' is a 'fear of falling', I assumed that by being in a high place increased the *possibility* of me falling. The higher I imagined I went, the more intense the fear, and rollercoasters do go quite high. The fear increased whenever I could see the drop, that kind of "don't look down or you will fall" message sprung to the forefront of my mind, and was magnified many times if *there was no barrier to keep me safe from falling*. The data that my friend gave me was based on her fear of motion, not falling, but I still wrote her data onto my hard drive as other 'possible visuals' riding the rollercoaster would bring. So, even though I did not have a fear of motion (motion sickness), I adopted the visuals. So, when my children asked me to go on the ride, I added my friend's visuals, which were nothing to do with heights or fear of falling and all about motion sickness, and the thing was, I didn't even realise I was doing it.

So, now knowing what I was doing when thinking of the rollercoaster ride, I decided to watch it a couple of times and see how great the risk was of me *actually falling* from this ride. Although people were screaming, I understood that they would not be screaming because they feared they were going to fall. The rollercoaster was being hauled up a steep track, quite high off the ground and then the carriages hurtled towards the earth, before spinning up another climb and repeating the process. The passengers on the ride were strapped into the carriage with a mechanical shoulder security lock. The carriages also had lap restraints and the carriages were secured to rails.

My fear of falling was based on having no barriers to prevent me from falling and nothing to keep me secure. I could now add some more information to my data stored under the label 'roller coaster', which was that it was quite secure, the carriage formed a barrier to keep passengers safe, lap restraints provided additional security, and the carriage was firmly connected to strong rails. Now, when I recalled the label rollercoaster, it did not evoke the same physiological responses because the 'fear' of falling data had been overwritten with information that the ride was actually very secure.

I told Mostafa that I *would* go on the ride with him, and he was totally shocked that I had agreed to do so. This was my first ever ride on a rollercoaster and although I did not enjoy it, I did not scream, become hysterical, panicked or terrified, my head did not feel as if it going to pull me 'over the edge,' and when I got off the ride, I was not nauseous or shaking. At no point on that ride did I fear I was going to fall.

What happens when we do this with children is that we increase our non-verbal communication to enable them to store our 'second-hand' data as visually as possible. We are identifying the 'cause' and then giving them loads of data of what the 'effect' will be if they do that particular thing and we are doing this all the time. We say things like:

- If you don't eat your greens, you won't grow into a big strong boy.
- It's a spider, quick, move!
- Don't pull that face or people won't like you.
- Don't play with dolls. People will think you're a girl, not a boy.
- Don't play with him, he's not nice and might hurt you.
- Don't listen to her. She's stupid and you don't want people to think you're stupid do you?
- Don't cry there's a big boy.
- I don't want you to go on the climbing frame. You might fall and break your neck.
- Don't go too fast, or you'll be sick.
- Hold on tight. Daddy doesn't want you to fall.
- If we don't invade Iraq, we are inviting terrorism to our doors.
- It must be true. I read it in the papers.

* * *

What we are doing is planting the *thoughts* in the minds of others, so that they will begin to associate certain effects with certain 'labels,' even though they have never experienced the effects for themselves. So, a small boy, for example, begins to associate crying with weakness and being seen as small, and even if crying is an expression of his emotions, he will suppress those emotions so that he is seen as 'big.' We do not realise how powerful our language, in all its forms, actually is. We pass our fears on to others and in turn are preventing them from experiencing life for themselves, in their own unique way.

One of the most visual ways to see this in action is to watch a parent and toddler interact when the toddler begins to take its first steps. The toddler starts to experiment with standing and supporting its own weight. It then goes to the next stage and will begin to release its grip on supporting objects, such as a table leg or sofa, to begin to understand, and *experience*, how to balance its body in an upright position. The child will then gain further experience by walking around the furniture, using it to maintain balance, until they can release one hand and still continue to walk upright.

After a while the toddler will hold their remaining supporting hand just above the furniture and occasionally re-establish contact, giving them a feeling of security. All the time the parents will be observing the child's progress, until one magical day the toddler turns their body away from the furniture and *towards* the open space. Now begins the first 'unaided,' faltering steps. The parent will crouch, a few paces in front of the child, and extend their arms and give words and expressions of encouragement, which the toddler focuses on, by making direct eye contact with the parent, before concentrating on moving one of their feet forward. Having achieved this first step, the toddler will regain balance and control and take another step, fantastic!

Where it all goes horribly wrong, is when the parents' language patterns suddenly change. So, if the toddler gets into a bit of a wobble when focusing on regaining balance, the parent might believe that the child is about to fall and suddenly make different facial expressions, or change the tone of their verbal communication. This, momentarily, distracts the child's concentrated effort on balancing, as they have moved their focus onto the parents' body language, and they fall.

Remember, our minds work with visuals, not words. Words are just a transformation, or an expression of our experience, based on five-sense constructed visuals. A way of understanding this is to think of what happens when you tell a child 'not to spill their drink.' The child transforms those words into pictures, so in their minds they *see* what they are *not* meant to do i.e. they get a mental image of a drink spilling. Now they have established the picture of spilling the drink in their mind, and their FG wants to make their wishes come true, so they spill the drink. Amazing! So, what should we say if we don't want our child to spill the drink?

I want you to think about how you represent the adjective 'not.' It is very difficult to express in a visual form, except by maybe identifying the picture of what you don't want someone to do and putting a red line through it. As adults, we understand that a red circle with line through it is a symbol for 'not allowed,' but young children don't, and even in bringing forth the image of what you *don't* want someone to do, you are still presenting the *image* of that to the individual's mind. As a smoker for many years, I understand how powerful visual stimulation is because I could be quite happy, not wanting a cigarette, but the moment I see a 'no smoking' symbol, the first thing I want to do is have one, because my mind has been stimulated by the image to *want* one.

If we do not want a child to spill a drink, we need to make them understand visually, what we *do* want them to do, so we might say to them, "Put your cup on the table" or "When you have had a drink, put the cup down next to you where you can see it." If we were to say, "Put the cup on the table so that you don't spill your drink," we have once more introduced to their minds the image of the drink spilling, and the chances are, it will happen. If we say, "When you have had a drink, put the cup down next to you but be careful not to knock it over," we have introduced the image of the cup being knocked over, and again, it will probably happen.

If we add even more information like, "and if you spill the drink, mummy will be very cross," the image they *see* is one of the drink spilling *and* mummy shouting at them, which, when they spill the drink moments later, is probably reinforced by mummy getting really angry and saying, "I told you to be careful not to spill your drink. You never listen do you? Always have to make mummy angry, don't you, you're such a clumsy child, you really are." The child has now received images of lots of 'labels,' which have been attached to them through spilling the drink, namely that they *never* listen, they *make* mummy angry and they *are* clumsy. The thing is the child *did* listen! This gives us, as adults, an understanding of how we should communicate with children to give them the best possible experience and to achieve the goals we would like them to achieve, which in this particular case, was not to spill the drink.

We all need to find *our* place in this world and have a desire to understand *how* we are represented as ourselves, in the minds of others. We do this by picking up the 'labels' that people attach to us, so if we do not want our child to be 'labelled' as clumsy and to manifest the 'label' as *who* they *believe* they are, by being clumsy, we should not mention the word at all in reference to who the child is. Once these 'labels' attach themselves, people find it incredibly difficult to detach from them and actually begin to reinforce it themselves by making statements like, "I could trip over thin air, I'm that clumsy."

Think of how this limits the child's abilities. We want to enable our children to express as much of their incredible potential as possible, and even 'quite good' parents are unknowingly restricting this.

There are so many ways that we can support children to develop their brilliance and probably the easiest and most effective way is to spend time with *them,* playing, reading and above all listening to what they are saying. I have spent so many years of my life working with children and their carers or parents, and the biggest cause of complaint children voiced was *not being listened to.*

One young girl I worked with, who was presenting so-called 'challenging behaviour,' I met in a secure unit. She was locked up 24 hours a day, at a cost of £2,000 per week. When I first met her she came across as very demanding and aggressive, always shouting and creating situations where she would be 'manhandled' by staff members which would, more often than not, end in some kind of physical restraint. She was also labelled a 'compulsive obsessive' and 'self harmer.' She did not stay in the secure unit for very long, probably less than a month, and was 'released' to the continuing care of the local authority.

Many years later, I met up with her again by chance, and she asked if I would like to go for a coffee with her, which I happily agreed to do, even though she didn't actually drink coffee. By now she had a daughter of her own, a gorgeous little two year-old who appeared content and happy. On that first meeting we did little more than talk about the past, catching up on old times and she asked me about my reasons for leaving social work, which at that point I didn't go into. I just shrugged my shoulders and said, "Just one of them, really" and left it at that. I really did enjoy her company though, and was very impressed by the way she *was* with her daughter. There was so much eye contact and exchanges of smiles, with the mother encouraging the little girl in everything she did. I will call the little girl Lee, and the mother, Patsy.

Patsy said that she was taking Lee to the Memorial Park, a short walk from the town centre, and asked if I would like to join them, which unfortunately I was unable to do. Patsy said that she had enjoyed meeting up with me again and that she would love me to have lunch with her sometime. She gave me her telephone number, commenting, "I won't ask for yours cos' you might not want to see me again, but don't know how to say it." As I opened my mouth to protest, she just put her finger to her lips, as if instructing me not to say anything, gave me a hug and then knelt down at the side of her daughter's pushchair and said, "Mummy's friend has to go now, and then me and you are going to go to the park and see the birds and play on the swings, so wave goodbye like a good girl," and with that she gave me a quick hug, and went on her way.

A few weeks later, I decided to give her a call and we agreed to meet up the following week at her home and she would prepare lunch. I can remember really looking forward to seeing her again; buying her some flowers before arriving at her two-bedroomed flat. The block, that her home was located in, was constructed from hard, unwelcoming concrete and all the glass was threaded with wire. The communal hall and stairwell smelt of stale urine and there was graffiti, lacking the artistry and creativity that some possess, sprayed here and there. At the side of the ground floor stairwell there was a broken pushchair, its small circular wheels twisted and fabric seat sliced into ribbons. I don't know why, but just looking at it made me feel sad.

As I climbed the stairs, my footfalls echoed, making me feel very alone, as if in some kind of concrete cave, devoid of life. There was nothing about this place that made me feel safe, comfortable or welcome and my feelings of warm anticipation had turned to ones of cold concern. My imagination now started to race ahead of me further and further with each step. At one point I thought my best option might be to give her the flowers as an apology for not being able to stay for lunch and then I chastised myself for even *thinking* such a thought.

Finally, I arrived at her floor and looked about for her number, and as my eyes scanned the doors, one stood out like an oasis in a desert. The door was painted a bright glossy blue, the number was in polished brass, to match the letterbox and lions head doorknocker, and there were two hanging baskets framing the door. Just above the keyhole there was a brass bell push, which I pressed, noticing that a smile had broken on my face. I heard a rhythmic tune fill the space behind the door, followed by the sound of Patsy approaching, obviously talking to someone. From behind the door Patsy asked in a very cheerful tone, "Who is it?"

"Rose," I replied, and with that the door opened and Patsy, who had just given me the biggest smile, stooped down to Lee's level, and said, "See, Lee, it's Rose. Rose is our friend who we had a drink with and she has brought us some beautiful flowers. Let's say hello to Rose and then we can all talk and put the flowers in some water so they can have a drink."

Lee smiled and in chorus they both said, "Hello Rose" and waved.

Suddenly I felt safe, comfortable and welcome.

We walked through the small hallway, which had orange-framed pictures on the bright yellow walls, displaying photographs and home drawn artwork. The living room was actually quite a good size and was just 'homely.' There was something indefinable that filled the space, and the only thing I could believe it to be was love, the energy of pure love.

Lee was extremely talkative and very sociable, her mother always including her in our conversation, which was mainly about their future dreams, places they had been to and people they knew. I spoke about my family, and as I did, Patsy would keep Lee clued up on what I was saying. We shared a lovely lunch, of grilled cheese on toast decorated with tomato and cucumber flowers, with the most enjoyable company and, having watched Patsy and Lee prepare the food with such enthusiasm; I relished the love in every mouthful.

About an hour after we had eaten, Patsy said that Lee would be going for her 'quiet time' now and both made their excuses and left. For a few moments, I sat alone and felt so relaxed in the tranquil atmosphere and then I stood up and walked to the balcony window at the far end of the living room. It, like the rest of the flat was colourful and invited you to step inside. I took in the view across the city and was amazed by how far you could actually see. Patsy returned after about five minutes and offered me a coffee, which I gracefully accepted.

As we sat back down Patsy said, "I don't drink coffee in front of Lee, that's why we had juice with lunch." She met my eyes and then said quite coldly and quietly, "At her age I was drinking coffee, can you believe that? When I use to ask my mum for a drink, she used to tell me to hang on a minute and then give me the last slurps of her coffee. Eventually she just tipped some of hers into a baby cup for me."

She stood up and asked me if I still smoked and, when I said I did, she said, "Come on then, let's go on to the balcony, and you can have one there."

As I took out a cigarette, I wanted to ask her how she knew her mother did that, when she would have been so young, but then, as if reading my mind, she said, "I watched her do the same to my little brother, it was like she never kind of made anything for *us*, and it was so disgustingly strong and sweet, so sweet."

"Do you see her, your mother?"

"Do I *see* her? I've seen her, as in 'with my eyes', but not as in 'seen her' seen her."

We has a really good talk about many things that day, while Lee had her 'quiet time,' and I met up with them every three months or so for a couple of hours until I moved to another town, often going in the evening after I finished work.

What Patsy said to me that day, and on the other occasions we had chance to talk privately, stayed with me and I will share some of it with you now, most of it connected to her past. I am going to write it as if I am Patsy, in the first person, and I will not include any of my comments.

I don't think she liked me. I don't think she ever really wanted me, or my brother. I don't think she ever has or ever will.

I can remember always wanting to please her, but I never did. I don't think I ever made her happy, or proud. I've never heard her use that word except when she said, "You have nothing to be proud about. Think you're clever do you? I'll show you what clever is, if you're not careful."

I stopped asking for things, even when I really, really wanted something, I stopped asking.

It was my brother I felt sorry for cos I knew he'd stopped asking, too.

When we started to fight, that's when she paid attention to us, and that's when we saw her face. I mean *really* saw her face. Most of the time she was on the phone or watching the telly. We never really *saw* her; do you know what I mean?

Most of the times we did it, fight I mean, it was worth all the pain, just to *see* her.

I hated her washing my face. I just use to hate it. She was so rough and the flannel smelt horrible, and I knew that the smell would stick to me and that I wouldn't be able to get rid of it. I hate flannels. I never use them, do you?

I didn't like it when my brother or me wet the bed because we knew we would have to lie in the smelly sheets. Most times, we would drag a blanket on the floor, take off our wet clothes and just cuddle up together. The next day the bed would usually be dry. I love clean sheets now. I change them twice a week and I always sleep better on those nights.

I can't remember her actually talking to me, *at me* yes, but not *to me.*

I was told that after she had me, she got bad post-natal depression and then my brother came soon after me, and that just seemed to make it worse, but I don't know if that's true, cos *she* never told me nothing.

Yes, there were some good times, but not too many, and you hold onto those good times until they can't hold *you* any more, and even when you think of them, you think of *her* and then stop thinking anything was ever really nice.

I hated it when dad left us and kept thinking he would come back, like he had done before, but he didn't, even though I prayed to God every night that he would.

I wanted to ask questions, but I was too young to know what questions to ask. I just wanted her to say something, but all she did was cry and say that *we* had driven daddy away.

School changed things really, being away from her I think. I remember 'storytime' and hearing a story about a happy family. They actually said in the book, 'they were a happy family' and I can remember thinking how lovely the story was and wishing that I was part of a happy family. I'm not saying I liked school, actually I fucking hated it, it was like all the teachers knew about my life, that my mum was a crazy person and it felt like they knew it was my fault. They would say things like, "Now, Patsy, play nicely or we will have to tell mummy and that will make her upset, and mummy is upset enough, isn't she?" I wanted to scream that I was upset too, but they didn't give a shit about me.

I remember a boy in my class. I can't remember his name but he was a real bully, always making someone, somewhere, feel uncomfortable. I used to be really quiet, but one day he took a toy off me that I was playing with, and that's when it happened. I lost the plot and went berserk. It wasn't about the toy. He had taken toys from me before and I had 'let' him, but this time I felt an explosion inside me and a roar came out of my body like a volcanic eruption. I grabbed the toy, a wooden xylophone, and hit him with it until the teacher grabbed my arm, then I dropped it and bit her, to make her let go of me. She ran out of the classroom, calling for assistance, while I continued to scream and throw toys in all directions. They said, "I had no control" over my behaviour and now I look back and think how couldn't they see that what I did was a result of *always* having to be in 'total control' of my behaviour. Do you know it was the first time I felt really free.

My mother never really used to be violent. She was just absent – not physically – I mean she was always there in body, just not in any other way. I used to try to get her to hit me because I thought if she could get really angry and explode like I had done, she might feel free as well, and then things would be all right. The thing was though, she didn't, she would shout and scream and give us a slap or two, but she never exploded, she would just turn up the volume on the TV and shut us in our room, jamming the door handle so that we couldn't get out.

I don't know when I started with my rituals, or how I even knew about rituals. I just used to make a 'deal' with God, that if I did 'such and such' he would make everything alright, but do you know what? God never kept his part of the agreement; no matter how well I performed the task or how much I pleaded. In the end, I hated God as much as I hated everyone else. He was just like them, promising and never delivering. The thing was, that in school they told us that God loved little children and sent his own son to help us, so why didn't he help my brother and me? Why didn't he *love* us and want to see us happy?

It was my brother I felt sorry for because he followed me in school. He was in the year below me and even though he was good, they treated him differently and that was my fault. In then end, he exploded too, just like they said he would. We became a 'double act' then, causing as much trouble as we could, not just at school, we started for 'real' at home, too. When mum was watching the TV, we would stand right in front of it, so that she couldn't see, or we would scream, so that she couldn't hear, and when she eventually threw us in the bedroom, we would make so much noise that she had to come back and open the door to try to shut us up.

When I was nine years old, I was taken into care for about six months, and so was my brother, but they wouldn't let us go to the same place cos they said we were too much 'trouble.' She had gone into a mental health unit, because she had had a breakdown. Funny that really, how can something that never worked, have a breakdown?

When we went back, things were different. We didn't live in the same house any more. And then mum was different too, like I could *see* her for the first time. Things were kept clean and tidy and this woman used to come to the house a couple of times a week and do things with us all, but even though this was what I had always wanted, it was as if God kept his part of the deal too late, and even though things were much better at home, the damage had been done and there was no way back.

She met another man, my so-called 'step dad,' and she would try to make deals with us so that he would stay with us. She would say things like, "Now, if you two are good, I will give you money to go to the cinema. Please be good, please." It was too late for deals, far too late. I used to really enjoy seeing her get so hopeful and then watching her fall. I can remember being *so nice* to him and then, when everyone was happy and smiling, letting rip.

'Step dad' was, looking back on it, quite a nice guy. We just never gave him a chance, and sometimes my brother used to say that he *liked* being with him and doing stuff together, but I would manage to persuade him to do as I asked and because he didn't want to lose me, he usually did what I wanted.

They got married eventually and we moved to his house, and that was just how it felt to me. *His house*, not *my home*. She was so fucking happy, always smiling and tidying up. She even made dinners and expected us to sit around like the 'Waltons',' all sweetness and light, but I was having none of it and started to cause all kinds of shit so that I didn't have to be part of the happy family dinner.

Then she got pregnant and I hated her more than ever. When the baby was born, I was really frightened for her, and wanted to warn her of what was to come, but do you know what, it never came. She was different with her, and every time I saw her with my sister, it reminded me of all the things I never *experienced* as her baby, and I hated her more and more.

I was taken into care when I was 12. My brother stayed with them. I was allowed 'home' on supervised visits and I hated seeing the 'happy family' that I had once dreamed of being part of. The visits were meant to help me 'integrate' with the family, but all they did was made me realise how *my* family had disintegrated, in that I was no longer part of it. My brother and sister seemed to get along fine together and sometimes when I visited, he would take me to his bedroom and beg me not to cause any trouble and I began to hate him too, for betraying me, for betraying us, and all the pacts we had 'sworn down to' over the years.

I didn't last very long with any of my foster parents, no matter how nice they were to me. I didn't want anyone to be nice to me; I wasn't *nice*. I was a bitch, a troublemaker, and a bad influence. Patsy didn't do 'nice.' But you know something, deep down inside, somewhere so deep, it was almost hidden away even from me, was a part of me that did believe that underneath it all, I was a good person, I had just forgotten *how to be* that person.

I was put into a residential unit when I was 14, after being moved from one foster family to another. My rituals were taking over my life by this point and I would go crazy if anyone interrupted them. Like I would have to clean each of my teeth individually, which took time, and then I intensified my rituals, so that I had to clean each tooth twice and if anyone tried to prevent me from doing this I would just totally lose control. And that was exactly what was happening, I was losing the control that I had been suffocating under for years and the experience of that, for others, was me being abusive, threatening, aggressive or whatever.

When I couldn't perform my rituals, I found another way to deal with this shit life I was living. I started to cut myself and it gave me the same safe feelings of being in control that my rituals did and soon this became my most important routine.

You know the secure unit bit, but after I left there I found someone who really loved me. He had had a shit life, like me, and we just understood each other's crazy little ways. We use to smoke weed and feel so happy. We used to laugh, and it was great. I felt like I had met the only other person in the world who really knew what I had been through, because he had experienced the same. I even stopped most of my rituals and enjoyed doing things, especially laughing.

He wasn't happy though, not really, really happy. He did 'stuff' for these men. I don't know what 'stuff' cos he used to joke that if he told me, he'd have to kill me, like he was some kind of secret agent, and I instinctively knew that if he didn't want to talk about it, then that was the way it had to be.

When I realised I was pregnant, I was scared to tell him at first and when I did finally let it out, he started to talk about us being a 'happy family' and getting a flat together, somewhere nice, and living 'happy ever after.' At first, I joined in the fantasy with him, but those thoughts of my own childhood would come thundering through my mind, full of 'what if's.' What if he left us? Would I hate my child for sending him away? What if the 'stuff' he was involved in was real bad shit? The social would take my baby away and give her to foster parents, and I knew what that was like. What if we didn't live 'happily ever after'? So many 'what ifs.' Then I understood. I could only depend on myself; even my brother who I thought loved me more than anything on earth had eventually turned his back on me, so why would this guy be any different? The only person I *knew* I could depend on was me, and my baby was going to have everything I didn't have.

When I told him I didn't want to be with him any more, at first he begged and pleaded with me, but it wasn't long before he gave up his declarations of love and never-ending happiness and instead called me a "cold hearted little slut," "bitch," 'tart" and saved the greatest insult for last when he said, "No wonder you've had such a shit life. You are a shit person that's why, and you'll always be a shit person. I hate you and hope the fucking social take the baby off you, you pathetic little bitch" and he left. I have seen him around, but he never speaks or comes near Lee, thank God.

I went to stay with 'special' foster parents who look after pregnant girls and the woman I stayed with was brilliant. I didn't mess her about because I wanted to keep my baby and after a while I actually got to like her. She told me all about her own life. She was in her forties and she had two daughters of her own who had grown up and got their own homes, one in Australia and the other quite close by. She herself had her first child when she was 16 and the next when she was 18 and had faced lots of prejudice from others, but she didn't care and proved everyone wrong by being the best mother that she could be. That was what she taught me, to be the best mother I could be.

I was the only foster child she had at the time, although she had supported others before me. I loved being with her and listening to her stories. She let me talk about things that had happened and she never interrupted, she just listened, and when I cried she just hugged me and allowed me to cry.

Patsy's story is not what many would class as a 'horror' story of childhood and I have met countless children who, like Patsy, experienced similar tortuous journeys, during my working life. I understood much of what she was saying, without asking for deeper explanation, because I had done so much of what she had done, but for very different reasons. Different journey, same destination. What strikes me more than anything else is that these journeys *do not need* to happen. In Patsy's case, her mother was suffering from postnatal depression and rather than address the illness, let alone prevent it, with appropriate care and attention, it was masked and made worse by medication.

If we look at the financial expense to this country, with the eventual costly interventions, it makes you realise how much money is spent trying to *deal* with the problem, rather than an initial outlay to *prevent* the spiral of decline. There is no need for this. We should invest money into our children and parents and really value their potential brilliance. Parents, mainly mothers, should not be isolated and disengaged *from* society, especially when they are performing the most vital role *for* society.

In our schools, we teach our children so much useless crap that has no relevance apart from brain washing them into regurgitating the 'party line.' We should be enabling them to express their own brilliance, not turning them into robotic parrots, unable to express a unique thought. Who cares if Henry VIII had six wives? Who cares if he broke away from Rome and Catholicism? Why are we taught to believe that he was such a great leader and king? In my mind, he appeared to be a woman-hating dictator who was only interested in exploiting his position as monarch, to bed as many women as possible and when the church i.e. God, did not agree with his misogynistic ways, he turned his back on the religion that had ruled everyone's behaviour for centuries, and created his own. Maybe he was a prophet, too! Due to his lust, hatred and exploitation of women, many more were killed and sacrificed. Why weren't we told the truth, if there is anyone out there who actually *knows* what the truth is, and why, when we tried to get answers to questions, were we told to "stop disrupting the class"?!! We are slowly destroying the brilliance of our future's potential, the planet's future potential, and in my mind, the government *must* realise what they are doing.

To 'save' Patsy would have taken a few hundred pounds of care and attention for her and her mother, who was *ill*. Instead it cost the government, read that as you and me because we foot the bill, thousands and thousands of pounds on ineffective and destructive interventions and then they inform us with great rhetoric and reverence, of how much money *they* have spent to *support* families and children. This is crazy!

So, what could be the real reason why the government does not want to develop the potential brilliance of our children? Well, I am not alone in thinking that maybe they don't *want* our children to develop independent thought, because if they do, they might not be so *easy* to manipulate and control. They want to control us, because they are scared of what *we* could be capable of, if *they* relinquish that control. They are terrified that we will see through their lies, propaganda and bullshit and demand a different way of experiencing life.

Schools would be places to create dreams and deliver new realities. There would be no such things as 'teachers'; the whole school would be a developing environment where everyone shared in the creation of brilliance. Parents and children would come together during the day, to share the experience of learning, where both felt safe, welcome and valued. Skills would be passed from one to another, without the need for certification and gold stars. Children would have the ability to explore their own unique abilities and utilise areas of their beings that you and I may never have had the opportunity to do. The school would be multi-generational with everyone supporting each other to live truly interdependent lives connected by love and respect. Children would learn all the skills and develop all the resources they would need to live their independent reality. What would the government do then? It would have to do something *real* for a living itself, rather than live at the expense of everyone else who is actually *doing, generating and creating* wealth for this country. The thing is that they don't have to be scared of the alternative future that brilliance can bring. Like Patsy, they can become the 'best that I can be' and enjoy contributing to a peaceful, creative and rewarding experience of life.

Then we have to consider the cost in human terms of the government's lack of effective intervention. Although we do not have the facts, in Pasty's case it is fairly safe to assume that prior to having postnatal illness, Patsy's parents were quite happy and probably looking forward to their lives together. Maybe they believed that this would be bringing another dimension to their expression of commitment.

Let's just focus on this for a moment.

I want you to clear your mind and take a good, disassociated look at the scene I am about to show you. I want you to imagine it as if you were watching a movie where you are the projectionist. This means that you have control of the film and can pause, fast forward or stop the movie when you choose. You are sitting in the projectionist's box and there is an audience watching the movie. However, whatever you do to the movie, you do to the audience as well. So, if you 'pause' the movie, you also 'pause' the audience. OK. So, now imagine yourself as the projectionist and let's start the movie.

The film is entitled 'Happy Families.'

The opening scene shows us Jack and Jill meeting for the first time. They are both working at the same office and over time, their friendship turns to love and romance. They date each other for a couple of years before getting engaged, throwing a party to celebrate. Their families, friends and colleagues cheer their health and future happiness. The couple work hard and save up for their wedding, and continue to love and worship each other. As they work together, they have many experiences to share, and when one is feeling low about work, the other can fully understand the *environment* the other is talking about. They go out and have fun, celebrating with each other the total freedom they feel they have.

Let's jump ahead to their wedding day. By now, both are in their mid twenties and have progressed at work, meaning they have more money. They had decided to spend some of that hard-earned cash on a romantic honeymoon after the wedding. The wedding itself was a fantastic affair, with Jill looking radiant in her fitted 'Audrey Hepburn' styled gown and Jack all kitted out like James Bond, in dark suit and bow tie. The church they were married in was dressed in red roses to match the ones in Jack's lapel and Jill's bouquet. We watch them take their solemn vows to love each other in sickness and in health, and hear that "those that God has joined together may no man put asunder.' Then everyone claps as they are declared 'man and wife,' and he is told he may "kiss the bride."

Ahh! Look at the audience; do they share in Jack and Jill's happy day?

The wedding reception is held in a hotel and the bridal party had endless photographs taken, as an eternal reminder of their 'happy day.' A video was taken of the speeches, recording her father's hopes and wishes for his little princess and the best man's anecdotes and laughter, as he recounts tales of Jack's indiscretions over the years they have known each other. Then everyone cheers the bride and groom, as they cut the wedding cake.

At the evening disco, we watch them dance their first dance, as a married couple, to a song that has now come to represent their love for each other.

The honeymoon is spent on a resort in Majorca and they exhaust their love-filled two weeks going to discos, clubs and of course, lying next to each other on a sun-drenched beach. Here they talk of their future, their hopes and aspirations. They would love a little cottage in the countryside eventually, but decide to try to save for their first mortgage, as the first step to this dream. They discuss different possible locations for their first home and dream of how they will furnish it, and cement their dreams, while they are still fresh in their memories, by making love.

We next see them as two very hard-working office executives, both still with the same firm. They now live in a small semi-detached house, with a postage stamp garden, in a fairly nice part of town. They are saving to take a step up the property ladder, and have put a deposit on a larger semi-detached property on a new development, that will be completed in six months time. Even though the mortgage on this will be substantially higher, both are in progressive positions at work and believe that, by the time they move into the new property, they will be just about able to afford it.

They both get up early at least four times a week to go to a local gym together before work, and after work they often meet up with friends, or stay home and watch a movie together. On Friday night's, they both go out with their own particular friends to maintain those important friendships, that may have preceded their own relationship, and on Sundays they always bathe together before sleeping. These are their routines and they both get enormous pleasure from them.

Jill misses a period and then another. She tells Jack that she thinks she might be pregnant and neither of them is initially happy. It doesn't fit with their plans, with everything that they have been working towards. For their dreams to become reality, they both needed to bring in money *and* they both need to progress in their jobs; having a baby would change all of that. We see them spend many hours conferring about what they should do, with anger, recriminations, frustration and tears becoming the overriding emotional outcome. Discussions have become heated disagreements. In a bitter compromise, it was agreed that the pregnancy would continue at the expense of buying their new property, even though this would mean losing their deposit.

Jack will try to talk to the developers to see if there was a way around the problem, but to no avail. Jill was not too happy about losing out on the house, as it was a good 'status' move for them, but did not want to terminate her pregnancy; this baby was an expression of their love for each other. Jill tried to persuade Jack that they should carry on with the purchase, saying that she would go back to work as soon as the baby was born, and Jack reminded her that nursery care costs a lot of money; money they *should* be spending on their new home. So, to stop the constant disagreements, the decision was made and although they *spoke* no more about the subject, they realise that it is ever present in their lives.

Jill really enjoys her pregnancy and feels as if she belongs to a new club, meeting expectant mums and talking to them, even though she may not have met them before. They would chat while waiting for antenatal checks, or walking around Mothercare, a store Jill now visits on a weekly basis.

Jack and Jill decide that Jill should return to her job after a break of six months to relax after giving birth and nursing, which her employers agree to, and Jill is quite looking forward to having a break from the frantic existence called 'work.'

Now, it is the last few weeks of Jill's pregnancy and she has spent a month on maternity leave to prepare for her new arrival. She reads all the

'Mother and Child' magazines she can get her hands on and fantasises about how good life will be for her, Jack and their new addition.

The week before Jill is due to deliver, Jack arrives home with some good news. He has been promoted to the head office of their company and will be earning quite a bit extra, after his initial six months probationary period. The company understands that Jill is due to have her baby at any time, so have told Jack to take a week off with Jill after the birth, and then report to his new manager at the new location, which is only 20 minutes down the motorway. His boss is taking him out to dinner that night especially to introduce him to his new manager. For the first time, Jill feels a touch of exclusion and wants to ask if she can go to dinner with him, then looking at her huge abdomen, decides against doing so.

Jill goes into labour and baby Leone is born, fit and healthy. Jack is there for the delivery and when he holds his daughter in his arms for the first time, is overwhelmed by the emotions he feels for her. He looks into her screwed up eyes and, with her whole hand embracing his little finger for security, makes a promise to make all her dreams come true.

Jill tries to breastfeed but Leone doesn't seem to want to take it, making Jill frustrated and the baby cry. The midwives try to encourage her, but as her breasts begin to fill with milk, they ache and throb with pain. One of the other mothers advises her, "I wouldn't breastfeed if they paid me; you want to give it up as a bad job. With my first I breastfed and my clothes stank of stale milk, my tits constantly leaked, leaving stains where the milk had come through, and every time my first needed a feed in the night, who do you think got the job? And you'll end up with saggy boobs, and for what? No it's not worth it love, not worth the tears and not worth the effort. No one will ever thank you for it."

Jill responds thoughtfully, "But I thought that 'breast was best'."

"Best for who, love? If breast milk was that vital to a baby's health and wellbeing, they wouldn't have invented formula would they? I'm just saying that you don't have to do this to yourself, that's all. We're liberated now, you know?"

Jill gives up her attempts to breastfeed after two days.

For some reason Jill doesn't feel herself but everyone she speaks to, about her feelings, puts it down to a wide variety of differing reasons, from 'three-day baby blues' to lack of sex! The overriding message is, "Don't worry about it; just let your body settle down and everything will be alright." Jill is discharged after three days in hospital and declared fit and healthy, as is Leone.

Jill and Jack have two days together alone, not counting the visits from the midwife and health visitor, to adjust to the new arrival, before Jill's mother arrives to stay with them for a couple of days to help out, returning home the day Jack starts his new job.

Jill does not know what to expect, being on her own with Leone, but her mother and Jack left contact details, should she feel the need to get in touch. Jill had woken at the same time as Jack and fed Leone while he showered, then she went downstairs and made him a cup of coffee, wanting to tell him how apprehensive she is feeling about being left on her own. When Jack comes down, he says that the baby is crying and that she had better go and check on her. Jill goes upstairs and instead of going into the nursery, she just stands holding the open door, before reaching the plug socket and switching off the power supply to the 'babycom.' Jill then closes the door and stands with her back to it for a moment, her heartbeat thumping in her chest, before putting on a smile and going back downstairs to Jack. Jack gives her a grin and then starts to talk about his own apprehensions regarding his day ahead. At 8.00am Jack kisses Jill on the cheek before getting into the family car and driving away.

As Jill watches him go, waving him off at the front door, she thinks of what lies ahead for her and does not want to shut herself inside with her fears. Instead, she just stands there looking at where Jack had been standing, almost as if he had never left. Then, looking at the vacant space that the car had recently filled, she realises that she is not even able to get in the car and escape. What once they had shared, the journey to work, was now just a journey for Jack.

Jill goes straight into the kitchen and makes herself a cup of coffee, trying not to hear the cries of Leone, but eventually realising that she has to go and to attend her. When she gets to the nursery, Jill listens outside the door, before taking a big breath and walking into the room. Leone is still crying, twisting her face and clenching her tiny fists. Jill reaches in to her cot and holds her hand, making 'shushing' noises to quieten her, but the crying continues. Jill lifts her out of the cot and supports her on her shoulder. She pats Leone's back in the hope that trapped wind is the cause of her discontent, but this also fails to calm the baby.

Jill thinks Leone might need to have her nappy changed and lays her back in the cot, while she goes to get a clean nappy and wipes from downstairs, but on reaching the living room, she closes the door, turns on the television and sits on the sofa. Eventually the cries stop and Jill relaxes, turns down the sound on the programme and drifts off to sleep. She is awoken by the sound of the doorbell accompanied by the crying of Leone. Her health visitor has arrived and Jill welcomes her into the house, offering her a cup of coffee and some biscuits. The health visitor agrees to the offer, but only after they have attended to 'baby.' Once in the nursery, the health visitor picks Leone out of her cot, after asking Jill's permission, and starts to fuss and comfort her. Jill watches the health visitor with a detached silence, before the health visitor suggests that Jill prepares Leone's bottle, while she changes her nappy. Before the health visitor leaves, she agrees to come the following day, to show Jill how to bath the baby.

Jack said that he would return by 6.30pm, but he doesn't actually get home until after 7.00pm, by which time Jill is extremely agitated. Jack can't understand why she is so tearful and is disappointed that she seemed disinterested in his first day at his new job. Jill is tearful because Jack just wants to talk about his day, but has no regard for hers. Jack asks what they are going to eat, quite without malicious intent, but Jill sees it as an indication that she is 'useless' and storms off to the bathroom, locking the door behind her.

When she returns downstairs, she finds Jack enjoying a glass of wine, while chatting to his brother on the phone about his new job, all laughter and smiles. On seeing Jill, he raises his glass and nods his head towards the kitchen where Jill finds a glass already poured for her. For some reason, this makes her cry.

As the weeks pass by, Jack leaves for work earlier and returns home later and Jill, feeling more and more isolated spends much of her time in the company of the television. Her friends and colleagues do visit from time to time, but she hates it when they come, as she feels she has to put on an act, and pretend to be what they expect her to be, so she does not encourage their visits. Jill has become very good at wearing masks. She has one for the health visitor, who doesn't come to her home any more, one for the clinic and one for her friends. She feels as if the 'real' Jill is disappearing under all the different masks she has to wear.

Jack, not wanting to upset Jill, doesn't really ask her about her day. He has learnt that if he asks, she will often get tearful, or complain of tiredness and in the end he feels so helpless, and she so frustrated, that they blame each other. Jack does talk to Jill about his new job, but she seems detached, or maybe resentful, and sometimes he feels a twinge of guilt. Instead he talks to his friends and now meets up with them on Wednesday evenings, as well. When he is out he feels guilty at first, thinking of Jill at home with Leone, but after a couple of glasses of whisky, he starts to mellow out and enjoy the banter.

One Friday night, after a row with Jill about his planned evening, he storms out of the house and goes straight to a bar and then on to his best mate's house. Jill sits by herself, watching their wedding video and looking through their photographs, remembering a time when they were happy. She wonders why it has all gone so wrong; she loves Jack so much and just wants him to come home. Jill feeds and changes Leone, crying bitterly as she does so and then lays her in her cot, while she opens a bottle of red wine and eventually falls asleep on the sofa.

Jack is also 'drowning his sorrows' and becomes a tearful drunk. His mate, John, asks him what's going on, saying he's looking worn out and tired. Jack tells him that it's so hard trying to make the targets with this new job and it's not that he can't do it, it's that he can't do it *and* take total responsibility for all the bills *and* Jill's emotional shit. Jill is meant to be going back to work soon, but she never wants to talk about it, in fact she never wants to talk about anything. Their sex life is shit as well, and he hasn't even been able to touch her since she had Leone. Jill doesn't take care of herself any more and because of the baby *they* can't go to the gym, even though Jack *needs* to go. Jack says that Jill no longer wants to go places on his days off and would rather just hand Leone over to him while she veg's out in front of the TV. Jill use to be a good laugh, and now, he never sees her laugh. Nothing is the same.

John listens and makes appropriate noises in appropriate places and when Jack finishes, he says, "I don't know mate. I've never been through it, and don't want to either, but I am sure that it is just hormonal and everything will get back to usual *given time*. You just need to take care of yourself. If you aren't there to bring in the money, then you'll really be in the deep and sticky. The thing with women and babies is that they don't understand what it's like for us, the men. I mean it's hardly a difficult job is it, looking after a baby? I mean all you have to do is feed them and change them a couple of times a day, how difficult can that be?

"Look at what we have to do to bring in the money to support the baby. I know it must take some getting used to, but I don't think you are helping her to get used to it by giving up stuff that is important to *you*, like the gym. If you keep doing stuff for her, then she'll never get the hang of it. If I was you, I would pay her some compliments, give her some flowers or chocolates, maybe take her out for a meal now and then, but let her get on with it. It's called 'hard love' mate, but then again, Jack; I'm not a woman. Hey, maybe that is what you should do! There must be some woman at your new place who doesn't know Jill. Why not ask her advice? Maybe there's something going on that only women understand."

So, that is exactly what Jack does.

OK, so now I would like you to scan the members of the audience, who have been watching the movie. Take a good look around. It's your audience and you can have whoever you like sitting in those seats. Now imagine that you have to give that family some advice so that they can have their 'own' happy ever after, and that includes Leone. I want you to select four members of the audience to assist you. When you have chosen them they will come up to the projectionist's box with you and the film can be used to revisit scenes, replay words etc. The audience members you choose should have many skills and can come from any walk of life. If you want Carl Jung to assist you, he will be there. Now take your four guests up to the projectionist's booth and find some solutions.

When you are doing this, I want you to imagine five clearly marked out circles on the floor of the projectionist's booth. In each circle, place one expert and have their name clearly written in chalk in front of their circle. Now you have to discuss the solutions, by giving each expert a chance to offer their thoughts. Before they speak, they must say their name and they must not be interrupted until they have finished what they have to say. Any expert can make comments as long as they offer solutions and they should not dismiss another's advice unless they have an improved alternative. You have the role of observing the discussions and ensuring no rules are broken.

Unfortunately, this kind of 'movie' is being played out by hundreds of families every day and we have to find solutions so that this systematic torture of parents, mainly women, is stopped. Children, as we have said before, do not need 'good enough,' they need the 'absolute best.'

I want to move on now to what I believe is happening to our children, in this free and open, democratic country we call 'home.' I believe that children are born with additional senses that we slowly deactivate as we 'teach' them how to exist on this earth. I believe that there is some 'power' out there that wants to control how our children behave and to do this they engage us – the parents – and the rest of society, to ensure it happens. I think that this has been an ongoing agenda for centuries and many people have already written excellent material on the subject, so there is no need for me to add my thoughts to either whom 'they' may be, what 'reasons' are behind it, or where 'they' can be found. What I *do* want to discuss are the methods that I believe, as do many others, they are using to de-sensitise our children to their own unique, limitless possibilities.

The other day, I decided to spend an entire day watching CBeebies (British TV channel for children), just to see what young minds have to cope with as entertainment. Then, a few days later, I 'experimented' with a 14-month-old child to see how she reacted to a couple of hours of the same. What struck me most of all, when I watched CBeebies, was how *visual* it all was. Everything was animate, with the brightest colours you could imagine. The scenery, in some of the backdrops, looked as if four year-olds had drawn it, and sometimes wobbled when the 'hosts' walked around. If the 'hosts' were people, they were always adults, who dressed and spoke like children, only more exaggerated, with loads of gesticulating and other body language.

The colours kept enticing me to watch the screen, even though I didn't really want to. The sound was also loud, exaggerated and repetitive. When the 'hosts' spoke, it was all very precise and each word was expressed with total animation of tone. The sound seemed to fill the entire space and made it difficult to focus on any other noises. The other thing that surprised me was that the same programmes kept repeating themselves, until everything sort of merged together into one huge jumble of colour and sound.

For you to experience this for yourself, I would suggest that you pick a morning when you have no distractions and turn on CBeebies. Now, do not adjust the sound volume from where you last had it, unless of course you had the volume muted, in which case put it at dead centre level. I would then ask you to just sit, watch and listen for the next half an hour. As soon as the half hour is up, do some constructive 'thought' work, maybe Sudoku or a crossword, or write a letter, for at least ten minutes, with the programmes still running and the sound at the same level. Then, I would like you to turn off the volume completely and do another 'thought' task for five minutes. Finally, close your eyes with the volume at a slightly higher than normal level, and just listen to what is being said.

Reflect on your experiences of all the different situations. Was it difficult to concentrate? Did you get 'drawn' in by the colours and did you find your eyes being pulled to the screen? Did the sounds start to agitate you and did you hear yourself responding to the television when questions were asked? What other sounds were you aware of when you were just watching the screen? Did you hear different sounds when you were just focussing on the volume? Could you do that for more than three hours in one stretch? For those parents who say that they have it on all day everyday, the difference for them is that they do other things to entertain you, such as talk to friends on the mobile, read magazines, drink coffee, and work on the computer. In other words, CBeebies is not there to *entertain you*. It is there to *entertain, distract and enthral your children*. You just regard it as *background* sound, which you will process and may decide to discard; preferring your own *selected* entertainment.

I am not here to judge, nor am I here to say I am any better than 'quite good' as a parent. I am only offering different perspectives and options for consideration. I *know* what I *believe* to be *truth* but I have no such knowledge of what *you* know and believe to be the truth, so these are my thoughts.

When my children were able to sit in a bouncy chair, at eight months old, I would strap them in, hand them a bottle of juice and sit them in front of the TV. This enabled me to do 'essential' jobs, like vacuuming, washing, writing and getting ready to go out. When I think of my experiment and how much it nearly drove me crazy, I feel dreadful about subjecting my children to such torture. I have seen so many small children, babies really, strapped into bouncy chairs, pushchairs, baby walkers, high chairs or even propped up on sofas surrounded by cushions, fixated for hours on this mind destroying, collision of colours, tones and totally false representation of the world we inhabit and the *way* we inhabit it.

I decided to see what would happen if I offered Shania, a 14 month old baby, the choice of CBeebies or me. To do this I had to break the session into four half hour segments. In the first half an hour, I placed Shania on the living room floor, having removed everything portable, so that the only 'play' experience open to her was the TV or climbing around the furniture. Shania was not strapped into her chair and had free scope to roam around at her leisure. When I left her to her own devices, she did initially look at the screen, but only during her general surveillance of her environment. She then began to pull herself up various bits of furniture, so that she was now scanning the area from a higher perspective.

Every now and then, as she continued her journey, she would stop and watch the screen and then continue on her way. I noticed that she did actually stop and fix her gaze on the screen, which she was not doing for any other part of the room. Whenever anything caught her attention, she would drop down to the ground and crawl over to whatever the 'thing' was, to investigate further. Once she had reached the object, she would explore it briefly with her eyes and then touch it with her fingers before picking it up and observing it a little more closely, and then putting it up to her mouth for further data.

I noticed that when she was absorbed with something, she would look up at the screen when the tones fluctuated from high and low sounds, which was most of the time, so even though it appeared that Shania *wanted* to concentrate on the object she was currently observing, her attention was constantly broken and interrupted by the noises coming from the TV. The screen also created a constant flickering display that was difficult for her to ignore because it actually affected the light in the room. The flickering makes you search for the source and then you are hooked by the images to keep looking.

For the next half an hour, I made Shania a bottle of milk and strapped her into her chair in full view of the TV screen. She became agitated after a short while and threw her bottle on to the floor, which I picked up, cleaned and gave back to her. After a few minutes, she threw the bottle again and then tried to look around for me. I did not meet her eyes and she became frustrated and started to whimper and bang her legs until I responded. As soon as I entered her field of vision, she started to smile. I gave her back the bottle and stood next to her for a moment and as soon as I turned to leave, she once more threw the bottle on to the floor. This time I did not give her the bottle back and after some initial crying and struggling she eventually watched the screen. Her body language was 'quiet' and she did not display any signals that she was enjoying the entertainment, such as laughter, in fact I did not observe a single smile and after 20 minutes she fell asleep.

For the next half an hour, it was just Shania and me, entertaining each other. I had a selection of playthings out of sight, but within easy reach for me. First I allowed her to explore the environment, as before, and this time I noticed that she kept checking me out every couple of seconds. When she was at the farthest side of the room, I called her over to me and she made direct eye contact, stopped what she was doing and sat down. Then she again scanned the path from where she was to where I was, and crawled across to me smiling and making verbal noises as she travelled. Once she arrived at her destination, she sat down and clapped her hands together, smiling as she did so.

We then played 'peek-a-boo,' which I tired of long before she did, and then a clapping game. In these games I didn't make any physical contact. Shania smiled a lot and tried to copy my actions and continued to clap her hands after I stopped. Then I played a game where I did make physical contact, called 'leggy over leggy' and in this game you sit the child on your lap and have them facing away from you. With each of your hands, you hold the child's ankles and while bouncing, in a 'singy songy' rhythm, sing "Leggy over leggy, the doggy went to Dover, when he came to a fence, the doggy jumped ovvvverrrr." As you sing the words, you cross and uncross the child's ankles and, at the end of the rhyme, you rock back lifting the child's ankles up in the air while supporting the rest of their body with your own.

Even though there was no eye contact during this game Shania really enjoyed it and was laughing and bouncing about to the words of the rhyme. Next, I played a game that involved eye contact *and* physical touch, 'never smile at a crocodile.' This game involved us both sitting on the floor and I make my forearms take the shape of a crocodile's jaws, which I open, and close while singing the rhyme. Then when the song has ended, I chase Shania with my 'snapping jaws,' trying to catch her. She loved this game. She laughed and squealed, moving really quickly at a high-speed crawl to try to escape 'my jaws.' Then, when I moved back to my starting space, Shania would follow, laughing and giggling as we did so. Shania was very good at maintaining eye contact and looking for 5 sense 'clues' as to when to make her escape from the snapping 'jaws.' I really enjoyed this game as well, and found that I was laughing almost as much as she was.

Next, I gave her a teddy bear to play with and I walked away and sat at my computer. Shania inspected it for a while, and then dragged it with her a few feet on her journey towards me, before dropping it with disinterest. When I picked up the teddy and encouraged her to play with it by waggling it in front of her face, she did engage, but as soon as I handed it to her and moved away; she would disengage from the teddy. I then left her to play with a musical press and activate toy, which she played with by herself for a couple of minutes before discarding it and searching for other interesting bits of rubbish off the floor. What amazes me about toddlers is how they can manage to find every bit of fluff and dirt that you thought you had managed to clean off the floor. Shania found so many interesting bits of debris to explore, making me get up and down constantly, to make sure what she was exploring was 'safe,' i.e. not a pin or shard of broken plastic.

For my final experiment, I turned on CBeebies again, and left a variety of toys scattered over the floor and then moved away. Shania did approach the toys, but they only interested her momentarily, certainly not for longer than one minute. The screen constantly distracted her, and her eyes kept making contact with it, as she explored. After about ten minutes, she became agitated and would pick up different objects, and in some cases she threw them. I then called her name and she instantly came crawling over to me, full of smiles and lots of eye contact. Shania was making a wide range of noises and squeals as she sped up to get to me. I then sat on the sofa and started to sing the crocodile rhyme and she became very excited and sat in front of me clapping her hands together. I kept singing and handed her a teddy, which she immediately discarded, before continuing to jog up and down and clap. Shania did keep flicking her eyes to the screen, becoming momentarily distracted as we played. After I turned off the television her enthusiasm for the play increased, with far more animation, verbal response and movement.

By strapping a child in front of a screen for hours, we are limiting their experiences of this three-dimensional existence, by offering them two sensory-based entertainments. Having the TV on in the 'background' distracts children from their immediate focus of attention, and prevents the child becoming animate as part of the experience, thus restricting physical exercise and movement. For parents to subject their children to such restrictions, these programmes should be 'teaching' our children something worthwhile, for us to be content to let them suffer such limitations. Well, once again, I suggest you actually observe the programmes *before* you let these 'teachers' have your child's undivided (restricted) attention. During my stint of watching CBeebies I was horrified and shocked, as previously I have never really paid attention to the programmes in any detail.

The first programme was 'The Tweenies,' where some 'human type' costumes (with real people inside); again very brightly coloured, let us 'join' them in their play. One of the characters, Fizz, was sucking her thumb, so the others called her a baby and said if she was a baby, she should go to bed. Fizz went to bed and the other three characters, along with some old geezer (I don't really know who he was supposed to represent) offered to read a book to them. He did not choose a normal words and pictures book, oh no, he chose a book where you could touch the pictures to *experience* how the pictures felt. In other words, the book attracted three senses: sight, touch, and hearing.

The other three characters sat around the old geezer and became very excited as he read and even more excited when they were allowed to touch the pictures, which made them all giggle and laugh. They experienced 'fluffy', 'scaly', 'rough' and 'shiny.' They had as much fun teasing poor old Fizz as they did experiencing the book. One would say, "Oh this feels so lovely Fizz and you can't feel it because you would rather be a baby and suck your thumb." As the characters touched the pages they would make some comment to Fizz about how lucky they were and how unfortunate she was. Just as the old geezer closed the last page, Fizz jumped out of bed saying, "I don't want to be a baby any more. I want to touch the book."

Sadly, the old geezer told Fizz that she was too late and had missed the experience, along with heckles from his entourage of 'good grown up' Tweenies, confirming that Fizz had missed out on all the fun. Fizz reacted to the news badly with a violent outburst, stamping her feet and then kicking over the furniture, and finally standing in defiant solitude, which she emphasised with a scowl and folded arms.

I was totally stunned!

The next programme was a kind of story with bright pictures and 'high tone, low tone voices,' and was about three little foxes that see a rainbow in the sky. They are out playing on their own without a grown-up fox anywhere in sight. They decide that the rainbow is so pretty that they would each like to turn their (already beautiful and don't need artificial colour) boring coats into a different colour from the rainbow. The trouble is they don't know how to do it. One has an idea and climbs up the side of a building, possibly someone's house, as the rainbow appears to be in the sky above the house. The other two follow this fox, neither protesting about what the first fox is doing.

When the first fox gets onto the roof, he falls through some kind of open skylight window and lands on the building below. The other foxes do not raise the alarm; instead they follow the first and slide down through the skylight to be with their friend. Once in the room they notice that it is full of paints and they start to squirt the paint all around the room making multi-coloured splatters everywhere. Their play is interrupted when one of the foxes hears someone approaching, and shouts, "Someone is coming, quick hide in case we get into trouble." And they all run off and hide. We do not see the whole picture of the person, but by his check slippers and bent knees, I guess he is a fairly old man. He is surprised by the mess and looks around. Meanwhile, the foxes manage to escape outside and start laughing and giggling about their adventure. The rainbow has gone when they get outside and the moon is in the sky instead. They realise that while they have been splashing about in the paint, that they have achieved what they actually wanted to achieve. One of them is green, one purple and one yellow. Hooray for breaking and entering, and when they go back home to mummy fox, who has obviously just been chilling out for the day, she laughs at her little foxes' adventures, too.

Next, I watched some total garbage called Granny Murray and, even though I work in London, I saw a totally different multi-coloured London than I am used to experiencing. Everything was colourful, and empty of people, yet fun and exciting. In this episode, the 'doctor' was the main focus, maybe she always is, who knows, and 'time' came a close second. The message was about getting everything done on time and when the people began to get stressed about not completing things on time, they were told, "not to worry because all the colours of the harlequin are there to help you," and shown a slightly more colourful representation of Canary Wharf than I have ever seen. It did make me think that I could shorten my 'work/life balance' training session substantially, because all I need to say to delegates is, "Don't worry because you have all the colours of the harlequin to help you."

We heard all about the 'doctor's' tough schedule, hour-by-hour, and watched as she questioned her own abilities to achieve her targets. And then, as if we weren't stressed enough, the 'doctor' made some poor male nurse, dressed as a clown, wash his hands and then put them under a special light so we could 'see' how dirty they still were!! He was told to wash them again.

The final crock of shit came from a couple of 'cooks' called 'Big Cook, Little Cook.' This involved some pretty awful 'trick' photography that made one 'chef' appear normal height and the other, tiny. Now, by the way they were dressed, it was obvious that the 'little chef' was the comedy part of the duo, while the other, the 'grown-up' representation, was in the role of advising and correcting the other. This means that the children are more apt to connect with the 'little' human representation. So what kind of a role model was the little guy? Well, for the first five minutes, he just bounced up and down and jigged this way and that, seemingly unable to sit still. Even though 'little chef' was told not to, he ran and jumped straight into the mixing bowl and splattered the flour everywhere and everyone laughed at his antics. In this programme, they made food to eat and we were asked to comment on whether we liked it or not!! Have I lost the plot completely?

We are allowing and, in some cases, actively encouraging our children to watch shit. In one short hour I saw: name-calling, bullying, stereotyping, selfishness and teasing, attempts at behaviour modification (which I might add gave no reward when the subject finally responded appropriately), neglect, exploring unsafe environments, climbing into other people property, wreckage and devastation, wanton waste, inappropriate behaviour, encouraging children to run away from their negative actions, non acceptance of blame (responsibility), collusion of parents by rewarding inappropriate behaviour, hyperactivity as a funny thing to do, and finally, behaving in a way you have been told not to and making everyone laugh.

The other thing that struck me about these programmes is they way that they are constructed *as if* the children could use their five senses to participate in the programme. For example, in the Tweenies, the children *watching* the programmes are excluded from experiencing the 'touchy feely' book as much as Fizz was excluded, and during the cooking programme the children could not experience the taste of the 'yummy' food that the brattish chefs had made.

It's all totally crazy to me, and people call *me* mad!

What *is* going on and if we don't have any idea, then why are we *allowing* something *we* don't understand to happen, especially to our children?

I believe that there *is* a purpose to all this; the isolating of parents, the 24-hour children's 'entertainment' networks, the colours, tones and constant flickering, the messages that are 'hidden' to us but 'obvious' to the children, the focus on a two sensory experience of a three dimentional world, the earlier age at which children start school, to begin the indoctrination in earnest, the foods, the additives, in other words, almost everything.

Our children are being programmed to focus their attention, and then process data through a fraction of their senses, limiting their experience and therefore their ability to generate options and choices. In NLP, there is a theory that the part with the most flexibility has the most choice, therefore as *experiential* flexibility is restricted, so are the choices or options. We, as adults, have already been processed, so we have a lesser degree of flexibility in the choices we tend to make and, as we have already been programmed, we 'educate' our children using the same programming, only maybe we are not *aware* that that is what we are actually doing. If a child does not conform to what we consider the correct way to respond, we chastise them and tell them to 'behave properly' or people will not like them.

How many brilliant young minds have been wasted, by the programming of adults?

When my eldest daughter Faye was around two years of age, she began to talk about her 'other' life, before she was with me. At the time I was around 19 years old and living in a fairly 'rough' part of Coventry. I had very little money to buy life's essentials. My husband at the time used to work night shifts in a car factory, so for most of the working week, Faye and I had to be very quiet while her daddy slept. On Thursday nights, he would go off to work on his shift and, as this was his final shift of the working week, he would receive his weekly wages in small brown pay packet; all of it was cash. Consequently, I rarely saw him from Thursday evening at 9.00pm until Tuesday morning at around 8.00am and when he did appear, there was little or no money left.

This meant that there was hardly enough for food, let alone toys for Faye to play with. To get out of the house during the day, we would walk into town and then go to the library, where it was always nice and warm with plenty of books to look at. Once we had finished there we would go to the Memorial Park and play on the swings and slides, or go for a walk across the fields to look at the horses, cows and ducks.

At the time, I didn't have a TV, hi-fi or radio, as there was no money to buy these 'luxuries,' so it meant that Faye and I spent a lot of time playing 'imaginary' games. I even had 'imaginary' creams that I could rub on her cuts and grazes when she hurt herself and, miraculously, she would feel better. Faye's vocabulary was extensive for her young years and she could maintain a conversation quite easily. One day we went for a walk to Nors Mill Park where there was a small boating lake, and people would bring their model yachts to sail. Faye had told me before that I was not her first mummy and I never argued with her, I would just comment that I was her mummy now. On this particular day Faye watched the men with their boats playing on the small lake and then asked me if she could have a drink. I told her that I hadn't brought one; but that we would go home now and then she could have some water.

Faye said, "There's some water, mummy" and pointed at the lake.

"You can't drink that Faye, it's all dirty and will make your tummy sore."

Faye looked on the ground for something and then stooping down, picked up a stone and said, "Come on mummy" and took my hand and led me to the side of the lake.

I asked Faye what she was going to do and she said, "My other mummy showed me how to make the dirty go away." And with that she threw the stone into the water laughing and crying gleefully, "See mummy, it makes the dirty go away."

She pointed at the water and said, "We can drink now, mummy" and pointed to the centre from where ripples emanated. I can remember wondering how she knew that dropping a stone into the water would make it ripple, and that the ripples would clear some of the debris from the surface.

A few weeks later, my father came to stay in Coventry for a short holiday and we met up at my brother's house. My father adored Faye and always spent time amusing her, and himself, by chatting away to her and making rabbits out of handkerchiefs that would 'scurry' up her arm, as if it was heading for a rabbit hole. My father stopped playing while he drank some tea and commented on how good she was at speaking now, and I told my father that she sometimes came out with really strange comments. I explained what I meant by telling him about Faye's other 'mummy' and then told him about the day at the park.

My father was an amazing, eccentric man, who was employed in Her Majesty's Inspectorate and in his spare time he practised faith healing, contacting aliens, and other spiritual activities, so he became very attentive to what I was saying. He asked me to tell him what other things Faye had said or done that appeared 'different' so I told him how she would talk to her 'friends' sometimes (not visible to me) and would play with one special friend all the time. I often heard Faye in fits of giggles even though she was sitting in a 'barren' living room. A bit later on, after Faye had woken from a nap, my dad asked if I minded if he spoke to Faye about her other 'mummy,' and friends etc and I said I was hoping he would.

I was amazed by what Faye told us. When dad asked about her other 'mummy,' Faye said, "Mummy doesn't like me to talk about my other 'mummy,' granddad," shaking her head. I told her that I wanted to hear about her and so Faye began to tell us. Her other 'mummy' was old and had hair like her great-granddad's (silver grey). It fell below her bottom, and she twisted it like rope. It was hot where she lived and at night-time the family would sleep outside together under a sheet, which was above them. Her mum used to do magic with food, and would dig a hole in the ground and put a big, flat stone in the hole. The food was wrapped in leaves and put on the stone and then the hole was covered up. Later they ate the food. When it was cold outside, they slept inside on some sticks covered in yellow grass.

They didn't wear clothes like ours; they would wrap themselves up in a nice sheet that was very pretty and colourful. Her mum would tell her stories and sing songs. They had different bread; it was flat and yellow and her mum cooked it on a big flat stone. My father asked why she didn't live with her other 'mummy' any more and Faye said that she had to go to the other place and they showed her mummy, she pointed at me and continued, "Mummy was sad. I came to make her better."

I didn't know what to think and put it down to Faye's imagination, but my father did not agree. He said that there was no way that Faye could have *known* about the things she had talked about without experiencing them in some form or another. I commented that I took her to the library nearly every day and read books to her; maybe that's where she had experienced these things. So my dad asked me if I had ever read her any such books, which I hadn't, meaning that either she'd somehow, unbeknown to me, managed to read the books for herself, or that she had gained that *knowledge* some other way. We agreed that the best thing to do would be to mention it the next time I went to the clinic, which I did, and I was basically told that it was just the imagination of a very bright child. However, a few days later, I received an appointment to see someone at the clinic with respect to Faye. I told my father about this and, as the appointment was only a couple of days hence, he decided to come with me.

When we got there, the clinic was very quiet and a nurse I had not met before checked my details and told me she would let the 'doctor' know that I had arrived. She reappeared a minute or two later and asked me to go through. When my father stood up to accompany me, he was told that only the mother and child were required, but that he was more than welcome to wait. He tried to protest, but failed to jump over the hurdle named 'hospital policy' so told me to go, and he'd be right there if I needed him.

When I went through, the 'doctor's' eyes were fixed on Faye and even as he told me to sit down, he never actually looked at me. He seemed a pleasant enough old man, dressed in an open white gown with a check shirt visible beneath. He said to let Faye settle herself, and then stated that he would be recording the appointment for further comment. He asked me to tell him the things Faye was doing which were 'concerning me' and although he listened to me, he was constantly watching Faye. Faye, by now, was standing beside me, holding my leg. I was in the middle of saying, "and when it was hot they would sleep outside with a sheet over them" and Faye interrupted me and said, "No, mummy, the sheet was up there," pointing to the ceiling, "not on me." She held her hand in front of her mouth, shrugged her shoulders and had a little giggle.

The 'doctor', or whoever the hell he was, then spoke to Faye suggesting, "Faye, why don't you tell me? Maybe I will understand better than mummy." He gave her hand a little squeeze and nodding his head, turned to face me and said that it might be better if he spent a little time alone with Faye. As I must have looked slightly concerned, he stood up and, after excusing himself to Faye, asked if he could have a quiet word and said that sometimes a mother's presence influenced the things a child was saying, or as I had just done, given out confused information. He said that if he was to understand, he needed to listen to what Faye was saying in her own words, continuing that it would only take about five minutes and that the nurse would be present throughout.

With that he opened a side door into a small internal corridor, which had a single seat ready for me to sit on. He reassured Faye that mummy was 'just there' and would come back in once Faye had the chance to tell her own story. With that, a nurse, who I had not seen before, smiled as she passed me and went into the room, cheerfully saying, "Hello Faye, how are you," before the door closed. A magazine had been left on the seat and I picked it up and flicked through it. It felt as if time was passing very slowly, even though I was alone for less than ten minutes. Occasionally, I would hear laughter or one of their voices shifting in tone and was reassured that Faye was all right. Eventually the door opened and Faye ran out smiling to greet me while the 'doctor' held the door ajar for me to join them back inside.

I noticed the tape recorder was still recording. He sat on the edge of his desk and looked down at me, and smiling briefly at Faye said, "Well you've got a really bright one there. Sharp as a razor, her little mind is, isn't it Faye?" He gave a knowing nod of approval before continuing, "Faye's a very special little girl but, and I must stress the 'but,' she has an overactive imagination, which if not properly channelled could cause her many problems in later life, especially during her school years. I am going to make a referral to a colleague of mine and, hopefully, you should receive a letter from him in a week or so, as there may be an option available that will be of great support to Faye, prior to her going into formal education. Give her a kick start, so to speak."

And with that, he shook my hand and gave Faye a pinch on the cheek, before turning and taking a file out of a drawer and opening it, silently dismissing us. I told my dad all that had happened and he kept asking if I had asked this question or that question and then heaved a sigh of regret, if I said I hadn't. My father had to return to Ireland a couple of days later and told me to keep him 'up to date' when I received any news.

I received a letter a few weeks later, asking me to make an appointment, with Faye, to attend an interview. As I didn't have a phone, or any money to make the call, I had to wait a couple of days before I could ring. When the call was connected I was asked my name, which I gave and then put on hold before being connected to someone else. The man said hello to me, not even giving me his own name, and then I recounted, talking to the doctor etc. I told him that I didn't have much money to speak, so he took the number and called me back. He explained that he ran a centre for highly gifted children and that he would be prepared to offer Faye a place. I complained that Faye wasn't even three years old yet, but he just kept on saying that the older Faye got, the more her imagination would run out of control and if she wasn't appropriately stimulated, it would cause her very real problems educationally. But it didn't matter how he tried to sell it to me. I wasn't buying! We ended up having an argument on the phone and then he went quiet and said he would only hold the placement open for a further three days, and then he would have to offer it elsewhere.

I finally got the chance to talk to my dad when I visited a relative, who let me use the phone. Dad listened and then asked me what I thought. I told him that I'd had a couple of days to think about it and had decided that I didn't want my daughter collected at eight o'clock in the morning and not returning home until after three. Dad said he had never heard anything like this before, pre-schools for gifted children, and he had even asked some of his friends in the Department of Education if they were aware of anything, but none were, although he did say that one guy said, "How would we know, we just work here."

I told dad I had made up my mind and that was that.

A letter arrived at my house about a week or so later and, as I was always in debt and receiving threatening letters, I frequently use to scan the envelopes for franking marks. I recognised that this had the same marks as the appointment card I'd received previously, so I set it on the fire with the rest of the demanding mail. I had no further communication with them, and did not attend the clinic again.

Since then, I have come across a few other mothers who experienced something similar and they, like me, chose to refuse the support. Faye did experience major problems at school, which became increasingly pronounced when we relocated from Ireland to Solihull in the UK. The sad thing is, that whoever those people were, they made me so concerned for my daughter's overactive imagination, that anytime she talked about her other 'mummy,' I would shift uncomfortably and say that I didn't want to talk about it any more.

There is so much that children, especially 'unprogrammed' youngsters, can show us, even if they can't express it in clear spoken language that we can understand, but we don't listen. We don't encourage and most importantly of all, we don't *believe*. Maybe we, the parents, get scared for our children because we want them to be 'normal' and not draw attention to themselves. We remind ourselves of the Japanese proverb, "the nail that sticks out is the first to be hit," Perhaps we are scared by what children are trying to communicate to us, reminding us of the worst kind of 'horror' movies that involve children, which have been around since the 'Village of the Damned.' Then, there is also the option that we don't even realise when they are trying to communicate something to us, because we are so locked in to our own reality that we can't understand that there may be an alternative option.

Children are our greatest asset, next to the health of the planet and universe, and we are willingly encouraging whatever 'powers' are out there, to disengage from senses and abilities that could make them 'a problem' to programme appropriately. We only allow our children to use their imagination in a way that fits with our own programming and if they move away from the label 'normal,' we quickly and quietly stick them back beneath, before they make a fool of themselves, or their stupid 'lies' get found out. The media is always reinforcing that 'different is dangerous' by ridiculing children, and their parents, who claim to have psychic abilities or talk of previous existences. So, instead of encouraging their children to express their own sense of reality, they make excuses for them, such as "Sarah has such a wild imagination," or, they put it down to something they've already experienced like, "Joe, I think you are getting confused with something you saw on television," or they just call the child an outright liar, "Stop telling such lies Megan, otherwise when you really want someone to believe you, they might not."

And if the children resist our explanations we, as adults, tell them to "stop talking like an idiot, or we won't take them to granny's at the weekend. Granny would not like to hear about those kinds of things.' Eventually, the children give up, as most children actually want their parents to like them and they can understand, like Faye did, that the behaviour they are exhibiting prompts the opposite emotions to the ones they want to evoke.

I watched a fantastic film a few years ago called 'A Beautiful Mind,' which really gave me the 'experience' of living another person's experience of reality, without knowing that this person's reality did not 'fit' with what the rest of society *believed* represented reality. The amazing thing about the film was that I, the viewer, did not know how much of his *experience of reality* was different to others until the physical representation of his interpretation of reality was removed from my vision. Where once the lead character had been physically, as well as emotionally and mentally, connected to certain people, now there was no *physical* presence. Where only moments before, I could believe in the people who inhabited his reality, because I could also physically see them, now it appeared that the man was 'crazy' because I could only hear his side of the conversations he was having. I could observe him apparently arguing, gesticulating and laughing with 'empty space' (if, in fact, there is any such thing as an empty space). I found the film so emotional that it brought tears to my eyes and I would recommend that you take a couple of hours to watch the film, even if you have already seen it.

The important thing to comprehend is that we *believe* that everybody experiences reality in the way that we do and that is just not the case. To understand this we need to become more aware of the way *we* experience reality in our *own* minds. We take in a vast amount of data through our five senses, which we then store as an *experience* of being. So, to give yourself an idea of what this means I would like you to just sit in a 'space' somewhere on your own. Now take in the five- sense experience of being in that space. Then turn your body around and sit facing the other way and repeat the experience. Although you are occupying the same space, simply by changing your physical frame in that space, it means that your interpretation or perception of that space changes too. The next time you are with another person, understand that what you are experiencing is going to be different to what they are experiencing, even if you *believe* you are sharing the experience.

A teacher, who stands in front of a class, has no idea what the students are experiencing from the lesson. I remember teachers telling me to listen and then telling me off, for questioning what I was listening to. To understand what we are hearing, we have to have awareness of what all the 'labels' we are hearing mean and sometimes the 'surface' information we are given does not provide enough data for us to process the words. For example, if I say to you, "Would you be offended if I asked to paint you in the nude?" what do you think I am saying?

Am I saying that I would like *you* to take your clothes off so that I can paint your naked body, or am I saying that *I* would like to take *my* clothes of while I paint your still clothed body? If you accepted the first interpretation and said, "No, I would not be offended" you might then shriek in horror if I began to strip off. To understand, we often need to ask for further information to make sense of what another person is actually communicating. And we often say words that we *assume* others have labelled with the same data that we have and that only adds to our confusion, when trying to make sense of what others are communicating to us.

When I deliver my training, I want the delegates to be aware that we do not always store the same data for the same labels, so I begin with an 'ice breaker' that enables them to raise their awareness. I will give each delegate a piece of paper and tell them that in a moment I am going to say a word and that I would like them to write down five other words that they *experience* as an interpretation of that word. I usually say the word 'dog' as most delegates have an experience of the label 'dog.' When they have written their words, we go around the group with each delegate offering one word from their list. The differences never fail to amaze them. When I say the word 'dog,' each person will construct a five-sense expression of the word. They do not see the letters d-o-g. They may get a picture of a dog they know, or they may recall the sounds associated with the word, or smells or the texture of the dog's coat. They may also include 'feelings' they have experienced. The list of five-sense experience (data) that people choose to express 'dog' (label) can be so totally different. Here is the feedback from the last group, of their experience of the word 'dog':

-   Friendly, happy, soft, yappy, small
-   Huge, fierce, big teeth, growling, horrible
-   Hairy, slobbery, smelly, shit, lampposts
-   Granddad, barking, ball, park, energetic
-   Cat, animal, bones, lazy, pedigree chum
-   Cat, cuddly, stroking, friendly, and warm
-   Kennel, Tom and Jerry, squat, fat, cute
-   Barking, snarling, nasty, dog catchers, unhygienic

- Muddy, playful, funny, helpful, makes me feel safe

Look at the differences in individual perception, from nasty to friendly, huge to small, and lazy to energetic.

We need to acknowledge that our perception of reality and other's perceptions can be extremely different, so in order to communicate what we want people to understand, we have to be clear that they are as close to our *experience* of our *communication* as possible. How many times have you thought to yourself that you understood where a person was coming from and then they say something that totally throws you off track? Say you are with someone and they say, "It's such a beautiful day, wouldn't it be lovely to go to the park and soak up the sun?" and you respond, "Yes, it's really lovely, that would be a nice thing to do."

They then say, "OK then, I'll just go home and put on my shorts and t-shirt and meet you there in about half an hour, by the coffee shop."

Now in your mind, you are thinking, "Hey, that didn't mean I wanted to go to the park. I was just confirming the *thought* that it would be lovely to soak up the sun."

However, as you are a good mate, you decide to change your plans and go with your friend anyway, even though it is not what you intended to do. So, as they have already left to put on their shorts and t-shirt, you visualise your intended journey and *see* the park in your mind, focusing on the coffee shop, where you are to meet your friend. Half an hour later, you are sitting enjoying a coffee, in the Memorial Park, wondering how long it will be before your friend arrives. Meanwhile, she is sitting on a bench, near the coffee shop in Coombe Abbey Park, wondering how long it will be until you turn up. When you finally contact each other by mobile, you almost 'blame' the other for the mistake and may say, "Well, how was I to know you meant Coombe Abbey? I thought you meant here, not there."

Both you and your friend visualised different places, stored under the same label and because you *visualised* it, you thought that your friend could read your mind and *see* exactly which coffee shop, in which park, you were referring to, when agreeing to meet her.

If I were to ask you what you think of the word 'lemon,' what visuals/data would spring to mind? Maybe you would be able to feel the texture of the waxy peel. Maybe the shape would present itself, and possibly you would experience the bittersweet taste in your mouth. Some of you may even imagine eating pancakes. In the instant I ask you the question, to make some kind of sense of what I am asking, you visualise what you *believe* I am saying, but maybe I am not saying what you *think* I am. I am thinking of decorating my living room. I just wondered what you thought of the colour lemon, and as I understand what I mean, I assume that you do too. So when you start to pull faces as you imagine the bittersweet taste of lemon on your tongue, I take that to mean that you don't think the colour lemon would be suitable. The next time you visit and I have painted my walls green, you may ask why I didn't choose a yellow shade to compliment my furnishings!

And if language is complex and confusing for adults then for children it can be extremely difficult to understand the grown-ups around them. When I wrote about my secret 'uncle' earlier, I didn't conclude the story, so I will now, to emphasise what I mean.

When Marion, Jessica and I ran off across the fields, I fluctuated between two very different states. First of all I felt exhilarated that I was free from him and then I felt terrified of what might happen next. My brothers were nowhere in sight and I asked where they were. Marion had felt really bad for leaving me and said that when they were nearly at the barbed wire fence, she came up with the idea of running back and saying that my brothers were on their way. She said she was sorry for taking so long but that Jessica had been very upset and she had to really encourage her to come back. When we were in view of the fence that led to the street, we decided to sit under a tree and collect our thoughts before going home. Marion asked what had happened when they left me with him and I said that we just talked, nothing else happened, and then they came back.

Marion said that Jessica was really upset because he had touched her and she didn't like it. Jessica told Marion not to speak about it any more. Marion asked if we should tell our parents what secret 'uncle' had done and when she mentioned telling our parents, I became totally panic stricken, feeling my heart racing and my palms becoming damp with fear. In my mind, all I could think was that if I told my parents, that the poison would kill me. I said that we should not say anything about it, and that if we did, then they would not let us play together any more. That we wouldn't be allowed over the fields, or that we might get 'belted' for being up Staircase Lane. My mind came up with a thousand excuses for not telling our parents anything and they agreed. So, we made a 'blood pact' where we broke a small twig from a hawthorn bush and in turn, pricked our fingers with one of the thorns, then each squeezing a drop of blood, touched our fingers to each other's and swore on our blood not to say a single thing.

As I approached home, my head was thumping and I felt really sick. Instead of going into the living room or kitchen, I ran straight upstairs and into my bedroom, and flung myself on the bed exhausted but unable to relax. It felt as if I was waiting for my mum or dad to burst into the room and ask me what was going on. After a while I went into the bathroom and scrubbed at my teeth and then filled the sink with cold water and kept washing my face, swishing the cold water around my mouth again and again. From my bedroom window I could see Marion's grandma's house and I would keep getting up from the bed and looking across to their house, checking that everything was as normal.

I heard my brothers returning from their play, and mum called me down for dinner, but I didn't want any, so stayed upstairs. When I lay on the bed, the words he had said to me kept coming into my mind, so I would get up and look out the window again in the hope that the voices would 'go away.' This went on for about three hours. Finally, I slipped under the blankets and waited for sleep to rescue me from the torment I was going through, but it never came, not then anyway. My thoughts were distracted by a knock at the front door and it was as if my ears zoomed in on the voices, not hearing any other sound. It was

Marion's mother's voice and I heard my mum telling her to come in. Even though I put my ear to the floor, I could not make out what they were saying, and I began to panic.

Next I heard my mother call out my name, so I jumped back into bed and hid my head under the blanket, pretending to sleep. Moments later, my mother was in my bedroom saying that Marion and Jessica's mother was downstairs, and then she touched my arm gently and asked if there was anything I wanted to tell her. I kept praying for this to stop; I didn't want to say anything. My mother persisted and said she would see me downstairs in a moment. I don't remember too much about the conversation that took place between the adults and me because I was totally shocked to find Jessica standing next to her mother, who was sitting on a sofa.

Jessica held her head down and when she lifted it briefly, to acknowledge my presence, it was obvious that she had been crying. I wanted to ask her secretly what she had said and why she had said anything because we had made a 'blood pact' and that should mean something to her. I didn't know what 'truth' to tell, as I didn't know what 'truth' the sisters had already told. I wanted to speak to Jessica on her own, and even though I knew this was not going to happen, I tried to 'read' her face, pleading her with my eyes to give me some clue about what I should say, but none was forthcoming. Jessica just *looked* ashamed, and kept averting her gaze. The adults decided on a course of action, which was to contact Mr. Sparks, who lived four doors away. He was a police officer, married with two young sons, one of who used to play with my younger brother after school.

When I look back on it all, I can begin to imagine how worrying all of this must have been for my parents. The year was 1966, which was famous for two things: England winning the World Cup and the arrest of the Moor's murderers.

Mr. Sparks was not in uniform when I was taken to speak to him. He looked like any other father, not a policeman at all, but he was kind and caring in his questioning of me. He began by telling me that I had nothing to worry about and that no one was angry with me, but that this man we had been with had done some 'not very nice' things to Jessica, and all he wanted to do was to make sure he hadn't done anything to me. I can remember blurting out, "He didn't do anything to me" and Mr. Sparks reassuring me, once more, that I hadn't done anything wrong and not to get upset.

He asked me where we had been that afternoon, and I decided that if I owned up to being in Staircase Lane, that maybe he would tell me off. Maybe I would get a hard slap from my dad, but at least it would be over, so I said, "It was all my fault, we were on Staircase Lane, we just wanted to sit in the tree roots, that's all, it's my fault…I made them come, they didn't want to…I'm sorry."

He didn't respond as I had imagined and said, "That's OK, I don't want you to worry about that. So, did this man just approach you?"

Now I felt nauseous; he had mentioned *him,* secret 'uncle.' My head started to feel as if it was about to float away and my body was being washed in alternate flushes of intense heat and then chilling cold. My stomach was churning and felt as if it was being tossed like a pancake, and I suddenly start to worry that because *he* had been mentioned, that maybe the poison was getting ready to work, maybe that was what all those feelings in my tummy were. I wanted to scream for him to stop asking me questions, telling him that I would die if he made me say anything. I wanted to shout, "Just hit me and let me go to bed, please just hit me because I'm the one that's bad; I'm the whore!" but the words just chased each other around my brain and never escaped through my mouth. As I hadn't responded, Mr. Sparks said, firmly but with kindness, "Look Rose, *you* have done nothing wrong. This man is not a nice man, he is a bad man, and if he has hurt Jessica, then we have to find him to stop him hurting another little girl, do you understand?"

I nodded and he continued, "We need to know as much as you can tell us because otherwise we might not be able to find him and the next little girl might not be as lucky as you." He leant forward, emphasising the seriousness of it all and continued, "Now, I want you to answer my questions, is that OK? It is better to talk here than at the police station."

As he was speaking, my internal dialogue was racing, "should I do this or that, say this or not, tell them everything or say nothing, lie or tell the truth, I don't know what to do." I am *scared*, not only of the questions, but also the answers. I'm not just scared of going to the police station, but scared *he* will *know* that I'm at the police station, scared to say the words that I spoke, words like 'whore' and 'fucking,' and scared that everyone will know that I was a whore. It was overwhelming me and I thought I would faint with the chaos of it all.

Mr. Sparks must have seen how distressed I was because he said he was going to fetch me a glass of orange juice, and have a quick word with my dad. Again, my internal dialogue spun like a pinball across my mind, one thought bombarding other thoughts into action, until my head was a mass of flashing lights and buzzing sounds, as all the thoughts had collided into each other and become a mass of terrified madness. I stood up and paced around the room, suddenly feeling like I needed the toilet, yet unable to leave the room, and even though I did not want Mr. Sparks to return and start questioning me again, I also wanted him to come back just so I knew where he was and what he was thinking.

After about 10 minutes, he returned and handing me a glass of orange juice, asked me to sit down and then said seriously, "We are trying to help, but we can't do that unless you help us. Now, this man, we need to know how you knew him. Jessica says he was your 'uncle' so I want you to tell me all you know about him. This is serious, do you understand, serious."

I nodded. He told me that my mum and Jessica's mum were very upset and that although they didn't want me to go to the police station, he had decided to call out some 'friends' of his, who were on their way to talk to me. As he told me this, my face felt as if it was instantly frozen, locked in time with his words, unable to escape. I had to tell Mr. Sparks something; maybe if I did he would tell his 'friends' not to come. My thoughts thawed my frozen face and I began to speak, "He wasn't my real uncle, I just called him uncle. He use to be at the bus stop on my way to school and he always said 'hello' to me. He would sometimes give me sweets, but he wasn't a stranger when I took the sweets, I never take sweets from strangers. He was nice to me, sometimes he walked me to school and he was never horrible. I don't know what he did to Jessica. I didn't see. Please can I go home now? I need the toilet, please can I go?"

Mr. Sparks smiled, "That's better, see it's not difficult, No one is angry with you. You pop upstairs to the toilet and then we can talk properly."

I was glad of the escape and ran upstairs, locking the toilet door behind me. At first I didn't do anything, I just stood with my back to the toilet door, focusing on my stomach which was bubbling and churning. I felt a wave of nausea flow over my body, then pounding in the front of my head and felt the bubbling and rising of vomit. I quickly lifted the toilet seat and dropped to my knees, struggling to keep the contents of my belly in, terrified that this was *it*; the poison was working and I was about to die. I wanted to be home with my family, not here. Then I vomited, again and again, until my retching stomach had nothing left to expel, and I slumped, exhausted, onto the cold bathroom floor.

The next thing I can remember was hearing knocking on the bathroom door, and Mrs. Sparks asking with concern, "Please unlock the door, are you alright…open the door, there's a good girl."

I got up off the floor and realised that I was still alive. I flushed the toilet, watching as the watery mess spun around before disappearing from view. Then I splashed some water over my face before unlocking the door. Mrs. Sparks seemed relieved, "Thank goodness, I thought I would have to break the door down. Are you alright?"

I nodded and Mrs. Sparks held my hand and gave it a squeeze before leading me downstairs. She opened the living room door and ushered me inside, where I was shocked to see not just Mr. Sparks, but two uniformed police officers, who half stood and smiled as I entered the room. Mr. Sparks introduced his colleagues and said that they were here to ask me some questions and then nodded towards them. They asked me all kinds of questions; what did he look like? What clothes was he wearing? How old was he? What was his name? How long had I known him? What did he talk to me about? I answered all of these honestly, describing his clothing on that day, saying I didn't know his name I just called him 'uncle,' and that he was about as old as my granddad.

I told them that he used to talk to me about all kinds of things, school, family, animals, friends and that I had known him for a month or so. The officers were very pleased with me, saying how good I was and how brave. Then they asked about that afternoon and wanted to know the sequence of events so they could get a clear picture of what had taken place. I told them about him coming into the lane and saying he would walk us home and that I didn't want to go, and when they asked why, I told them that I didn't want to be with him, I wanted to play with my friends. Then they asked about Jessica and asked me if I saw what had happened. I told them that I saw him touch her, when she was climbing over the gate, but I didn't tell them how he had watched me watching him as he did it. Then they asked why I had not gone when my friends left and I burst into tears crying, "Because *it was my fault*. If he wanted to hurt someone he should be hurting me, not them, they were my friends."

The police officers kept reassuring me, telling me it was alright and not to get upset and apologised for having to ask me so many questions, while emphasising how important it was to get as much information as possible. I was then asked to tell them what happened when Marion and Jessica left and when I wasn't forthcoming with a response, was reminded, "This is very serious Rose. This man is a very bad man and if you don't tell us exactly what happened how would we be able to stop him from hurting other little girls? We know that this is difficult but we need you to be really brave, OK?"

I nodded and started to speak. I told them that he had asked me to go and sit with him and that he had put his coat on the ground and we had both sat down and that we just talked. When I was asked what about, I said that he had told me that he was going to go and live by the seaside and that if I wanted to, I could go with him. When I had finished speaking, I looked up and asked if I could go home now, but they shook their heads and said that they just wanted to ask me a few more questions. One of the officers came and squatted in front of me, gently placing a hand on my knee, which made me freeze, and said, "You have been very brave Rose, but we need you to be brave for a while longer and then we can all go home, OK?"

I held on to the words "then we can all go home" reassured that this meant no visit to the police station at least. I said, "OK."

"Now this might not be easy for you but I am going to ask you some questions and I want you to answer them as honestly as you can, OK?"

I nodded. My stomach had begun to twist and somersault again, giving me a warning that they could not hear, and possible questions flooded my brain making me feel like a pressure cooker ready to explode. The police officer returned to his seat and began. "Did this man touch you?"

"No"

"Did he ask you to touch him?"

"NO"

"Did he ask you to take off any of your clothing?"

"No"

"Did he expose himself?"

I didn't fully understand what they meant by this so said no.

"Did he kiss you?"

"No"

"Did he do anything to you apart from talk to you?"

"No, he just talked to me and then they came back shouting about my brothers."

"How long was it before Jessica and Marion came back?"

The only lie I told that day left my mouth, "Only about ten minutes."

"And in that ten minutes this man didn't touch you or make you touch him and he never exposed himself to you?"

"No, he just talked, please can I go home now? I am tired and I don't feel well."

"Just a couple more questions. Would you recognise him again?"

"Yes"

"Are you telling us the truth?"

"Yes."

With that the officers muttered something to Mr. Sparks and all of them left the room. I sat there on my own with thoughts swimming around my mind just wanting to escape to my room and to never leave it again, ever. The police officers returned and said that I could go as soon as I had given them more information about the way he was dressed and a good description of him. I can't remember any more of what took place on that evening apart from finally being safe in my bedroom and crying myself to sleep.

As an adult, looking back on the events of that day, I can now see all the things that they could have asked and didn't because of the way they communicated the questions to me. They *believed* that I understood what the word 'exposed' meant, but I actually didn't and when I had considered the question, I fleetingly thought that 'exposed himself' meant that he 'exposed' (shown) to me that he was a bad man. If they had given me more information, or clarified what they meant by 'exposed,' then maybe the whole tale would have come to light. They also asked if he had touched me, but never asked if I had touched him. In fact they asked me everything that he *didn't do* and never once asked about what *he did do.* When they used words like "be brave" they didn't understand that from my perception of the situation that meant, "be brave and don't tell them anything because then the poison won't work and you will stay alive." It didn't mean 'be brave and tell us what happened even though we know it is difficult for you."

In situations like this, it is all too easy for adults to *imagine* the sequence of events that occur when a child is molested, and that *limits* the child when they are being asked questions. At no point, for example, did I want to say, "He asked me to say that I wanted him to fuck me and he called me a whore and made me play with myself."

As a child, I would never have used those kinds of words and even if I did, I would certainly not say them in front of police officers. I had seen how parents admonished those children stupid enough to say the word 'bloody,' so I could only imagine the response to words like 'fuck' and 'whore.' And because they had preconceived ideas of what *may* have taken place, it *limited* the questions that they asked me to answer, so if they never asked it, then I never mentioned it.

This is where it all goes horribly wrong, and the processes we use to talk to children who have been abused, make it even more difficult for children to express what they have experienced. And things have not improved with time. Now the child cannot be 'led' by the person asking the questions! Let me just ask you this, at nine years of age would you have been able to say 'fuck,' 'whore,' 'I played with myself,' 'I asked him to fuck me,' and describe with clarity the disgusting things that *you* did and said, to your parents, or any 'authoritative' adult, for that matter?

In our world, we have things back to front and instead of enabling our children to express their abuse, leading the way to make it easier for them, we don't help them one iota. This is madness and children who have been abused have the whole guilty perverted mess of it trapped in their heads, unable to express what has happened because 'no roads led there' to enable them to say what they experienced.

Let me put it another way. Imagine that you are nine years old and you are asked by your parents to go alone into an isolated farmhouse at the end of a dark, empty lane and spend the night there. They are not going to go with you, but will communicate with you via a 'walkie talkie.' How would you feel about going there all by yourself? I'm sure that many of you would not be happy to do it even now as an adult, let alone as a child. Yet, this is what we expect abused children to be able to do. Revisiting abuse is as bad as the abuse you have already experienced, so why would anyone want to go back there? And we don't even help them.

Sometimes, we are so caught up in rights of the perpetrator that we forget about the rights of the child. The child doesn't stand a chance, they are wracked with guilt, they don't fully understand what has happened, or the implications of it and they are left to struggle alone, wanting to hear someone say the words, so that they can just 'nod' or 'shake' their head appropriately. They don't want to use those words, or explain the actions and child abusers *know* this. You don't think a child abuser, who gets excitement from exerting his power over a child, is going to follow a method of abuse that is easy for the police to break. No, of course not, the abuser is going to play with the child's emotions, guilt, and *the child's involvement in their own abuse*. The abuser is going to use words to make the child *believe that this is their fault*, that they themselves have made this happen and that they, the abuser, are not actually doing anything to the child that the child doesn't want to happen.

One of the most effective ways of ensuring that the child becomes totally confused is for the abuser to make *parts* of the experience pleasant or enjoyable for the child; this provides a maze of guilt for the traumatised child to try to negotiate. And to create as much devastation as possible, they will make the child aware that she is actually the one doing wrong, and that because the she has done one 'wrong' already, i.e. taken sweets, gone to see the puppies, or been where she shouldn't have been, her parents or whoever will be angry with her and/or not believe her story. Why would any child, no matter how traumatised by her experience, want to tell anyone the 'full' story?

We have to make it as easy as possible for abused children to inform us of their experiences, and we should be there supporting them and leading the way. By not offering them choices, we are limiting their ability to communicate with us, and in turn, ensuring that it doesn't happen again. There has to be a better way and maybe if we put our minds to it, we can make the whole 'abuse' issue easier for *children* to deal with. We are adults and it is our duty to protect our children and make our world a safe place for them to experience. How many children's experiences have haunted them for *years* because they cannot express, no matter how much they may want to, the abuse they suffered? In my own case, it has taken me over forty years to verbally communicate what actually took place! And how many children are abused and then murdered? In the UK, a report by UNICEF found that two children, under the age of 15, die from abuse each year and that 25% of all rapes, reported to the police, are committed against children (NSPCC). And, horrifyingly, it is estimated that there are 60 million survivors of childhood sexual abuse living in the United States of America today, 60 million! How many others, like me, are not reported because the child is unable to express their abuse? Things have to change.

Other research indicates that a typical child sex offender molests on average, 117 children, most of who do not report the offence (Pandora's Box: The Secrecy of Child Sexual Abuse). We only have to imagine the absolute horrors that children are experiencing at the hands of people like Fred and Rose West to realise that children do not know how to inform on their abusers. The West's home had children's dead bodies buried all over the place, and the children that were still living in the home were being physically, emotionally and sexually abused on a daily basis.

This was happening over a period of *decades* and the children, for whatever reason, felt unable to tell anyone. We have to change these statistics, because each single statistic equals more than just a number; it equals a child experiencing guilt, physical pain, emotional torment, fear, hatred, confusion and it affects each of them on levels that we can only begin to imagine. Statistics from the US indicate that approximately 95% of teenage prostitutes have been sexually abused, and that approximately one in three girls is sexually abused before the age of 18. (Pandora's box)

Years ago, as part of my job, I was asked to support a 14 year-old girl during the trial of her abusive mother and stepfather. I cannot go into too much detail but we had to remove the girl from the children's institution where she resided, and take her to a safe house about 20 miles away from where the case was being heard. I will call the girl Sophie. She had suffered horrendous abuse. We stayed in a cottage in the countryside and although she was very anxious, as we had to move on the advice of her solicitor for her own personal safety, she was incredibly strong. Sophie had the body of a woman, was extremely curvaceous, and very pretty.

During the lead up to the trial, Sophie had been very attentive and was asked if she would like to visit the court so she would understand who would be sitting where, and how the actual day would proceed. I went with her on this visit and Sophie was very concerned that her mother and stepfather would be sitting at a 90% angle from where she would give her evidence. We asked about Sophie providing video evidence, but they would not agree and instead said that they would ensure that Sophie was completely screened off, so that she would not see them, nor they her. I can even remember saying that I hoped the screens would not be the rail and gathered curtain affairs that they have in hospitals, and the woman who took us on the tour, assured us that this would not be the case.

The first day of the trail arrived and Sophie woke very early and spent ages pacing back and forth, until we left on our journey. When we arrived, we were ushered into a small waiting room and told that Sophie would be called to give evidence, probably before lunch. The wait was dreadful, with nothing to take her mind off what was taking place, apart from interruptions from barristers, fully gowned, coming in to use the coffee machine.

As Sophie's case was so atrocious, I was to go into the witness box and sit a few feet behind her, while she gave her evidence. The idea being that if she found the experience too difficult, I would signal to the Judge and would be allowed to offer her support. Finally Sophie was called, and we both entered the courtroom and were shocked to find that no screen had been erected and Sophie's parents were glaring at her with total menace. This obviously had a tremendous impact on Sophie, and she turned and walked straight out of the courtroom. I caught up with her and she was crying, sobbing, "They saw me, they saw me, they promised me, didn't they? They promised me."

A court official approached us and asked what the problem was, so I explained what had been agreed on our visit previously. The official said they would see what they could do, and scurried off back towards the courtroom. Half an hour later, during which time Sophie had become very quiet and withdrawn, we were once more called and when we arrived in the witness box, the only screen provided was the rail and curtain affair, which had gaps where the material had gathered so did not obscure the view.

On the third day of the trial, Sophie was again to give evidence and we both took our places, which faced the jury. In the jury there were people of all ages, including one young male. The jury was looking at photographs when we entered the court, although at that point we did not know what the photographs were. Sophie was questioned about one particular incident, when her stepfather had pushed meat forks into her breasts, and she very bravely recounted the incident.

The jury was told to look at the photographic evidence and I could *feel* Sophie's pain and embarrassment before I saw it. It was awful. Sophie's shoulders started to move up and down and I realised that she must be crying silently to herself, as there was no noise, so I moved closer and was immediately instructed by the Judge to move back. I did as he said and then heard Sophie start to make sobbing noises, so once more moved forward only this time when the Judge told me to move, I refused saying that the child was very upset and obviously needed a break and that I was taking her out of the courtroom, which I did. When we got to the waiting room, Sophie sobbed her heart out and we just hugged each other. I never spoke a single word. After a while, her sobbing ceased and she lifted her tear-stained face and said, "They were looking at photographs of my naked breasts, weren't they?"

I replied honestly that I didn't know. Sophie continued, "I *know* they were, because when they took the photographs, they said that had to take them for evidence, so that people would be able to see the scars left by the forks. How can they just expect me to sit there, while all those people look at my naked breasts? And that young bloke sitting at the back, he couldn't take his eyes off me. He just kept staring. I can't go back in there Rose. I want to go home, I can't do this any more."

Sophie never went back to finish giving evidence.

Another young boy I worked with used to ask me to tell him fairy stories where he would change the names of the 'bad' characters to the titles of family members, while the main character's name remained the same. He would add in more 'nasty' characters as the fairy tale was told, giving each a personal twist. He was without a doubt, one of the most beautiful young boys I have ever encountered, and I became quite close to him over the years. His behaviour was bizarre to say the least and many of the staff found him difficult and effeminate, not wanting to be left on their own with him, fearing accusations. I will call him Daniel.

The thing was that Daniel needed physical contact. He needed to be hugged and cuddled, but due to the nature of his sexual abuse, this was not encouraged, so Daniel would find his own methods to get the physical attention he desired. He would behave in such a way that he would end up being restrained and if it was by grown men, it made him more excitable. Daniel had been sexually abused by both sets of grandparents, uncles, cousins and both parents all of his life and the family had albums full of photographs of his extensive abuse. I became Daniel's 'special support worker' and spent hours talking and cycling with him around the countryside. Once I took him to London for a day trip and it was great to just see him smile. I worked with him for about a year before I moved to another residential unit across town and lost touch with him.

A few years later, I moved unit again and made good friends with another social worker, who had also supported Daniel, as his 'special support worker' and we exchanged notes on his progress. My colleague had been with Daniel when he gave his evidence and said that the whole process had been disgusting with Daniel exhibiting incredibly childish behaviour and avoiding direct questions, making his version of events seem dubious. He said that the whole affair had changed something in Daniel and throughout the trial, once he was back in the unit at nighttime, he would just close himself off from everyone. After the trial had been concluded, Daniel was moved into specialist foster care and from there had ended up in the secure unit, for his own safety, due to self-harming.

I didn't hear any more about Daniel for around two years and then one day my colleague came into work and asked me if I had heard the news about him. When I said I hadn't, my colleague said I should sit down and then said, "Daniel hung himself two days ago; he's dead!"

He was 17 years old. This was when I decided I needed to leave residential children's social work. There has to be a better way. We have to listen to children. We have to listen to the adults who never spoke out as children, and ask them why? Then we have to find solutions so that the awful aftermath of abuse is minimised. Prevention is better than cure and one of the ways that we can prevent some of the child abuse that occurs is to make our children aware of all their senses.

We need to understand what subliminal messages they are hearing and seeing, by watching the TV, even CBeebies, and making sure that the messages they are receiving are ones that we want them to hear. We should make children explore with their senses to develop them as much as they possibly can, so that they understand the internal messages they are receiving. Showing them cartoons about little foxes going out on their own and breaking into people's houses, and running away when you feel guilty is *not* the message that will enable children to remain safe! We should stop classifying our language, giving power to certain words, so that children feel unable to express them. I was more worried about my family finding out that I had said a certain word than anything else! Crazy!

People should take the box of their heads and see what is going on, and not make comments like, "But I don't want my children to know about that sort of stuff. I want my children to have an innocent childhood." They need to wake up and smell the coffee. If we don't find ways of equipping our children to understand how to protect themselves, then they will lose more than their innocence. I would rather have learnt how to prevent myself from being abused than about some pox-ridden misogynist who just happened to be king. Parents need to be supported to raise our future generation, and children need to be encouraged to explore all their senses and develop their amazing potential. Who knows what Daniel may have become? I don't, but what I do know is that *all* life is precious and *no* life should become just another tragic statistic.

The Bit Where I Rant About...
Relationships

Ah, relationships! Our lives are full of relationships of all different kinds, and many of us will wear a 'different hat' for each one. To explore a little deeper, I would like you to think about the diverse relationships you have in your own life. All of us exist in our own little soap operas really, so imagine all the different characters that are written into your script. Now think of a situation. Maybe you need advice about something personal, say, for example, that you are contemplating having an affair with someone who really excites you, and makes you feel alive. The only problem is that he is married, even though he has told you that the marital relationship is no longer what he wants.

Who would you go to for advice and support? The chances are that you may choose a 'special' friend and seek their advice. Maybe you would write to the problem pages of a magazine, or just keep it secret and try to deal with the emotional turmoil yourself. As you start to really think about your relationships, you begin to realise that they all serve different purposes, or fulfil numerous needs in you and, possibly, the other person. We are, as a species, very social and we rely on these social relationships to keep us connected to the whole, or society.

Throughout my life, I have met many people who espouse to be totally independent and who rant on about how they are self-sufficient and don't need anything or anybody. Well, I have news for them; no one on this entire planet is independent, not even a hermit living in a cave, or a bird flying in the sky. This planet and everything on it is

167

dependent upon everything else for its continued survival and maybe if we really understood that, we would take care of every single living thing, as well as ourselves. We are all part of the same whole and we can never be anything but. Anything that has ever been, will always be; something that 'is' can never be 'was,' it will always remain 'is.' To explain this more clearly, if I were to hand you a glass of water and tell you to get rid of it, in other words, turn the water (is) into something that no longer exists (was), how would you do it? Maybe you would drink it and if you did, has the water gone? No, it has just become part of you. Possibly you would pour it onto the garden, but it is still there. If you were to boil it, it may turn to vapour, which would eventually condense back to water. How about freezing it? No, it's still there. Tip it into the ocean maybe? It simply becomes part of the ocean.

There is no way that you can actually make something that 'is' into something that 'was,' even if you separate the different elements; they still exist in their own right. It makes you begin to realise that even water is made up of separate parts. And like the hermit in the cave and the bird in the sky, we need to drink water for life, as we are dependent on it. We are the perfect recycling machines, what we take in, we recycle and without the ability to do this, humans would not exist. I am sure that the hermit and the birds also eat and both are dependent upon the earth to provide that food, whether it is a worm, carrot or fish.

Without the sun, there would be no heat, providing the warmth for plants to grow or the fruit to ripen, or life itself to survive as, without the rain, lakes, oceans. We can become so wrapped up in our own estimation of how 'independent' we are that we begin to believe it. We are part of the *whole* and no matter what we do we can never be a *'was.'* Not understanding this can become one of the greatest downfalls to our liberation; we are *one*.

I saw an amazing programme on TV about a fig tree. David Attenborough narrated it, telling the life cycle of the fig tree and all the insects, animals and birds that visited the tree for their survival. There were literally hundreds of different species and some were almost totally reliant on the figs to sustain them. The most amazing fact of all was that a single wasp was responsible for fertilizing the tree and without it there would be no figs. Without that wasp, many other living creatures would not have such abundance. Some may have the ability to adapt to new environments for sustenance, some may be able to exist without the life of plenty that the fig provides, but some, like the fig wasp, would not exist. The fig wasp and the fig tree are *one*.

Humans can be so arrogant; we think we know so much, yet in reality, we are aware of so little. How can we learn, when we limit our own abilities to gain knowledge? We keep our heads inside the box, like ostriches with their heads in the sand. And even when we do gain knowledge, do we always learn?

No.

The earth has so much intelligence to offer us, so much wisdom to pass on, yet even when it is staring us in the face, we can't see. It really is a case of not seeing the wood for the trees. I believe that each living thing has something to contribute to the existence of all of us. The planet is a recycling machine, with each part contributing to the whole again and again and, while everything is as it should be, the balance is maintained. Where it all starts to go wrong is when we, as in humans, start to put things where they shouldn't be and then the balance tips. Say we explode an atom bomb. The balance is shifted because we have made a mistake with our experiments of all things natural, and created imbalance, albeit briefly.

The earth will show us with its wisdom, by providing us with knowledge, so that we can learn from the experience of exploding an atom bomb. We experience this knowledge through our five senses, so we see the devastation, the destruction of land, the death of people and animals, the disease and fouled farm lands, the genetic deformities, the infertility in everything, and the stench of decay. We feel the pain.

Once the earth has provided its wisdom and we have experienced the five-sense reality of it, we are supposed to learn. We are supposed to learn that 'doing this, causes that' and why would you want to cause that to happen again? And if we repeat the process and drop another one, do we think the result of the five-sense experience to be any different? Of course it won't. Why don't we learn? Because we do not *experience* a relationship with the earth, we do not see ourselves as part of the whole. We see ourselves as part of a country, or state, or army or group and we don't take any individual responsibility for ourselves, let alone the earth.

We are not separate; we are whole.

Change the way you perceive yourself to be. Presently, we believe ourselves to be an independent being. If you're not the one who gets cancerous tumours, gives birth to a baby riddled with life-threatening deformities, buries your parents, or becomes infertile, then why should you see yourself as part of the whole? I mean no one wants to be part of that do they? No way! So what do we do? We stick our heads firmly in our boxes, or up our asses, or hide in the sanctuary of dogma and pretend that in our 'world,' it doesn't touch us. Well, here's some news. It does!

The most important relationship you have is the one you are part of and more dependent upon than you are on your own mother. It is your relationship with the earth, and by earth I mean *everything*, even things you don't yet know exist. Your existence on this planet was meant to be experienced through *all* your senses, including your intuition and most of us can barely see...*even when it is held up in front of our eyes*.

Pictures of screaming children, running naked down dusty roads, burnt by napalm.

Newspaper columns informing us how many civilians were killed today in a roadside bomb blast.

Children maimed by cluster bombings.

Land rendered useless.

Cows falling over, going increasingly madder, until they die.

People addicted to crack cocaine and babies born to addicts, struggling to 'cold turkey' from their first breath of life.

Children playing at being real soldiers, with real guns and bullets.

A mother with empty breasts, struggling to keep her child alive.

We open our eyes and don't see a thing. We cease to experience life and allow others to tell us what our experience is going to be *and they are making it all appear so normal.*

When we feed cows with meat, the earth, in her wisdom, sends us five-sense experience of what this does. We can see it, we can smell it, we can touch it, we can taste it (or in this case wouldn't) and we can feel it. From this five-sense data, we bring our sixth sense into play. Our sixth sense will give us a gut feeling, or intuition, as to whether the experience in doing that particular activity, in this case feeding cows with infected sheep carcass, was 'good'or 'bad' and we then react to the learning and either do or don't repeat the process. This is how the planet maintains its balance and continues to thrive. When we limit our five-sense experience, we don't have a balanced view and do not bring our sixth sense into play. So, if we hear of an event, that is all we do, hear it. If we watch TV we don't feel, touch and smell what the experience is, we base our reaction on two senses: sight and sound. Most of the time we rely on government 'controlled' media to deliver our news and, as they are spending *your* money, they are going to want to tell you what *they* want *you* to hear, so that you continue to give them *your* money. You have to understand that this means that *you* are responsible. It's no good sitting back and saying that you don't agree with what they are doing, but it doesn't really affect you; it does. And *they* know that it does, that's why they don't want you to know!

Imagine that if every pound you paid to the government, out of the hundreds we give them to spend on our behalf, was engraved with your name, and that whatever that pound was spent on, your name would go with it, so that you could actually see where your money ended up, would that make a difference? If you had to account to this earth for every single pound you have ever paid to the government, what do you think you would experience? If you knew that one of your pound coins ended up as a bullet lodged in the brain of a six year-old girl, would you be happy to account for it, to take responsibility? No? But hey, this bullet has your signature on it. If we do not experience this earth through all our senses and realise that it is the most important relationship ever, that we are responsible for our actions, even if that just means paying tax, we have little hope for our own future, let alone our children's.

The next most important relationship that you will ever have is with yourself. It is my belief that we have a 'part' of our being that inhabits this recyclable body so that we experience terrestrial life through it. I cannot define or label that 'part' but it exists to me, and many others have labelled this essence as spirit, energy force or consciousness. Which label it is, I am not sure. This is the authentic 'you' that exists within and outside of the body. It is the part of you that uses the body to experience the essence of being and has no limits because it will always be. Whereas the body will decay and separate into different elements, which will all be recycled no matter how we ritualise burials, cremations or even freezing ceremonies, the knowledge and thought exist forever in a form that we may not be able to touch, but which can touch us in so many ways.

How many of you truly believe you know yourself, the person who lives inside the body, the person who looks in the mirror and sees a reflection of himself?

Describe yourself to me, tell me who you are.

Get a sheet of paper, or bring up a document on your computer and write out a description of whom you are.

Now, a bit like before, I am not going to comment on that for another short while. So that you are not encouraged to look down at what I write next, I will move on.

How many of you like yourself? Do you open your eyes in the morning and give thanks that you can experience a new day on this planet? Do you relish the thought of each and every breath?

OK. Back to the list about whom you are!

How many of the following did you list?

- What gender you are
- How old you are
- What colour your hair is

- What colour your eyes are
- What your star sign is
- What job you do
- What qualifications you have got
- Your marital status
- How many children you have and then lots of additional information about them, rather like the list you have made for yourselves
- What car you drive
- How tall or short you are
- How fat or thin you are
- Your weight
- How many brothers and sisters you have
- What your parents do
- What religion you are
- What ethnic origin you are
- Where you live
- What your accommodation is like
- What pets you have

* * *

Well done! You have been successfully programmed by the powers that be in this world. None of this information tells me anything about *you*. I want to know about you, so give it some more thought and get back to me. If, on the other hand, you did not include any of the bullet pointed statements then well done, you know more about your self than most.

I want to know what it feels like to experience being you. If I posed this question to David Icke, he may possibly respond that he is infinite love. Now back to you. I want to know how *you* experience being you.

So many people are hypnotised into believing that they are their body, or their star sign, religion, sibling number, job title, relationship titles (in their hundreds), bank balance or social status. This is not what it is to experience being 'you.' If I were to share some of my own official information with you, what would it tell you about me? Let's give it a go and see.

- I am fifty this year
- I have brown eyes and dyed hair (my original colour was brown)
- I have five children and 12 grandchildren
- I live with Mostafa
- My house is a little mid terrace property, close to the city centre. My front door opens onto the street and I have a view of a factory from my back garden.
- I drive a 10 year-old Pajero
- I am small in height
- I am a Gemini

So, what have you learnt about me from that?

You may have thought, "Oh, I knew she would be a Gemini. Communications, Mercury and all that. I didn't think she'd be that old though, do women of her age really use the word 'fuck' that often?"

You might think, "Ah, now let's see. Five kids of her own and 12 grandchildren and she's only pushing fifty! I bet she's had a hard life!"

None of that is relevant to what makes me experience life the way I do. For instance, you may think that being born a Gemini means I love training people, all that communication and being able to perform with mercurial speed, darting from one topic to another with air-like ease. But what if that is not they way I experience it? Or possibly I believe I should love it because I am labelled Gemini! You are putting your own learned perception of reality onto me. Maybe I would really enjoy experiencing life as an accountant, as I actually prefer numbers to words. What I am saying is, that those bullet-pointed answers give me such a limited description, they just give me a visual description and even then I interpret it my way, not yours.

When we do this we are giving power and control to the body (humanbot) and not accepting the responsibility of controlling our physical beings. We are allowing people to tag us with labels that say absolutely nothing about who we are and then we buy into the labels and limit ourselves beyond belief, *or* imagination. We become the status and the status becomes us. Once we have given over control to the body (the humanbot), then the humanbot rules the mind and not the mind ruling the bot.

An example of this might be someone who sees him or herself as 'fat.' Maybe when they were younger they may have been heavier proportionately to their height and age. Possibly 'official' experts made the young person think that they were 'fat' because they were told that they were 14lbs overweight against 'official Government guidelines.' They then start to accept the label by thinking "Well I must be fat because 'they' say I am."

This could end up one of three possible ways that I can think of:

1.   The young person accepts the expert's judgment and begins to exercise and eat a more healthy diet until they fall within the recommended guidelines.

2.   The young person accepts the expert's judgment and begins to believe that they are fat. Every time they think about it they reinforce the belief because they are telling themselves, and therefore FG, that they are fat. FG will make their wishes come true and will start to bring food into their mind which will awaken the desire to eat, and low and behold they will start to get fatter. Then other people will notice that they are putting on weight and confirm the label, making you believe it more, until the body, fuelled by FG, takes over control. Then you have to buy larger items and start to wear baggy clothing until that is no longer baggy and have to buy the next size. Now even your clothes labels are telling you that you are fat! And you tell anyone who asks, "Honestly, I hardly eat anything. Nothing I try seems to work. It must be hereditary or chromosomal and not forgetting I have 'big bones.'"

So you do the 'same old, same old' and get fatter and fatter until your energy levels are so depleted because they have to constantly divert their attention to food processing that there is little left for anything else; so exercise stops as well. If you keep doing the 'same old, same old,' soon everything will stop, including your own heartbeat.

3. The young person accepts the expert's judgment and begins to believe that they are fat. They start to become obsessed with food and the desire to reach the officially perfect weight for their height and size. At first they are quite sensible and begin by cutting out the usual crap, like 'takeaways', chocolate, pastries and sweets. They continually motivate themselves by saying that they don't want to be fat, and they want to lose weight. FG picks up on what they are saying and acknowledges that they see themselves as fat, and that you *don't* (FG attaches no meaning to the word 'don't') want to be fat.

So, even though you know you are losing weight, when you look in the mirror you still *believe* yourself to be fat. You will then reinforce that by telling yourself that no matter how much you stick to the healthy eating, you still end up fat. As people begin to notice your weight loss (which is generally after you lose more than 18lbs.), they begin to make comments like, "Wow I can't believe how much weight you've lost, you look really good." This equates, in your map of the world, to, "Wow, who would have thought a fat whale like you could lose weight. You look really good now but wait till the fat cow you really are breaks free. Diets never work but, hey, good luck porky."

This reinforces to your FG that you are really a fat person and, no matter how little food you eat, you always will be. Deep down inside, where you once believed there was a thin you trying to escape, now you visualise it as a fat you! No matter how thin you become, somewhere deep within you have programmed yourself to believe you are fat and that is that. Full stop. So what do you do? One of a couple of things; binge and starve, or starve, or eat till you're sick (with the help of a toothbrush, until it becomes an habitual reaction to food), or become so limited by your behaviour that you cease to function even at the most basic survival levels and starve yourself beyond physical intervention.

* * *

This is what happens when you believe yourself to be any kind of label; fat thin, Gemini Taurus, big small, Conservative Labour (sorry about that one, there really is no difference), plain attractive, funny serious etc etc. FG wants to make your dreams come true, so if you keep telling FG, "I'm a Gemini and they are great communicators" FG will keep making you aware of opportunities to display your Mercurial banter.

The thing that we need to remember is that the longer we have bought into this label, the more our physical and emotional being reacts as the label dictates, with the benevolent support of FG who flashes images of inspiration our way constantly to remind us of what we are believing our self to be. Then sooner or later, someone will ask how you always have a quick response to any question, and you might shrug and say, "Maybe because I'm Gemini."

FG will be really happy with that, you are what you wanted to be, a Gemini. When you get asked your star sign from then on people will say in amazement, "Do you know what, I just *knew* you were Gemini!"

So, what we are learning here is really quite amazing!

Inside every single one of us is a dream maker, waiting to fill our being with the resources to achieve anything we want to achieve! Why be just Gemini? Why not be as flamboyant as Leo, tidy and organised as Virgo, home loving as Taurus and sexual as Scorpio? In fact why not be all the admirable and enjoyable aspects of all those zodiac signs? Why do you limit yourself by saying, "I'm Gemini!"

If you wonder that you might be limiting yourself, think about this. Have you ever met someone you really fancied and found out when their birthday is and then checked them out, by reading up on their star sign? Then, when you find out that you are not compatible, as far as star signs go, you thank your lucky stars for not finding an appropriate opportunity to get a date. After all, Leo's are extravagant and like to show off, and you are more about intellectual discussion than flamboyant chitchat. A few weeks later, to your utmost surprise you find yourselves at the same event, and begin to talk to each other. You notice how well groomed the Leo is and how their hair really is their crowning glory and when they do show off a little, trying to impress you, you understand it's just that they are a Leo. You get on well together and you even find yourself liking their cute little Leo ways, until the day you fall out with each other and then you tell yourself, "I should have known, bloody arrogant Leo, prefers to spend an afternoon getting pampered than discussing something of interest with me."

What was happening here was as follows:

You fancy them but don't seem to be getting anywhere, so gather more information. At present, FG has very little data to go on apart from the images and feelings you get, when you think about the person.

Further information provides the knowledge that their star sign is Leo. Get as much information as you can about Leo. Apply the data for Leo when you think about the person. FG now has special 'characteristics' to look for and highlight your attention to, reinforcing your belief that this person is a Leo.

In doing that, the other person, who also believes themself to be Leo, gets this validated when you notice their Leo traits.

FG becomes very limited in what other visuals evoke thoughts of the Leo, so you begin to see their Leo traits more than any other.

The cycle continues.

People get so hooked into their 'star sign' that it can limit their choice of partner and create enemies where there was the potential for friendship. We are so connected into it that some companies give preference to candidates of a particular birth sign! You might think they are crazy, but are they? Many of us *believe ourselves* to be Gemini, so constantly reaffirm to the rest of society that we have the characteristics of Gemini. So if I was applying for a job as a journalist against say, a Scorpio, if the company bought into the star sign hypnosis and believed that *I had too*, then I would have the perfect characteristics for the job.

And many organisations realise how effective the programming has been and will *expect* the candidate born on 1st June to display more communication skills. It's totally barmy!

*   *   *

I am everything and it's fabulous! Never put limitations on your self. Learn to be, to experience, to be liberated and start to visualise exactly what you *want* to experience in and through this body that you call 'myself.' FG will open your mind to possibilities that have been there all the time, you just never *visualised* them to FG before. If someone asks you what your star sign is say, "All of them."

Stop *doing* what the label/government/powers that be tell you to *do* and start *being* whatever it is you want to *be*. This is your chance to experience with all *your* senses to make your own choices and decisions and take responsibility for them, not blame it on your star sign. Remember, the label we all exist under is human *being* not, human *doing*. Be your self and awaken your mind to the possibilities that could be opened to you, by FG, if you take control of the body and awaken the mind with a multitude of sense-based experiences.

We really do need to understand our self before we can accuse some other poor bastard for not doing it! You see the thing is, that even if FG focuses our attention to the characteristics of being Gemini, we all still have all those other characteristics that are not mentioned under the label Gemini; FG only alerts us when we behave *as we intended*. So, when we do things that are 'out of character' we don't notice them, but often others will and make comments like, "She's not usually like that, it's not her style" or "he acted totally out of character. I've never seen him like that."

We need to free ourselves from as many restrictive labels as possible. Then you will get to know yourself and take control of wherever you go.

I want you to do a bit of visualisation. I want you to see a beauty of a road curving down the slow slope of a mountain in Scotland. You are standing at the top of the track. The dusty road stretches out before you inviting you to speed down its twisting curves. You look about you and take in the view; blue skies, drifting streaks of washed out clouds, the colours ever changing on the mountainside, and not a soul in sight. You breathe in the mountain air and its clarity gives it a taste sweeter then the best wines. You feel exhilarated and reach your arms high above your head and shout your name into the atmosphere and hear it again and again as it drifts down the track.

You wish that you had a real good car and imagine a red convertible Golf GTI, perfect to experience the thrill of such a track. And when you open your eyes, you are sitting in the driver's seat; holding on to the leather wrapped alloy steering wheel with one hand, while the other is caressing the stainless steel gear knob. You take control and then go! You feel as if nothing is impossible, like you are free to just experience the absolute brilliance of this moment. You take it all in, the sound of the tyres on the gritty track, the smell of the leather, the feel of the wind blowing over the top of your head, the view cascading into your present and the taste of freedom.

OK. So, now imagine that really happened. See it, hear it, taste it, feel it, smell it. Do it in your mind as you would do it in real life, in other words, see it through your own eyes. You love this car, it might not be a Ferrari, but for what you wanted to experience, it was perfect. Now repeat the whole experience as if beginning again, only this time as you rev the engine and scan the road ahead, you see a series of speed cameras, one every ¼ mile, and the track is eight miles long. They are preceded by a series of flashing signs screaming '30.' The cameras may be active, or they may not. The choice, the experience and the responsibility are all yours!

Now, before anybody starts preaching that I am encouraging people to break the law, I am not, it was all visualisation. But let's just imagine that it wasn't. If you had enjoyed that track before and driven at just over the speed limit because of all the twists and turns, then your driving experience and ability to use all your senses to enjoy driving the car would've ensured that you arrived safely at your destination. You are in control because you are utilising your senses and past experiences to guide you. If you drove at the speed limit and were not in touch with all your senses, then you are more likely to have accident. Think of all those times when you have taken a wrong turning, or slammed on the brakes when you realised the traffic lights were actually red, or answered your mobile and kept swerving out of the lanes (don't even say you don't do it! I drive behind those kind of people all the time!).

What is the usual list of excuses?

- Did I nod off then?
- I was trying to listen to you.
- Hang on a minute; some moron's flashing me. "Who the hell are you honking at? I'm in my lane." Sorry about that, yes anyway…
  - I was thinking about the meeting with my boss.
  - My head was thumping from partying the night before.
  - I only took my eyes of the road for a minute.
  - The baby dropped her bottle; I just reached down to get it.
  - I was getting a blowjob, what's it to you?

* * *

You were not in control. And because we do those things, when the government (local or otherwise, it all goes in the same pockets) wants to put speed cameras in every possible place to protect us from those 'thoughtless people,' we go with it because we recognise the experience of being, or being involved with, one of those 'thoughtless people.' You are so busy being told what to do that you forget how many things you have, albeit unwittingly, *agreed* to do in the first place. It's all a huge con.

Take the 'Congestion Charge.' On the face of it, very commendable and I am sure that it has relieved the bumper-to-bumper traffic chaos in the Congestion Charge zones. It might not seem that way to me when I drive through London, but hey, that is just my experience, maybe I just go at the wrong time.

So, what do they decide to do? Extend the Congestion Charge zone, oh and, raise the price of the charge, which they do under the guise that the zone is proving very popular with local people and appears to be cutting congestion (maybe that's why the charge went up, not enough punters, victims of their own success). Well, of course the locals are going to be happy, why wouldn't they be? I would be happy if my street charged every one else a fine, for using it. It would make it easier for me to get home, and park, every evening. This is what this really is, a fine for driving on roads that you actually pay tax to maintain for driving purposes. Sorry, can someone just run that past me again? So, I am being fined for using something that I am actually paying for in the first place, is that what you are saying? Darn right it is! And the cheeky bastards even have the nerve to mesmerise us with the voice of some husky streetwise Londoner, telling us not to worry if we have forgotten to pay our Congestion Charge; they understand life doesn't always go to plan.

If we like we can pay online or, if we prefer, we can pay tomorrow for an extra bit of cash! And because it is done in such a sweet kind of "look, we know you're guilty of driving on roads that you pay to maintain, but we are nice people and are here to help you pay the fine," we pay! "Mate, I've been at work all day and have got to get to the hospital to pick up my sick daughter and drive her to her aunt's house for some care and attention, as my partner left us last week, under the pressure of it all. I won't get to see a computer until tomorrow morning!" They understand. We can pay an *extra* fine tomorrow for the audacity of having a life.

Do you know how they teach traffic cops to fly around London breaking every speed limit and committing hundreds of other traffic violations? They send them to a special driving school where they learn to activate all of their senses. I live near MIRA, which is where they come to drive skid cars to gain experience, in a safe environment, of driving in extreme conditions, so they can drive safely in busy cities and on country lanes. I was married to a traffic officer once and when he was learning, we all had to learn with him. He modelled the behaviour and evoked the responses of seen it, heard it, tasted it, smelt it, and felt it. After modelling a qualified instructor for a sufficient period of time, he went to experience it for himself as he took control of the car. Once *he* passed the course *my* driving abilities were criticised more than ever with comments like, "You really are so totally useless. If you look over the hedgerow, further ahead on the lane, you would've seen there was no traffic coming and you could have overtaken." Yes, thank you, fuck off.

One day when we lived in the perfect 'happy ever after' village of Bradby, I had to make a trip to Coventry, so I got in the car, which happened to be Primera SRI, and set off on my way. Bradby was surrounded by well-used country lanes, normally by mud-ridden tractors. The farmers had been doing some planting and there was a handwritten sign on the turn into a lane that said 'Mud on road.' Well, I must admit that I had only been driving for about a year and, living with my perfect traffic officer husband, only added to the limitations I put on my own abilities. Also when I was learning the 'Highway Code,' ready to regurgitate on demand, I obviously did not take in the bit about the effect of mud on the roads.

I carried on driving at around 35 miles an hour, taking in the beautiful view, as the road was one of those long slow downhill twisting kind of roads, so there was plenty to look at. Suddenly, a baby rabbit appeared and looked as if it was about to run under my wheels, so I turned the steering wheel (power-assisted of course!) to avoid it and the bastard thing switched direction, so I twisted the wheel again. The significance of the sign declaring 'mud on the road' suddenly became scarily obvious as the car went into an uncontrollable (for me, anyway) spin. I came to a rather smashed up standstill in a ditch.

I was not aware of time passing but another driver stopped, and I remember him asking for my mobile and somehow alerting my husband, about five minutes drive away (if you heed the 'mud on the road' sign). I was still stuck in the car when my knight in shining armour, known as 'traffic officer husband' turned up. Can you guess what the 'I'm labelled as a traffic officer so I am going to behave like one even though I'm also labelled as your husband' did? He only started to measure the scene, can you believe it, while I'm still in the car! Then, when he came to speak to me his first words were, "Well, what a surprise! Do you realise what speed you were doing? The farmer had put out warning signs." One of the passengers from the car that stopped to assist said to me, "Are you *sure* that's your husband?"

At the time, I can remember recording that memory as really sad and an indication of the state of our crappy relationship, and now I actually just laugh about it.

We are allowing the powers that be to dilute our senses and limit our behaviours, until we believe what they tell us to believe. None of us, apart from the police, of course, has the sensory acuity to drive above a certain limit and to make sure, and protect the rest of us, we are going to put cameras in the most dangerous of places, like er…at the bottom of a straight hill that has no other roads leading onto it. Now, we know that the car naturally speeds up as its weight carries it down the hill, so understand that this might mean that you have to apply the brakes abruptly, or nearly drive into the rear of the proceeding car, that has come almost to a standstill (they've already been caught here and can't afford another fine, three more points and an increase in insurance), but we just want to keep you safe.

Now, I am not telling people to drive like maniacs and break the law. I am merely commenting that they call us all thoughtless people and we all get punished and labelled equally, even if we are totally in control. If they are so worried that someone might get hurt, then why don't they put fucking cameras in children's playgrounds?

Why don't they stop selling alcohol?

Why don't they put cameras in nurseries?

Why don't they put cameras in schools and watch the brilliance of children erased by the government's pathetic curriculum, which leaves no room for individual discussion?

How can we know ourselves if we allow people to limit our experience of being? That is why so many relationships go wrong and our relationship with our *self* is, frequently, the one we get wrong more than any other. Seriously, if you don't know who you are, underneath all of those labels, then how the hell do you expect anyone else to?

The thing is, FG is really the *self*. The body, the conscious mind and the whole world just exist in our own selves as expressions of our five-sense, sometimes sixth sense data input. The conscious mind has to inform FG of *all* the experiences that are possible so that the self can record them and then decide whether to repeat the experience or not. If we lose conscious control of our bodies by feeding our *self* (FG) the wrong information, our self will experience what we have *programmed* it to experience. If we keep telling our self that we are a 'useless driver' the self will visualise ourselves to be a 'useless driver,' and the body and senses will confirm it.

Wake up to who you can be. How can you experience being a human if you don't open your brilliance to what *being* can really be? Don't look at everything with your head in a box, take it off and see what's really going on and get to enjoy being you! Let me tell you that once you taste the freedom, you will never want to limit your experience of *being* again. It doesn't mean that you have to abseil off tower blocks, just don't label yourself for *not* doing it and if you feel like being a sexy Scorpio, be one. Once you start you will not want to stop and you will begin to recognise some of the scams you have been buying into for so many years. You may even find that you like being your self and eventually love *being* you and that's when the magic begins. Oh, and before any of you start limiting your self immediately, by saying, "But I've always been like this!"

STOP.

There is one more thing that I should tell you about your amazing self. FG has no concept of time with regard to experiences. This means that what *has* happened and what you *would like* to happen, exist at the same time as your *self imagines or remembers it*. You can experience this by doing a little bit of visualisation. I want you to think of the last time you ate ice cream. If you believe that you don't like ice cream, remember why you believe that, or choose something you *do* believe you like. Recall as much data about the experience as you can. Who were you with? What flavour was it? Was it a particular brand? Where were you? What did it taste like? Visualise it with all five senses, as if you were experiencing it again.

OK. Now, I would like you to think of the next time that you think you will eat ice cream. Who will you be with? What flavour will it be? Will it be a particular brand? Where will you be? What will it taste like? Visualise it with all five senses and see yourself, through your own eyes, experiencing it.

Where did you experience the *recall* of yourself eating ice cream? Was it in your mind or did you have to get in a car and travel to the exact location to relive the experience? And when you imagined eating ice cream in some *future* location, where did you experience it? Was it in your mind, or did you have to build some futuristic time machine to take you there to experience it? Both experiences could be brought to mind almost simultaneously, or within seconds, of each other. This is because in *self,* time does not exist as recordable, so we can jump backward and forward, days, years, decades and in some cases, lifetimes. And we can still experience things that happened years ago, in almost the same thought *as things that have yet to happen.* So, anyone who believes that behaving as a label dictates is behaviour that cannot be changed believes something that is not true, not in my map of the world anyway. We can, and already do, time travel!

None of us are broken. We are all capable of experiencing anything we want and freeing ourselves of the labels we limit ourselves with. Rip off the label and tell FG what you want. Visualise it, experience it through your own eyes and then watch as, somehow, all kinds of opportunities you were never aware of before, start making your dream a reality.

When we arrive at this point, of being able to *know and love* our self, then we are able to enter any relationship from an honest and open starting point. If you do not understand the way you communicate with your own *self,* no one else will ever be able to understand what *they* believe to be you. Once you know your *self* then this is what you have to offer to a relationship, endless possibilities. Fabulous, eh!!! Imagine telling your mates that you had just met this fantastic new lover, and when they ask what he or she does, you respond, "Anything you can imagine and then some!"

It would leave them with their chins on the floor.

Another magical thing about going through this is that when you know yourself, then you let FG (self) know exactly who you are trying to attract, and suddenly many possible candidates appear before your very eyes, as FG makes you aware of all possibilities of which you have requested. That's when you can start to form relationships knowing who your really are, and what you really want. Love has to start with the self, otherwise how can love be offered? If you do not posses love of *self*, how can *self* offer something it does not possess?

Why do so many relationships that start out with so much promise, end up in so much pain? The answer lies within you.

Think back on your past relationships and begin to understand what part *you* contributed to the break up. It is all too easy to tell our side of the story, eliciting from others the words we want to hear. This is not taking responsibility and life is all about being responsible. There is a reason for whatever we go through in this existence, no matter how clichéd that sounds. However, in order to understand the reason, you have to appreciate *your own responsibility in the experience*; if you don't do this, then you may never understand the reason. Many of us give away control of *our being* to others and then get stuck and don't know how to get it back. Imagine if you had a really good computer game where you controlled this fantastic 'human being' called "Insert Your Own Name," but I will use the name 'Humanbot.' You, the game player, are not of human form. You are pure energy and with this energy, you power the game. 'Humanbot' progresses in the game to higher levels by using its 'special powers', its five senses, to remain 'full of life' (FOL).

To get onto the next level 'Humanbot' must achieve 200 FOL points.

Also, on your monitor you can see the 'power meter' which must register at least 200 Power Tokens (PT) in order to progress.

Your role as the game 'player' is to make sure that 'Humanbot' negotiates all of the challenges in front of them, with enough FOL and PT points, to safely go up to the next level. The only guidance you, the Game Player, has to enable this achievement is by deciphering the 'messages' that 'Humanbot' sends you through the energy cord that connects you to the computer terminal. The end prize of the game is that you, the player, have an experience of what it is to be confined by a physical body, able only to utilise a maximum of five out of a possible 10 senses and take all of the knowledge, experience and increased energy with you to, maybe, a central energy bank or possibly, the next game. The next game might not even be an'earth' game; it may be situated in a totally different 'time' in a totally different universe.

Imagine how well you have played the game so far; you have already reached level five, which is called 'Relationships.' You have been looking forward to this level and hope to complete the challenge with maximum FOL points. The game begins and then ends: sadly you fail to achieve enough FOL and PT's to reach the next level. In order to find out *how* to progress to the next level you will need to assess your game plan to find out how to improve your FOL and PT's.

This is how you are going to do it!

I want you to imagine that in front of you are two seats. You (the game player) sit on one seat, and you (the Humanbot), on the other seat. You are in the role of 'Solomon' and will ask questions of the 'game player' and 'Humanbot.' Examine the way 'game player' and 'Humanbot' communicate with each other. Allow each their turn to respond and just absorb the lessons on how to progress.

The assessment might go something like this:

Solomon: Why did the relationship not work out?
HB: He just wasn't my type.
GP: What do you mean, wasn't your type? You didn't specify a type. I can visualise it now. You were noticing how many people had partners and you were getting more and more unhappy with the situation, and remember that day, when you sat all alone in your

bedroom, playing all that sad music? Here, I'll let you rerun the experience. Can you visualise it? Good. As you can see and hear, what you actually said was, "What is wrong with me? Why doesn't anyone ever want to be with me? I don't want to be on my own any more. I just want someone, anyone. I just want someone."

Did you hear that clearly enough? Thought so!

HB: Yes, well I didn't *mean* 'just anyone.' I *meant* someone who will love me, or even like me. The person you sent me was totally unsuitable.

GP: If I might just say something. You never mentioned the word *love;* you never even mentioned the word *like*, if you had, I could have brought up all the data on those labels and heightened your awareness of appropriate partners. You said that you 'didn't want to be on your own,' and I did as you asked.

Solomon: Thank you. Let's move on. What made you realise that this was not an appropriate partner?

HB: Well, when we first met, quite accidentally, I actually thought he was kind of cute, so when he asked me to have a coffee I thought, "Why not?" To begin with everything was fine. We had some things in common and did a lot of talking, but then things started to go wrong. Things he did started to annoy me, like always turning up late and making me hang around. Then it was like *I* had to pay for most things and there were the little annoying habits. I tried to get along with him but the longer I stayed with him, the harder it became to break up. In the end I just began to feel trapped and depressed with the whole situation. I didn't know what to do and so just kept on doing the same. I began to lose touch with who I was and the only way I could get any peace was to try to block out of my mind the situation I was in. When he really pissed me off, I would have a drink, or turn on the TV or even go to bed. Anything to just take my mind off the situation really.

GP: First of all, the meeting was no accident. I alerted you to the potential partner as one who could fulfil your specific request, which as we have already covered was totally lacking in specificity. I would also like to mention that when your partner first began to pick his nose and eat the contents, I did react to the data supplied by your five senses, but you rewrote the data by saying, "I'll pretend I didn't see that," as you did for a lot of their behaviour. When I attempted to alert you to the fact that I could see the FOL and PT's getting lower, you didn't acknowledge me and when I could see that this relationship was actually reducing the levels so much that they were lower than *before* you began the relationship, you just kept telling me that it was better than being alone, even though *I* could feel that it wasn't. And to make matters worse, whenever I did manage to alert you and you didn't like what I was saying, you would disconnect by drowning me out with the television or alcohol and, on many occasions, both. If you had listened to me we could have ended this relationship much sooner, instead of losing all those points, making us worse off than when we started.

Solomon: Thank you both for your time. I will now assess the best way to learn from all I have heard and instruct you on how to use this new knowledge on the Relationship level of this game.

Report from Solomon: Lessons to assist with completion of the level.

• When HB is requesting something from GP, the request should be specific. If HB requests 'just anyone' then that is what GP will make available.

• HB needs to provide GP with as much five sense information as possible about their experiences, so that GP can process the data clearly and as fully as possible.

• HB and GP need to understand that they are in this together and that no blame is attached to either for the failure to complete the level. In order to aid communication it might be an appropriate action to spend time in direct communication with each other. This could be achieved through 'thinking and visualisation' time, which should be experienced alone without the distraction of alcohol or any other interference.

• HB should understand that GP could see the FOL and PT's on the monitor and trust that GP is acting in a benevolent way to achieve the best outcome. That outcome has to be expressed by HB in as many ways as possible, using all of HB's powers, to ensure that what is communicated is ecologically sound, in other words, is the best possible outcome to achieve points.

The meaning of your communication is the response you get. If you say your life is shit, then you will get shit. If you look for problems you will find them. If you tell yourself that you are a crap lover, then you will be a crap lover. Instead, tell yourself that your life is brilliant, look for solutions and become the amazing lover you know yourself to be.

* * *

To anyone reading my rantings who is not involved in a relationship and would like to be in one, get to know and love yourself before you enter into another potential partnership. Find out who you are and what you really want from life, at least then the potential partner has something to go on. So many times in my life, I have heard the same phrases, regarding relationships, come out of people's mouths:

- They never listen.
- They have no idea what I'm really like.
- It was all their fault.
- I tried my best.
- I did it all for them.
- They made me do/feel/act/ that way; I didn't want to, they made me.
- I knew it wasn't going to work; I just didn't want to accept it.
- I loved them more than they loved me.
- We just had nothing to say to each other any more.
- I didn't want to hurt them and in the end they hurt me.
- I stayed for the kids.

Each one of the above statements is an abdication of *your* responsibility for *your life* and the way *you* experience that life.

Let me use my own experience to highlight my point. When I was 14 years old I met the man who was to become my first husband. I met him through a school friend, who had, at 14 years of age, just given birth to his child. I will call this man Stuart. My school friend put the baby up for adoption.

At this time in my life I was in a strange place myself. I was still living with the torment of the sexual abuse and believed myself to be a whore, often behaving as befitted the label. I rarely spent any time in school and when I did attend, I would cause as much disruption as possible. I spent most of my time alone, walking over the fields, trying to make some sort of sense of what life was all about. I smoked and drank alcohol as often as possible. I hated myself and felt so out of control that I self harmed.

My father had been accepted into Leeds University where he was studying for an MSc Degree, which meant he lived away from the family home for the majority of his time. My mother was doing the best she could to take care of us all, and work, so things were fairly strained for everyone really. As my mum had three children younger than me, the youngest being eight years old, her time was always in demand, meaning that I exploited the situation and often shouted that I was going to a mate's house, when I was really doing other things that I know she would never have approved of. I could have been helping my mum but didn't often volunteer, preferring to get out as much as possible.

I met Stuart again, when I was almost 15. He had started to hang around the school gates, and somehow we just got talking. Usually I would just go into school to register and then run off over the fields. By this time I had been told by my school not to return after the summer holidays and even though my father was furious about it, he tried to prevent me sliding down the slippery slope of delinquency by convincing an old colleague of his to accept me onto a catering course at a local college, where he was head of a department. The course was due to start in September and I was kind of looking forward to it, even though it was not the dream career that I had hoped for.

During the summer holidays Stuart and I spent more time together, just talking really. He had a very sad life story, telling me that he had been adopted himself when he was born, then his adoptive parents split up when he was five, the break up of which was extremely tragic, with his adoptive mother stabbing his adoptive father. They divorced and Stuart stayed with the father in the family home. His adoptive father then remarried a woman who had a son of her own, who was exactly the same age as Stuart. Stuart began to suffer emotionally and physically and felt neglected by the family.

He told me that all his past relationships had been crap, especially the one with my old school mate that had ended with his own child being adopted. He said that he hated himself for that, and that one day he would find his son and make it up to him. He spoke of how he had tried to find out *who* he really was, who his parents were, but that his dad and his wife, wouldn't give him any information. I felt so sorry for him and believed that there was some special connection between us; both of us had been through troubles and basically felt unloved and/or unworthy of love. Stuart and I began to meet up more regularly and he would give me cigarettes and cider as we talked. He said that he wished he had a girlfriend who was like me, someone who understood him and as soon as he uttered those words I wanted to make his wish come true; I was 15 and he was 19.

Stuart was not the most articulate of people, whereas I was always very good with words (Gemini, Mercury and all that crap!) and this started to become apparent in our relationship. If we had a disagreement I was always able to use rhetoric to swing the conclusion my way and even though I knew Stuart did not like the outcome, he could not put up a good enough argument to change it. At first they were just little disagreements about what we were going to do, but soon they started to affect other things like what clothes I was wearing. I didn't let it worry me too much because I believed at this point that we loved each other and that our love would jump any hurdle. Most times, when he said he didn't want me to wear whatever it might be, I would just say something like, "If I go back home and change then we are not going to meet up with our mates till later, they'll all have had a 'few' by then and may go on somewhere else, just leave it eh?"

And Stuart would listen to my reasoning and then reluctantly agree. Then one night, in 1973, the pattern changed. We were meeting up with some of our mates and going to a local disco and I had arranged to meet Stuart at the bottom of the road. My mum did not approve of Stuart, so most of the time I met him without her knowledge, let alone consent. As we were going to a disco, I had bought this really gorgeous short mini skirt and matching top, which I was wearing with a pair of high blue platform heels.

As I approached Stuart I noticed that he wasn't smiling and had folded his arms across his chest; a sign that I knew meant he was pissed off about something. I guessed it was going to be about my outfit, the thought had actually crossed my mind when I had tried it on in the store, but I really liked it and felt good, so I had already rehearsed this situation. I went up to him to give him a kiss, but he moved away shrugging his shoulder. I reacted as normal, by asking him lovingly, what was wrong with him, even though I already had a damn good idea. We followed the normal routine, with me suggesting that we go anyway so that we didn't miss out on the fun, expecting him to remain in a mood for an hour or so, but at least I would get to wear what I wanted. This time the routine changed. He started to get really agitated and said, "I don't want you to go out looking like that, OK. I don't want you to. Do you want every other man looking at you, is that what you want, eh, is it?"

I told him that of course it wasn't what I wanted; I was only interested in him, no one else. He grabbed both my arms with his hands and pushed me so that our arms were extended and then said, "OK, so I've had a good look. Now go and take them off!"

It was not a request. Once more I tried to reason with him, still locked in position, and he shouted, "You are not listening. I am not asking you, I'm fucking telling you go and get changed or we ain't going fucking nowhere." And with that he pushed me away.

I did what at the time I thought was the best option; I went home and got changed. Stuart waited across the road for me and when I came out in trousers and a jacket he smiled and called, "Come on then, we don't want to waste any more time."

That night he had loads to drink. Normally he drank pints, but that night he was having shorts as well *and* he appeared agitated. While he was standing at the bar another man accidentally spilt some of his drink on the counter and Stuart reacted quite verbally, which made him even more fidgety when he came back to the table, and soon after he said that he wanted to leave. All the way home he was going on about how he'd seen me looking at other men and that he was pissed off with my behaviour. I told him that he was wrong, I hadn't been looking at any one, but he just called me a lying bitch and said that if I wanted to look like a whore then maybe he would start to treat me like one.

I can remember thinking that maybe I should split up with him, as I didn't like the way he had treated me, but the next day everything was different. He was happy and smiling and said we should go and sit over the fields, but I wasn't keen to go. He wanted to talk to me, he begged, then touched my chin to lift my head, and looking into my eyes, added a few more 'pleases.' So I went with him and we talked. He said he was sorry about the previous night and that he didn't mean to upset me, it was just that he loved me and couldn't stand the thought of anyone else looking at me, or me looking at anyone else. He just wanted to be with me and he was going to show how much he loved me; I would see the proof at the weekend. So instead of splitting up, I eagerly anticipated his demonstration of love. On the days leading up to the weekend he was especially attentive and we didn't argue once; we were all loved up again.

On Saturday evening he kept his word and revealed his declaration of never-ending love; a tattoo of a rose on his forearm with my name emblazoned beneath. This was indeed a true affirmation and I was almost in tears by the visual impact of it; someone really loved me. Stuart told me that this meant I belonged to him; I was his and he was mine. At that moment I felt blissfully happy, declaring my love to him by doing almost everything he asked me to do, whether it was what *I* wanted or not.

The first time after that when I didn't agree with him and said I wouldn't comply to whatever request it was, he reminded me of how he had got his arm tattooed with my name, a tattoo, and I couldn't even do the littlest of things for him.

The first time he hit me, it was *just* a slap and it shocked me so much that I did nothing in retaliation. I just stood there with my cheek stinging wondering what had just happened. As the realisation slowly began to filter through, I turned and walked away. Moments later Stuart was behind me, begging me to forgive him; he didn't mean to do it, I just drove him crazy, why couldn't I just do what he asked instead of always trying to cause a problem. I just kept walking. He caught up with me and took hold of my arms and then hugged me, crying as he spoke, saying that he was sorry and that he would never hit me again. He didn't mean to do it. He said he didn't know what he would do without me and that he loved me. We stayed together.

The first time he knocked me unconscious was at my college's Christmas party in 1973, which was held in a club about five miles from Coventry. I was having a brilliant time, listening to the likes of David Bowie and chatting to all my college mates, one of whom was a guy I got on really well with. I liked him a lot and we would make each other laugh during the practical cooking sessions. Stuart did not come to the party until about an hour after I'd arrived and when he walked in I got up from the table and walked over to greet him. He took hold of my arm and forcefully escorted me to another empty table and told me, quite aggressively, to wait there while he bought himself a drink. When he returned I suggested that we go and join my friends instead of sitting on our own and he asked why I had to sit with them; he was here now. Stuart didn't talk to me, instead he just kept glaring over at my friends and then, when I asked him why he wasn't talking, he told me to go and sit with 'them' if he was boring me. Suddenly the Christmas party lost all its festive spirit.

Moments later, one of my mates came over and grabbed my arm saying that she wanted me to dance with her. I looked sideways at Stuart and, as he made no attempt to prevent me from going, went with her and started dancing. Over my friend's shoulder I could see Stuart watching me, only taking his eyes off me to drink his beer. The dance ended and as the next song began, Michael, the guy I had been speaking to, came onto the dance floor to join us. I knew that Stuart would not like this, but reasoned that as Michael was dancing with my friend and me and we weren't even touching each other, then I was not doing anything Stuart could object to. I thought wrong.

Just before the dance ended Stuart came on to the dance floor, grabbed my arm and pulled me outside the building. As we got onto the gravel car park I fell, but he just carried on dragging me, by my arm, calling me all the names under the sun. I pleaded with him to let me go, or at least let me stand up, but he just kept calling me a 'slut' and a 'whore' and to 'shut the fuck up' or he'd give me something to shout about. Finally, he had dragged me around the side of the building where he roughly hauled me to my feet; shaking me and spitting his anger in my face, "See what you make me do? See how you get me angry? Why do you have to do it, eh, why do you have to make me so fucking angry? Do you like me getting mad, eh, do you?"

By now I was crying, almost hysterically, shaking my head and begging him to stop, but it seemed to just fuel his fury and he continued to accuse me, blaming me for what was happening, saying that I didn't know when to stop, and I just had to keep pushing him.

I was really scared now and told him the relationship wasn't working, accusing him of not trusting me. I explained that Michael was just a college mate and nothing more and that if he didn't believe me then I didn't want to be with him any more. He glared at me for a split second and then uttered the word 'bitch' before slapping me so hard across the face that my head spun violently with the force and smashed into the brickwork of the building. I fell to the ground.

When I opened my eyes, I became aware of the shouting before I realised what had happened. My college friends were all ganging up on Stuart, not physically but verbally, telling him to 'fuck off' and Stuart was walking away from me towards the entrance of the car park, shouting abuse, telling Michael I was nothing more than a whore, and he was welcome to the 'dirty bitch.' Once Stuart had gone, or had at least appeared to go, my friends comforted me and said I should go home and get my mum to take me to the hospital. Michael offered to call me a taxi to take me home, but I said it was better that I go on my own. I didn't want him to come with me because my father was home for the Christmas holidays and I didn't want to give my parents any reason to be more pissed off with me than they already were.

Michael insisted on paying for the taxi, waiting with me until it arrived, and then explaining to the driver that I'd had an accident and to make sure I got home safely. While we waited he said that I shouldn't ever let any guy hit me or call me those names and he gave me a small kiss on the cheek before the taxi pulled away. My head was thumping at this point and I just wanted to get home and forget I'd ever set eyes on Stuart. Just as the taxi turned out of the car park it abruptly stopped and Stuart began talking to the driver, explaining that he'd called my house and there was no one there, so he'd been sent by the others to go with me to the hospital. I wanted to tell the driver to go, but there was something so scary about seeing him, that the words never left my lips and the passenger door opened and Stuart climbed in next to me. He put his arm around my shoulders and told me that he was going to "take care of me;" he was here to make everything right. The driver dropped us off at Accident and Emergency and drove off, but we never set foot inside that hospital. I asked him to leave me alone, to just go away, but he didn't.

That night was the first time he raped me and as he raped me, he told me that if I ever tried to leave him, he would find me and kill me. He knew everything I did, everywhere I went, and he would be waiting. He wouldn't let me go home until I had promised that I would never leave him and that I would tell no one about that evening. Hours later, he walked me home and waited while my father unlocked the door. It was the early hours of the morning, maybe 2.00am, and my dad had his dressing gown on and was obviously angry asking me "what time to do you call this?" and after smelling the alcohol on me, he shook his head saying that he couldn't understand my behaviour. I raised my head and, when he saw the swelling on my brow, he asked me what the hell had happened to me.

For the first time in my life I felt more scared of someone other than my father; my dad might get really angry, but he would never kill me. Stuart would, so I gave my dad some smart-ass reply, so that any sympathy and potential support was gone and I was ordered to go to my room. When I got up to my bedroom I closed the curtains and as I did so, noticed Stuart smoking a cigarette, at the side of the entry across the road. He smiled at me, raised his thumb and then blew me a kiss. When I looked out fifteen minutes later he was still there, standing in the shadow of the entry.

There is so much more to the part of my life that involved Stuart, but I don't want to say any more for now. I want us to have a look at what took place to see what we can learn.

The first thing that comes to my mind is that I had never dealt with 'secret uncle.' I went from a straight 'A's student to a teacher's nightmare within a year. My mind was in torment and during the monotonous drone of the teacher's voice; I would hear the words 'whore' again and again. It got to the stage where I couldn't hear the teacher at all and didn't care about whatever *important* thing we were meant to be learning. I felt as if everyone secretly *knew* what had happened to me so I started to isolate myself from the one or two pupils who spoke to me. I did not have an easy time of it at school, as most of the other girls bullied me, so school was a horrible place for me to be.

I knew of Stuart and that he had already had sex with a 14-year-old girl, so that should have put me on my guard, but I didn't pay any attention to my FG and actually *looked* for reasons to like him. I did not love myself at this point so was in no position to offer something *I did not posses* to another person. I knew that Stuart was not able to 'beat' me in an argument and knowing this to be true, offered him no way to express how he was feeling about decisions that in essence *I* made. I knew that my strength was 'words' and when I became aware that he was frustrated at never being verbally my equal, I should have ended the relationship.

When Stuart first started to 'dictate' to me about my clothing, or the way I expressed who I believed myself to be, I should have understood my emotions well enough to know that the *feelings* that were constantly making themselves apparent were 'telling' me that something wasn't right. Instead of acknowledging them, I made excuses to make myself *believe* something different, when my FG was doing its best to get me out of the situation.

Once I let Stuart know that I would do what he wanted as long as he put enough force behind the demand, then essentially I was making him aware that physical strength would compel me to do things that, given no physical coercion, I would not choose or want to do.

The first time I decided to end the relationship, I should have focused on the reasons that had made me even consider breaking up. If I had assessed what was really happening in the relationship, no amount of 'material' declarations of love, would have enticed me.

In accepting his tattoo as a sign of his devotion to me, rather than being some ink pressed into the skin, I also accepted his claim that this meant 'I belonged to him.' I gave him all the wrong signals and allowed him to then use this 'declaration of love' as a stick to beat me with, whenever he wanted to *prove* his love. For example, 'I know that I call you abusive names and give you the odd slap, but don't forget, I went through agonies and paid good money for this tattoo, just to show you how much I love you.'

The first time he slapped me, in not walking away and ending the relationship, I was actually giving him a very clear message that I did not like what he had done, but as long as he said he was sorry and promised not to do it again, it was all right.

At the Christmas party I had the option to go with Michael to the hospital, or to my father, but I didn't, because by that time I had given Stuart so much control of my emotional well-being, that I was more scared of leaving than staying.

Now, I am not saying that it is right for any individual to hit, or otherwise express violence, in any kind of relationship, I am just saying that no one can *make* you do anything. We have *choice* and we have the right to say that we are not happy with the relationship and do not want to continue with it any more. If one person in the relationship is not happy, then it is impossible for the other to be content. If you think you are, then you, like me, are just fooling yourself and not taking a good look at the bigger picture. We are *all* responsible for the choices we make and we have no right to blame those choices on other people. I had no right, for example, to believe that Stuart *made me* get changed into other clothes. If I did not *want* to dress differently, then why did I give my power away to him? I could have just said, "Sorry but this is how I choose to dress, so if you don't like it, then that is your problem, not mine."

Once *I* agreed to get changed, *I* and not Stuart, gave a clear message that if you exert enough pressure then *I* will do what you say.

One of my favourite books is 'The Arabian Entertainments', which many people know as 'The Arabian Nights'. One of the first stories in this book is called 'The Ass and The Ox' and it tells the tale of an ass and an ox who live on the same farm and work for the same owner. One day the ox is bemoaning his life, saying how he has to work from sunrise to sunset, weighed down by a heavy wooden yolk and being hit continuously with a stick. The ox says that he is so tired at the end of the night that, although he does not like the dry dusty feed that is put out for him, he knows that if he doesn't eat it, he will go to sleep tired and hungry and the following day's work will seem twice as hard. He says that the farmer no longer makes him a bed of thick straw, but just scatters a scanty amount on the cold hard stable floor, that make him awaken with aches and pains. The ox says he has the hardest life of all the animals on the farm.

The ass listens to him and observes that the ox never shows his disapproval of the way he is treated and says that he himself has quite a nice life. If he doesn't want to do something he will dig in his heels and if they try to beat him with a stick he brays and whinnies as if he is about to die. The ass says that once they brought him dry and dusty food and even though he was tired and hungry, he did not touch it, and when they came to get him from his stable the next day, he lay on the floor as if he was about to take his last breath. Now, the ass continued, I have a fine bed of straw, fresh water and carrots and turnip mixed with my meal.

So, they hatch a plan and the next morning when the farm boy comes to harness the heavy yolk to the ox's neck, he is surprised to see the ox lying down, hardly moving even his eyes. The boy tries to encourage the ox to move, and even beats the ox with the stick, but the ox remains still on the stable floor. The boy notices that the dusty, dry meal has not been touched and begins to worry about the health of the ox and runs to inform the farmer. The farmer, on seeing the ox, believes that the animal is ready to die, and suddenly realises the ox's worth. If the ox dies, who will till the soil and who else would be strong enough to drag the heavy plough? All at once the farmer realises that he must do his best to make the ox well again, so he tells the boy to give the ox some carrots and turnip with his food and to make him a good thick bed of straw to keep him warm and comfortable.

The story does go on from there, but the point I want to emphasise has already been made apparent. The ox was treated so badly because he *allowed* people to treat him badly. The ox could not speak the same language as the humans, yet he was able to change the way he was treated by making the farmer aware that he was not going to allow his poor treatment to continue. The ox took responsibility for the way his life was and once he understood that this was his right, things changed. I never wanted Stuart to hit me, or abuse me in anyway, but I did not take responsibility for myself, I *gave* him permission by allowing it to continue.

In relationships, no matter what kind they may be, we always blame other people and when we do this once and then *continue* to do this, it is no longer the other person that is to blame, it is *ourselves*. In many cases of domestic violence, even though I have experienced it myself during two marriages, both partners are participants in the abuse. In staying with someone who we know is causing us *harm* or those whom we are supposed to protect, we are participating. The problem lies in the fact

that people get stuck; they limit their choices. I can remember being in
a refuge and it wasn't the most luxurious place on earth, but it was safe,
and even though I hated *being* in a refuge, it was a better *choice* than
experiencing various forms of abuse on an almost daily basis. There
were others in the refuge that missed the *material* benefits of being in
their own house and so made the choice to return home, usually coming
back to the refuge one or twice a month.

After I had left the refuge and been re-housed, I went back later
as a volunteer worker and often saw the same women and children
going back and forth, that had been there when I was a resident. One
woman, in her mid-twenties, told me that she really wanted to leave
her husband, but she hated living in the refuge so much that she always
returned back home. One day, while we were talking, she asked me
how long I had stayed in the refuge before I was rehoused, which was
around six months and she said, "See, that's the difference between
you and me, I couldn't stay in this shit-hole for that long, neither could
my kids, it wouldn't be fair on them. They like to have their 'things'
around them, home comforts, you know?"

She then asked me where I had been housed and I said I had a
two-bedroom flat on Botanic Avenue, Central Belfast, and that I loved
being there because it was so peaceful and safe, if there wasn't food
in the cupboards then that was my responsibility, no-one else's. My
children were happy, one was in school and the other nursery and
that I now had time to do the things I wanted to do, like study and
voluntary work. She commented that her husband only usually 'lost it'
at the weekend and although she didn't love him, she didn't want her
children to grow up without their father, so as long as he didn't start
on them, things would probably continue on the way they had done
for nearly three years.

For whatever reason, this woman was *telling herself* that the way
she existed was OK and was almost blaming her children for remaining
in this situation. At the same time she was *telling herself* that it would
not be 'fair' on her children to leave the family home and spend six
months in a refuge, in order that they could be housed somewhere

safe. Her children were witnessing the abuse and being forced to leave the family home nearly every weekend. I asked her if she thought this was fair, and that maybe she should ask her children what option they would prefer. When we have children it is our *responsibility* to keep them safe and to actually recognise what safe *is* for them. No child likes to hear their parents argue, let alone see one physically assaulting the other, and why should they have to become *unwilling* participants in something that they have little power to change.

I stayed married with Stuart for three extremely long and difficult years, leaving when my son was six months old, because I knew if I didn't, either he would kill me, or worse, I would kill him. When I spoke to people about Stuart, the moment domestic abuse was mentioned, people automatically took my side and even I blamed him for four extremely unhappy and abusive years. No, he should never have hit me and, once that had happened, it should have made me consider the choices available to me, which were to stay with him, or leave him. As far as I am concerned now, the first time he hit me I should have walked away, and if he came after me, then I should have informed my family, or the police or a friend who could have ensured that I was safe; I should have taken responsibility for myself. The thing is, I didn't, and this made me a participant in my own abuse.

There may be many reasons why a person stays with another who is abusive to them but, at the end of the day, it is still their *choice* to stay. My children and the children of the woman above and countless other children do not have the choice and I know without a shadow of a doubt, that in my choosing to stay with Stuart, my daughter was experiencing trauma from the behaviour of adults, who were meant to be responsible for her health, safety and wellbeing.

When we enter into any kind of relationship it must be on an equal plane, based on trust, without possession and with respect for that person's personal belief. All this crap about one being older or younger than the other, or differences of social status, gender, religions and so on, is nothing to do with whether a relationship will be good or bad, yet we set so much store by them. These are all labels, all of them.

When you meet someone, find out about *whom* they *know* themselves to be, not *what* they *think* they are.

Honesty is incredibly important in any relationship, and vital in a sexual one. If you are after a 'one-night stand' then don't bullshit that you want anything more and if you know that the other person wants nothing more than a night of passion, then don't agree to it if you know that this is not what you want. There is just so much bullshit going on and so many people, including myself, blame others for hurting them, when they themselves hand them the ammunition to do it. In other words they are hurting themselves!

One of the major contributing factors to relationship breakdown has to be possession and not just tenure of the person, but of their time, choice of friends, contact with their families and even their past. The thing is that we actually believe that this person, who has entered into a relationship with us has not, nor in fact could, agree to become an extension of the other, living their life at the other's dictate, liking everything that they like and wanting to spend every single second in that person's company. Yet *many* of us seem to think it does. If you have children, then I agree the responsibility for caring and supervising the children belongs to both parents (even if you have separated from each other), and if one parent goes out all of the time, leaving the other with an unequal share of that responsibility, then that is something that should be talked through. If, however, we are talking about two individuals with either equal responsibility for children, or no children, then things are a little different.

Many times over the years I have heard women complain about their partner's thoughtless behaviour and one of the greatest causes for complaint is 'timekeeping,' especially the time the partner returns home after a night out with friends. This is generally how the tale goes:

"Well it all started because he wanted to go out with his mates, and although I was knackered, I said I was hoping that *we* could spend a quiet night in together, get a DVD and a bottle of wine, and maybe have an early night. Anyway, so he says that if I'm knackered then I should have a bath and chill out a bit and he will go and get *me* a bottle of wine, cos he isn't feeling tired and wants to go out as he's been working all week, like I haven't! So, to be honest, I wasn't too happy about that, but he started to get all stroppy, saying I never let him do anything, which is such a lie because I always let him do what he wants. So, when that doesn't work, he starts to be all nice saying he will get me a 'Chinese' *and* a DVD before he goes, so I think to myself if I say 'no I don't want it' he'll just think I'm being awkward, so in the end I agree and he goes out and picks the stuff up for me."

"When he came back he started sucking up to me, saying how we'll do something next weekend, that he'll look after the kids tomorrow night if I want to go somewhere and all that kind of stuff. Well, I was having none of it and just didn't say anything either way. Then, when he's getting ready, he's all happy and trying to make conversation, like he's only doing it cos he knows he's going out, know what I mean? Anyway, he goes to give me a kiss before he leaves and I turned my head, so he kissed me on the cheek, and he asks *me* why *I'm* being funny with *him*, like he doesn't know or something."

"So, I ask him what time he coming back and he starts to get all cagey, saying he doesn't know who's going yet, or what they'll be doing and then he even had the nerve to say that it might be late, so as I'm tired I shouldn't bother to wait up for him! I thought to myself, oh no you don't mate, so I say to him, if he can't tell me what time he's coming back in then he needn't think he was going anywhere. So then he says he'll probably be back around 1.00am, so not wanting to cause a row I got up and went into the bathroom and started to run my bath. He follows me in and looks all sheepish and then says he's put my food in the oven and he'll try and get back for midnight and turns to go, so, I call him back and say that he better be back at 11.30 cos I'm tired and I don't intend to stay up half the night waiting for him. Anyway, he agrees and then goes.

"So, I have my bath and then eat my 'Chinese' and watch the DVD and then I dropped off to sleep for a bit and when I woke up it was

10.45pm so I thought I would tidy myself up a bit for when he came back, you know, to show him I cared. Anyway, I started to put on a bit of make-up and looked at my watch and it was 11.15pm, so I put on some chilled out music and lay on the sofa, expecting him to walk through the door at any minute. At 11.30pm he was not back. So, I made myself a coffee and put his ready in a mug for when he does come. Now it's 11.45pm and still no sign of him. By midnight I'm starting to get well pissed off and make myself another coffee. Then I call his mobile, but he's got it switched off and that really made me angry.

"By 12.15am I am pacing about, looking out the curtains to see if I can see him and then calling his mobile again, but it's still off. At 12.30am I start to get worried cos he knew I'd be waiting up for him, so I call one of his mate's mobiles, but that's off too. So now I'm starting to get really worried in case he's had an accident, or got into a fight or been mugged or something. Then, at 12.45am, I hear him coming down the path, so I just sit on the sofa and I'm fucking fuming. I can hear him struggling to get the key in the door and I think, here we go, he's too drunk to even open the bloody door.

"So finally he comes in and I can hear him creeping about, so when I hear him going upstairs I get up and go into the hallway and he turns and looks at me and has the cheek to ask me why I'm still up! Well that was the final straw so I let him know it. We ended up having a huge row and I made him sleep on the sofa. He's so fucking inconsiderate sometimes, didn't give a shit that I'd spent half the night worried that something had happened to him, I mean he could have called me, but he couldn't even be bothered to do that, do you know what I mean?"

Why is it that when we enter a relationship with someone, we believe that to mean that they only want to spend time with us and that their world must revolve around us and not themselves? So many relationships break down because of one individual believing that another should put aside their own interests, activities and individual freedom, to follow them around like some dependent puppy. Why do so many people expect this from a relationship? If we are never alone how can we ever get to know who *we* are and what we *really* want from life? How can we make ourselves independent in thought, deed and action, if we constantly depend on another to occupy our every waking moment? We all need space to be with *ourselves,* to develop our potential for brilliance and to enjoy the reality we call life.

The issue to do with 'timekeeping' is a prime example of this craziness and dependency on a particular person to make us feel we are wanted and belong. We rationalise our actions by saying, "Well if he loved me, why would he want to spend time with his friends?"

This is mad!

Think of something else you enjoy, say swimming. Now would you be happy to spend your entire waking hours swimming and nothing else? Imagine if every moment you were consciously awake you had to immediately jump into a swimming pool and swim. In the beginning you may well enjoy the experience and because you love to swim, you may wake up each morning relishing the thought of diving into the pool, but after a while, the novelty begins to wear off, and if you are forced to continue to swim every moment of every day, you would slowly begin to resent the swimming pool *and* all it represents. Instead of being an enjoyable experience, it becomes a prison that prevents you from experiencing all the other magical gifts this world has to offer. This is what it can be like when we enter a relationship with someone and if we compound that by not being authentic about who we are and what we enjoy then, what started out to be something good, slowly turns into a nightmare reality.

I have met so many women who are not honest right at the beginning of the relationship and then blame the other for their behaviour. An example of this from my own experience was when I was about 13 years old. I had a friend in school called Noelle, who had an older brother called Phill and the first time I saw him I thought he was gorgeous and this developed into a major crush. Noelle and I would often stop over at each other's houses, one Saturday night hers, two weeks later mine and so on, and I couldn't wait for the one Saturday a month when I would be her guest.

My experience of how good the 'sleep over' had been, would depend on whether I managed to see her brother or not and even though Noelle would have thought up things to occupy us, if Phill was at home, then I would make up excuses to stay in. I wanted to find out how I could make Phill notice me and so began to pay particular attention to his likes and dislikes, one of which was Arsenal football club. Now, I had absolutely no interest in football and as I had brothers who supported Everton and Liverpool football clubs, around me, I actually got totally fed up of hearing about bloody football. I remember that during this period we even had two goldfish named Alan Ball and Joey Royal, in honour of two Everton players of the time. It used to drive me crazy when the television was monopolised by my brothers, mainly over the weekend, when a variety of football programmes were broadcast and if I wanted to stay up, rather than go to bed, it meant watching something that bored me senseless.

So, when I found out that football was Phill's main interest in life, it should have given me a major warning that if I wanted to begin any kind of relationship with him, that football would be something he would, in all probability, continue to enjoy. I needed to accept and understand that and hope that there would be other interests that we could share jointly, when he wasn't enjoying his passion for the 'beautiful game'. The problem was that I never really got a chance to talk to him, so didn't find out what those other interests might be. The only way I could think of getting an opportunity *to* talk to him was to develop an 'interest' in football, so I started to pay particular attention to Arsenal football club.

The problem was that as I did not have a *genuine* interest in football, I found it hard to retain facts and information about the club and would spend hours trying to memorise the players names and positions. In my bedroom I started to put up posters of players, like Charlie George, to support my own emerging *belief* that I enjoyed the sport. I bought myself an Arsenal scarf and sewed an Arsenal badge onto my jeans and couldn't wait for my next 'sleep over' at Noelle's house, hoping that Phill would notice them and therefore, me.

I can remember arriving at Noelle's, all kitted out in my Arsenal paraphernalia early one Saturday morning and having a coffee in the kitchen, as we talked about options for the day. I wanted to ask her if Phill was in, but before I got the chance to ask the question; he came into the kitchen, having just woken up. He looked like a 'god' to me; bare-chested, bare footed, with tousled 'sleepy' hair. All I could see was him; all I could feel was him, almost as if we were the only two people on the planet. He looked at us and yawned, muttering 'hi' before opening the fridge and helping himself to some orange juice. Noelle continued to talk about possible activities that we could do, but I wasn't listening, I was just aware of the movements of her mouth, of gestures, but nothing more.

Then it happened.

I had tied my Arsenal scarf through the belt loop of my jeans and his eyes fixed on the red and white 'bait' dangling temptingly down the side of my leg. To make sure he got the message that I was also an avid Arsenal fan, I moved across their huge breakfast kitchen and stood by the side of the table, with my back slightly towards him so that he could see the club badge sewn onto the back pocket of my jeans. That did the trick and he spoke, "Hey Rose, is that a 'gunners' badge?"

I replied almost with disinterest, "What, oh yeah, Arsenal are brilliant, why who do you support?"

Inside I felt as if I had struck gold, the lure had worked and suddenly he had noticed me. The thing is, he hadn't actually noticed me, he had noticed his team's colours, but to me, that fact never registered.

My infatuation with Phill lasted a whole year and we did spend time together, well in my mind we did anyway, on the Saturday nights I spent at Noelle's house watching 'Match of the Day' together with, I might add, the rest of his family. While I watched the game all I could think about was 'us.' Throughout the match, my gaze would fix on him and fantasies would develop, whereas he never took his eyes from the screen.

Now imagine what would have happened if I had managed to entice Phill to want to get to know me better, by say, asking me out on a date. Maybe he would have invited me to watch Arsenal v Coventry at Highfield Road and maybe, if he did, I would have enjoyed the experience *because I would have been with him,* not for the actual football. Possibly we would have seen each other again and gone to other matches or sat watching the many 'football type' programmes on the TV, or I could have spent lazy afternoons watching him kick a ball about with all his 'footie friends' or got up early on at the weekend to watch him compete with his own team in the local league; who knows? But what I do know is this: I had absolutely no interest in football whatsoever.

During the 1966 World Cup, a particularly bad year for me, there had been an explosion in the growth of football mania, which continued into the 1970's and with it came 'football hooliganism' meaning that 'football' was everywhere; on the TV, in the papers, in the terrified town centres, bus and train stations, in playgrounds and parks, everywhere, and I hated it. Sometimes, when my brothers played the game with their friends, I would watch them, especially after 1966 as I was not supposed to go over the fields by myself, and would occasionally be asked to be the 'goalie' if they were a 'man' down, and no matter how hard I tried to get involved, it just totally bored me to the point that I would often get sworn at by my brothers for 'letting' goals in, while my mind was elsewhere.

Occasionally they would let me play a game called 'World Cup' with them, which involved one person playing the part of goalkeeper while the other players would represent individual countries. It was a kind of 'sudden death' competition where, if you failed to score a goal from a penalty kick, your team (meaning you), were eliminated from the competition. On all but one occasion of playing 'World Cup', my country was always the first to be purged.

Phill and I would not have stood a chance in any kind of relationship because *I was not being honest*; I was trying to be what I thought *he* wanted me to be. So, maybe after one or two visits to the stadium, I might have made some excuse *not* to go, the conversation sounding something like this:

Phill: (Cheerfully) I'm looking forward to the match tomorrow, aren't you?

Rose: (Hesitantly) Actually Phill, there is a gymkhana on that I would like to go and watch, and I thought, as we *always* spend our time doing something associated with football, that it might be good to do something different for a change. What do you think?

Phill: (Disbelievingly) What are you on about? Me miss the match, you've got to be joking!

Rose: (Petulantly) But we always watch the match. I just think it would be nice to do something else.

Phill :(Factually) But I always go to the game.

Rose: (Excitedly) Exactly! Why can't we do something else for once?

Phill: (Questioningly) But I thought you enjoyed it?

Rose: (Assertively) I do, just not every week.

Phill:(Factually) It's not every week Rose, it's just one day a week, not even a day, just one afternoon.

Rose: (Questionably) Yes, but then there is 'Match of the Day' and your league games and then midweek fixtures. It is always about football. Why can't we do something else for once?

Phill:(Uncomprehendingly) We do other things as well Rose so don't say we don't, anyway I don't know what you are complaining about, I mean we support the same team, it's not like I support Arsenal and you Chelsea or something. I don't understand you, but if you don't want to come then don't bother, I'll catch up with you after.

Rose: (Adamantly) And what? What will we do then Phill eh? I'll spend the entire evening listening to you going on and on about the bloody match. Why can't we do something *I* like for a change? Why does it always have to be about bloody football?

Phill: (A little aggressively) I thought you *did* like bloody football!

Rose: (Smarmily) I do, but not *all* of the time. Please Phill, let's do something different, something we can *both* enjoy for a change.

And with that, the cat is finally out of the bag and once it is, something has to give! If we are not honest then, as someone famously once said, 'the truth will out' and, when it does, many relationships will flounder.

Why is it that when we enter into relationships, we believe that we have to do *everything* together and that if we don't, then it means that we don't *feel* anything for each other? Why do we use 'cause and effect' to highlight our insecurities by saying things like, "But if you loved me you would want to spend time with me/ wouldn't want to go there or do this, or eat that or even *think* of something else!"

Why do two completely unique individuals, suddenly start to speak in 'we's' instead of 'I's'? So many times I hear one person in the relationship make comments such as 'we love to go shopping don't we, dear?' or 'we don't like that colour do we, darling?' What is that all about? Why do we get *so possessive* about our partner that we have to try to absorb them entirely into our own character, our own expression of who we believe we are?

Why make your self into something that is really a replication of another's exclusivity, and surely if we do this, then unique no longer exists. This is yet another way that we limit our selves. Instead of experiencing life and making our own independent decisions, we become the shadow of another's experience and thus, limit our own expression of reality.

There is something that we all need to understand about this life we are experiencing, and that is that *you* are the only person who can live *your* life and *you* are the only person that will be there from beginning to end. Parents may be there for some of the time, as might children and possible partners, but eventually they will move away to continue their own life experience, maybe in another form that we express as death, yet *you* will always be there. You cannot live your life through another person, you have to experience things for yourself and make your own evaluation; you cannot exist in anyone else's reality, only your own. Truth is *what* you are. So, let's remind ourselves of what truth means…

Truth, *trooth, n.* faithfulness: constancy: veracity: agreement with reality: fact of being true: actuality: accuracy of adjustment or conformity: that which is true or according to the facts of the case: the true state of things, or facts: a true statement: an established fact: true belief: known facts, knowledge.

Truth is *what you are.*

So, why do so many of us try to be something *we cannot be?*

When we are not truthful, especially with our self, we find life difficult to understand and experience reality as something we don't fit with. On occasions this can manifest itself in a physiological way, such as headaches, or tension and at other times it can be more psychological, and whether we experience it in one way or in a combination of differing ways, the message is the same, 'this is not truth, this is not myself'. And this is how your *self* is expressing the mismatch. It is the 5-sense experience of not being *truth.* The amazing thing is that this happens all the time and we often just ignore our *self* and continue to do whatever 'it' is. Let's think again about Phill and me. The first truth that springs to mind is that I didn't like football. Football did not give me any kind of enjoyable five-sense expression and often evoked experiences from my past that were unpleasant. If we then look at some of the other truths:

- I liked Phill physically and I wanted to get to know *him* as an individual and fantasised about enjoying spending time with *him,* in pursuit of this knowledge
- Phill liked football and expressed this through his physiology, emotional expression and time he spent involved with this activity

If I understand these statements of truth as the 'true state of things: known facts or knowledge', then to try to be something that was not *truth* meant that *I* was not *being* me, so not matter how much Phill believed that he liked me, he never really knew the true me.

Why do we give people ultimatums? Why do we say 'it's either me or them' or 'this or that'? Who do we think we are? Do we think they are we and we are they, or more cutely, two halves of the same body?

We are unique, every single, individual one of us is a distinct expression of 'truth' and cannot exist enjoying our five-sense reality by attempting to be anything less than 'truth'. If Phill enjoyed football, then I was 'wrong' to pretend that it was something that I personally enjoyed. I could have initiated a conversation with him about football and then told him of my love of horses and if we were individually enjoying the five sense reality of each other, then maybe we would have continued our conversation across many topics. If Phill then asked me to go to a game with him and I agreed, and consequently found that I did not enjoy the experience of the game, I could have told him and he could then make his own individual choice, whether to carry on going as he had previously been doing for years, or spend that time with me. That way we could both individually have enjoyed our 'time', together and apart.

If you know that someone enjoys doing or experiencing a particular thing, then why do we believe we have the right to prevent him or her experiencing that, just because we are in a relationship with him or her?

It's crazy, really.

We say totally ridiculous things like, "Oh he showed me how much he loves me by giving up his Friday nights with his mates" or "I know how much you love me now because you've stopped wearing those clothes."

Bullshit. That is limiting, not infinite possibility. You don't *own* a person; in fact you cannot ever *own* anything apart from responsibility and truth. How many times do we have to keep repeating the 'same old, same old', before we learn the lesson? How many times do we have to say 'he broke my heart' or 'I gave up everything for her', before we understand that only *you yourself* can break your heart. And that if you give up something that you enjoy, you will have enough resentment of the limitation inside you that you eventually make statements like, 'I gave up everything'?

If you are in a relationship and do not particularly like certain things about the other person's behaviour, then don't *experience* it. If it is a habit, say for example smoking, then you have to understand as clearly as you can, how *they* experience smoking. To you smoking may represent something smelly, dirty and anti-social, yet to them it may mean relaxation, time out and a brief high. When their experience of smoking changes into something that makes them cough, leaves them breathless and is no longer enjoyable, then if they want to try to break the habit, it is their individual choice, not yours or mine, or the government's, but their personal choice. You might want to expand their knowledge of the so-called dangers of smoking but ultimately, if you don't like it then you don't have to experience it. Move out. Move on. Get a life and stop trying to live someone else's.

We have to stop blaming other people all the time. No one can *make* you do anything, only you can do that. All my life I have blamed people for my experiences and, in not taking responsibility for myself, I never learned the lessons, or made myself acknowledge that I had other choices. This is my life and therefore my responsibility and if I don't like the five-sense reality of it then *I* have to change it and that goes through every expression of my reality.

Briefly look at 'global warming' and your belief around this subject. Do you really give a damn, or do you just go with the flow and rabbit on about how concerned you are about it all, while driving to the airport in your two litre car, before hopping on to a plane for a holiday in some tourists 'paradise' that has destroyed the local habitat? If you really don't give a hoot, then that is fine with me, just be truthful, don't bore me to death with how you can't stand the thought of the world you are leaving for your children and grandchildren.

I am truth therefore I want truth and need truth, to exist.

I remember about 15 years ago, my sister asked me if I wanted some tuna fish sandwiches that she was about to prepare, and knowing that I was vegetarian, tried to persuade me that eating fish did not mean that I was *not* vegetarian. She held up the can and said, "See it has a label which says 'Dolphin friendly'" and I replied, "Yes, but not very friendly for the poor tuna fish!"

Understand your truth and then live it. Don't jump onto someone else's bandwagon if it is not what you believe. Be your self, even if you are the only person who thinks that way. To quote Ghandi again:

'even in a minority of one, the truth is still the truth'.

Relationships need truth to exist and if truth does not exist, then neither does the relationship; instead it becomes an autocratic power game that destroys rather than develops. When we enter a sexual relationship we need to be true to ourselves before we can be true to anyone else. We need to spend time understanding who *we* are and what *we* want from life, instead of just latching onto the dreams and ambitions of another.

At the present time, I am involved in a sexual relationship with Mostafa and so far I have spent six years enjoying the experience of the relationship. I do not see him belonging to me, nor vice versa, I see myself in a relationship that I am currently enjoying but have made it clear that as soon as I wake up and think to myself 'I am not happy with this relationship any more' that I will walk away from it and Mostafa has said the same.

I do not want to experience life in a way that I am not enjoying because some culture, religion, government or bullshit piece of paper says that I am committed to this person for even a day, let alone eternity. If Mostafa wakes up tomorrow and says that he doesn't think this relationship is working out and that he would rather move on, then what the hell is the point in me trying to prevent that from happening? Would I be happy if the tables were reversed? No, of course I wouldn't.

In my relationship with my dentist, would I be happy if he said that he wanted to keep drilling my teeth even though it no longer served any possible purpose for me? No, I would be out of that chair the moment I got the chance, I wouldn't say, "Oh ok I'll stay, being as you get so much enjoyment from drilling my teeth!"

I would be gone like a shot, so why do we expect someone to stay with us when the pleasure has turned to pain?

I remember years ago, I met a guy called Neil and I thought he was totally amazing and I loved being with him. Then one day he told me that he didn't want to be my boyfriend any more and walked away. I was in such a state, crying, begging, pleading, and promising to do anything he wanted as long as he didn't leave me. Neil would not change his mind, so I decided to do everything in my power to get him back. I turned up at places I knew he was going to be, I sent him gifts and letters and generally bombarded him from every angle I could, in the belief that my behaviour would make him understand how much I loved him and in turn, love me back. Do you think it worked? Of course not, it had the opposite effect and he really started to get pissed off with me, until eventually I gave up, telling my story of how he broke my heart to all my friends.

Why on earth do we believe that we can make someone love us? We can't make anyone do anything. And it is so embarrassing for everyone, and those who don't squirm at the behaviour, have a good laugh about it with their mates, "Bloody hell did you see the way she was parading about, dressed up like a dog's dinner? What a stupid idiot, she looked so bloody ridiculous and I had to laugh when she tried to look so surprised that he was there. Right old 'bunny boiler' she is."

Once I went out with a guy who 'loved me more than life' and, at the start of the relationship, I believed I felt the same. After we had been dating for about three months my feelings towards him started to change. Things that had once seemed 'cute' now proved 'irritating' and then became 'annoying' and finally 'infuriating'. Where as once I had looked forward to being with him, my desire for the enjoyable parts of the relationship were being overshadowed by the anticipation of his annoying little ways. In the end it was hard to see any enjoyable parts and I realised that the relationship was no longer beneficial to me on any level, so much so, that even what I once considered 'happy memories' were now tainted.

I decided to tell him, in as nice a way as possible, that the relationship was over, but he refused to listen and repeated back to me words I had so recently said, declaring my everlasting, undying love for him. It was incredibly traumatic, with tears and accusations, and eventually with him proclaiming he would change. I gave in and remained with him, but nothing could awaken the passion and desire that I had once felt; the absolute reverse happened. Instead of looking forward to seeing him I began to make excuses, saying that I wasn't feeling particularly good, or that I had to study, and this only led to more accusations and disagreements, which increased my desire not to be with him.

After one particularly huge dispute I decided that enough was enough, so when we met up that particular day, I once again said that I couldn't stand it any more, nothing had changed, in fact things had got worse and I was ending the relationship. He responded by telling me of all the things he had done differently, just to please me, and how he was more attentive to me than he ever was and finally shouted, "What do you want? Blood, do you want blood?" and with that picked up a discarded ring pull from a can off the ground and started to twist it into a point and drag it across his wrists dramatically. I was horrified and pleaded with him to stop but he kept doing it saying that without me he was dead anyway.

In that moment I knew that there was no way back; I had to leave the relationship completely. I hated watching him in so much pain and in such an emotional state, but I also knew that together we would experience no real happiness, as I no longer loved him. If I had made the decision to stay, knowing the truth of my own self, I would have been the one to die. It was incredibly hard to walk away from him that day, but much easier than remaining with him.

By staying in relationships that are no longer of any benefit to us, we are also making what could be happy memories painful reminders, and therefore, no longer enjoyable experiences. When I think back to that time with him, I don't remember anything really good about the relationship. Even though, I am sure that we did have some very happy times; this is sad. When we take time to review periods of our life experiences, we should be able to visualise all of the enjoyable times instead of just having a series of 'failures' haunting us. All we get from that is a feeling of constant disappointments, which some people actually begin to believe, is due to their own personal failing. So many people believe that they are no good in relationships, they always go wrong, no one ever likes me, I always get dumped etc, because they can't visualise all the times they went right, or were liked, or were attached. To enter into a relationship, even if it is just for a single night, there must be some kind of attraction. It therefore follows that you attracted someone, and if you can do it once, you can do it again.

When relationships end, we are always left with some sense of regret and in many instances, especially if you are the partner who has been rejected, much time is spent lamenting the break-up. In itself this is no problem, but when we start to self accuse and feel hatred towards our self, then real difficulties can happen with our self-belief, self-respect and self-esteem.

* * *

First of all, let me make one thing clear. There is no *right* partner and no *wrong* partner in a break-up no matter how the divorce courts try to apportion blame. If we think back to my relationship with Stuart, it could be argued that I was beaten because I stayed, or, that Stuart beat me because I didn't leave. The point is that 'there is no such thing as failure only feedback,' and the feedback is a mechanism to learn. When my relationship with Stuart ended, many people were incredibly 'supportive' to me and my children and I thank them for their consideration, however it is also true to say that due to their compassion *I did not learn* from the feedback. Let me list some of the comments:

- No one ever has the right to hit another.
- He's just inadequate.
- How could he treat you like that?
- Violence should never be an option.
- If I see that bastard, I'll kill him.
- You're safe now; no one can hurt you.
- The poor kids imagine them seeing him do that to you.

- I'll bet you never trust another man again, will you?
- Oh you poor thing, how did you cope?
- And you stayed with him for three years and that's how he repaid your loyalty?
- All those years just wasted.
- You did nothing wrong.
- He was the one at fault, so don't you dare go blaming yourself.

All of the sympathy, which I might add, was very welcomed at the time, did nothing to make me look at *my* part in the abuse and my involvement was actually worse because it was directed at myself. When Stuart hit me the first time, it should also have been the last time. I shouldn't have been rewarded with tea and sympathy for allowing another person to abuse me and by *staying*, that is exactly what I did; I became a participant in my own abuse. When a relationship ends the last thing we actually need is the sympathetic ear of a well-meaning friend. They are going to tell you what you want to hear and not always what you *need to learn* to enable you to grow from the experience. Why do so many of us say, "I always seem to pick the same type" or "I must have the word 'IDIOT' tattooed across my forehead" or "I don't understand why this always happens to me."

It is because we are not learning and every single thing we do in life provides us with a lesson, we just have to acknowledge the learning and then we won't keep attracting the same type of relationship.

So many women who have experienced a 'domestic abuse' relationship, go straight into another one; I did myself, and refuges should start to work on the whole 'responsibility' issue so that future abusive relationships are prevented rather than offering unconditional support to the 'victim' without enabling them to learn from their own participation in the abuse.

We can be very selective when recounting our personal 'life experience' stories and the way to really support someone who has been through this kind of trauma is to let him or her see the *whole* picture rather than just the part. To really enable them to make the best choices for themselves in the future we need to expand the way they view their choices, so that they have more options. People will make the best choice they can at the time, so if they believe there is only one option, then they have no choice, if there are two possible options they may face a dilemma, but if they have a wide range of choices then suddenly there are endless possibilities.

Many women that I have spoken to over the years use the words, "I had no choice," when what they really mean is, "I didn't know what other choices were available to me."

I said it myself about Stuart when I was asked why I stayed with him for so long, but it wasn't that I didn't have a choice, I just didn't know what choices were open to me and, more importantly, didn't open myself to the choices. Taking responsibility can be difficult because deep down inside we believe that we are 'right' and the other person is 'wrong'; this confuses us making it problematic to accept that we had anything to do with whatever went 'wrong' in the relationship. There is no 'right' or 'wrong', just learning, and if we don't learn we will keep on repeating the 'same old, same old' until eventually we do.

Here is a way that you can really learn from relationship break-ups.

First of all you need to think of a particular relationship, either past or present, that you wish to examine.

Take six sheets of paper.

On three, write one of the following words 'PAST' 'PRESENT' 'FUTURE.'

Now write your name on another sheet, the partner on the next and on the final sheet write the name of the greatest 'counsellor' that you can imagine (this can be anyone living or dead).

Next, put the sheets out on the floor so that 'PAST' 'PRESENT' 'FUTURE' is in a horizontal line and the sheets with the 'names' are facing them.

Step 1: Think back to when you first met the partner. Watch the experience as if you are seeing it happening. Pay careful attention to everything that is taking place as if it is a movie. Look at the colours, the smells, and the sounds. Look at how you are behaving, your body language, and your words. You are watching the movie as if it was the present day.

Step 2: Step onto the paper marked 'PAST' and experience that first meeting as if it was happening right now. If the experience was in any way traumatic do not move 'into' the experience, instead continue to view it as a movie. Now step off the 'PAST' and stand in a neutral area and think of what you are going to eat later. This clears the association of being 'in' the experience.

Step 3: Step onto the paper marked with your name and talk about how you experienced that first meeting. Think about your initial impressions, your hopes and aspirations, and any particular intuitions or concerns.

Step 4: Now turn to the sheet marked with the partner's name and ask them what impressions they had of that first meeting. Think about the meeting from their perspective.

Step 5: Step on to the sheet marked 'PAST' and imagine that you are experiencing the 'movie' as the partner and that it is happening right now. When you have done this clear the association and think of the next holiday you are going to take.

Step 6: Step onto the sheet marked with the partner's name and talk about how 'you' the partner experienced that first meeting. Think about initial impressions, hopes and aspirations and intuitions.

Step 7: Repeat the process but this time visit the 'FUTURE' sheet for both yourself and the partner.

Step 8: Ask the counsellor for their impressions of where the relationship began and where it is headed for the future, looking at both partners. Stand on the sheet marked 'counsellor' and when giving 'feedback' to each individual they should face that particular sheet.

Step 9: Step on the sheet marked 'PRESENT' and with the knowledge you have gained express how you feel being in this relationship right now. Be aware of your physiology and emotions. Repeat for the partner.

Step 10: What have you learned about this relationship?

What have you learnt about yourself?

What responsibility do you need to accept to enable you to learn from this relationship?

How can you use this information to ensure that you do not need to learn the same lesson repeatedly?

At any time during this process you can ask the counsellor for their advice or guidance. Remember you are not here to point a finger of blame; that is not learning. You are doing this to learn about *you* and how to improve your chances of participating in enjoyable and pleasurable relationships. By 'blaming' the partner for everything you are abdicating responsibility for your own life, so you need only to focus on your own role, as that is where the learning happens.

If you do this with a couple of different relationships, you may become aware of patterns in your behaviour. Maybe you actually respond to negative behaviour and not positive, so when your partner has tried, in the past, to show his affection with compliments, you have ignored the behaviour possibly because you find it difficult to receive praise. However, when your partner is critical towards you, he or she gets a response. This is an amazing way of understanding 'the meaning of your behaviour is the response you get', so with the example above you do not know how to respond appropriately to flattery, so you ignore any admiring comments. Your partner wants to express their feelings by complimenting you and would like you to respond with some emotion. Neither partner's behaviour is eliciting the response they want. Your partner criticises you and you respond emotionally as you *do* react to negative depreciation. In future, to elicit an emotional response, the partner will use criticism and if the negative behaviour continues to reward them with an emotional response, he or she will use scorn more than flattery. Who do we afford blame to now? Who is responsible for all the arguments and disagreements?

In order to learn, we need to accept responsibility and to learn from our own behaviour and not point the finger at someone else. When we can understand our own behaviour, then we will be better equipped to begin to understand another's.

What about working relationships?

Well, there is as much misunderstanding going on in the workspace as there is in the bedroom. However I do think work has a specific 'donkey' strapped to its back that maybe sexual relationships don't and that is that as far as sex goes we are really producing something, by ourselves, for ourselves to share and enjoy with someone of our own choosing. The choice is ours, the effort and energy is ours and the reward is unimaginable pleasure. Work is slightly different. I believe that if each person was choosing their own business to run, and being creative in their idea and choice of business, people would be far happier and less fixated with the monotony of television and 'takeaways.'

Creating your own business is like watching your thought develop into an image and then become a reality, with you as the originator and creator. You are as dependent upon your business as it is on you and this creates a drive inside that is hard to compare to any other feeling. Maybe building your own home from design through to completion would be similar, but that does not bring in the 'people' side, the physical interconnection between producer, competitor and customer. Anyway, I believe that if each of us were in control of our own enterprise then going to work would become far more rewarding on so many levels, and challenging, bringing us more knowledge and awareness of ourselves as well as others.

So to get back to the point, most of us are working *for* somebody, and maybe we don't even get to see the finished picture of whatever it is we are working to create. Many of us are forced to work set hours and days, whether we are stimulated at those times to perform the job or not. Some of us feel trapped by the lure of the money and sit and dream of what *could* be, if only we won the lottery. There may be those amongst us who just sort of 'fell' into the job and even though it's not what they want to do, well, maybe in a couple of years they'll do something different. And of course there are those who are stuck at a certain level of progression, sick of being overlooked and remain stuck doing the same thing day in day out, in the hope that an opening will come along. When you think about your reasons for doing what you do for work, why do you *really* do it? For a moment of two I would like you to close your eyes and imagine that you could pass any course, or be given any amount of money, to do anything for a living that you wanted to, what would you choose to do?

For most of my working life, my job has involved working 'with' people, either social work, family support or teaching, and even though I have enjoyed each of them, there was always something missing. Maybe I didn't like the way things were managed, or I hated to see so much waste and sometimes it was about the staff and their aptitude and/or attitude to perform the task. When I thought about what I *really* wanted to be, for as long as I can remember I have wanted to be a writer, and here I am now writing for 'real.'

What did you come up with? Was it the same as the job you are doing now?

I would guess that a fairly high proportion of you would have chosen something other than what you are currently doing and even if I gave a very conservative guess at 50%, then even if you are one of that 50% it still means that you will be working with some of the remaining 50% who *wouldn't* choose the same job. This means that an awful lot of people are not living their dreams and ambitions, instead they are going to work, for however many hours, doing something *less* than what they desire to do. When you put that many people together and ask them to achieve something, lets say load pallets, half the 'team' don't give a damn about the pallets, some of them are dreaming of how they could organise this far better if it was their factory, others are doing as little as possible and some are doing the best they can, but wish they were somewhere else all the same. Do you think that this combination brings with it harmony and job fulfilment? No, neither do I.

When we go to work, we should know why we are going there, but we really don't have a clue about why most other people are there. We may think we do and they may tell us whatever they like, but we don't really know. I used to work with a woman once who always appeared to enjoy her job and when I met her six or seven years later she told me that she was singing on leisure cruises; I was stunned. She said that she had always dreamt of being a singer, and although she felt she was too old to be the 'pop' star she had once wished, this was her dream come true. I had always thought that she wanted to qualify as a social worker and when I mentioned this she said, "Well, you have to look willing, say all the right things because you think, well what else is there? Now look at me eh!" This is what I mean when I say that we can never really know what another person is thinking, or even if what they are telling us is true. So, in a work situation, the dynamics can already be lively, shall we say, before colleague conflict rears its nasty little head. Often a 'work' problem is the tiniest tip of a rather complex iceberg, so the way to sort out any kind of conflict with colleagues is to isolate the tip, so to speak. Leave the rest of the iceberg right where it is; don't even go there. If you look for 'problems' believe me you will find them, so instead look for solutions because that is what you will discover.

My other bit of advice is to deal with one 'iceberg tip' at a time. If I were still a manager, and one of my staff came in to see me with a complaint about another staff member and when I asked what the issue was, they began to rant on about half a dozen different things, I would be questioning their own skills and abilities around communication or assertiveness before dealing with anything else. If you have a work colleague who does something to you that you feel unable to address yourself, then take that issue to your line manager and get it sorted out; don't store it up for the day when you can take a whole trolley load of gripes with you. This is how resentment develops. For example, imagine a work colleague doesn't get some paperwork to you on time for you to complete the work you need to do. Instead of confronting them about it, ahead of time, you waited until the final half hour of the day it's due, before approaching them.

They say they won't get it finished for another 45 minutes, but if you are prepared to hang around they will be as fast as they can. So you wait because you don't want to confront them or get into trouble for not completing your part of the paperwork. A few days later, the same thing happens and you respond in the same way, only you are a bit more pissed off this time. Two days later, you go to the photocopier and find that the work you have been struggling to get printed off in time has been cancelled and your 'favourite' colleague mumbles an apology but says theirs was urgent. You decide that even though you are really angry you will 'let it go' for now as you have to get your work copied before it's too late.

The next day you arrive in work late, after a breakfast disagreement with your partner, and getting cut up by some thoughtless driver on the ring road. You sit down at your desk and look for a copy of a report you left out and after searching for a good ten minutes, ask your colleagues if they have seen it anywhere and one says that they saw your 'favourite' colleague reading it. That is it, the straw or, the 'tiniest tip' of the iceberg. The manager is then called, either by you, your colleague or another member of staff to sort out the dispute and instead of just clearing up the case of the 'missing report', the manager is suddenly dumped with a whole host of shit to do with photocopiers, staying late, etc., etc.

All of us need to be aware of how and *what* we are communicating when we are in work. We are supposed to be part of a team, no matter how big or how small, all working towards the same goal and sometimes it's a bit like watching the 1966 World Cup, only with Bobby Moore and a couple of others every now and then, just switching to the opposing team. Imagine how the outcome would have been so different if that had happened, yet this is what's happening in work all of the time.

Not only does it mean that whatever business we may be working in is losing productivity, very possibly quality and money, but also staff members are experiencing stress, meaning they are more likely to take time off work which again will not only affect the business but also the health of the individual *and* create an increased workload for the remaining staff; all this for the 'tiniest tip' of the iceberg. Maybe, if you had taken some responsibility for your *own* health and safety at work, you would have time managed your day more effectively so that when you had not received the paperwork the first time, at the agreed time, you could have approached your colleague to find out if they were on schedule and if not, asked if there was anything you could do to support them, after all, you are on the same team.

This is how teams are built that enable businesses and people to flourish. Take responsibility for your working experiences and look at how you can improve the ways in which you work, rather than creating an inner feeling of resentment that you then announce was the 'handiwork' of someone else. It is your creation, not theirs and maybe they were actually totally oblivious to how exactly they were supposed to be 'making' you feel. Remember the meaning of your communication is the response you'll get, so if your colleague does not get work to you on time and you did and said nothing, then nothing is what you will get. How are they supposed to understand that you were not happy with the situation unless you communicate that message?

We don't say what we should say to get the response we *really* want. If you *want* to be happy at work, then the best person to make that a reality is yourself, so start smiling because smiles are contagious, if you smile at someone almost invariably they will smile back. Be responsible for your emotions and listen to them. No one ever 'flies into a rage'; the rage is the end result of a whole series of events and emotions, never a single incident. If you are stressed about something that is unrelated to work, then acknowledge that fact, don't dump whatever disagreement you had with someone else on to a work colleague; it really isn't fair, and if you have an issue with a particular person, then mention it to them first before you annihilate their professionalism in front of other people. I have always thought that someone who is prepared to talk to me behind a colleague's back is also probably talking about me behind my back to someone else.

It is very dangerous to get caught up in colleague's disputes, as I have learnt to my cost. I thought that I was just offering some friendly advice and support to a work mate of mine who was having a difficult time with another worker, so when I was called into the manager's office to give 'my side of the story,' I was surprised to hear that I too, apparently, had experienced problems with the worker in question. I found myself in the awkward position of not wanting to comment officially on something I had been quite happy to voice my opinions about, unofficially. In some kind of bizarre twist, I was seen as the one 'stirring up trouble' when that was exactly what I had been trying to prevent and when I tried to explain that, it somehow just didn't sound right, "Well, no that is not exactly what I said, well, I know it may sound like that but I didn't mean it that way, if you know what I mean."

If we all took a little more responsibility for ourselves, communicated effectively and focused on being part of a winning team then the only issues we would have to deal with would be the tiniest tips of icebergs. Show your colleagues that you are approachable, friendly and a team player and that you want to be valued by your colleagues as much as you value them and remember that you control your emotions, nobody else, so if you want to have a good day in work then make it happen. You are in control of whether you do or don't, so if you are having a bad day you need to take a good look at why, and then change your perspective.

If you are not happy with the work you are doing, period, then do something about it. Here is a way that you can focus on your future:

Imagine that in front of you there are two chairs (if you can physically put two chairs in front of you, all the better). Both chairs are set in your future, five years from now. When you look at the first chair you can see yourself living the life you do now. The only difference is that you are five years older. Take a good look at your future self.

What do you look like?
How do you feel about your life?

Now sit on the chair and see the future through your eyes, as if you were experiencing it now. Talk about your job and the people you work with.

Have you progressed? Do you enjoy work more or less now?

Do you have any regrets?

If you could turn the clock back five years, what would you do differently?

Take in the experience for a few moments and then move off the chair.

Now, think about your favourite colour and imagine your mind is a blank canvas and write your name on the canvas using paint in your favourite shade.

OK, now look at the second chair. There is another future, as you did not stay in your current job, but instead followed your dream.

How does s/he look?

How does s/he feel about life?

Now, sit on that chair and see the future through your eyes as if you were experiencing it now.

How does this future feel?

Have you progressed?

Do you enjoy your work more or less than you did five years ago?

Do you have any regrets?

If you could turn the clock back five years, what would you do differently?

Take in the experience for a few moments and then move off the chair.

Now picture and elephant in your mind and colour it your favourite shade.

OK, now look at both chairs, with their future 'you' seated on them. What differences are there between the two?

Describe what you see, hear, feel, smell and taste.

You now have the option to choose which future you would prefer and to sit on that chair again and examine how you got there. Think about the life you are living, now that you have chosen your future. What do you do each day?

What do you enjoy most about your life?

How do you see the next five years developing?

What is your state of mind like now, do you feel happier, richer, and healthier?

Now you are going to rerun the events of the last five years so that FG can notice, and pay particular attention to all the information contained in the movie, which you will play on rewind at quite a fast speed. You will see the past five years flash past and you will catch glimpses of your journey, until you end up at the present day. This will be like playing a movie in reverse and you should ask your FG and the two future 'selves' for their guidance. Once you reach the present day ask your FG to provide you with all the resources you need to complete the journey to this future. Finally, thank your FG and both future selves for their support.

Your future is literally in your own imagination; whatever you want and wherever you want to be is open to you, the only thing preventing you achieving your dreams is you. You need to see yourself living the life that you want because once you create the thought FG can deliver the means. If you are not happy in work, then take responsibility, stop keep blaming other people for the way you feel, you are the only person responsible for the way you feel, no one else.

If I was to say to you that I could *make* you really laugh right now, would you believe that I could do it?

Let's give it a try; laugh.

Did it work? Are you laughing out loud, with tears in your eyes? If the answer is 'no,' then I have proved my point. If the answer is 'yes' then I want you to consider what and *whom* it actually was that made you laugh. Now, I would like you all to think about the last time you had a really good laugh. Bring to mind the event and replay it in your mind as if you were experiencing it again for the first time. See everything, the colours, the sounds, the smells, and feel the atmosphere. Now tell me about it. Probably, just thinking about the last time you had a really good laugh; a smile crept onto your face. If you were very visual with your recall of the event, you may well have burst out a small laugh and if you really relived the experience you will be laughing out loud. *You* can make you laugh, not me or anyone else. It is how you interpret events and experiences that make you laugh and how you experience humour. I have heard some comedians being called 'funny' yet when I have listened to their jokes, I have not found them to be in the slightest bit witty and the reverse is also true.

If you don't feel able to change your current job, then at least take responsibility for your *experience* of work. You don't have to like everybody, but you do have to work with him or her, so make the best of it. All relationships are basically of your own making, people will respond to the way you communicate with them, so if you want them to be good, set out with that intention and they will be good. Take responsibility for the way people connect with you, don't always point the finger towards someone else without first looking within, to understand your involvement, remember a relationship implies more than a single individual.

The most important part of any relationship is the part that happens even before it begins. This is the part where you *imagine* how you want them to be, in as much detail as possible. If you are looking for a sexual partner then imagine how they will look, what they will feel like, how they will smell, what kind of things they will talk about, the kind of places they would like to go. Picture yourself talking to them, laughing, kissing, holding and touching. Really get into the role; this is your perfect creation and you can choose all the characteristics, the attitude, the way they will be with you, anything, and it is all down to you.

Once you have created the perfect partner make the colours brighter, the images sharper, and the picture larger and then turn it into a movie and watch as your relationship develops. Everything about the movie should be positive; all words, all sounds, all feelings. This is your dream, where you control absolutely everything and feel so good about yourself. Once you have played the movie, see yourself put the film in a can, label it 'Perfect Partner' and store it in your mind in a filing cabinet marked 'Relationships', then shut the drawer. At least once a day, for thirty days, you need to sit quietly, maybe with some appropriate music playing in the background, and play the movie. After watching the film, ask your FG to provide all the resources you need to live the reality and then believe it will happen.

If you have a relationship at work that you would like to change, you can follow the same process, this time replacing the 'perfect partner' with the image of the colleague in question. You can imagine going for a 'truth talk' together along a pretty canal bank. Imagine that the sun is high in the sky and that wild flowers grow along the banks. It is an idyllic day and you have the afternoon to spend together. You can take food and drink if you like or maybe a dog, or even just walk yourselves. As you walk along you can ask each other any question that you like and the other will respond with a truthful answer. There will be no embarrassment or ill feeling, just a sense of relief that the air is being cleared and that you are both beginning to understand each other.

When you finish your walk, you will embrace one another in friendship and respect, knowing that you are part of the same team, working towards the same goal and thank each other for your honesty. You will put this film in a can and mark it 'Work Relationship (add the person's name)' and then store it in your mind in the filing cabinet marked 'Relationships.' Play this movie as often as you need to and remember to play it before you have any meetings with the particular colleague, it will enable you to enter the meeting feeling more in control.

Relationships are vital to our five-sense experience of being on this planet and without them, life would have no real purpose. Relationships totally dominate our lives, yet most of them we don't even see and of some we have no awareness of at all. We are not independent, we are inter-dependent and we need to acknowledge and give thanks to every single thing that contributes to our being and realise how much poorer we would be without them. Today, for example, I had some lavash bread with pure honey and it was so beautiful. The bread was baked in London to a recipe created in Lebanon and the honey was from Turkey, complete with honeycomb.

As I sat squeezing the honey from the comb with a warm spoon, I thought about all the bees that had worked so hard to gather the pollen from thousands of flowers to enable me to enjoy the experience of tasting the honey. This may come as a shock to some people, but Tesco doesn't magically produce the honey that they sell in their vast stores.

Look around you at everything you have and give thanks for it. Start to appreciate the things in life that you have forgotten contribute to your experience of *being* and start to see the good in the world; once you do the good will see you and life will become somehow more wonderful and amazing.

Relationships with people are only as hard as *you* make them. If someone is treating you badly then take responsibility and move on; if you don't then *you* are treating *you* badly and they are no longer to blame. Stop thinking about what you don't want, start believing in, and creating what you do want. Imagine it in as much detail as possible, see yourself living it and experiencing it with as many of your senses as possible and then believe that you will have it. Dreams do come true, but it all has to start with the dream.

The Bit Where I Rant About...
Sex

ex can be really fabulous and it can be a way to go beyond the five-sense experience of this existence into other realms of wonder and pleasure. So why do so many people have a problem with it?

I absolutely love sex and spend as much time in the pursuit of its manifold treasures as I can and I don't just mean the physical. There is so much to sex and when it is good, it's pretty damn cool, but when it is brilliant there is nothing on earth, in my estimation, to compare to the pleasures it brings. For many years I did not think like this; I was totally screwed up about it. The whole subject seemed totally confused as I didn't understand how I should be feeling, let alone how I should be reacting to it, or responding to others who may be commenting about it.

I guess that I was brought up in the twilight years of 'prudishness,' when it was considered to be something that was 'done' to women, rather than something they participated in, and if you did willingly co-operate, then you were considered to be 'easy meat.' So whenever I had sexual urges, it just confirmed in my own mind, what secret 'uncle' had told me I was years before that I was a whore. I can remember spending a lot of my time totally hating myself for enjoying sexual self pleasure or of becoming aroused by another human being and it was a tortuous battle that, over many years, caused me so much self-shame and self-loathing that at times I found it hard to understand who the hell I was and why I appeared to behave differently with other 'nice' people, especially females.

When I was a teenage woman no 'decent' girl would do anything with a guy before committing herself to 'have and to hold him' or vice versa, for eternity, so any woman who managed to 'get herself pregnant' (however that was meant to happen) was seen as *less* than other women in terms of *purity* I imagine, than those who managed to control their natural bodily instincts. And some of the most fervent believers of this crazy idea were women themselves, who would take great delight in ripping a 'sister' to shreds, calling her all the names under the sun, while at the same time thanking her lucky stars that it wasn't herself that the (her own) condemnation was directed at.

I remember when I was around 14 years of age, participating in a 'truth talk' with some of the 'rebel-type' girls from my school. This was a very secretive activity, which involved finding somewhere secluded and huddling together in a small group of maybe five or six girls, talking in whispers and sharing the odd cigarette as we answered questions 'truthfully.' Most of the time the questions were about boys, who fancied whom, but for the rest of the time the questions would be sexual. On this particular day one of the top 'rebels' was participating in the 'truth talk' and she seemed to be the one that most inquisitors addressed their specific question to, while the rest of us would wait with baited breath to hear her words of infinite wisdom. I recall that she spoke to us about her various 'sexploits' with some of the boys from a neighbouring co-ed school and I am telling you she had us all intrigued by what *really* goes on when you have a 'proper' boyfriend, meaning one you actually 'did things with' rather than just write his name all over your pencil case and meet occasionally to watch him play football.

All of us were in total awe of her, including myself, and the way she just talked about things so casually so, for example, when she was asked if she had 'done it with two guys at once,' she replied nonchalantly, while inhaling the smoke of a cigarette, "Yes, why not, I mean if you have done it with one, then what's the harm in two even if it is at the same time, I mean you will at some time do it with two, no one in their right mind is going to just shag just one guy in their life!"

I can remember a communal gasp move through the group a bit like a Mexican wave, and she just smiled and repeated the words, "Why not?" more as a statement than question. A few 'boring' questions later and it was her turn again and this time she was asked if she had ever given a 'blow job' and she replied, "Yep, quite a few actually, this one guy, you know the one that hangs out at the youth club on his Lambretta? Well, I did it to him until he came."

The rest of the group were totally shocked and disgusted, pulling faces and making noises to indicate their abhorrence of such things, then one of the group asked, "Did you swallow it?" and when the top rebel nodded she asked excitedly, "Oh my God, really, what did it taste like?"

The 'top rebel' became, to me, the 'top bullshitter' when she replied, "Actually it was quite nice really, a bit like honey, but not as sweet if you know what I mean."

In an instant I hated her; I knew she was lying but I couldn't say anything without making the others aware of *why* I knew she was lying and thus exposing myself as a whore. Instead I silently got up and walked away.

For many young girls, this is how they learn about sex; through so called 'truth talks' and it is a very sad indictment on how we prepare our children for sexual relationships. Some may say that it is a better method than the use of ignorance which, it is also sad to report, has been the technique utilised over the centuries, especially in Western Europe, but I think both are equally objectionable. I think that a person's sexual identity is of equal importance to their social distinctiveness and that to develop *who* you are or what you *want* to be, each of us should be made aware of all the choices and options open to us, as it is only in this way that we can have greater flexibility in the way we lead our individual lives.

If you look at the differences between women and men with regard to sex, it comes as no surprise that the minds of men are full of it, while women often see it as a necessary evil that has to be endured in order to experience childbirth. The way that sexuality is expressed to males is very overt and 'in your face' with magazines and clubs ready and willing to encourage men to 'spread their wild oats' as often as possible, even if that entails nothing more than a quick wank over a girlie magazine. Yet women are not encouraged to express themselves in a sexual way and, should they dare to try, are often ostracised from the rest of civilised society. No one talks to girls about masturbation and of how to pleasure themselves, and because no one does, girls either remain ignorant, or are disgusted with themselves for doing such things.

Young girls are brought up, in the main, on fairy stories and, whether they are written by Brothers Grimm, Sugar Magazine or the lyrics to a Backstreet Boys song, they are all fairy stories. The important thing is that they are mainly auditory; they are words that we hear. We listen to the meanings; we store the words with as much, if not more detail, than the vision. With young men it is usually more visual. Magazines display overtly sexual images whether the magazine is about fishing, biking, computers or photography. The words are also backed up with lots of images, graphs, and technical data so that they can see what is happening. Men tend to store the visual image first and then auditory, so they *see* what is meant. This, obviously, is not always the case and it can be different in each gender, the point is that you have to understand the way you communicate sexually and be aware of your partner's preference, otherwise you could be in for some major misunderstandings. To find out which your preference is I have listed a few questions to help you on your way.

You tick either 'red' or 'green' and then add up your totals for each.

1. When you are focusing on a task, do people have to touch you or repeat themselves before you can hear what they are saying? Yes=Red No=Green.

2. When you recall an argument you had with a partner, do you remember what they said to you in detail? Y=Green N=Red.

3. When you get upset about something do you like to talk it

over with someone? Y=Green N=Red.

4.   If the partner of your dreams were in front of you now would you a) imagine them totally naked or b) imagine the things you would talk about? a)=Red b)=Green.

5.   Do you a) show how much you care or b) say how much you care? a)=Red b)=Green

*   *   *

The more red points you scored the more visual you are and the more green, auditory. This is important to understand as once you are aware of the way in which each of you communicate, the easier it is to enjoy the differences between you.

An example of misunderstanding could be that the male in the relationship is visual and so shows his partner how much he loves them by doing things, such as putting up shelves or buying a present. If the partner is also visual then everything is hunky dory, however, if the partner is more auditory then they are more likely to want to hear how much you love them, so an hour spent talking to them about why you love them and what is so special about them would be more appreciated than an hour spent purchasing a present. Of course the ideal in any relationship is to be aware of your partner's preference and, if you are different, then do a bit of both, so buy a gift *and* tell them why you have bought it for them. Many men have a great deal of difficulty doing this. When they give the gift their partner will often ask, "Oh that's lovely. Why did you buy me that?" and the man will reply, "No reason."

I once visited a couple where the woman in the relationship was very auditory and said to her partner, "You never tell me that you love me, never, can you remember when you last said it?" and he replied, "I put up those shelves that you wanted and I bought you that CD that you liked" and she answered, "Did you hear what you just said, I am asking you when you last told me you loved me and you mention bloody shelves and CD's, I'm not talking about that, you just never listen…" and he interjected with, "And you never see!"

If we want to have a good sexual experience then begin by understanding how you communicate, otherwise you might not get the response you really want. Sex begins by knowing *you*.

How many of you have really had a good look at your own body and by that I mean in the way you would examine a leaf from the garden. You need to really explore your own skin, touch yourself and tell yourself how magnificent you are. Look at the contours of your body from all different angles, use as many mirrors as possible and tell your self how sexually fabulous you are. Explore your own genitals and feel what makes you tingle or feel good. When you have a bath or a shower, don't just do it as a routine method of getting clean, really enjoy your body and care for it, literally shower love and adoration on it. Eat food with your hands and lick the tastes and textures from your fingers, really understanding the nature of the experience, not just the taste and aroma. Sit naked to read a book or to listen to some music and start to get comfortable with being you, not some dressed up, and therefore hidden, clothes horse.

Each one of us is a unique masterpiece that can never and will never be replicated; that is amazing and worth celebrating. When you experience your own body, think of the wonder of it and how this is your physical expression of being. Once you are comfortable with being with you, then you can open yourself to another. So many women are so hooked into what they look like, and what is *wrong* with their bodies that they can no longer see all that is *wonderful* about them. When they do get into a relationship, they want to hide the very thing that they are supposedly offering to another person, themselves. Some may try to keep themselves covered up, or hide under sheets, or turn off the light or one hundred other excuses that prevent the partner from actually *seeing* their bodies.

Most men are visual. They have been looking at images forever and a day and now they want to look at you, totally naked preferably, and from every conceivable angle, and while they are looking they will probably not hear a single word that you are saying. They are absorbed by the vision of it all. I have watched quite a lot of pornography over the years and what always strikes me is that men do not seem to notice any 'faults' in the women in these movies, and even if they do, it does not interfere with their enjoyment of the entertainment, whereas women I have watched these movies with will always comment on the state of the porn star's teeth, cellulite, fingernails, toes, ass, boob jobs or tacky tattoos; they don't focus on what the men focus on.

If you are watching porn with your partner, don't keep pointing out the 'bad stuff' instead see it as a sexual, rather than a comparative or competitive experience. The whole porn industry is based on visual experience and even when it is in written form it is incredibly sexually graphic, so that the image of what is being said is very clear in the reader's mind. If you are spending a quiet night alone and you want to experience sexual arousal, then the chances are that you will have to sexually stimulate yourself and this always occurs *in your mind,* so if you want a quick orgasm then you are not going to want to read about the colours of the trees, or the intricacies of the layout of the city; you just want to cut to the chase and read explicit sexual content to enable your imagination to run riot.

If you are in a relationship where your partner does not talk to you enough, or express him or herself verbally, then you should ask yourself how visual you are being towards them. Sex needs to be expressive, it should never be something that is done to one by another, and it should be an expression of your sexual self, which is shared and enhanced by another person or person's sexual expression, or 'sexpression.' If you know your sexual self then you enable another to understand how to pleasure you and vice versa.

Too often we play games with one another, not mentioning what it is that we like and then get mad when they can't guess. For example, if I were to offer to buy you an ice-cream now and bring it to you as a token of my friendship and care, if I don't know what particular brand you like then generally I would buy the flavour that I like, at least that way if you didn't like it then I could eat it myself and at least one of us would enjoy it. I might take a wild guess and buy you 'rum and raisin' flavour and if I am extremely lucky I might get your taste buds excited, if not, then I will know not to buy this flavour the next time. I might get it totally wrong altogether, as you may hate ice-cream and you might even think I was being thoughtless by bringing you something that I liked, without finding out your preferences.

If you want another person to know what you like then tell them, and if you don't, then don't feel rejected when they don't guess right. About the ice cream, one other very important thing we should remember is, at least I bought it for *you* and do you know what that means? It means that at that particular time you were in the forefront of my mind; I was not thinking about work, or my house, or going to the bank, in that moment *you* were the focus of my thoughts. Always remember that; it is the thought that counts, and whoever brings you anything, be it ice cream or fluffy handcuffs, was thinking of you.

Another difference between auditory and visually stimulated partners is their physical involvement in sex. Auditory people will be having a conversation with themselves and, if their partner is not auditory, often these conversations can divert them from the physical experience of what they are doing. So, as I am an auditory person I will give an example. When I was with a partner, who was extremely visual, I did not like him to see me naked and would often jump under the covers before he came into the bedroom, or turn the light off before I got undressed. When we lay together I wanted him to say wonderful things to me, but he never did, so both of us became frustrated with our sexual encounters in our different ways. When we had sex I would tell myself what he was doing and imagine the words he would be saying to me, but when they never transpired I would start to have other conversations with myself about totally unconnected things, like the children, or my dogs or how tired I was.

I can only imagine that he must have been trying to visualise what my body looked like and if he couldn't then maybe he visualised a body that he could imagine. Our sex life was totally crap to the point where it started to become nothing more than a release of sexual tension, rather than an act of sexual enjoyment. When I try to understand why

I behaved like this it is actually a combination of many things, from my upbringing, to the media, from my own critical analysis, to a belief that to show my body it should be nothing less than perfect. The thing is that he didn't care about those things, he just wanted to experience it visually, to see what he was touching or tasting or making love to.

Once you have mastered the art of being naked, and are comfortable with it, then enjoy being naked together. Get naked as often as you can, not just for sex, or at least make it part of your sexual experience. This way you can talk to each other while you are naked and *not* having sex. Make some food together in the kitchen and play some music and dance close to each other. Enjoy the freedom of being as nature intended you to be, totally free of all inhibitors and inhibitions.

A few years ago, I decided to hold a 'Valentine's Party' for four other couples. Valentine's Day had never been a day that my partner and I really celebrated; it was always more a day for disappointment or misunderstanding, so I thought that this might be something that we could plan together and look forward to. I can remember paying so much attention to detail and secretly finding out each person's birth time, date, place etc and having compatibility horoscopes compiled for each couple, as well as ordering sixty silver and red helium-filled balloons which festooned the ceiling.

My partner helped me prepare the food which we had agreed should be consumed with fingers, and then to add some interest, with someone else's fingers and, if you wanted to drink, you had to ask someone else to hold the glass to your mouth while you drank. Everybody enjoyed this part of the evening and different friends would be feeding each other, regardless of their gender or whether it was their own partner or someone else's. There is something so intimate about sharing food and drink in this way, something observant and diligent, and it makes you feel cared for. It also meant that we were communicating verbally and visually, as to feed someone involves noticing and asking them questions, or discussing tastes and textures. Try this for your self with your current or next partner and if you can do it naked; sex, food and nudity are a perfect combination.

Another misunderstanding that happens all too frequently during sex is the accusation of being 'taken for granted,' when often this is *not* what is meant, by the partner's actions. I can't even begin to count the number of times I have heard women utter this charge and if men don't say the actual words, it's because they vote with their feet and go to someone whom they believe *doesn't* 'take them for granted,' even if that person is a sex worker, or a one night stand.

The first thing that we need to understand very clearly is that *no one* can take you for granted unless *you* give them permission to do so. This again, is about your responsibility for your self and your five-sense experience of reality. If your partner wakes up with an erection and decides to just 'slip it in' while you are still half asleep and you permit that to happen, then you are communicating to them that it is OK. There is no way that this kind of reaction can communicate that his deed is making you feel like you are being taken for granted.

If you communicate with your partner *then they will know* that this is something that you are not particularly ecstatic about and maybe they will then feel able to articulate to you why they feel the need to 'sexpress' themselves that way. If you cannot talk at this level then really there is little point in you continuing your sexual relationship. You have to take charge of your own experiences and should never force the blame for lack of sexual enjoyment on any other person. If you meet someone and have sex, and it's crap, then tell him or her what you like, listen to what it is that they like and decide whether to do it again, if not, then take responsibility and move on.

When people are involved sexually with another person they can often become possessive to the point that if their partner so much as gazes at another individual they are berated for it endlessly. The thing that amazes me is how anyone can believe that they cannot look. Sex is everywhere, on the TV, in the newspapers, magazines, billboards, shop windows and even walking down the streets; how can they not look? The whole point of using sex to sell or advertise is to *get* people to look and it is a *natural phenomenon* that happens almost automatically. We have a shop in a busy street and I often watch the men who gather outside, most days, in the village square. They generally gather on the edging walls of the raised flowerbeds, most sitting hunched over talking, until a woman comes into view, then their physiology changes, as does their engagement in conversation. When one of the group catches sight of the woman, he will generally show he has noticed her by raising his head and then straightening himself up a little. He may then nudge his companions, if they have not already been alerted by his altered state, and make some comment.

If the others are also interested in the *look* of the woman they will all alter their body posture and may even begin to groom themselves; talking is now minimal as the males focus their attention on the female until she passes from their immediate view and, once this happens, they will return to their conversation and original physiology. In some cases I have seen men move physically to a more advantageous position, becoming oblivious to what their friends are discussing until the woman has completely disappeared from sight. It is natural to look. Yet so many people who are involved in a relationship genuinely believe that their own particular partner has absolutely no interest in looking at any other individual, and that if they did, then this would be almost tantamount to infidelity.

Total crap! *Everybody looks including you.*

The reason that I know this to be true is because for you to accuse the partner of looking, then you must have looked too! And do you know what, in most cases the woman *especially* will actually notice the 'object of desire' before the partner does; it's called 'checking out the competition' and we all do it all the time. So, it is incredible to think that an awful lot of us blame and berate our partners for doing something that we have actually done before they have!

Of course we need to look and, if we like what we see, then we may try to emulate either their dress sense, or their demeanour or some other aspect of what we visualise by looking at them. On some occasions we may take in the whole picture and then, within seconds, have found the flaw in perfection, just in case our partner should decide to glance at them. We can then berate them *and* point out how far from perfection the person they have espied really is. A further reason for *looking* is that we are constantly assessing our current situation, gaining feedback from yourself that the choices we make are appropriate and still ecologically sound, so you automatically glance at the person and then continue on your way, unless of course your *self* tells you that this individual is worth pursuit.

Jealousy is not a good emotion and it is like a disease that flows through your entire being and in some cases, totally paralyses the sufferer to the extent where their whole life revolves around suspicion and accusation, until finally one partner leaves the relationship. Jealousy of *anything* will achieve nothing apart from harm, mainly to the person emitting the emotion. Jealousy and sex do not fit well together. I know of people who are envious of their partner's ex-partner's! How crazy is that?

Imagine that you are with someone who has recently broken up with a partner they had loved for a number of years. It would be expected that if they had loved that person, then quite a lot of their recent history would involve the mention of the ex-partner's name, unless of course they avoid talking about the person all together. Now, for whatever reason that particular relationship has ended, they have chosen to be with you and maybe, when they are talking about past events, they may mention the other person's name, or talk of how they felt about that person. What is there to be jealous of? You are meant to care about your partner; at least enough to enter a sexual relationship with them, so why would you *not* have wanted them to have experienced good, enjoyable relationships? As I have said throughout, all experience is learning, and if they have previously been in good, enjoyable relationships, then they have learnt many things to bring to *this* relationship. It is wonderful to have experienced the feeling of love and passion and maybe this is what you are hoping to experience with them, so you should feel safe in the knowledge that they have an awareness of these feelings and emotions.

Sex should always be honest for it to be pleasurable to the max. Trust is really the key word here; trust your self, trust yourself, trust your body, trust your intuition, trust your emotions, trust that this is what you really want and if you don't trust at *any* of those levels then don't do it.

I am saddened when I read through the 'Agony Aunt' pages of any magazine to hear young women asking whether they should have sex with their partners or not. I mean, what kind of education are we giving to our children when they feel the only way they can make an informed decision about something as intimate as sex, is to ask some so called 'auntie' who you know absolutely nothing about, and worse still, who knows absolutely zilch about your child and their situation.

Our bodies are armed to the hilt with intuitions, perceptions, physiological changes, and emotions, all of which are informing us of the choices available to us. We should be teaching our children how to understand themselves and to be aware of *their* responsibility for the choices that they make. We should be informing them of the power that they have to control their lives, not taking it away from them and offering them some 'auntie' in a magazine to advise them; they should observe the advice their self is giving them and we need to show them how.

Another thing that people are concerned about with regard to sex is their own private fantasies and how to express these to a sexual partner. Fantasies are just that; your own miraculous and brilliant movie theatres, where you get to allocate roles, write the script and direct the action. In your fantasies anything can happen, anything you can possibly imagine can take place and you can experience it as if it is real, or as real as you can imagine it to be. There is absolutely *nothing* wrong with fantasies. Fantasies can only exist in your own mind, and when they leave the mind and are acted out for real then they become actualities and that means that the people involved are no longer actors and have the right as such to *choose* to be involved, their level and role of involvement and the responsibility of such.

Fantasies are actually a good way to explore how you might *experience* a particular sexual event and can be useful in developing self-esteem, especially for men who are experiencing erection issues. If you are shy, or nervous, fantasies will allow you the space to practise skills to overcome these feelings. Now, some people might get a little fractious about imagining anything of a sexual nature, maybe believing that they will automatically become a 'filthy pervert' or something similar, well, I just want to ally that fear as best I can. Many of us have read books and when we read the words on the page we change the written word (2nd transformation) into images and symbols (1st transformation), so if you have read a book that included anything of a violent nature, or even murder, especially if written in through the 'eyes' of the murderer, then you have fantasised. The thing is that most of us, in fact the absolute majority, will have no worries that we will go and commit the atrocities described, which we have experienced in our minds. Problems only occur for people who have some difficulty defining the difference between reality and fantasy.

In order to understand what a sexual fantasy experience is like you can now create one. Remember that your fantasy can be any place, any time and with any one; it is a bit like daydreaming and you are in control, even if being in control is *not* what you wish to fantasise about. To do this in a way that is honest, you need to rid yourself of all the labels and boundaries that society, friends, family and *you* allow to restrict your individual choices.

Make sure that you are alone and make yourself very relaxed and comfortable. You should not need to use music or adjust the lighting because this sexual fantasy will exist in your mind, where you have the capacity to play any kind of music, or any other sounds you wish, and the lighting could be stars, sunlight or dark dungeons; the choice is yours completely. Once you are relaxed and comfortable start to think about sex in all its aspects and as you continue to think about sex you will find that the thoughts evoke different reactions to the way you are feeling. If something doesn't feel right then let it go and conjure up some different thoughts until you find one that makes you feel aroused and, once you have done that, the rest is up to you.

Many people feel guilty about their fantasies, as they don't 'fit' with how they perceive they *should* think about sex, so instead of enjoying their unlimited imagination they put brick walls up and refuse to look at what they may really desire. The thing is we all fantasise, we all dream and we all imagine and if we didn't we would find life incredibly difficult. Even reading these words now, you are using your imagination, to fit with your sense of reality and if we were unable to do that, then the written word would serve no purpose.

Have you ever read a book and then really looked forward to seeing the movie and feeling disappointed because the two didn't match in your head? If you have then you are not alone, and no matter how many people have read the book, all of them will have their own personal images; no one who has read the book and then gone to see the movie, will believe the visual interpretation of the book, to be the same as theirs. The only person who truly knows what you desire sexually is you, so if you have no idea, because you shut out all the thoughts and images that you believe you shouldn't fantasise about, then really, how can you complain when your partner gets it so wrong? To find out what turns you on sexually, and safely, you need to experience it in your mind first so, put all your inhibitions and limitations aside, and you can try anything you wish. The greatest universe is the one that exists in your mind, because you can make it whatever you want it to be; if you want to have sex in your mansion, or on the Orient Express or gazing up at the stars in the London Planetarium then visualise it, create the scene and away you go.

Once you begin to understand how you react to various sexual stimuli then you are in a better position to have all, or at least part, of your fantasies transform into realities. You, once again, have to take responsibility for the limitations of your sexual pleasure and stop blaming 'him' or 'her' for not knowing how to turn you on. When you are in a sexual relationship you need to be able to communicate your desires in a safe way to your partner and one of the best ways of doing this, is verbally. Spend time to get to know each other, talk about your fantasies and notice how *they* react, this way you don't arrive with a whip and handcuffs while they have dreams involving romance and chocolates. If you have no common ground there really is little point in continuing the sexual relationship because you will not be experiencing the sex you really *desire* which will cause untold stress and tension.

Anticipation is a great aphrodisiac and expectation is the creation of the mind. When you think about what you really want, the desire is so strong that sometimes the *thought* of what is playing out in your own mind, is far more enjoyable than the actual experience. This being so, doesn't it make sense to find a sexual partner who can make the reality at least match the anticipated encounter? Why bother to have sex with someone who is not on the same wavelength as you? There is nothing worse than waking up next to someone after a night of anticipated passion and thinking, "Well, that was nothing like I expected," especially if it encased in a crate of guilt. The only thing I can imagine that could be worse is to wake up feeling the same way year in and year out, waiting for the day that your fantasises become manifest, even if it is not with your current partner.

Although most men are incredibly visual when it comes to sex, most are more than happy to *listen* to sexual fantasies because they will picture them in their minds, making them visual and real, so if you are the partner that likes to talk, then talk, and make it as visual as you can and in this way your partner will not only get stimulated but also be aware of what *you would like* to experience. This is why Internet 'chatrooms' are so popular with both genders, because people can 'hide' behind a virtual identity and visualise who and what they want to be.

During my own years of incredible sexual frustration I would spend hours chatting online to people I hoped I would *never* actually meet, simply because they would write the words that I needed to hear to get me turned on. I also had a friend who lived alone and who didn't want to get 'involved' with another man until her children were older as she had heard so many horror stories of paedophiles taking advantage of lonely women to gain access to their children. She would put her kids to bed at 7pm and then, once they were asleep, she would have a bath, put on her make-up, dress in sexy underwear, open a bottle of wine and start surfing. She believed that cyber sex was the best sex she ever had and she could move from partner to partner almost simultaneously, without feeling the slightest trace of guilt. She told me that she has enjoyed 'kinky threesomes,' lesbians, orgies and a whole host of other cyber sexual fantasies that have felt so real, that she has no intention of doing them anywhere other than her cyber world where, she says, she can do and be whoever she wants.

Another friend, also a single parent with young children, shares a romantic glass of wine twice a week with a 'man' she has been speaking to for over two years! She says that they have sipped cocktails in Manhattan, trekked across the outback to sample Blossom Hill and ignited their passion with Champagne in Paris. Never once has she actually spoken to this 'man' but she says she has had better sexual experiences with him, than anyone else ever. He tells her what he wants to do to her and what he would like her to do to him and that makes her totally horny.

Both of these women are exploring their sexual imaginations in complete safety, with total responsibility and getting an immense amount of pleasure from the experience. I should add here that responsibility is yet again the key word as there are some Internet users who have a 'hidden agenda' when it comes to the pursuit of a partner, but acting responsibly, much as you should in any kind of relationship means that you are in control. Many people are put off cyber sex because of all the imagined fear that the web is only used by sexual deviants, yet those same people think nothing of crossing a busy road, even though there are a fair amount of dangerous drivers. Why should this be? The reason is because when they go to cross a road they are aware that most people have respect for human life and would not dream of actually running another human being over, in much the same way that most Internet users would not dream of abusing a child, so they keep a wary eye on all the drivers, but don't allow the imagined fear of the irresponsible driver to prevent them from getting to where they want to be.

Using the Internet to explore your sexuality will remain safe as long as you remain in control; if you don't like what is being said, or suggested, then click 'ignore' and the person will not bother you again and, if they try to, then report them to their Internet provider (the email address is all the information they will require) and they will take their responsibility seriously, and make sure that you are not bothered again. Also never divulge your address, as I have once came across a woman who was burgled by her Internet 'lover' when she gave him her address after previously informing him of the hours she worked.

If you have children then their safety is your responsibility so you must ensure that no one, no matter who they purport to be, has any kind of access to your children. Remember in cyber space you can be whoever you want to be and so can everybody else. If you should eventually decide that you would like to participate in any form of Internet relationship, or meet your cyber partner in reality, then here are some pointers:

• Never give your address or postcode. In fact it is safer to be quite general about where you live, i.e. Near Coventry, rather than, Rugby.

• Never give out your family name, choose something different. The reason for this is that many of us are listed in the telephone directory and our details can be easily accessed.

• Meet your 'date' somewhere public and if you can, ask some friends to mingle with the social group, until you give them 'the nod' about how to proceed. There are a couple of reasons for this, the main being to keep you safe however, should you get into any difficulties, then they will be there to offer instant support. Most of us do not want to get involved when we see what we *perceive* to be a couple, having a disagreement, so a couple of friends who know the score, will react the moment they see your discomfort. Another reason is that *should* you decide to leave with the partner, to go 'wherever,' your friends will have lots of relevant, factual information to pass on to whoever might need it. Make sure you give your friends as much information as you can about your 'date,' particularly the email address, make and registration plate of any vehicle and any mobile number. This is your responsibility, so make sure you look after *you*, before anyone has to.

- Take only the basic essentials with you. Do not advertise your wealth or laden yourself with a laptop, overstuffed wallet or festoon yourself in gold. Thieves do not wear labels *or* fit any particular stereotype. Many men have been exploited remorsefully by cyber partners they have met, and leave themselves open to exploitation by those who use the Internet for their personal financial gain.

- Don't be persuaded to 'go back to theirs,' no matter how attractive it might sound. Keep the mental fantasy going until you are as sure as you possibly can be that they are what and who they say they are.

- Remember that meeting someone through work, a friend, a social event or through local connections, often means that you have more information about the person and their local habits i.e. place they go for a drink, food, walk, swimming, dentist etc. On the Internet people can be from anywhere, they may even turn out to be your neighbour! This happened to a guy I use to work with; he had actually been having cyber sex with his neighbour and didn't find out for nearly two years. He thought she was a 22-year-old French student studying in Edinburgh and, as she returned home to her parents during university vacations, he fully understood how difficult it was for them to actually meet. In reality she was in her late forties and worked in a chemist. The awful truth for him was that she was aware of who he was and continued to participate. Although some people may find this situation humorous, he certainly didn't, and was actually off work for a while and eventually moved home, as he no longer felt comfortable living anywhere near her once he had found out her true identity.

- If you do decide to go on somewhere with your date, then make sure you tell someone where it is you believe you are going and then let them know when you arrive there. Most people have a mobile phone these days, so even a text message will do, just make sure you take responsibility for your safety.

- Don't drink too much alcohol.

- Pay attention to their body language and if you feel they are feeing uncomfortable, make it easy for them to leave. There really is nothing worse than a 'blind date' that doesn't know when to give up.

•   Do not feel pressured to do *any single little thing* that you don't want to do. If you do, then you are giving them permission to take control of your own personal choices and once you do that, you and only you are responsible for what you reap.

*   *   *

This may all seem a little 'OTT' but taking responsibility for your safety enables you to actually pay more attention to your date and you will therefore have more five-sense information available to either enjoy your date or make a swift exit.

The Internet gives so much pleasure to so many people who, for whatever reason, are unable to express that pleasure in other ways and I know that during my period of 'celibacy,' which lasted for 16 years, it enabled me to have some serious sexual fun, so it would be wrong of me to make anyone believe that it is not a safe arena for meeting potential partners; it is as safe as you make it. It is also a fantastic way of fantasising and experimenting with your own sexuality and that is something, which everyone should do more of.

If you are already in a relationship then talk to each other about things you have *imagined* you would like to do. It doesn't mean you have to do it. My partner loves it when I tell him fantasy stories, no matter how unlikely the content. I invent places, people and *write* either him, or me, or some times both of us, into the story; I just let my imagination run riot and the results are amazing. We both understand that this is pure fantasy and that should the situation arise to act out this fantasy, it would be a personal, rather than joint decision, first and foremost, as to whether one, or both of us, pursued the fantasy to make it a reality.

The most wonderful thing about imagination is that it can take you anywhere and it can make you anything you desire to be, so if you want to have a body of strong rippling muscles with animal magnetism, then guess what, that is exactly what you can be. And if you want to be a sex goddess who mesmerises your partner with your sexual passion, which makes him unable to say no to you, then that will also happen; the script is in your hands. Without fantasy and the ability to imagine we would not be able to exist in reality in any kind of meaningful way. Every moment we are planning ahead and to do that takes imagination.

Just think about how most of us begin our day; many of us are doing today what we planned the day before and if we can visualise what we want to happen, or what the outcome of our planned day will be, then we can influence the outcome, with intention. Too many of us blame others for future events not turning out the way we had envisaged, yet so many of us do not put enough effort into the intention, and this is especially true of sex. For example, if you know that you are going to meet your sexual partner tomorrow, how much time do you actually take to imagine what you would like to happen? Most of us just think, "Oh great, I am meeting up with my partner tomorrow night, and I can't wait. We will have a great time and everything will be brilliant."

Most of us do not focus, or intend, anything more than this, so that when we meet our partner we have an expectation that it is going to be good, without spending any time focusing on *how* it is going to be fantastic. There is a phrase that I use when training people on management techniques that states, "The person who sets the agenda is in control of the outcome" and we need to apply this to our sexual relationships as well. For most male wired brains, the outcome they want is to have sexual intercourse with their partner, so they focus on that particular outcome often anticipating how they can achieve this, whereas most female wired people want to experience an emotional connection and might run through the words, or expressions of love that their partner will articulate. If you can understand that male and female brains are wired in a totally different way, then you can communicate your agenda and listen to your partner's ideas and combine the two, so that you both achieve the outcome that you desire.

This also increases the depth of commitment to each other, as you are *showing* your partner that you care about their enjoyment as much as your own. This does require a level of confidence, but the amazing thing is that if you ask men or women about the qualities they admire in a partner, confidence and honesty are right at the top of the list, so be confident and be honest.

Take the time to *evaluate* what happens in your sexual relationships as well; as this is how we learn and choose how to move forward, and in your evaluation remain honest. Do not blame the other person for *making* you do things or *making* you feel a certain way; this is all in *your* mind, not theirs. If you haven't told them that you enjoy being massaged, then don't admonish them for not doing it, you never know, it might be something they would love to do to you, but are too shy or frightened to suggest for a whole myriad of reasons. Once you both understand what the other person desires, you then both have a choice as to whether you participate or not and then, if you choose to participate, you should both evaluate whether this is something you would choose to do again or not, and look at ways that you can learn and therefore improve whatever you have experienced.

Sex is, and should be, an incredibly magical and stimulating experience and the means to make it so are in your hands and your amazing imagination. Take responsibility for your sexual growth, erotic development and pleasure and think before you blame anyone for something that lies in your own limitless imagination.

The Bit Where I Rant About...
Religion

For as long as I can remember, religion has figured in my life in one way, or another. I was baptised into a faith, which I knew nothing about, before I could speak, and was even bestowed an extra set of 'parents' to ensure I was raised as a good 'Christian' girl. I was sent to Sunday school where I learnt all about Christianity, or should I say, someone's interpretation of what Christianity is, and given guidance on *how* I should live my life, so as not to be condemned to hell after my death; all this to a child who has only just begun to live, let alone have any real understanding of what death actually is. In truth, no one has an understanding of what death is; yet religions tell us what they *believe* it to mean and present that as an absolute truth.

As a child, I was also taught to respect my elders and do as I was told, so when Sunday school teachers spoke of 'hell and damnation,' I believed and respected the information they were sharing with me; why would I doubt them, they had years of life experience and were teachers of the subject? I also was enrolled as a 'Brownie' at my church and would take part in the grown-ups religious ceremonies, which was really exciting, as children were usually restricted from all but the 'family service,' so joining them as a 'Brownie' made me feel 'grown up'. It was also quite lovely to spend an hour with my entire family, singing and praying together in the same place *and* at the same time.

At first I didn't really understand *what* exactly I was being taught at Sunday school and most of my time there involved joining in various activities such as making palm crosses or singing easy to remember hymns like 'Give Me Oil In My Lamp.' As I grew older and started mainstream education, that which I was learning at school corroborated what I was being taught at Sunday school, meaning I had two distinct groups of informed, educated adults recounting the same stories. I had even less inclination to challenge what was being said, or have any reason to disbelieve.

I can remember vividly the day I started to question what I was being told. I was being prepared for my Holy Communion, which would make me a fully paid up member of the Protestant Christian sect and during preparation classes we, the ones to receive Holy Communion for the first time, were told that if we were asked if we believed in the Holy Catholic church and no other religion, we should respond in the affirmative. I started to get a little confused, as I didn't really know about any other religion that might exist, so how could I swear something to God that I did not know to be true? This troubled me as I did not want to be condemned to eternal hell when I died by lying to God and swearing the same, so I raised the point at our next instruction only to be told that I shouldn't worry about any other religion, I should just concentrate on learning the responses I needed to give to gain entry to this one!

This I did not like. No one was going to make me lie to God! So, I decided to find out what other religions there were and this actually proved to be a very difficult task. When I asked the Sunday school helper about this, she told me that there weren't any other religions really, as Christianity was the only true belief. I challenged her and asked why we would have to swear to God to believe only in this religion, if there was no other; surely God was already aware of this fact. Her response to this was that I should just do it; God would understand the truth and not judge me. The Sunday school teachers were not helpful either and implied that I was being 'difficult' and not taking the importance of confirmation seriously enough!

So, I decided to start to look for information on religion where ever I could find it and even went to another church to see if it was any different or better than my own parish. As I was still quite young there was a limit on where I could get information from, so my sources were nearly always Christian-based. Eventually I did get confirmed into the church, even though I spent most of the ceremony with my fingers crossed.

I can also remember after my experience with 'secret uncle' feeling incredibly scared and isolated and when I went to bed at night I would sleep on the floor and offer my bed to Jesus, thinking that as so many people had been cruel to him, and he was born in a stable and slept in a manger, that he would enjoy the comfort of my bed. I actually believed Jesus to be there and would speak to him before I slept, finding him so easy to talk to, a real good listener.

Religion has played such a major part in so many different aspects of my life that it is difficult to separate it from any part of my existence; it has been inherent throughout. I always considered myself to be 'deeply' religious and one of my favoured career ambitions was to become a nun even though, at the time, I did not realise that nuns belonged to a different sect to my own. All I know with absolute certainty is that I wanted to *know and belong* to the truth, the true religion, whatever it might be. So, all my life I have searched and my conclusion is that religion is almost the polar opposite of what I have been searching for; religion *of any kind* that involves a personal 'god' is not truth.

Once I arrived at this conclusion, which I have to add, has only been over the past six years, I started my journey of self-discovery, of my own truth and this really has set me free. I look at the world I inhabit in a totally different way and actually see religion as a reason for hatred, discrimination, disfiguration, mutilation, depravation, exclusion, torture, war, violence, self-denial of a whole host of 'god given' wonders, misconceptions, suspicions and lack of responsibility.

I believe that some of the greatest 'spiritual' orators have been hijacked by religious groups, who twist their words to fit the latest 'prophet based' created dogma, almost with total disregard for what the 'prophet' was *actually* hoping to enlighten us about. Jesus is a case in point and throughout the bible, it is clear that Jesus did not believe in man made religious ritual. He told his stories of enlightenment on hillsides and in God's created universe. He told us that God was within each and every one of us and that we did not need to go to temples with their rich trappings; look at the churches now, draped with all kind of idolatry shaped in his vein, in exact contradiction of what he believed. Why, I ask myself, did this happen?

My search for truth has been an evolving journey, where every time I reach a point of exhaustion, another avenue opens up before me for further exploration. I have read books by Mahatma Ghandi, Tuesday Lobsang Rampa, David Icke and various other spiritual thinkers and I have to agree with Ghandi when he wrote after opening himself up to a wide variety of religious teachings, including Hinduism, Islam and Christianity, " I do not know where I am, and what is and what should be my belief" and concluded, "I have made the world's faith in God my own, and as my faith is ineffaceable, I regard faith as amounting to experience...I have no word for characterising my belief in God."

As my search expanded, I realised that many others have set out on the same journey; in search of truth and most have arrived at the same place that Ghandi reached when he said, "This truth is not only truthfulness in word, but truthfulness in thought also, and not only the relative truth of our conception, but the Absolute Truth, the Eternal Principle, that is God.... but I worship God as Truth only I have not found Him, but I am seeking after Him... but as long as I have not realised this Absolute Truth, so long must I hold by the relative truth as I have conceived it. That relative truth must, meanwhile, be my beacon, my shield and my buckler."

What I have realised is that if 'truth' is created in my own mind then truth cannot be what someone else says truth is, as we have no real idea of how they actually *see* their truth. To make it slightly easier, imagine that you are sitting having a meal in a restaurant with three other friends and you are seated at a square table with each of you sitting at a different side.

Each of you will have a different experience of that restaurant and that, in turn, can influence the enjoyment of the meal and your participation in, and understanding of, your conversations with friends.

Imagine that you are sitting facing North, which is where the entrance is located. You have full view of the door and every time it opens or closes you will become momentarily distracted and even more so if there is a waiting area or bar situated there. You might not want to look every time someone walks in or out, but you will do it all the same, sometimes losing track of the social interaction between your friends, or asking for a story to be repeated.

Your friend 'A' is sitting facing South, exactly opposite you, so has no view of what is going on behind, instead 'A' can see a young couple, seated behind you to your left, who are behaving very romantically: holding hands, lots of eye contact and touching; really quite intimate and tender. At one point 'A' loses contact with the group altogether as she leans to one side, when she notices the young man reaching into his pocket, pulling out a small, red velvet box.

Friend 'B' is sitting facing East and has some peripheral vision of what the other two can see, but has to turn her head to understand what you and friend 'A' are being distracted by. 'B's view is of the toilet area and she becomes momentarily preoccupied with the people who enter the toilets, wondering why they are taking so long, or if they have washed their hands. All manner of distracting thoughts pass through her mind.

Friend 'C' is facing West and has a view of the passage that leads to the kitchen. As the food comes and goes she makes comments on the wonderful dishes that are about to pass the table. 'C' is also rather taken with a waiter and watches every time he passes to enter the kitchen, once or twice as he returned to the restaurant, he caught her gaze and this is exciting her.

Even though all four of you are eating in the same restaurant, dining at the same table, eating food cooked by the same chefs, your experience of the restaurant will be slightly different to each of theirs.

Now imagine that the restaurant, we will call it 'God's Pantry,' represents 'truth' or God, and that many people eat there every single day of the year. Each individual person is going to experience 'God's Pantry' in a different way and will pass on that 'truth' in the manner in which they themselves interpreted it. They have no control over the way that *you* experience that truth. You can listen to them intently and even ask them for more detail, but a bit like the way we saw how each individual comes up with different images for the word 'dog,' each of us will transform that 'truth' into descriptions that we ourselves understand.

Right, so let's go back to 'God's Pantry.'

Years pass and 'God's Pantry' begins to earn a reputation as being a good place to find truth, and as the word spread, many people travelled to experience truth. They would then broaden the potential customer base by telling everyone they knew, their version of truth, so that they could experience it for themselves. Eventually its competitors decide that they have to get rid of 'God's Pantry' otherwise they will go out of business, so they first call in environmental health inspectors to try to damage 'God's Pantry's' truth, and when that doesn't work, they try adverse publicity, anything to stop people from experiencing the truth.

Finally, the competitors feel that there is only one option left open to them; they will have to kill the truth. People are saddened when they hear that 'God's Pantry' is no longer there and talk about the happy times they had there and before long it becomes almost a legend. The problem is that no one will ever experience 'God's Pantry' again and so people decide to spread their version of truth and as it passes from one to another, until one day, a smart entrepreneur decides that if he can replicate 'God's Pantry,' he could develop a thriving business of his own. He sets out to achieve his goal, talking to as many people as possible to discover the restaurant layout, the menu and dishes served; everything he can to replicate the truth. He calls his restaurant 'God's Pantry – The Sequel' and begins to spread the word that soon the truth will be available to everyone.

At first, trade is slow with people coming in dribs and drabs. Some had visited the original 'God's Pantry' and even though their experience is different, they *want to believe* that it is the same, because they know that the truth, as they knew it, has gone and they don't want it to be forever. Because they want to believe so desperately in truth, they encourage as many people as possible to go and seek it for themselves which, of course, can only be found in 'God's Pantry - The Sequel.'

Soon people are travelling from far and wide to visit the one place on earth that holds the truth and the restaurant is full to overflowing, so the entrepreneur decides to open a chain of 'God's Pantry's' across the land and that is exactly what he does. They are now everywhere and people visit the restaurants because they believe that they will find the truth, and because they believe it, maybe some of them will and this will benefit the entrepreneur who will ride off the back of the original creator of truth, making millions out of people's ignorance of the same, rather than enlightenment; in other words, it's all a con.

You are truth, I am truth, and we are truth. There is no need for us to pay for the privilege of knowing truth; it is always within us. As I believe this to be true, why is it then that I took so long to find it out? I mean, if the truth was always inside me, why didn't I know it?

The answer is that I have been brainwashed, since birth, into a belief system and in order to maintain control of me, in other words, keep me hypnotised, the organisers of the belief system created something called 'religion' and this system influenced everything I saw, everything I read, everything I heard and continued to reinforce itself through education and learning development. If I did anything that went against their religion, then I would be called 'mad' or 'crazy' or possessed by some demon spirit, so it would not be in my best interests to do or say anything that contradicted their dogma. I suppose as well, there was a part of me that wanted to believe it was the truth, a bit like the people eating at 'God's Pantry,' I wanted to believe that the brilliance I felt, somewhere deep inside, had to mean that there was more to life than I was experiencing, so maybe all these other people were right, and the religion was the truth.

What happened to me was that I really believed there had to be a religion that was right, so I carried on looking, desperate to find the right prophet to pray to, who could make my life good. And the more you believe it to be the truth, the more you are scared to even think that it might not be, in case you are damned to eternal hell; meaning I never looked within, just in case.

History has also cemented our ideas and fears of religious power so that we can witness for ourselves how women were burnt in their thousands, or ducked under water until they drowned, or men tortured to confess their belief and others fighting for their lives in a pit of lions, as penance for their belief. And even though we are aware of the history of religious violence, we never really question why any 'god' would want this destruction to be wrought in his name and should the question raise its controversial head, we push it out of sight as quickly as possible.

Throughout my life 'things' to do with religion have never quite added up somehow, and over many years it has felt as if veils were being lifted from my eyes one by one; each new veil revealing more of the stupidity and arrogance of religion, until I eventually reached the point I am at now. I am the truth.

Think about religion for one moment and ask yourself what do *you* really believe?

There is no right or wrong answer; this is your life, your experiences create your reality. I would like to write about some of my thoughts and this may offer you something to think about to widen your possible choices.

The first time I really questioned the existence of God, as represented by the church, was when my baby daughter, Rebecca, died. I was living in a women's hostel in Portrush, Northern Ireland at the time, with my three children. I can remember feeling so relieved to be away from my partner and thinking that I would have a new start, in a new town far away from his influence. Rebecca was only four months old and somehow I always knew she would die, even before she was born. I contracted encephalitis when I was four months pregnant and I was really ill, losing lots of weight and strength in my body. I can remember the doctor trying to give me some medication to ease the pain and refusing to take it, in case it affected the baby. My delivery date came and went, with no sign of arrival, so the birth was induced and Rebecca was born weighing 4lbs 14ozs. On the day I was due to leave hospital the doctor told me he thought I may have TB and so I was to stay for a few more days until test results proved otherwise, which they eventually did.

It's strange thinking back to this time because it almost feels like someone else's life. I can remember I only had two visitors, apart from my children, during my eight-day stay, my husband and a volunteer from the Samaritans who had supported me through a very difficult couple of months. Rebecca was born on November 14th 1979 and I was so happy to take her home, not because I wanted to be at home, but because I was aware that my husband was leaving my other children alone while he went to the pub every night. I have very few photographs of myself with all three of my children and the image is so sad to look at now. There are no happy smiles; you can smell the poverty and the children look terrified. Life was really hard for all of us, including my husband who had a serious alcohol addiction. I did my best to manage our social security money, but my husband would keep taking it to go to the pub, not returning until he was hardly able to stand.

Rebecca was so tiny and the winter was coming, with colder nights and therefore more heating costs, and I was so worried that we wouldn't be able to pay the bills that I would hide money to make sure we had enough to see us through the winter. We had received a final demand for the electricity when I was in hospital and I had given my husband the money to pay the bill, which he assured me he had done, so I thought that with the little bit I had managed to save, we may even have some left over to give the children a Christmas present each.

Not long after Rebecca had come home, we were all sitting in the kitchen, which faced the front of the house, when a knock came at the door. My husband told us all to be quiet and then crept to the window and looked out to see who was there. Then he made his way back to where we were sitting and told us to get under the table and keep quiet. I couldn't understand what was going on, so I asked him who it was. In a hushed whisper he replied, "It's the electric" and then huddled back down under the table. I couldn't understand why he was hiding, so got up and answered the door.

A rather large, officious looking man was standing there and I can remember smiling and asking him what he wanted. When he told me he had come to disconnect our electricity supply, I was briefly stunned and argued with him that he was mistaken, the bill had been paid, but he assured me it hadn't. I asked him to wait there, but he insisted on stepping in to the house, so I left him in the hallway while I tried to sort out the mistake. As soon as I saw my husband's face I knew that the man at the door was right, my husband had not paid the bill and had spent the money on his addiction instead.

I wanted to scream, but instead I remembered my secret stash, thinking that if I paid him now, then he wouldn't disconnect the supply. I dashed upstairs, excusing myself as I passed the unwelcome visitor, and reached under the bed for the box containing my money, thanking God for its contents, but when I opened it, there was nothing left in it. I sat looking at its empty insides for a minute or two and only put it down when I saw a tear stain the white inside of the box, to a watery grey colour. I made my way slowly down the stairs and told the man that I had no money to pay him and he replied that if I had no money, then I had no electricity. I can remember begging and pleading with him; telling him I had a new baby under a month old and two other small children, but no matter what I said he just responded that he was 'just doing his job.'

After he left I just sat there feeling numb until my husband came and apologised saying he wanted to pay the bill but went for a 'quick one' on the way and he didn't mean to take the money from the box but added that I shouldn't have been hiding it from him anyway. I didn't respond; there didn't seem any point. He then tried to cheer me up by saying, "Well, thank God the heating and cooker are gas. At least we will be warm and can heat some food."

I just continued to sit, as if I was glued to the step of the stairs, until finally my husband returned and said he couldn't stand to see me like this, so he was going to the pub. That night was a very cold night, and after my husband had left I had looked to see why the central heating had not switched itself on, only to find that the heating system was activated by an electric switch, meaning we had no heating in the house whatsoever.

When my husband returned much later, I didn't even say anything; I just lay there while he babbled on in his drunken state. The next morning when he came downstairs, he asked me why I hadn't put the heating on as he was freezing, and if he were cold then Rebecca would be as well. That's when I broke down. I held my head in my hands and just cried and cried, until the snot and tears soaked through my jeans, until I couldn't even breathe, let alone speak.

A couple of days after this, we received our benefit cheque, so my husband said he would go and collect it. I was not at all happy about this, but he insisted, asking the children what they wanted him to bring back from the shops for them. I remember James saying, "Bring me some Cornflakes daddy, please", and my husband ruffling his hair and saying, "Of course daddy will bring you some Cornflakes back." Faye asked for nothing, because I think she already knew that that was exactly what she was going to get. As he made his way to the door I begged him to stay at home and look after the kids and to let me go, but he just kept smiling and insisting that he went and, in order to prove that he wasn't going to spend the money on booze, he would take Rebecca, in her pram, with him. This concerned me even more, but now he had got the idea into his head, there was no shifting it, so I wrapped her up in extra blankets and watched as he waved goodbye saying he'd be back in under half an hour.

After he had gone I started to get anxious and then told myself not to be stupid as he had Rebecca with him, and he would be back. I looked out at the skies, which had those heavy clouds suspended high above, and I just knew that it was going to snow. Almost as soon as I thought it, the clouds burst and heavy snowflakes rapidly changed the dismal landscape of the estate into to a picturesque snow covered image of 'peace and goodwill.' The snow continued to flutter from the sky until the garden and pathways merged into a blanket of whiteness, removing any trace of where one began and the other ended. I guess maybe an hour had passed by this stage and I decided that I had better go and find my husband, so I took my children to a neighbour's and began to search for him.

There were six different pubs in Craigavon and as the snow settled thickly on the ground, I crunched and slid my way to four of them, without any luck. By this time I was freezing and getting more and more fretful with each pub I visited. As I approached the fifth pub I noticed something by the entrance covered in snow, it was hard to define what it was at first, but slowly the object took shape and I realised that it was my baby's pram. I ran towards it calling, "Rebecca, Rebecca" and on reaching it, frantically brushed the snow from the outer cover, and there looking at me with beautiful brown eyes, was my baby. My sense of relief lasted only long enough for me to tickle her cheek, before it was replaced with anger.

I slammed open the doors to the bar and saw him sitting on a stool, laughing and joking with the other drunks, a whisky and a pint at his elbow. My anger developed into rage and I lost all control of my senses. I screamed like a banshee and then charged at him; grabbing his jacket collars and almost lifting him off his stool slammed him against the wall next to the bar. I was so fired up with rage and fury that I couldn't make an understandable sound at first and then, shaking with the energy of the rage that was exploding throughout my body; I banged him a final time against the wall, before letting him slide to the floor at my feet.

I staggered outside and bent my head over, coughing and retching, and threw up a pool of hot, pungent watery bile that almost instantly began to dissolve the purity of the snow. My head began to spin making me feel like I was about to fall, so I lent against the wall trying to control my breathing. I regained as much of my composure as possible before walking back in the pub. The barman told me to get out saying, "You're barred for life, you fucking madwoman, now fuck off before I throw you out meself!"

I ignored him and approached my husband who was back sitting on his bar stool drinking his whisky and held out my hand for whatever money remained, but there was none. He said he had bought everyone drinks to "wet the baby's head" and cleared his slate at one of the other pubs, so I told him to carry on and not to bother coming home again. Needless to say, he did come home, and life continued as it always had.

The house was freezing and we spent our time sitting wrapped in blankets for most of December. A day or so later, I noticed that Rebecca wasn't feeding as well as she normally did; my breasts would ache with milk, yet she seemed too tired to make any effort to drink. I decided to take her to the doctor's; he said she was 'very poorly' and admitted her to hospital immediately, where she was found to be suffering from pneumonia. Rebecca stayed in hospital until December 23rd when she was allowed home, by which stage I had been given the money by my parents to pay the outstanding electricity bill, so we were reconnected.

Nothing much changed in my life for the next couple of months, except for my feelings towards my husband; I couldn't stand him near me any more. I would make sure I was in bed before he came home and if I wasn't asleep, I would pretend that I was, and even when he put his freezing cold hands on me or kissed me with his disgusting alcohol-laced mouth, I would remain as still as I could until he gave up trying.

Then one day he came home earlier than usual and he was not alone; he had a sex worker with him and, he informed me with great pride and joy, that she was here to show me 'what a woman should do for her husband.' The woman was almost as pissed as he was and she wrapped her short leopard print dress around his jubilant form, laughing and kissing his neck. For a brief moment I thought I should get up and scream at her to 'get out of my house,' but for some reason I just sat there and let them continue with their drunken display. After a while they were no longer in my focus; my mind was drifting somewhere, I don't know where, all I know is that it was no longer in that room. For me that was the end and I knew that I had to leave and get out of this madness.

The following morning, when he came downstairs, I told him that

I wanted him to leave and that if he wouldn't I would take the children and go myself. He seemed quite shocked and asked me why, so I told him my reasons and again I asked him to leave. He didn't and instead threw me through a kitchen display unit and continued to beat me, until the police, who had been alerted by a neighbour, rescued me.

The police sent me to a 'battered wives' home,' as they were so quaintly known, in Portrush, miles from where I lived; I was told that this was for my own safety. After a long journey we arrived at the refuge where the staff welcomed us and I was shown to my room with my children. After being there for nearly three months I was actually starting to enjoy life again. The staff members at the refuge were easy to talk to and most of the other women were friendly enough. The good thing about living at the refuge was feeling safe and warm; nothing bothered me. There was food in my locker and money in my pocket. This was the warmest and safest I had felt for a long time. I felt like I had taken control of my life and would often just smile to myself at the sheer sense of freedom I now had. I was 21 years old at this stage.

The staff at the refuge would sometimes organise a little 'get-together' for the resident women, and maybe bring in someone of interest to talk to us, or we would just sit and chat about life. The mothers were asked to settle the children first and then go into the lounge where tea, coffee and cakes would be laid out, along with chairs and any information leaflets that they thought we could benefit from reading.

On this particular night, Rebecca would just not settle, she was not crying or fretful, she just wouldn't sleep and I did not want to leave her lying awake in her cot, so asked if I could bring her to the 'get together.' Throughout the evening Rebecca sat wide-awake and was passed from mother to mother, everyone talked to her and she smiled and gurgled happily. Everyone commented on what a lovely child she was and how content and happy she appeared. As the evening grew late, I made my excuses to leave saying that I was tired and both Rebecca and I needed to sleep, so each of them gave Rebecca a kiss and we went to our room. This had never happened before and it was so wonderful to see all the mothers and refuge workers being so attentive and kind towards my baby. I thanked everyone for a lovely evening and Rebecca and I made our way to our room.

The room I slept in was not particularly big so the children and I shared a double bed and Rebecca slept in a cot by the window. As I was breast-feeding Rebecca, I got her changed and into her nightclothes before slipping beneath the blankets naked and tucking her up next to me. For some reason Rebecca just wanted to play, so I talked to her for a while and she 'talked' back to me and just enjoyed some moments of happiness before I put her to my breast. As she suckled I spoke to her of my hopes for the future, that one day soon we would get our own place and maybe we would have a garden for the summer, as she would be crawling by then and would need some soft grass beneath her knees. Eventually she drifted off to sleep, so I laid her beside me and cuddled up next to James.

I woke with a start at about 6am and knew without even looking, that Rebecca was dead. I pulled back the sheet and grabbed her body next to my naked skin and ran from the room screaming for assistance. People came out of rooms, confused by all the noise, some yelling through closed doors to 'shut the fuck up.'

I was totally naked and ran up and down the flights of stairs screaming for a member of staff, but it was too early and no one was there to take control, relieve me of this nightmare and bring everything back to normality. Finally I sat on the bottom stair, cuddling Rebecca to my chest and I rocked back and forth, repeating over and over again, "Mummy loves you, Rebecca, please don't leave Mummy. Mummy loves you, Rebecca, please don't leave Mummy."

I don't recall much of the rest of the day, not the spoken words, but I will always retain the images and even now as I write these words, I see snatches of what took place on that awful day: ambulance men, police, frantic staff members arriving, women crying, my children confused, Rebecca being stripped naked on the kitchen table, me begging to hold her and being denied, my last look before she was taken physically from me forever, a doctor arriving with a hypodermic filled with some substance 'to ease the pain,' me screaming at him to leave, falling in a heap and begging God to take me, being left in an empty room, a black pit of silent pain.

My daughter died on 21st March 1980; she was just four months old. My body ached in a way that only a mother who has lost a child will ever understand; there is no other pain on this earth that is comparable. It invades every single cell, every individual particle of your being and tortures your mind endlessly, forcing images into focus that you don't want to see, but they are relentless and never stop.

My breasts were aching with the pressure of milk that she would never drink; my heart was full of love that she would never feel and my soul felt as if it had been torn from my body and thrown into hell. But I was not dead and I was reminded, sometimes by strangers, that I should begin to prepare for my baby's funeral. The first time someone uttered these words to me, I looked at them with disbelief. How could I bury my baby? She's only four months old, it's all a mistake, a big mistake and if I even *think* about burying her then that means she really is dead and that is just incomprehensible.

I began to think that maybe Social Services had concocted this conspiracy and that Rebecca hadn't really died at all, she had just been 'taken into care' by the authorities until I could show that I could afford to look after her. The thought grew in my mind until I convinced myself that it was real; Rebecca was alive and well and being looked after by some kindly foster parents. I mean if she was really dead, they would have given me some time to say goodbye to her, they would have returned her clothing to me, but they hadn't.

I can remember thinking to myself, "OK, if you want me to think she is dead, then I'll play your stupid game and arrange a funeral and behave like a woman who has lost her child, and then, when you bring her back to me, I will act like I am totally surprised. I *know* my baby is still alive. I'm her mother and I have milk in my breasts to feed her, how can she be dead?"

I had to keep myself busy and as I cleaned and wiped and polished and moped I would concentrate all my focus on Rebecca's return, but if I didn't concentrate, my mind would be filled with images and snatches of speech that confirmed my worst fears and imagining. One of the refuge workers spent some time talking to me about my feelings, but I couldn't tell her what was going on in my head, because if she found out that I knew Rebecca was alive, then maybe she would tell Social Services and then I might never get her back. So, when she began to talk about arranging the funeral, I agreed that I would start the preparations.

The first church I visited was the parish church that served the refuge and I don't remember much of what was discussed, but I do remember with absolute clarity the vicar informing me that he could not provide a service for my daughter, as we were not 'of this parish.' This only served to confirm in my mind that my baby was still alive; I mean what church would refuse a burial service for a *baby*?

I went to another church which was close by, but they also refused to provide a burial service for her, and with each refusal my hope and joy grew, because I knew that my baby had committed no sin, so if she really was dead, all of the church people would be supportive and agree to provide for her spiritual needs.

After visiting four different churches in Portrush, I decided to call it a day. I contacted my father and explained that I was unable to find anyone prepared to offer my child a service and he muttered something about 'religious bigotry' and said he was collecting me and the children the following morning and arranging for me to meet with my family's local vicar. I had attended this church when I lived at my parent's house, so my father didn't think we would have any problems.

My father had informed the vicar of the situation and he had done some preparation work ready for our meeting, which was held in my parent's home. As we drank tea, the vicar began to explain that the reason that it was proving difficult to provide a service for Rebecca was that she had not been christened and that she did not really 'belong' to his parish or the parishes in Portrush; it was a rather difficult situation all round. I can remember thinking, "They must think I am totally mad. Jesus loves the little children. If my daughter was really, truly dead, how could Jesus *not* allow her to be buried? They have my baby and they are just fucking with my head."

I decided to ask him some questions, "If no one will provide a funeral service for an innocent four-month-old baby, then what am I meant to do? Do I just dig a hole in the sand on the beach and dump her body in there? Or should I dig a grave in my dad's back garden and lay her to rest? Why is it that a representative of God cannot perform a service for a child of God? What am I supposed to do for God's sake, tell me and I'll do it, just tell me."

I left the room, ran upstairs and locked myself in the bathroom. My mind was filled with images of her lifeless body, of the ambulance driver holding her in his hands, of hypodermic needles and I began to scream, *"You fucking bastards, you're all bastards!"*

My father knocked quietly on the bathroom door and spoke to me, the soothing, loving words of a father distraught at his child's pain, asking me to come back downstairs as the vicar had a suggestion that I should hear. I lifted my head, which felt as heavy as lead and looked at my reflection in the mirror above the sink. When I looked into my own eyes, they filled with pools of water, which tumbled silently down my face, making my image blurred and unrecognisable. I turned on the cold water and splashed my face with the freezing liquid until it tingled. Then I made my way downstairs and into the lounge, where the vicar and my father were waiting.

The vicar explained the predicament he was in, protesting that it wasn't his fault; it was 'just the way things were,' before proceeding to tell me of his plan for Rebecca's burial. Although he would not be allowed to perform a service for Rebecca in the church, he was quite prepared to say a few words for her and he had been frantically contacting other colleagues over the past 24 hours. One of them had come up with a suggestion that might *appeal* to me. I raised my eyes to meet his, giving him silent permission to continue. He lent forward, clasping his hands together, as if in prayer, and said, "My colleague has found a family who are prepared to have your baby buried in one of their family graves," he rocked back and forth before continuing,

"It is the grave of a woman who was loved very much, and her family would be more than happy for Rebecca to be laid to rest there."

He sat back on his chair and both he and my father looked at me, waiting for some kind of reaction, and when none was forthcoming the vicar asked to be excused, leaving my dad and me alone. My father took hold of my hands in his and spoke with heartfelt emotion, "Rose, I understand that this might not be what you want, but your baby is not coming back and we have to make sure that we can bury her with the love and dignity that she and you deserve. If you don't want her to be buried with this woman, then say so and we will try to find a better alternative, but you need to think about it and make some kind of decision, so that the vicar can make the arrangements."

I looked into my father's eyes and nodded my head, "Tell him to come back and I will listen to him. Okay, you're right, it isn't what I want; none of this is anything that I want, but what else is there? To the church she was a sinner, just because she wasn't baptised, or she was from the wrong parish, the wrong religion, the wrong everything. She was my baby, a baby. What has she ever done wrong really, nothing, it was me who did wrong, why don't they punish me?"

Dad put his arms around my shoulders and gave me a squeeze before saying; "None of this makes any sense to me either." And with that he went to bring the vicar back to join us.

The funeral was conducted in my parents' house, in the morning room, on a circular dining table covered in a white linen cloth. Rebecca's tiny white coffin looked lost in the centre, surrounded by flowers and cards. My husband turned up just before the coffin arrived and the funeral director shook his hand and asked if there was anything he could do. My husband said that he wanted the coffin lid removed, as was traditional, so to my horror the coffin lid was slowly unscrewed and placed at the side of the coffin.

Family members and friends had started to arrive and my parents were doing the best they could to welcome the mourners. I didn't want to speak to anyone and asked to be left with my baby for a few moments. Everyone left the room, I heard the door close quietly behind me and then I approached the open coffin and held onto the edge of the table as I looked inside. The tiny baby was covered in a white sheet, exposing just her sweet little face, and on her head was a small white covering, almost like a skullcap. My mind began to go into major denial again; this wasn't my baby, she didn't have a skullcap, her ears were not in the right place, and her lips were the wrong colour. I touched her cheek and was shocked by how cold and hard it was; Rebecca's was soft and warm. I had been right all along.

I silently left the room, then the house, using the back door to avoid bumping into anybody, and walked off towards the shops at the bottom of the road. One of these shops sold designer baby wear and as I walked in through the door, I looked at all the fabulous clothes hanging on the rails and draped artistically about the walls. I would buy my baby the most expensive clothes in the shop and take them home with me, ready for when she returned. One of the shop assistants approached me and asked if she could help, so I asked her to hand me certain items to look at before making the choice of the most beautiful dress and bonnet I had ever seen. Just as the assistant was folding the tiny outfit, the shop door opened and my father's voice spoke gently, but with a certain firmness, "Rose, come on sweetheart, your baby needs you now to take her on her final journey."

"It's not Rebecca, Dad, honestly, it's not my baby, they have made a mistake... her ears don't look like that, she's so cold, I touched her cheek..."

"Rose, it is Rebecca and you have to be really strong now because you have two other children who are desperately upset back there and they need their mummy to help them to understand what's going on. Come on sweetheart, let's go home."

The funeral service was, in essence, a few words spoken by the vicar about how Jesus died on the cross. It was over in minutes, then the guests filed out into the front garden of my parents' home and watched sympathetically as I carried the tiny coffin past them. The funeral director held open the rear door of a black saloon car and gestured for me to approach. When I reached him, he extended his arms, saying that he would hold the coffin until I was seated. I sat on the back seat and held out my arms for the coffin and as the funeral director handed it to me, he moved his mouth as if he was speaking, but I could hear no sound; it was as if all the noise had left the planet: no birds singing, no cars passing, no dogs barking, no sound of tears, no beating of hearts, no children's laughter, just silence.

I held the coffin on my lap, felt the movement of the engine and then began the 45-minute drive of silence. Although outwardly I may have resembled a marble statue, with a fixed expression, eyes hardly blinking and mouth firmly closed, inside my mind there was a battle between two conflicting sides of me; one, total denial and the other, the beginnings of grief. Inside my head there was so much noise; shouting, screaming, crying, begging, pleading and screeching, "PLEASE DON'T LET THIS BE HAPPENING, PLEASE."

I was only aware that the journey was over when the driver opened my door, and suddenly all the sound and noise exploded in my ears, like a tidal wave, washing away all my privacy and leaving me naked in this place I didn't want to be. He nodded his head in acknowledgement that we had arrived and then extended his hands for the coffin. I tried to give it to him. I really did, but I just couldn't do it, if I did I would never hold her in my arms again; she would be gone. He interrupted my thoughts, as if reading my mind, "Madam, you can have her back as soon as you are out of the car" and again proffered his extended arms.

We were in a small graveyard at the side of an old church; it looked almost neglected with headstones that were worn with time and a path that competed with the grass to remain visible. I looked ahead and could see the vicar, complete in black and white flowing robes, standing by a raised pile of fresh mud. I felt as if I was in some kind of horror film and kept trying to move my feet forward, but they wouldn't move. My father came and supported my elbow with his open hand and gently started me along the path. It was as if I was walking to my death; with each step I could feel a lump grow in my throat, until it felt as if it would suffocate me. I tried to speak but couldn't form the sounds and once more I was encased in silence.

Eventually, we reached the open grave that already contained a coffin and the funeral director approached me with open arms, indicating that I should give him Rebecca, and I tried, but I just didn't want to let go. What if it really was her, what if this small white casket really did have my baby inside it, what if, what if, and what if? Gently my father unfurled my fingers from the box and placed my dead baby in the arms of the funeral director.

I didn't see him put her in the grave; I didn't see anything. The world was spinning around me and everything was a blur of black, white and grey; nothing was distinguishable.

The vicar brought me to my senses by calling my name and offering a small handful of dry earth. My father walked with me as we took the crumble of mud and approached the grave. Inside, just underneath my skin, I was screaming, begging, pleading, bargaining with God, promising to do anything, anything at all, no matter how big or difficult. I would do it, just as long as you give me my baby back. Please God, just let me have Rebecca back, she's too little to be buried in the ground, please God.

Then it was over, at least for the vicar, the funeral director and the mourners. For me the nightmare had just begun, but that's another story.

The children and I stayed at my parent's house for the rest of the week and on Sunday I walked down to the church and straight into the middle of a sermon being given by the same vicar who had attended Rebecca's funeral. He was ranting on about the passion of Jesus on the cross and the whole church was full of people, all dressed in their 'Sunday best' and something inside me exploded and I started shouting, "You're all a bunch of fucking hypocrites… you don't give a shit about anything, not Jesus, not each other, not anything… I hate you, all of you, you say you care but look at you, the fucking fur hats you have on your head cost more than my electric costs for a year… you're meant to be Christians, but you're not, you're just fucking hypocrites and I hate all of you."

Even as I began to shout, the vicar was making his way up the aisle, raising his hands at the startled congregation indicating to them that he would 'deal with the situation'. By the time he finally got to my side, I was finished anyway and turned to walk out of the doors before letting out a final explosive outburst, "Jesus died thousands of years ago. My baby died a few days ago, but then I guess my baby meant nothing to any of you, did she?"

And with that I left.

This was the first time I really questioned the existence of God as represented by the church. It never made any sense to me then and it still doesn't make any sense to me now. How can a child be refused a church burial?

Why did she have to be put into the grave of a person I never knew, just because she wasn't christened?

Why was I told that I could never put a marker on her place of rest?

Why would God allow this painful discrimination to happen?

Religion is the craziest of man-made creations; I mean why do we all buy into it? Fear is the answer, total fear.

Let us just for one moment think about the magnificence of whatever it is that we perceive to be God. What do you actually believe God to be?

Really think about it and then ask yourself some questions.

Do you think that if God wanted to get a message to mankind, that he might be powerful enough to let each of us know what the message might be, or do you think God would need to communicate the message to one particular 'prophet' in the hope that it was interpreted correctly, translated into every single language known to mankind and reached every individual on the planet?

God does not need prophets, religion does.

Who do religious leaders really think they are?

Do they think that God prefers them to any of his other children; after all we are all created in his image, so we must *all* be his children?

It's all there to keep us under control, spawn fear and generate enormous amounts of money.

Look at the atrocities that are performed during religious rights, female circumcision is a case in point; there is actually no earthly, or heavenly, reason to mutilate a young girl. What do the people who do these disgusting practices actually believe? Do they think that God got it wrong and that they can perfect his creation? And nuns who for years have denied the greatest of God's gifts, procreation, why do they rebuff themselves and God?

Do they imagine that God will thank them for their sacrifice?

What about priests who deny their sexual existence, is God rewarding their abstinence with a special place in heaven? How impertinent are these people, the very people who rant on about how they give their lives to God, deny the lives that God has given to them; it's all bollocks. In the name of religion, God's creation has been hunted and slaughtered; genocide has taken place on countless occasions in God's name. The very symbol of Christianity is the cross on which God's 'son' was tortured and crucified in the name of religion, spawning yet another dogma for believers to follow.

You don't need to follow any religion. God is within, You are God, I am God, we are all God and all the 'prophets' over countless centuries have been trying to get us to understand that one simple fact; we *are* God. So where did religion come from? Well I have my own ideas; so will explain them to you in a story:

Once upon a time, long ago, when humans lived in social groups, a bit like gorillas do now, man had no need for religion. Each social assembly worked together to provide a lifestyle that supported *all* the members of the group. This meant working with nature, understanding the seasons and tapping in to the awareness of the group. Each member of the social group would have a function within it that contributed to the whole, and no member would be 'carried' or given a 'free ride,' as every single member was valued for their part in the greater whole.

In one of these groups, long ago there was a young man named Oracle, now he did not like to perform hard tasks, preferring to sit under the trees and watch as the others gathered food, or drink. Oracle was one of those people who can *appear* to be working when, in reality, they only spring into action when they think they are being observed (mmm… a bit like an atom). As time passed Oracle had perfected his art of deception so well that no one realised he was doing only half of the work of the others. This was because everyone was working so hard to contribute to the group that there was no time to observe whether others were doing the same; it was just assumed that this was so.

Oracle knew this, so exploited the labour of all the others at every given opportunity. While the others toiled, Oracle would sleep, making sure he was well hidden, and creating alibis should anyone complain about his contribution. As Oracle was still an adolescent, when he was supposed to be hunting with other members of the group, he would be told to hang back behind, almost like a rear look out, and so while the others risked life and limb in the hunt, he would sit back and rest, often gorging himself of fruits he found close by. Every now and then he would make some form of contact with the group, just to support the fact that he was engaged in the activity. After a successful hunt he was part of the victorious hunting party honoured for their bravery by the rest of his tribe. Oracle thought how good his life was and had no concern that other group members were often hurt or exhausted by their pursuits. He just knew that he was on to a good thing and had no interest in fighting fearsome creatures, especially as there were many eager students not much older than him who were vying for the more reckless positions. No, Oracle was just fine where he was and had no intention of changing his role within the hunting party.

One day, Oracle heard two other members of the group talking and hid, close to a nearby tree, so that he could listen to their conversation. Brados, the elder of the two, spoke first, "You are tired Lugus and need to rest. That last hunt caused you an injury that I don't think you have recovered completely from. Maybe tomorrow you should stay in the village, and join us next time in a less physical position, as you are always one of the lead party, which demands the greatest concentration."

Lugus sighed and replied, "Brados, you are observant and a good friend. I am tired and in need of rest but I have an obligation to the village. What would I do with my time if I were to remain behind? Let me join you tomorrow and if I am unable to lead then there will be other ways that I can contribute. Let's see what the new day brings and then act accordingly." And with that the two friends retired to sleep.

Oracle did not sleep and, as he did less work than the others *and* found time to rest during the day, he could often stay awake long after the rest of the village was asleep. Most of the time he would just watch the nocturnal animals or become engrossed in the positioning of the stars, but on this night his thoughts turned to the conversation he had overheard. He thought to himself, "What if Lugus is unable to remain one of the pack leaders during the hunt? What if Brados suggests that Lugus might be more useful as a rear guard, what would I do then? I have to find a way to make Lugus believe that the position at the rear is more exhausting than that of leading."

So, as the other villagers rested in preparation for the coming day, Oracle hatched a plan to ensure he remained at the rear.

The next morning the group rose early and readied themselves for the day's hunt. Oracle was quite tired from a night spent hatching and plotting but decided that this was all for the good and would make his story more believable; on this hunt he had no intention of sleeping.

As the hunting party made its way into the dense forest, Oracle made the others aware of his presence, which was something he never normally chose to do; it was easier to blend into the background and become almost an afterthought, but on this day he joined in the hunting conversation and general camaraderie. When the time came for the hunting party to split into their various roles, Oracle asked if he could join the lead group, but Brados refused his request saying that Oracle was not yet skilled enough to take on such a responsible position. Oracle was happy with this response, but feigned disappointment and with a rejected shrug of his shoulders hung back while the others moved into their own positions.

Oracle knew that he would have to work hard, at least for this one day, so set about climbing the tall trees to gain the greatest vantage point, and rather than taking care not to injure himself as he would normally do, he took no care whatsoever and, within an hour, his body was covered in scratches and welts. Oracle also set a trap to catch a rabbit and from his position high in the tree kept checking to see if he had caught his quarry, and when he wasn't climbing he would be wading through rivers or pools, the mud of which stained his skin and angered his cuts and sores, making them appear worse than they actually were. Oracle put all his energy into that one day and even though he was desperately tired, he fought the very suggestion of sleep and continued his energetic vigil.

Eventually, he saw a rabbit struggling to release itself from the trap, which ensnared it and Oracle quickly made his way to the ground and broke the struggling animal's neck. Then he took the point of a sharp stick and stuck it into the flesh of the animal, tearing it open to reveal its innards, which he extracted and smeared over his body, before throwing the carcass as far as he could into the dense undergrowth to be disposed of by scavengers.

A short time later, Oracle heard the chanting of the hunting party caught on the breeze, indicating a successful kill, and he knew that the group would soon be united for the jubilant return to the village. Oracle was truly exhausted, but prided himself on a job well done and secured himself in the highest tree to await their arrival. Normally, when the group were on the return journey, Oracle would just slip in behind as quietly as possible, in an attempt to draw as little attention to himself as he could, but on this day he had other plans. As the group approached Oracle made himself ready and looked at his outward appearance with satisfaction.

When the group was directly below his tree, he called down to them, making them stop and look around. Oracle then began the long descent from the high tree and when he finally arrived at the bottom, the group was aghast by his manifestation; he looked as if he had fought a battle with a terrifying beast, so bloodied and cut was his skin. The group gathered round the exhausted Oracle and questioned him about what had taken place, but Oracle fell to his knees in a state of collapse and was carried back to the village by members of the group. Whenever any member of the group was harmed, or unwell, the rest of the villagers would take care of them, in the belief that every member had a vital role to play in the group's overall survival, so Oracle was made comfortable before being asked to recount what had taken place.

Oracle was desperately tired and it showed in his expression and speech, which he used to his advantage as he told his 'tale.' He began by saying how everyone assumes that the villagers involved in the actual 'kill' are more at risk and have greater skills than those who attend the rear; this, he stressed, is not so. At the front there are many hunters, working closely together, communicating with signs and sounds and making sure that each of them is safe from harm. Not so at the rear. He was left alone to keep his own safety secure *on top of his* responsibility to the leaders of the hunt, who had their backs to many potential predators. His role was exhausting enough, climbing from tree to tree to ensure the safe passage of the lead group without having to confront wild animals by himself. "Who is there to watch my back?" he asked, "If anything was to happen to me, then all of you in turn, are exposed to an ambush, maybe from the rear, or on your return journey. Imagine what would befall the village if that were to happen? There would be no food and maybe fewer members of the hunt would survive the ambush and then what would become of our village?"

Villagers nodded in agreement, or shrugged their shoulders, before he continued, "My position is vital to the kill and I have developed my skills in climbing to the top of the highest trees and swinging amongst the flimsiest foliage in order that I can ensure the village is sustained by the very survival of the lead group. And I have increased my own ability to hear and distinguish between the sounds that filter through the forest, so that I am alerted to the noises of predators that could be the hunt's undoing."

The villagers continued to nod in agreement and Oracle continued to speak, "I never ask for recognition as I believe a successful kill and jubilant return home is testimony to my skills, yet no one even notices I am there most of the time." Some of the villagers begin to protest, commenting on how they always noticed him, Oracle raised a weary hand to dismiss their protests and continued, "*but,* if you will allow this poor wretched man to continue, that is exactly *why* I am so skilled in my lonely task; because no one even notices I am there!"

Some of the villagers slowly nodded their heads with dawning understanding as Oracle continued. "Today as you may recall Brados" he weakly nodded in Brados's direction. "I asked if I could become part of the lead group, do you remember?" Brados acknowledged the earlier conversation and satisfied, Oracle proceeded, "Did you ask yourself *why* I made this request?"

Brados shook his head a little and replied; "I thought that you wanted to be with the leaders, at the front, where the action takes place, I suppose."

Oracle slowly nodded his head thoughtfully up and down, "Yes, I knew that would be your answer. Well you are completely wrong. Let me explain."

The villagers began to sit on the floor, all of them engrossed in the tale being told and looked with anticipation towards Oracle, who, realising he had now got their undivided attention, built the anticipation by requesting some water, which was duly given. Then, pulling himself up a little, he began. "First let me address the point you made about the 'front.' You, the lead group, as you so rightly stated, face 'front,' in other words you have but one direction to focus on. I, on the other hand have four sides to concentrate on, not just one, and while the lead group stay on the ground, cutting a path, I have to swing high between the branches and then drop down to the ground, before scaling the trees again, so that I can ensure your safety from all of the best vantage points at the top of the forest. I have to listen intently to the sounds that filter in from all directions, estimating their proximity and possible threat to your survival and this has enabled me to understand the forest. The forest is communicating with me and I with it." He paused for effect and took another sip of his water. "Yesterday, the forest spoke to me about Lugus." He focused his gaze on the man in question and all eyes followed his, "The forest said that Lugus was exhausted and in need of rest and that if he didn't, he would be unfit to continue with his role."

All eyes turn to Lugus, who slowly nodded his head in conformation, "Just as the forest said then?" commented Oracle. Lugus gave a slight shrug of agreement as Oracle continued, "When the forest spoke of Lugus I asked it what should I do, but I received no response, so I decided to speak to you Brados in the hope that you would listen to me, but you only complained about my lack of responsibility and dismissed me, but," he added swiftly before Brados could comment, "that is not of any relevance to the events of today."

Oracle had twisted the conversation between himself and Brados but quickly asked, "You recall our conversation?" Brados attempted to speak but only managed to utter the words, "Yes, I remember..." before Oracle moaned in fake pain. He opened his mouth as if to speak but paused and lay wearily back on the soft grass and then yawned, "but I am tired now and need to rest. I should tend to my wounds before I sleep."

People protested, saying that he must eat to keep up his strength, or at least allow them to tend his wounds but he refused, offering exhaustion as his excuse. His wounds looked severe, especially where he had used the blood and guts of the rabbit, blended with mud to such dramatic effect. Some of the villagers were gravely concerned but Oracle insisted that rest was what his body required to begin the healing process and so the villagers begrudgingly removed themselves and set about preparation for the night's meal and celebrations.

Oracle quickly fell asleep, even though it was only early evening, but this was what he had planned all along; he wanted to sleep now so that he could wake before anyone else. The villagers prepared the food and began to discuss the events of the day and the obvious bravery of Oracle. Others commented on his ability to communicate with the forest and debates broke out, with one side calling it an impossibility, and the others arguing its probability. All the villagers enjoyed the evening and men and women would select each other as company for the night while the children slept in a huddle under the trees.

There were no clothes in the village, neither was there any adornment or monogamy; the village was as a single entity working together to sustain life, vitality and pleasure. No woman slept with a particular man, or favourite woman and no man felt bound to sleep with women in preference to men; every contributor enjoyed the bounty of the village. Relationships did not exist in the 1-2-1 kind of way that we now believe they should operate. The intimacy that flowed between individuals surged between the groups with each person experiencing another. When the children of the village reached puberty they would celebrate and express themselves in their own separate clearing until they were ready to join the larger adult gatherings. There were no laws and no rulers; the village operated at a co-operative level, everyone contributing and developing the productivity of the village and therefore receiving and benefiting themselves.

Oracle had slept soundly enough, only being disturbed now and then by concerned villagers offering food, drink or company, and he woke while the moon was still high in the sky. With practiced skills in moving silently, he left the village encampment and made his way to a small pond not far away. He then immersed himself in the cool water and rubbed at his skin until all traces of the rabbit's blood and guts, as well as the muck and filth were gone. Then he searched out pungent leaves and edible berries and pummelled them together between two pieces of smooth tree bark, until a dark purple paste was formed. He took large waxy leaves and spread the paste on one of the leaves, placing another leaf on top before making his way back towards the edge of the forest clearing where he lay down, placing the large waxy leaf poultice over the areas of his body that had looked the worst, although once cleaned, were nothing more than small cuts and grazes. Then he closed his eyes and drifted in and out of half sleep, until the footfalls of an approaching person alerted him to feign 'real' sleep.

The first villager to approach was surprised at what he saw and bent to gently shake Oracle to his senses, but Oracle remained still, so the villager called out to others, who gathered round wondering what the fuss was about. That's when Oracle opened his eyes and with dramatic effect sprung to his feet, making the leaf poultices drop to the floor revealing his 'healed' body. The villagers were amazed even though they had vast knowledge of the healing properties of plants, herbs, fungi and fruit; they had never seen such a potent recovery of such brutal wounds.

Oracle was now in his element and strode towards the clearing where the remaining villagers were preparing the morning breakfast and sat on the soft grass. Quickly the others surrounded him, prompting him to continue with his tale of the previous night, the others urging him to explain how he came to be healed this morning. Everyone was asking questions at the same time and Oracle raised his hand to silence the group and then continued his tale of the previous night. He began by telling the assembled crowd that he was thinking about poor Lugus as he sat listening to the sounds of the forest, when the forest again spoke to him and told him that *he* the forest, had prevented him from becoming part of the lead group, because the forest has eyes and ears everywhere, not only below the ground but at all levels, from the deepest root to the highest leaf on the tallest tree. The forest knew that there would be great danger present in the exact location of the hunt, and wanted Oracle to be able to protect the lead party and therefore made sure he was in his usual place.

The forest then told him that a great tiger was prowling close by and that if it picked up the scent of the hunters they would be sure to die. It told him that he would protect Oracle when the tiger approached and that it would provide a heavy branch to beat the tiger with. It told him that there was no time to alert anyone or call for help as he would only notify the tiger to his presence and the forest said he needed to stay high in the sweetest smelling of all trees until the tiger passed, and then launch his attack.

All the villagers were engrossed in his story and Oracle realised, as he looked at the group of astounded, yet accepting faces, that if they believed what he had told them so far they would believe anything, so he continued, explaining that the forest began to shake its leaves gently to alert Oracle that the tiger was beneath his tree and that he'd used all his skills to remain silent as it passed quietly beneath. Then he told them that the tree moved its branches to enable him to climb inaudibly to the ground and stalk the tiger. The forest made sure that not a twig snapped under his feet as he approached the tiger unnoticed. Then as he moved to take his next step, a branch lifted itself from the forest floor and he grabbed it just in time as the tiger turned to look directly into his eyes. He continued his tale of heroic valour, of how he struggled with the tiger amid the leaves and branches, of how the tiger clawed at his flesh and of the final blow that sent the tiger defeated, running away from whence it came with its tail between its legs.

People were amazed and couldn't comprehend such a thing to be true yet they had seen his wounds, felt his exhaustion and watched him sleep rather than join in the festivities. Then they began to ask about the events of the morning and Oracle related his tale. "I was lying in a tormented sleep, when I heard a voice calling me to go into the forest. My body was aching with the pain of the fight with the tiger and my energy was low, but I felt as if I could not refuse, so I struggled to my feet and followed the calling. The moon was still high in the sky and no one else was woken by the voice, so I carried on until my energy gave out and I fell in the exact spot where you found me. I have no idea what happened, all I know is that my wounds are healed and I feel better than ever and ready to take up my position as usual!" Oracle jumped to his feet indicating that he was ready to go and soon the rest of the hunting party assembled and went on their way to search for the day's meat.

Oracle was extremely happy with his life. He spent his time in lazy pursuit of idle pleasures, gorged himself on fruits and slept on and off throughout the day. Occasionally, he might have to throw some sticks at passing animals, but most would meander off and posed no threat at all. Everyone had accepted Oracle's tale and on occasions he would be asked questions about the events, but mostly it was forgotten. He had achieved his goal and continued this way for quite a while.

Although Oracle knew he should be content, as he was living the lazy lifestyle he had wanted, there was something missing; we know it as purpose, but Oracle did not understand it as such, he just felt lethargic and had no zest for life. Soon he became quite bored with his self-imposed lifestyle and he began to notice that he was not as agile as he had once been. The day also began to stretch out before him, and where once he had enjoyed the solitude, it now frustrated him. He wanted the day to pass so that he could enjoy an evening of sexual pursuits and social entertainment. There had to be a way to achieve it and he began to think about how he could utilise *the already accepted belief* that there was some kind of 'all seeing' entity that had knowledge and authority over their environment. What if he built on this misguided belief? A plan was beginning to form in Oracle's mind.

He began in much the same way as he did before, listening to snatched conversations, or noticing if people rubbed or touched certain places on their bodies, indicating the presence of an ache or pain and he began to 'prophesise' many problems that the villagers were having, almost before they had consciously noticed them themselves. Then he started to create 'healing' potions that he said were a 'gift' from the forest and informed his 'patients' that the medicines would always return a person to health, if they *believed* in the wisdom and healing power of the forest. The forest was their life force and without it there would be no shelter, no food, and no warmth. They would have nothing without the forest, which, in its infinite wisdom, provided for their every need. And the strange thing was that even though everyone in the village had *always known* this to be true of the forest, for some unknown reason, they responded to Oracle's words as if hearing them for the first time.

He began to plant 'seeds of doubt' into the mind of every person he spoke with, turning them away from previously established medical treatments by inferring that they were inferior and that the poultices and herbal remedies that the forest provided were proving much more effective. As everyone knows, health is top of many people's agenda and the same was true in the village, which meant that most people turned to Oracle's medications.

Soon there was not enough free time available for Oracle to keep up with the needs placed upon him, so he began to casually plant the thought in as many people's heads as possible, that it might prove more beneficial if he was allowed to spend his time freely in communication with the entity that was the forest. Within a short space of time this is exactly what was proposed.

Oracle was amazed at the stupidity of his fellow villagers and felt something that he had never experienced before, individual power. Now he had all day to do what he wanted and as long as he kept vigilant, listening to whispers and noticing people's body language, he could create a *need* for his fraudulent services. So, for a while that is exactly what he did, and while the others provided for the villager's group needs, Oracle gratified their individual health requirements. But the contentment Oracle felt was short lived and, deep inside, he became aware that he could actually control his own future personal enjoyment and pleasure at the expense of the group, purely by influencing what they *perceived to be* truth. He decided that he would spend his time studying the plants and wildlife that thrived in the forest; this way he could dedicate his time to the pursuit of *independent* knowledge that could enable him to create the belief system that would provide *him* with maximum gain, rather than the group as a whole.

The first thing he had to do was to convince the group that he should be allowed to work purely in the quest of beneficial medications to maintain the health and wellbeing of the villagers. He decided that the best way to approach this was to work with the villager's *fears* so he hatched a plot to hasten the appropriate moment.

Oracle knew which plants to use to generate a fever in humans, especially the young; this information had been passed down through the generations, as had the antidote, should anyone be unfortunate enough to consume the poisonous plant. Thankfully, this had not happened for many generations. What Oracle was about to do had never, in the history of the village, been done before; he was about to risk the lives of the village children for his own personal gain and he was *totally* aware of that fact. The thing was, the more he thought about it, the more excited he became by the created image. For as long as he could remember, everyone had performed every single task and action for the benefit of the group and he began to see himself as above the group, superior to all of them. The more he thought about his plan the more excited he became; he would play the imagined scenes over and over in his mind and let the insatiable desire for power run riot with his imagination.

He decided to act that very night and, while everyone else was sleeping, he crept silently into the forest and made his way to the pond, which reflected the dim light of the moon, enough for him to clearly find exactly what he was searching for. He selected a few of the fever inducing leaves and wrapped them carefully in a large waxy leaf and then returned to the village. Oracle then began to pulverise the poisonous leaves onto the waxy leaf until a liquid began to separate itself from the bulk of the mashed leaves. Once he had extracted as much juice as possible he carried the wax receptacle to a bowl of berries, ready prepared, for the children to eat on waking.

Holding the leaf above the fruit, he pierced the tiniest hole in the centre to allow the juice to filter through onto the berries below. He then carefully tossed the bowl of berries to ensure that the juice touched as many as possible. As he moved the bowl around Oracle felt a feeling inside himself that he had never experienced before. He felt as if he had the power of life and death and he was about to prove it to the rest of the village. Oracle was so excited by his actions that he could hardly sleep and was awake well before he heard anyone else stirring. He continued to feign sleep until most of the villagers were up and about and then he joined the group for breakfast. He found it hard to control his feelings. He felt the same way he did when he was a young boy on his first hunt; although he had not been involved in the capturing of the deer, he had watched, fascinated as it lay pinned to the ground by the hunters. One of the elders had called him to come and give thanks to the animal for the life it was giving to the village, and he stood looking into the animal's eyes as its throat was cut and its blood collected in bowls and vessels. The power of life and death made him feel almost invincible.

Oracle watched as the large bowl of berries was placed before the children for them to share and he wanted them to stop their incessant playing and squabbling and eat. He could feel his heart pounding in his chest as the children's hands reached into the bowl, selecting the succulent berries and then placing them in their mouths. For a brief moment it felt to Oracle as if time stood still as he watched a young girl crush the tender fruit in her mouth. As she swallowed, she continued to laugh with her friends and then reached back into the bowl for more. Oracle felt as if he was going to burst; they were all eating the berries and no one knew they were poisonous apart from him. He felt as if there was nothing he couldn't do.

While everyone ate, Oracle began to address the villagers saying that the forest wanted him to learn more of its knowledge and that he had been told to construct a shelter amongst the trees where he could gain wisdom without interruption. The villagers reacted, as he knew they would, saying that they had always lived together and should keep things the way they were. Brados commented that if everyone worked in this way and constructed shelters in isolation, it would make the village vulnerable, and so a discussion ensued, which lasted until the meal was finished; the end result of which was that Oracle was denied his wish, but told that he could continue to spend time in the forest searching out remedies and medicines. Oracle pretended that he was happy with this outcome, but inside he was seething; Brados would soon learn that Oracle was a force to be reckoned with; he would make sure of that.

Oracle knew he had to act before the poison induced a fever in any of the children, so he stood up dramatically and began to speak as if he was having a conversation with someone. The other villagers were alarmed by his behaviour but gathered closer to hear what Oracle was saying. Oracle held his hands outstretched towards the forest and spoke, "I did as you asked 'magnificent one,' but they will not agree… what can I do to appease you…they do believe in your knowledge and wisdom… please don't do that 'magnificent one' they are only children…don't go, please I beg you, there must be something I can do…wait…come back" and with that he fell onto the ground and began to behave as if he were having a spasm.

People clamoured to observe the scene and when Oracle was sure he had the benefit of a large audience, he raised himself to a sitting position, before holding his head in his hands and shaking it back and forth. Brados was the first to speak, "What has happened Oracle, are you ill?"

Oracle raised his head slowly and looked into Brados' eyes and said, "The forest, which is known to me as the 'magnificent one,' is insulted by our ingratitude. Magnificent One is the creator of everything that lives in this forest and that includes us, the villagers. We have denied Magnificent One his request and he is angered by our lack of belief in his magnificence. He is going to prove that he holds life and death in his hands this very day. Magnificent One has the power to wipe out the future of our village and will release his power before the sun leaves the sky," and with that he fell dramatically so that his body was face down on the grass.

The villagers began to huddle together, some worried about what the message meant, others saying that Oracle had become unbalanced by spending so much time alone. Brados clapped his hands loudly and stood on top of a tree stump to raise himself above the assembled crowd before addressing them in a loud, clear voice, "Quiet everyone, quiet please!" Silence replaced the muttering and everyone looked at Brados expectantly as he continued, "Friends, our village and many other villages, have existed in the vast forest for generations, and we have always respected the forest and it has respected us. We have nothing to fear, the forest needs us as much as we need it. We have always lived together, eaten together, hunted and gathered together, raised our children and educated them in the ways of our people and our ancestors; this is our life, a shared existence with each person contributing to everyone else's life. If just one of us leaves the group, we are weaker and more vulnerable than if he stays; we have to protect and care for each other. Now I think it is best if we all go about our business and make sure that we have food for everyone for this evening, instead of wasting our energy worrying about something that will never happen."

A cheer went up as Brados stepped down from his vantage point, casting a sideways glance at Oracle as he did so. Oracle decided in that moment that he would exact his revenge on Brados in the most publicly humiliating manner he could imagine, but first he had the next step in his plan waiting to kick in; it was just a matter of time, so he smiled at Brados and slapped him supportively on his shoulder saying, "Maybe you are right Brados, maybe I spend too much of my time alone, maybe I don't expend enough of my energy foraging, maybe I have had too much sun, who knows? How could a forest exact revenge upon us?" And with that he smiled and then shouted above the crowd, "Brados is right everyone. We have nothing to fear as long as we do what he says," emphasising the point by raising his fist in the air and letting out a whoop, which the relieved crowd heartily joined in with.

It was early afternoon when the youngest and weakest of the children began to show signs of a fever. One of the villagers was sent to find Oracle, but he could not be found, so instead one of the elders, who had some knowledge of medicine, examined the child. Before the examination was completed another child was complaining of feeling dizzy and sick, and then another and another, until all the children were calling for help and assistance. The elders, who remained in the village to educate and care for the young while the more youthful went hunting and foraging, were the ones who used to dispense all medication before the rise of Oracle, but lately so many villagers had become apprehensive about the effectiveness of their prescriptions that their stocks of available remedies were drastically depleted.

Some elders ran into the forest to seek out a selection of herbs and fungi that may provide the remedy to the burning fever that, by now, most of the children were suffering from. The problem was that they had no idea what could have caused the malady, so didn't know which remedies would be useful. Two elders, who had recently stopped being involved in the hunt, were sent to try to track down the hunting party, so that they could return and help them to collect the medicines, while another was sent to alert the foragers.

Oracle observed the unravelling commotion from the top of a tall tree and had an uncontrollable urge to laugh. It was all happening exactly as he had imagined, better than he imagined. Beneath him he could see the elders rushing about in panic trying to gather as many potential remedies as possible and in their haste and with a lack of diagnosis, they were walking past the very leaves that would provide a remedy. Oracle put his hand over his mouth to stifle his glee and once again felt a surge of power rise in his being. He was finding it difficult to contain his patience as he waited high above the frantic villagers for the return of the hunting party and Brados.

In the clearing the children were laid out, some rolling and twisting with pain, while others, mainly the young and the weak, were as still as death itself. Weeping elders fanned them with large flat leaves in an attempt to control their raging temperatures, but to no avail. Oracle estimated that he had until sunset before any lasting damage was inflicted on any of the children, and hoped that the hunting party would soon return, but his impatience was not generated to save the lives of the children, it was for his own anticipated humiliation of Brados. He continued to watch the scene unfold in the village and then turned in the opposite direction to see if he could see the returning hunting party, before focusing his attention to the village. The elders were rushing back and forth, some bringing water, others crushing herbs, some discussing possible remedies, but nothing was improving the children's situation. Finally, Oracle heard the hunting party before he saw them, as they cut their way through the undergrowth at a rate he had never seen before. At last the moment was almost upon him. He watched as the group ran into the clearing and dropped to their knees around the sickly children, not knowing what to do for the best. Lugus was the first to speak, "Where is Oracle?"

The villagers looked at each other waiting for someone to speak, but no one had seen Oracle since the morning. Lugus advised that it might be prudent to search for him, Oracle understood the remedies and how to apply them, and so a party was dispatched to alert him to the crisis.

Oracle could see a small group of villagers running towards the forest and he felt the surge of anticipated excitement course through his veins and with it came a realisation that he had no care for the suffering of the children, no concern for the tears of the villagers, he only cared about how wonderful he felt. He watched as the group dispersed into the forest shouting his name as they progressed and he revelled in their pain and desperation until at last, unable to contain his silence any longer, he dropped down. Oracle called out so that the search party were aware of his presence and waited with a smug smile until the first approached and relayed the devastating news. At first he stood silently, as if disbelieving what he was hearing and then he shook his head and sped towards the village. On arrival, the villagers ran towards him, reaching out to touch him and imploring him to make the children well again.

Oracle approached the children, some writhing in the unbearable feverish heat, some hardly moving at all and dramatically held his head in his hands, before springing to his feet and shouting at the top of his voice, "WHY?"

Then, running towards the forest, he kept repeating the word over and over again, "Why?" Then he did something extraordinary; he lay face down on the grass at the edge of the clearing and began to jerk his body in all directions for a few moments before slowly rising to his feet and returning to address the desperate crowd, where he raised himself above the mass on the tree stump that Brados had so recently occupied and held his arms aloft as he began to speak, "I tried to warn you all, but you didn't listen to me, you preferred to follow Brados, so now you turn to me to correct what he created with his lack of respect for the 'Magnificent One.'" Oracle turned slowly on the tree stump to measure the crowd's reaction and then continued, "But we have to put our feelings to one side, for the present, and find a way to appease 'Magnificent One' and hope that he shows mercy on the young of our village. I will go into the forest alone and face its wrath, offering my life if necessary, and try to gain the knowledge to heal our children." And with that he jumped down from the stump and met Brados' eyes saying, "Maybe I had too much sun eh, Brados?" before running triumphantly into the forest.

Oracle made his way to the pond and gazed at his reflection in the still water and believed he was staring at brilliance. He then gathered the required antidote, before pulling four giant waxy leaves from a huge plant. He laid them on the ground and then climbed a tree and began stripping the old twisted vines that hung amongst the branches, into long threads before dropping to the ground. Oracle then began to weave the threads onto the large leaves and when he had achieved his task, he tied the vine about his chest, spinning around to ensure the garb would not break or fall down. He picked up the antidote, wrapping it in a leaf and binding it to his outfit, and took a final look at himself in the clear surface of the pond. Now he felt truly magnificent and was ready to wreak his revenge and take hold of as much power as possible; from now on his life was going to be different.

Just before he entered the clearing he picked up two short, thick branches that had fallen to the forest floor and began to bang them together in a slow, loud rhythm. Most of the villagers were now engaged in sheltering the children from the heat of the afternoon sun, holding large palm fronds above their bodies in a feeble attempt to keep them cool, but when they heard the beating of sticks they raised their heads to see what was happening. Oracle was now ready and he relished the way the villagers looked at him; some rising slowly to their feet in amazement. Oracle wasted no time now, he could tell by the lack of movement coming from the children that the poison had now reached its peak of potency and the effects would soon slowly begin to wear off; he needed to complete his 'miracle' before that happened.

Oracle made his way to the stump and stood aloft, continuing to bang the sticks until he had everyone's attention then he spoke in a loud, confident voice, "The children will be healed." He hesitated and listened to the clapping of hands and the expressions of joy that filled the clearing and then continued, "Yes, 'Magnificent One' will spare the children, but not before I relay a message to you from the 'Magnificent One.'" A gasp sped around the group, with people looking questioningly at each other before fixing their gaze back on Oracle.

"The message is this. 'You have shown disrespect to me and all I have ever shown you is love. You have fed for generations on my bounty, yet have never given me any form of thanks for my ever-plentiful gifts. I hold the power of life or death over each one of you and of the survival of your village. I have now shown you my power. From this day forward, Oracle will be my voice and shall wield my power. You must provide for him *anything* that he requests without question. Oracle will adorn himself with my leaves and vines to remind you all of his direct connection to the 'Magnificent One' and when you address him, you also address me. None of you should ever doubt my power again. Do you all agree to my terms?'"

Oracle stood expressionless, as if in a trance and waited for the response from the totally confused group of villagers. Slowly, at first, people began to nod or vocalise their agreement, until there was a sea of voices calling out the word 'yes.'

Oracle scanned the crowd for Brados and noticed him standing at the back with his arms folded across his chest; he was not joining in with the others and just kept shaking his head from side to side. Standing next to him was Relta, one of the village women who chose to spend many of her evenings with Brados. There was nothing outstanding about her appearance, but she was intelligent and kind hearted and that made her popular with many of the villagers, both men and women. Oracle hit the sticks together to gain everyone's attention, "'Magnificent One' has prepared a remedy for all of the children. Take the contents of this package and mix it with fresh rain water and then administer ten drops of the potion to each child."

He released the package and handed it to a host of outstretched hands before continuing, "'Magnificent One' is full of love for each one of you. Once the children have recovered you must show your respect and gratitude. Oh, and one final thing, 'Magnificent One' will spare the lives of all the children, if you offer one life in return; the choice is yours!"

And with that he stepped down from the stump and assisted the elders who had already begun to mix together the potion as instructed.

Oracle could see that some of the children were beginning to breathe more easily, so he quickly hastened the production of the antidote and administered the first drops himself. Moments after the children had been given the fluid, they began to apparently 'return to life'; sitting up and commenting on how much better they felt. The villagers were joyous and surrounded Oracle, touching his hands and falling at his feet in total gratitude. Oracle felt like a god and surveyed the scene as if it was his kingdom and then announced, "We should have a special feast in celebration and give thanks for the lives of our children."

Everyone seemed so happy and thankful, almost like they had forgotten the deal that had been agreed, but Oracle didn't mind; he would attend to that later.

Oracle decided to return to the forest while the others made ready the feast, but before he left he approached Relta, who was hugging one of the children in a loving embrace and stood in front of her, "Relta, you have to come with me." He held out his hand, but she refused to accept it asking him instead what he wanted her for. Oracle was not happy about being questioned but gave her a smile and extended his hand again, "Relta, you are to come with me now, these are not my words, but the words of the forest. Please do not disobey, just do as 'Magnificent One' asks, please."

Relta reluctantly accepted his hand and with a backward glance at Brados, walked across the clearing and into the forest.

Once they reached the pond he indicated for her to sit and then paced back and forth in front of her before sitting down and taking her hand, "Relta, it has been decided that you are to help me with my work. This is a great honour for you. Tonight will be the last night you spend in the village."

At first Relta was shocked and made a move to stand, but Oracle took hold of her arm and eased her back by his side saying, "There is nothing to fear. Enjoy the festivities and we will speak again in the morning." And with that he indicated for her to leave.

The villagers prepared for the festivities, every one of them happy and carefree. There were two other people who had taken their leave from the clearing that late afternoon; Brados and Lugus, but Oracle was unaware of this fact, as he was too involved with his own imaginings of what could be. This festival was to be the best celebration ever as, in the minds of the villagers, their children had been spared and there was much to rejoice. Most other evenings, after the day's tasks had been completed and the food had been eaten, the villagers would spend time socialising with each other. Sometimes they would dance to a rhythm created by the pounding of their hands and feet or to beats created by drumming with the hands on a hollowed out tree trunk. This was always the time when the villagers relaxed together before selecting sleeping companions to share the night's comforts.

However, this evening, everyone was contributing in his or her own unique way, to ensure that this would be a night remembered for generations. The amazing thing was that no one had to organise the festivity; it just fell into place. Have you ever seen ants work together? Look at the incredible anthills they construct, the food that is sought and returned to the colony and the manner in which young are cared for. There is no leader ant telling the others what to do, it is just achieved by individuals behaving intuitively for the benefit of all. This was how the village worked, everyone instinctively contributing to the whole. Of course there were mechanisms that allowed for ideas to be shared or individual voices to be heard, but the supreme power collectively belonged to the village.

Over the past generations there were those who had left the village to seek out a new life in one of the neighbouring tribes and stories had been told about their reasons for doing so; most having a unknown desire somewhere deep inside that, although they didn't know what the passion was directed towards, nor what it would bring them, understood that they had to move to a place where they could find peace. The tales that had been passed down told of men or women who were tormented or who behaved in ways that were different and unexplainable. Oracle's character was not dissimilar in disposition and it was this singular thought that gave Brados comfort; maybe Oracle would leave the village and that would give Brados cause for double celebration.

Oracle admired his reflection in the cool, motionless water of the pond. He was pleased with what he saw; he looked different and he felt different and although he did not understand what this feeling was, he loved the way it coursed through his veins, making him feel that anything was possible. He picked some supple twigs that had flowers springing from them and began to twist them together until they formed a complete circle of perfumed blossom. For a moment he spun it idly on his wrist thinking about the evening ahead; he would show Brados, he would show them all. He held the power of life and death, no one else, and as he thought about it he felt ecstatic. He looked again at his reflection and began to pull at his hair, which hung around his shoulders. Absentmindedly he placed the garland on his head and then, on seeing his reflection, twisted his head from side-to-side. From the clearing the sound of drumming reached the pool and Oracle held himself up tall and straight and began to walk towards the sound of the drums. The throbbing of the beat pulsated in his veins and he felt immortal.

Food was laid out on huge woven platters at various locations across the clearing and groups of villagers were laughing and dancing as others beat the rhythm. In the centre of the clearing was the stump which some of the younger children had surrounded with flowers and which they now danced around, holding hands in a large circle. Oracle was inspired by their dance and approached the frolicking youngsters, flipping the garland onto his head as he joined hands with the children and skipped around the stump with them; he felt high.

After a short while the drumming stopped and all eyes turned towards Brados who was striding towards the stump, which he jumped onto before addressing the crowd, "Villagers this is truly a day to remember. Thanks to Oracle and his amazing skills in medicine and plants, our children are saved and our village will carry on over many future generations. I ask you all to give thanks to Oracle." And with that the crowd started to shout out their appreciation.

Oracle approached the stump and Brados held out his hand, pulling him gently to his side and then with both arms he hugged Oracle and then jumped down and walked to where Relta was standing. Oracle held up his hands to the group to ask for silence and spoke, "It is not I who should be thanked. It is not I who saved our children. It is not I that can decide what or who should live, nor what or who should die!"

He looked at the silent crowd before continuing, "It is the forest, the 'Magnificent One' who should be praised, not I. The children *know* that this is true, that is why they have laid flowers at the stump and why they dance around it for joy. 'Magnificent One' speaks to me; I hear the words yet I am but a messenger. I understand the power and the wisdom that the forest has and, after the events of this day, you must understand it too. We have to give the forest the life that it has asked for and we should give thanks that one life is all that has been requested!"

He stopped and looked at the assembled group who were looking around for someone to offer an answer; then Brados stepped forward, with his hands raised and stood before the stump, turned and addressed the group, "I have a life to offer the forest, if it is indeed a life that the forest wants." He looked up towards Oracle, who was almost beside himself with joy thinking that Brados was saving him the trouble of getting the villagers to agree that Brados should be the life sacrificed. Oracle answered him, "Of course it is a life; that was the agreement. The lives of the children for a single life."

"Good", said Brados, before shouting to Lugus, "Bring the life forward."

The villagers began to part as Lugus led four other men who carried a live deer, which had been tied with vines between two braces, the animal weary from its endless futile struggle. They stopped next to Brados, still supporting the weight of the large animal on their shoulders. Brados spoke, "We offer this life to the forest in thanks for the lives of our children." And with that he slit the animal's throat and once it was dead the men let the carcass slump at the foot of the dead tree stump. Oracle had speckles of blood on his headdress and body and as the crowd let out a triumphant cry he smiled to himself, silently thinking that even though Brados was still alive, it was Brados himself who had brought the animal to be sacrificed, he had slit the animal's throat; he, Brados, had complied. The rest would now be easy.

That night, as the celebrations wound up, Oracle searched for Relta, but she was nowhere to be seen and although others approached him to join them for the night Oracle was only interested in Relta. Eventually he saw a small group of maybe eight individuals making their way into the forest, so he followed silently behind them, until they stopped by the pool. The evening sun was beginning to fade, but it highlighted the one person he was interested in, Relta. He fixed his gaze on her to follow her movements and watched as she lay down on the soft edge by the pool. Then he saw another body lay next to her, which began to embrace and caress her; it was Brados. Oracle watched as they laughed and found comfort in each other before he skulked off to sleep alone.

The next morning, Oracle was awake early and helped the other early risers to prepare the morning food. There was much talk about the previous day and of the night's celebrations and Oracle appeared to all, as bright and cheerful. Slowly, the villagers began to congregate for their food before setting out on their tasks for the day. Oracle noticed Relta and her companions approaching and helping themselves to various fruits and berries, so he walked towards her and caught her arm saying, "Relta, don't forget that you are to work with me from now on. I will be going to the forest soon, so will meet you there once you have finished your food." And with that he released his grip. Relta agreed, somewhat hesitantly to join him before turning her back on him, commenting on the sweetness of the fruits to another villager.

Oracle made his way to the top of a tall tree and sat amongst the branches, his mind thinking of ways in which he could exploit his newfound power. He put his first thoughts into action when Relta appeared. He told her that the forest had said that she must stay in the forest and learn the ways of medicine to protect the villagers should anything happen to Oracle. This she reluctantly agreed to do, as her first priority was always the group.

Oracle realised that now the villagers had experienced 'fear,' in this case the fear of losing their children and therefore their survival, they would do anything to prevent the fear becoming a reality so all he had to do was to manifest a *fear* of an event, he didn't have to *manifest* the event; this made it incredibly easy for him to manipulate the villagers to do as *he* wanted, behind the belief that it is the forest, or god, that was actually 'doing the deal.' He was also secure in the knowledge that even the most articulate and verbal of the villagers, namely Brados and Lugus, had already proved their belief in the new 'god' as they had brought the animal for sacrifice. Oracle decided to exploit this to access as much free food as possible, after all, why should he have to share the limited food stocks when he could have as much as he wanted when he wanted?

He introduced the new 'law' that 'God' had instructed him to carry out at the next evening meal, by informing the villagers that the forest, or 'god' as it was now to be known, was unhappy by the way its glorious bounty was never shared with 'god,' and so from that day forth a portion of all foods were to be taken into the forest and offered as a gift for 'God's' wisdom, protection, guidance and continued provision of abundance. To Oracle's surprise no one vocalised any argument against the new law and at the end of each day a share of the bounty would be left at the edge of the clearing. Oracle would then collect this, after the villagers had retired, eating only that which would spoil and storing the rest in the hollow of a tree trunk. Oracle also set Relta to work collecting the various fauna, fungi and fruits to prepare into medicines, so this gave him more time to relax and focus on his personal ambitions.

Oracle's physique was now beginning to show the signs of inactivity and even though he was still a very young man, he was losing his muscle mass and body definition. He thought to himself, "Why should I, the great Oracle, have to compete with other men, who only remain muscular because they do not have the brains that I have? Why do the women always select the men with the best physique and not the man with the most power?"

He pondered on this for a few days and then decided on a solution.

At the evening's gathering, he approached the villagers and

informed them all that 'God' wanted everyone to display their *belief* and gratitude by wearing symbols of the abundance of the forest's greatness. Oracle, of course, entwined fear into the story by inferring that 'God' was all-seeing and all-hearing and would be able to use those 'god given' abilities to see who truly believed and who didn't, adding that it would be foolish to deny 'God' such a small token of respect, when the power of life and death, as had already been proven, lay in 'God's' hands.

At first, only a few villagers took to displaying their *belief* in the forest by wearing strings of flowers about their waists or threaded through their hair, but after a few months every single villager was adorned with some form of leaf or flower attire, mainly due to being reprimanded by those who felt it foolish to even chance a repeat of the near loss of their village. Oracle was in his element as once, not so long ago, certain villagers had found his display of leaves and garlands rather self-indulgent, now everyone was following his lead.

By this stage Oracle had mastered as much as he could learn about the medicines available and was in demand for his lotions and potions whenever anyone fell ill, but this was not enough for him, he wanted more, much more. He knew that he already held the health of the village in his hands, now he wanted to hold the bounty of the village in his hands, too. Relta shared her nights only with Oracle and, as she believed that she was doing it for the benefit of the rest of the village, she never complained and was a faithful companion to Oracle. Having Relta submit so easily to his every command, he soon became bored of her and wanted fresh meat to play with. He decided that as the health of the village was of prime importance he should be able to decree that other workers were made available to work for the forest exclusively. This way he could have another two women to share his forest tasks and, more importantly for Oracle, his amorous attention. Besides, he could really do with someone to prepare his food, as there was so much sacrificed these days to keep 'God' happy and imagined fears at bay.

Oracle did much the same as he had the first time he wanted the village to support his ideas, only this time he dropped small amounts of laxative into the drinking water for the elders. Once again Oracle was careful in his contamination of the water so that the elders would recover speedily once he administered the antidote. This time the villagers didn't have any form of discussion about who had the ability to save the elders they just summoned Oracle who told them that 'God' had sent the illness in retribution for a general lack of respect for the power of the forest.

A day or so after the elders had recovered, Oracle informed the group that 'God' wanted more women to support Oracle in his important work and the villagers readily agreed. He also said that the forest wanted Oracle to be provided with a woven shelter that would span between four huge trees, providing cover and safety for his work and also provide security from any wild animals that roamed the forest. Once more the villagers agreed and some, who would normally join the hunting, or gather food, were secured to construct Oracle's forest retreat.

Oracle now had his own shelter, four women to cook and provide him with an abundance of medicinal materials and all the food he could ever imagine; best of all the villagers were now so 'hooked' into the belief of 'God' that even when the hunting and foraging did not provide enough to feed the whole village sufficiently, Oracle never did without, nor did his women.

Oracle was happy with his lifestyle but he did miss the company of the other villagers and so decided that he could invite some friends to join him in his man made paradise. The question was, who should he choose? The first requirement would have to be that they believed completely in 'God,' so he had to find a way that would ensure that those who came to join him had complete *trust* in 'God.' He would spend hours trying to think of a way that he could prove the individual's strength of belief until finally he came up with the perfect ordeal.

A year had passed since the day the children's lives had been spared and Oracle suggested to some of the more obedient villagers that they should spread the word that a celebration should be held to mark the survival of the village which, they readily agreed, was a wonderful idea and set about to encourage others to think the same.

On the day of the celebration, Oracle told his women that they were to be allowed to join in the festivities and that they should adorn themselves from head to foot in garlands to show their compliance and belief in 'God.' He also told them that they should not venture away from him, but follow wherever he went and only speak when he permitted them to do so. The women were so excited about seeing their fellow villagers again that they did not care about the restrictions and set about collecting flowers for their adornment.

Oracle and his entourage entered the clearing some time after the celebration started; Oracle wanted to make a grand entrance and anyway, he and his women always ate the best foods the forest, and villagers, could provide so he had decided that they would not eat with the rest of the group. His late entrance afforded him the welcome he had wished for; everyone looked at the flower adorned group as they entered the clearing, some even stood up and made 'whooping' sounds showing their happiness. Oracle waved and acknowledged their welcome and then made his way towards the stump, which he did not climb upon. Instead, he stood before it and spoke to individuals who approached him with hugs and good wishes. He sat down and as he did so, his women seated themselves a few feet to the side of him. Friends approached the women and Oracle gave his consent for them to spend some time in sharing news and information.

Many commented on the healthy appearance of the women, two of whom were now pregnant, remarking on the glossiness of hair and their wholesome look which, of course, was in the main due to a fairly easy lifestyle, shelter from the weather and an abundance of healthy foods all provided by the villagers, although none of them seemed aware that this was the real cause of their hearty look. The women themselves put their health down to their dedication to 'God' and as Oracle had explained to them "reward for their selfless devotion to the wisdom and brilliance of the forest."

Oracle caught the comments of the women and, as they were saying exactly what he had hoped they would say, allowed them to continue the social conversations. Even when he saw Brados approaching Relta, he did not prevent them from talking and instead lent his head to one side so that he could overhear their conversation. Brados began by telling Relta how good she looked and of how much he missed her company and then he asked her if she was happy, to which she replied, "I am very happy, Brados. Oracle treats us kindly and looks after our every need. At first I was lonely, but now, with the other women, life is easy. I do miss the children, but soon I will have a child and Nelta is also pregnant, so it won't be long before we hear the cries of children again."

Brados gazed at her and he wanted so much to take her somewhere where they could be alone, but Relta did look happy and appeared content catching up with old friends, so he never let his desires slip from his mouth. Instead, he took hold of her hand and said, "You have always been special to me, Relta and I miss being with you, but I can see that you are happy living in the forest and, as long as I can see you, then I should be happy, too." And with that he got to his feet and went to join a group who had begun drumming. Oracle was bursting inside with glee; Brados would never again have any woman he chose. The only person capable of that was Oracle.

After a time, Oracle decided to make his latest decree ordered, of course, by the forest. He moved into the centre of the clearing with his entourage and clapped his hands while his women 'whooped' to get the crowd's attention then, with his women seated at his feet he awaited the gathering of the rest of the villagers before speaking, "Friends, thank you all for such a wonderful celebration of the "saving of the children." The forest is conscious of your devotion and will continue to provide for your every need. In order that this day should never be forgotten, the forest has ordered that the 'stump' becomes a place of sacrifice and worship. Any of you who are experiencing problems can communicate with 'God' through the 'stump' and you may leave any offerings you wish there. The 'stump' must be protected and anyone found defiling it would be punished by the villagers for disrespect and for tempting the wrath of the forest. There should also be a larger retreat constructed within the forest so that others can join in service to 'God.' As you can see, the forest bestows health and wellbeing on those that choose to serve with loyalty and who show allegiance."

He stopped briefly to measure the response of the villagers, who all seemed fairly excited at the prospect of possibly being selected for such beneficial positions, before continuing, "However, in order to show your commitment to the forest's service any potential candidate must be prepared to show their dedication through a personal sacrifice which will last for as long as forest deems necessary. Also, any candidate who does not serve the forest well will be sent back to live in the village and will never again be allowed to rejoin the retreat!"

Oracle watched as the crowd began to chat amongst themselves, some commenting that they would apply no matter how steep the sacrifice, while others proposed certain villagers who they thought would fit the role. Oracle held up his hand for silence and continued, "The sacrifice that is required to show obedience is celibacy."

He paused while a buzz of chatter passed amongst the crowd and then continued, "The period of celibacy will only last until the forest is certain that you have proved without a shadow of doubt that you believe in 'God's' magnificence. For some that might be only one or two seasons, for others it might take longer, so I advise only those who are strongest in dedication and belief to consider these positions. I will return to the village before sunset to meet with any of you interested in joining the service of 'God' in the retreat."

And with that he waved his hands in dismissal and wandered about the group looking at all the beautifully adorned women, before dismissing his own women to return to the retreat while he spent the night in pursuit of personal pleasure.

The following evening, Oracle recruited four men and two women to join him and his women at the retreat, their first task being to construct another shelter close to the existing one. Oracle wanted a shelter to himself, so that when he was supposed to be in private communication with the forest, he could really have a sleep or spend his time imagining other ways in which he could exploit his power. The construction was completed in days, with the help of many villagers who wanted to gain favour from 'God,' so spent long evenings threading leaves through vines to build a secure shelter in the hope that their labour and duty would be acknowledged. Oracle did bestow favours on those who showed such dedication by rewarding them with fruits that were stored in the retreats, which would need to be eaten before becoming ruined.

So, once again Oracle had his private space to fantasise, sleep and plan while others did his work for him. It was on one of these lazy afternoons that Oracle was alerted to the impending birth of Nelta's child, by one of the new disciples who was himself afraid to inform Oracle of the news, as he knew the penance he would have to pay for disturbing Oracle's time with 'God'. The others urged him to call out to Oracle who although angry at first, soon became calm and ordered Nelta to be brought to his retreat. He laid out a bed of broad leaves and began to organise his various medicines ready for her arrival. When Nelta arrived with the other women, who were expecting to attend to her, Oracle ordered them all to leave saying, "Nelta is to be attended to by me alone. If, at any time, I call out to one of you, then you may enter, but until then I want you to remain outside."

He then ushered them all out of his retreat and gently assisted Nelta on to the bed of leaves. He reassured her that she was in the best possible hands and told her that he was going to do a special dance to invoke the wisdom and guidance of the forest, to assist with her delivery. Nelta had total confidence and belief in his abilities and did as he asked.

Nelta's labour was fairly swift and soon she began to moan with the pain of the head 'birthing' and Oracle, who had done little more than dance around and watch the unfolding birth in amazement, stopped and brought a leaf for her to chew. He told her that the leaf would take her mind away from the pain and allow him to deliver the child as painlessly as possible; in truth the leaf had no medicinal powers that he knew of, but somehow Nelta believed his words and on the onset of a pain requested another leaf. Outside all the disciples could hear the words being exchanged and were amazed at Nelta's resistance to pain, which must, they concluded, be due to Oracle's prowess in medicine.

Oracle positioned himself so that he could see the birthing child and when he saw the head crowning on the final push to birth he felt a surge of excitement that he had not felt before. Then, with a final twist of the shoulders, the baby was born and so was the father. Oracle held the tiny child in his arms, still attached to Nelta by the umbilicus and watched as his tears fell onto the newborn's head. He was totally overcome with emotion and would not take his gaze from the child's perfect form. With a realisation that was almost overwhelming he said under his breath, "This child is mine!"

He then handed the infant back to its mother and called for Relta to assist him with the delivery of the placenta before leaving the women alone with the newborn infant.

Oracle felt a strange sensation rise up inside his being and he ran stumbling out of the forest into the clearing. He threw his body prostrate before the stump and emptied his soul into the ground beneath his crying eyes. He had a daughter and he knew the daughter to be his; no one else could have impregnated Nelta, this child was his and he once more felt immortal.

Some of the elders approached him and asked what had disturbed him so and he replied, "I have witnessed the birth of a messenger from 'God,' a birth without pain, with a message for us all that 'we can have a lifetime without pain if we believe in the forest.' The child is to be named Glory and she will be raised in the retreat, learning from her first moments to her last, the wisdom and beneficial abundance provided by 'God.'"

Oracle was soon blessed with a son by Relta, who was also delivered by Oracle's own hands and, once more, the stories were related of how the birth was painless and of how the women now thrived with health and an abundance of milk. He named his son Sequoia in recognition of the forest's blessings and all seeing eye.

Years passed and Oracle's group of disciples had grown, leaving the villagers with more work to do to keep up with sacrifices and ever-growing numbers in the retreats. Oracle was concerned about the welfare of his children, not the minions in the village; they had become nothing more to him now than moronic idiots who deserved to break their backs for his chosen 'family.'

One day, one of the followers informed Oracle that he has heard that Brados had been breeding discontent amongst the villagers, complaining about the lush lifestyle of the followers and how they, the villagers, have to work as hard as two people and then sacrifice the best of the food to the forest. Oracle thanked the follower for his insight and went to his quiet retreat to think. He had to find something that would quieten this discontent without compromising his own opulent lifestyle. So he decided to decree another law to avert any damage that Brados might be implanting in the minds of the villagers; Oracle was the only person allowed to do that.

He ordered a celebration to thank the forest for its continued abundance which was to be held in the clearing after two mornings had passed, and he told the villagers to bring only what they could spare for the festivities. He then brewed a concoction that he knew would cause infertility and poured the greenish coloured sticky liquid into the empty shell of a nut and then bunged the top with a small lump of clay. For two days he dropped the potion into Relta's drink and watched with a quiet satisfaction as she drank every last drop. And for two days he sent all his followers to hunt, trap and forage for fruits and berries. Each follower was taught how to find certain leaves, fungi and berries from all levels and areas of the forest, so were quite adept in the art of the work, they had just never had to do it for the provision of food, or in such great amounts, but they were spurred on by their belief and returned laden with succulent provisions.

The evening of the celebration arrived and Oracle made his followers construct lightweight woven carriers, which they straddled between their shoulders to bear the abundance that the forest had provided. All of the followers were clad from head to toe in garlands and leaves and were like a moving garden of colour as the entered the clearing. Oracle led the magnificent procession with Glory on one side and Sequoia on the other. The villagers cleared a path for the triumphant entrance where the food was laid out in the centre of the clearing. Oracle raised his hands to the happy throng and said, "The forest, your 'God,' wants to reward you all for your devotion and has sent his followers out into the forest with empty hands and returned them to you with hands so full. This is in recognition of your devotion. The forest has also instructed me to bring you some more guidance which I will do, but only after everyone has enjoyed the feast." And with that he threw his hands up into the air and the villagers stamped their feet and 'whooped' in delight.

When everyone had finished eating, before the dancing was to begin, Oracle called everyone to his attention, "Friends, I think it is time that I informed you of the words of the forest."

A hush came over the groups and everyone gathered closely to hear what was said and, once Oracle was assured of their undivided attention, he began, "The forest has provided well for us for generations and has blessed us with the magic and wisdom of its abundance. Without the forest where would we be and what would we have? Nothing! The forest wants to reward our dedication by affording some amongst you some special gift."

He paused and watched the amazed faces that sat before him. "The first gift will be bestowed upon the first followers who have lived a chaste life for many seasons. God has seen your strength, perseverance and dedication and I will tell you of your gift in a moment."

He turned to acknowledge the followers who were smiling in anticipation of their reward before turning back to the assembled mass. "The elders that live here will each be given extra fruit. This will be given to them by my followers who will gather the fruits themselves and prepare them for the elders."

A chatter of approval rippled through the group and content with the response Oracle continued, "There is one amongst you who has received special recognition from 'God.'" He paused for effect and watched as the group looked from one to another trying to guess whom the celebrated person might be. Oracle's eyes moved across the crowd, seeking out the person he wished to honour and when he saw him, pointed and watched the crowd stretch and raise themselves to catch a glimpse of the identified person, "Brados," said Oracle, "You have been given special recognition for your strength of character, your diligence and commitment to this village and everyone who lives here, your hunting and tracking abilities and your devotion to the forest, shown by your tremendous leadership and unfailing ability to provide fresh meat and fish for so many people."

Brados was being 'whooped' and congratulated by many and Oracle had to shout above the noise of celebration, "Brados, step forward so that you may hear of 'God's' gift to you."

He held out his hand as an indication for the crowd to part and for Brados to step forward. Brados was confused; this was not what he had expected and at first he thought that maybe Oracle was trying to trick him, but when he looked at the assembled villagers all cheering him, he became swept up in the adulation and walked to stand in front of a smiling Oracle, who pulled the other into his arms and whispered, "My brother, I am so happy for you," before turning Brados to face the crowd and then, addressing them, rather than Brados himself, continued, "The forest knows a great leader and you, my friend, my brother, are a great leader. You are to be given a special role, a role that will honour your strength of character, your strength of commitment and of course, your physical strength." He swept his eyes across the crowd and allowed them to come to rest on Brados. "You are to lead a group of highly skilled villagers to escort me to other settlements, to learn about their knowledge of medicine and return this to *our* village so that everyone may prosper and benefit from good health."

He held up his hands to silence the 'whooping' crowd, "This work may take you away from the village for many sunsets and the forest recognises that all sacrifice made by one for the benefit of many, is the greatest of all sacrifices so, as the forest is All Seeing, this has not gone unnoticed." Once more he paused and scanned his eyes across the group. Everyone was stamping their feet and Oracle encouraged their appreciation by starting to call out, "Brados, Brados" and soon the crowd took up the chant.

Oracle turned to look at the recipient of the ovation and saw in Brados' eyes a reflection of what he had seen in his own many seasons ago; in that moment Oracle knew that he had Brados exactly where he wanted him. He smiled as Brados continued to bask in the addictive high of adulation before raising his hands to silence the crowd.

"Brados, this job that has been given to you, is not an easy path to follow. There will be many as yet, unknown struggles that you will overcome, the biggest of which will be to leave the village and the comforts provided by such. So the 'All Seeing One' has asked me to bestow upon you a gift."

Brados turned to face Oracle, who extend his arm and wrapped it around Brados' shoulder in feigned camaraderie, "Brados, you shall not spend one night without the comfort and passion one such as you deserves. You are to be given a companion to share your journey and care for your every need!"

Brados looked quizzically at Oracle, not understanding his words. Oracle walked forward and took the hand of Relta who was bedecked in garlands and sweetly scented flowers, bringing her to stand at the side of Brados, whose eyes widened at this vision before him. Oracle took Relta's hand and placed it on Brados' shoulder and then settled Brados' hand on top of hers. "Relta will be your companion from this day on. Relta will always be with you and will obey your every command." Oracle turned to face Relta and said, "You, Relta, have thrived through your obedience to 'God.' You have carried out the forest work diligently and without complaint. The forest has heard you call for Brados in your sleep and understands that you too have sacrificed much to serve, without disagreement. The forest now instructs you to serve this mighty leader well and to give up all other physical involvements and be just with this one man. You will always remain covered in the presence of others, so that no other being may gaze upon what now belongs to another, do you understand?"

Relta acknowledged Oracle's words and, with a nodding smile, spoke "Oracle, as you know I would give my life for the forest. If this one small request is all that is asked of me, I am both humbled, and honoured, to do as the forest dictates."

Oracle let out a huge roar of approval that was taken up by the crowd and filled the clearing with a triumphant bellow of sound. Oracle smiled at his success, which turned into laughter as he looked at this once heroic man. Brados would never experience the recognition of his own child gazing into his eyes. The amazement of his control made him feel heady with the delight of his revenge, and the total ignorance of the assembled masses, who joined in with his laughter. Brados did not know what to think; he felt simultaneously confusion and elation. No woman belonged to anyone, all were part of the community; how could one own something that had no single owner? It didn't make any sense, but his doubt was slowly submerged and replaced by the incredible feeling of lightness that invaded his body, almost raising him above the crowd.

Oracle clapped his hands together and once more began to speak; "Now to the matter of the first followers." He turned his gaze in their direction and asked them to step forward. "You have shown the depth of your belief by denying to yourselves the delights and sexual passion of life in your endless devotion to an All Seeing forest. You may also select *any* woman or man, *of your own choosing*, to be committed only to you. This is in direct recognition of your own commitment to that which is greater than you and provides everything to you. It knows your thoughts and can see inside your head. The forest has recognised the unspent passion that you have each struggled to contain and has heard the silent cries begging for release. Now is your time. Each of you can select any person you choose and they will serve you as you serve the forest."

The first followers jumped and stamped their feet, throwing their arms about each other in congratulation. Oracle gave each an embrace and ushered them to make their selection, before smiling at his children and, lifting each to his side, turned and left the ecstatic mass to continue their celebrations.

Hours later he heard the return of his group of followers, laughing and chatting to each other and hugging and embracing each other.

Each had selected a partner and was intoxicated with the anticipation of sated desire. He moved to a position where he could observe the group, amongst who were Brados and Relta, and watched as the passion withheld for so long exploded in an orgy of crazed ardour. As he watched, he realised that he could direct every single individual any way he wanted. Not one of them had argued that one person cannot hold another unless it is what that person desires, and then, only in that moment. No one had shouted out against one person controlling another. No one had done anything, except praise the wisdom of the forest. Now he could take them wherever he wanted and he knew exactly where that would be. He grew bored with the lustful orgy that was being played out before his unseen eyes and in the relative quiet of his retreat, he turned his mind to his next challenge.

Oracle understood that to have power, one had to evoke fear in the people one wanted to exert power over. Fear itself was no more than a belief, so if he could make them fearful of some imagined event or instant then he could also make them believe in something else that was imagined; he had begun to understand the incredible power of the mind. Oracle was by no means a stupid man; he was actually very intelligent and perceptive and, due to a host of followers who were prepared to perform every little task he requested, it meant that he had endless amount of time to devote to his favoured pastime of observing people.

One of his preferred group of subjects to study were the elders, especially when they were telling the children tales passed down through the generations, of heroic acts of selfless courage, usually referenced against a triumphant hunt or never repeated talents, such as the tale of one of their forebears who fell from the top of the tallest tree in the forest and landed feet first in a pile of fallen leaves without a scratch. The tale had changed even since Oracle remembered hearing it many seasons ago. In his time the hero had walked away with "a mere twisted ankle and a few cuts and grazes," now it would appear he walked away without a mark at all.

Oracle began to ponder on this, wondering when it was the tale changed and if in the passing of his lifetime the hero would fall not from the tallest tree, but from the moon. When he watched the children, listening to the stories, he was fascinated in their animation and expression. Some children would cover their eyes and others shake their heads from side to side, frantically shouting out words to alert the hero of the tale of impending danger. As Oracle watched he wondered to himself, "What do they see? Is the tree in their mind tall, narrow and straight or is it bushy, twisted and heavy with leaves? Why do they stamp their feet when they know that the hero is about to step on the branch that will give under his weight and why do they put their hands over their mouths as he starts to fall? If they can experience all of these emotions connected to an event that they have never witnessed with their own eyes, what does that mean?"

Oracle spent hours pondering on these questions and slowly came the realisation that the individual does not have to experience an event in reality to experience the emotions that they would have *if* they *had* experienced the event in reality; in other words he realised that he could generate those emotions in individuals, or maybe even groups of individuals, if he could make them see in their *own* minds certain images. This was an astonishing discovery for it meant that he did not actually have to poison the children, for example, to make the villagers believe them to be ill; he just had to generate the *belief* that the children were ill. This would create images in the minds of the villagers and these, in turn, would evoke the emotions.

Oracle had also stumbled upon another amazing fact and this was that whatever he focused on in his own mind and imagined to be really happening, for some strange reason nearly always transpired. Like the night with Brados; Oracle had imagined the scene and played it over and over in his mind, speaking out his words and acting out his gestures, he had even imagined Brados' responses and, if necessary, rewrote the script before playing it to himself again and again. When the time came for the 'live performance' it played out almost exactly as it had in his mind. Oracle pondered on this long and hard but never really came up with any explanation as to why it happened and instead contented himself in the fact that "it just does" and began to ferment his plans based on this wondrous intelligence.

The other settlements in Paradise were scattered throughout the forest, which itself covered most of the land, and different groups of people lived in a distant kind of harmony with each other. Sometimes individuals would leave one settlement to seek out other groups, and on occasions new settlements would form, but there was no hatred between the groups. Every few seasons nomadic tribes would camp close to an existing village and they would be welcomed into the fold, sharing evenings of tale-telling, dancing and passion with the host group. In this way the gene pool was constantly mixed ensuring that genetic disease was almost unknown. No village used barriers or boundaries to depict what was theirs as there was an acceptance amongst all the tribes and settlements that nothing can be owned; everything was part of the whole and each living thing was dependent on every other living thing for life. Oracle had begun to change that long accepted view and no one had challenged *him* for doing so.

He decided to talk to the elders about introducing the children to the story of the forest and of his own involvement in communicating the forest's words into deeds that saved the village from extinction. The other heroes from the past probably never got to hear their own tales told, or witnessed the wonder in the faces of the children; but he would, he wanted to become a living hero, able to embellish his story his way, for maximum effect. The elders agreed and suggested that Oracle himself be the first to sit with the children and give them a first hand account of what happened. This amused Oracle and he told the elders that he would give it some thought, wanting to develop the tale in his own mind before implanting it in the minds of others; he also wanted to make sure that his own children were amongst the other youngsters, to hear the tale.

One afternoon, Oracle decided the time had come for him to speak with the children and to tell them of the amazing events that had taken place in the forest. He asked two of his most faithful and observant followers to accompany him and to bring the children from the retreat as well as instructing some other followers to bring plenty of fruits and nuts for the elders and the children. His arrival in the clearing was welcomed by a 'whooping' riot of voices and smiling, contented faces. Oracle ordered the fruit and nuts to be distributed around the assembly and then ordered the porters to leave. Then began his magical narrative and as he weaved an epic tale of heroic proportions he watched the awe-struck faces react to his every word.

At times he rose to his feet, pointing towards the sky and smiled as he watched the faces of the children and elders follow his movements. When he spoke, as if he was the forest, his voice changed and became deep, authoritative and strong and he authenticated sections of his tale by gaining agreement from the listeners; at one point he described a child hovering so close to death that his words were barely heard, but "I asked the forest to give me the power to hear, and to my astonishment I heard the child whisper 'Oracle, please don't let me die' and I held my head in my hands and pleaded with the forest to let that child live" and, as he finished speaking, Oracle scanned the crowd and pointed to an entranced child saying, "That child was you wasn't it?"

As Oracle fixed his eyes upon the child he also nodded his head in confirmation and, in turn the child mimicked the action and cried 'yes' even though no such words were ever spoken; it was almost as if he made the child *believe* that it *was* he who cried out 'yes.' At other times he would turn to his followers and get them to honour certain, insignificant comments he made, as this gave the *impression* that everything else was also truthful. Oracle delighted in this experience and realised that these were the minds that he needed to control first, the minds of the young and then, of almost equal importance, the elders.

After his storytelling session he instructed the elders that he would visit the children once a season to tell them further tales but, that they themselves should make sure that stories about the forest, and its power over life and death and, of great importance, its 'All Seeing Eye', should be told every other sunset. The elders agreed and thanked Oracle for allowing them to listen to his heroic and selfless tales of courage, alongside the children.

Oracle saw a way to exploit and further his megalomania. No

longer would the children and elders just gather to pass the time with storytelling, with some children choosing to weave garlands or rest away from the group, no, *all* the children and elders would gather together to be educated by new stories; his stories. How long would it take before the imaginary tiger, became a man-eating beast capable of killing ten men with a single swipe of its paw, and how long before his life threatening wounds became healed instantly? Yes, Oracle mused, education of the young minds was important and he would ensure that soon the tale of their ancestor falling from the tallest tree was a paltry matter no longer spoken of.

Oracle now put his other plans into action. Brados and Relta were ecstatic in each other's company and Oracle had no further fears of any issues with Brados. It never bothered Oracle to see them together, as he had only ever seen Relta as something he couldn't have, and that attracted him *more* than actually sleeping with her. He had not really understood the emotion when he felt it and now he began to try and analyse exactly what it was that had occurred. He reasoned with himself, that if nothing belongs to anyone why did he *feel* as though he wanted her to be with him? Any villager could lie with any other villager, or even groups would join together in sexual fulfilment, so it wasn't as if he would have been sexually bereft. Then the realisation hit him like a bolt from the blue; he *felt* the way he did because he *imagined* that Relta belonged to Brados, even though in reality nothing belonged to anyone. Wow! This thought started to snake around his mind awakening all kinds of notions. This was powerful stuff and he now held in his hand a further key to total control and, ultimately, power.

Oracle realised that he could only have *real* power if the people *believed* they had something to give, something that belonged only to them and that then and only then would they *fear* it being taken by someone or something else. In this settlement, like all the others, there was no sense of *being individual*, of wanting for wanting's sake, not for the benefit of some collective group. He realised that before he became powerful, he had viewed *all* the children as his, as did all the other men; in fact *all* children called *all* men 'brother' and *all* women 'sister.' Yet since the birth of Glory and Sequoia, he had not felt that way, something was different. He knew that if a fire raged through the forest he would run to save those two children before any other, no matter how many he passed in his search for Glory and Sequoia. The difference was that Glory and Sequoia were his *and that fact alone* made him defend and protect them above all others.

His mind continued to search, drastically trying to reach the conclusion of his mental struggle. And as he continued to toss thoughts back and forth, a realisation hit him, like the butt of a ram; if he *knew* these things, then what if someone else in another settlement realised them too? Now he felt another emotion rise inside him, panic. He was happy with his position and the way his life was. Anything he wanted was brought for him; he no longer had to root around in the forest, or swing from tree to tree risking life and limb to secure a particularly precious flower, he had followers to do that. What if the other settlement gained more wisdom than he has? Surely his villagers would desert him for the other and then he would have to forage for berries or prepare food.

The mere thought of it made him shiver and that night he returned to the clearing and released his energy in sexual pursuits, in the hope that it would clear his mind, but even the frantic delights of two women failed to pull his mind from its beginnings of paranoia. He had to find out what the other tribes knew.

Oracle set about organising a party to visit the other settlements, telling his followers that they would be exchanging knowledge to gain greater medicines and potions and, while in part this was truthful, only Oracle understood the visit was also to alleviate his persistent and ever-growing paranoia.

After a journey lasting six sunsets, the party of trackers, who had gone ahead, informed Oracle that there was a settlement close by. Oracle had never travelled more than a single sunset from the village and he was amazed by the incredible varieties of plant life that existed in the truly abundant forest. Some of his followers, who had been carefully selected for the journey, were picking various samples to take back to the retreat in the hope of introducing them on their return to the village.

As they approached the settlement a high 'whooping' of voices signalled them welcome and Oracle was relieved by what he saw and its resemblance to his own village. Local people approached them and at first they were amazed by the garlands and leaves that decorated their bodies, but extended their arms in open embrace to their visitors and took them to a clearing, much like their own, bringing fruit, nuts, honey and leaves as a tribute to their unexpected, but welcomed guests.

Oracle was overwhelmed by the friendliness of the settlers and realised that this was an exact replication of how his villagers, including himself, welcomed visitors or nomads. Almost spontaneously people began to drum and chant, while others rose to their feet and encouraged their visitors to accompany them in dancing to the heavy rhythm. Oracle watched the bodies moving in front of him and believed in his own mind that this dance was given just in his honour. One of the young women who was gyrating her naked body to the heady drumming, caught his eye and within moments she was standing in front of him, holding out her hand, and, when he reached out and accepted it, he felt as if lightning had shot through his body.

The young woman smiled as she flicked the garlands that hung about his waist, before asking him what they were for. Oracle returned her smile and said that he would tell her later, wanting only to watch her and stir his body to her own movements. Oracle did not want let go of this woman, there was something about her that made his pulse race and his heart pound, but he wanted desperately to talk to some of the elders about their potions and he knew that he would not rest until he was aware of the extent of their knowledge, so he thanked the woman for her attentions and made his way to the edge of the clearing where some elders were sitting engrossed in the goings-on of the surprised celebration. When he turned to look back, the young beauty was now dancing with another, who was caressing her body as they danced to the hypnotic beating of drums.

The elders rose to their feet in a gesture of warmth and welcome as he requested to speak with them for a while, and he sat on the ground and introduced himself. One of the older women asked him about his garlands and Oracle flicked at the flower heads and said that they were worn for protection, by all of their villagers and, as this journey had been a relatively unknown exploration, the party had wanted to gain as much security as possible. The old woman looked quite puzzled at first and then shrugged her shoulders and enquired as to the purpose of their passage. Oracle explained that he wanted to share knowledge of a medicinal nature that could prove mutually beneficial for all inhabitants of the forest and when the group of elders nodded their heads in appreciative understanding, Oracle smiled and asked when they could speak.

Another elder, named Drafos, advised Oracle that the village welcomed their visitors to stay, whether that be for a day or a lifetime, and then suggested that Oracle enjoy the bounties of the celebration, as the night would soon draw in; they had many sunsets to speak of medicines. Oracle smiled at the wise man as he rose to his feet and then stooped to put an arm around Drafos' shoulder, saying, "You are wise with the experience of seasons, so I will go and find a different solace this evening and look forward to meeting with you in the morning." And with that he made his way back to the milieu of the festivities.

Oracle searched through the sea of merriment until his eyes met with those of his desire. He walked to where she was dancing and removed a garland of flowers from his neck and draped it over her shoulders. She laughed and threw back her hair, stamping her feet in time to the pounding of the drums.

As the colours faded from the evening sky, Oracle asked the young woman to take him somewhere where they could be completely alone, so she led him by the hand to the furthest edge of the clearing where the grass gave way to the beginning of the trees and there they lay together as they watched day transform its beauty into night. Above the clearing, in the sky, they could see a bright moon hanging in a twinkling mass of stars and neither spoke as they just absorbed the magnificence of it all. Finally Oracle asked, "What are you called?"

"Rispie!" she replied.

Oracle whispered her name and held her throughout the night as if, without her heart beating next to his, it would mean certain death. As she fell asleep in his arms, he looked at her illuminated only by the moonlight and knew that not only would he leave this village with as much medicinal knowledge as possible, but with Rispie by his side as well.

Oracle had spent most of the journey formulating his thoughts into plans and now his plan was ready to be enacted. The most important objective was to gain as much knowledge as possible as he understood that health was the most vital of all human needs so, to control the health of each individual gave enormous power to the person who held that control. He also recognised that people experience fear as if the event they fear is actually happening, in other words the event does not even have to occur to experience the fear. It therefore followed, in Oracle's mind, that if the greatest human desire was health, as without health there is limitation on what a person can experience, that if he could generate fear in an individual, or group of individuals, they would suffer ill-health then he would gain control of their minds by implanting fear. With that control would come power, just as he had achieved previously.

Oracle met with his party of followers in the morning after sharing food with Rispie. He had woken before the sun had begun to rise and had gathered fresh leaves and threaded them into a garland, which he tied about Rispie's waist. He had learnt that Rispie was a member of the hunting party and that she would be gone for most of the day tracking animals suitable for the evening's feast. Oracle told her that the leaves would protect her and that every time she looked at them she would see his face in her mind and with that he kissed her before she left to join the group of assembled hunters.

Oracle's followers had all enjoyed the warmth and pleasures of the settlement and even those followers who were still in chastity had spent time in conversation with their hosts, enjoying the discourse. Oracle had sent two of his own hunters, one of which was Brados, with Rispie's group and requested that Relta and some of the others offer their assistance to the foragers in their search for fruit, honey and berries. He escorted the others into the forest and, after a short distance that put them out of earshot of the village, he gathered them about him in a close group and asked them to sit.

Oracle told the followers that they should casually join in with the settlers when they were at their work and begin to tell them about the wonders they had experienced in their own village through the guidance of 'God.' He said that he feared that these settlers may suffer the same dilemma that had befallen their own village when the children became ill and, as no one was wearing the insignia of the forest 'God,' it followed that there was no one in this settlement who had the ability to communicate with 'God' therefore, if the same fate did befall them, their children would die and with it the settlement itself.

The followers agreed with Oracle's analysis and began to show concern about what could transpire if the settlers here did not possess the belief, or indeed communicate, with the forest. One of the followers, a young man named Brekno, commented on how he thought it strange to see the settlers totally naked about the village; it had long been the custom at their own village to adorn the body with the fruits of the forest and total nudity seemed almost disrespectful to 'God', in that there was no recognition of the forest's magnificence and bounty. Oracle acknowledged Brekno's words and then posed a question to the follower, "How do you *feel* wearing the forest's treasures?"

Brekno was silent for a moment and then lifted himself up slightly and said; "Different, it makes me feel different!" And he nodded his head to affirm the words. Others in the group also recognised the same feelings within themselves and began to mutter in agreement. Oracle raised a hand for silence and then bending forward, he spoke in hushed tones, as if he was afraid that they might be overheard, "That feeling of being different is exactly that, we are different. We have been *chosen* by the forest to learn knowledge, knowledge that will make our village strong and healthy, we *are different!*" And with that he sat upright and held out his hands to the group in a final gesture of affirmation. The group followed suit and one asked, "Oracle, what does being different mean?"

Oracle let out a small laugh and replied, "What does it mean to *you?* That is the question that needs to be answered; what does 'being different' mean to you?" The follower, a young woman named Shelpie, shrugged her shoulders so Oracle turned to the rest and stated, "You must all *think* about what this means and we will meet here again at noon and speak again."

As he dismissed the group he reminded them to talk to the settlers as they went about their tasks and to *notice* how they felt when in the company of their hosts. Oracle then rose to his feet and made his way back to the clearing to seek out Drafos, the elder he had spoken with the previous evening.

Oracle found Drafos engaged in instructing the young how to clean fruit and for a while sat and observed the elder with quiet fascination, much like the assembled group of youngsters. There was something magical in the way he instructed them; he engaged them with all of their senses, inviting them to taste, feel and smell the fruit as well as visually exploring it. As he worked with the enthralled gathering, he told funny tales of other youngsters who had eaten fruit infested with ants and made the children giggle as he described, in a most animated fashion, the ants dropping from a poor child's nostrils. After a time another elder relieved Drafos of his duty and the children 'whooped' in delight in their enjoyment of his education.

Oracle approached Drafos and helped him to his feet and the two walked together, embracing the other's shoulder, to a quiet spot near a hollowed out tree stump at the edge of the clearing. Oracle and Drafos talked for quite a while about the different antidotes and potions that they shared in common and then Drafos reached into the hollow trunk of the tree and pulled out a variety of shells with clay bungs that contained some potions that Oracle had no knowledge of. As Drafos delighted in his explanations of what each shell contained, Oracle made careful mental note of what he had learnt.

Oracle noticed that the top of each bung had an impression on it, some kind of a mark pressed into the clay and he enquired about this phenomenon. Drafos explained that there was a time, not many seasons ago, when one of the elders gave the wrong potion to another, who had been bitten by a serpent and instead of the elder recovering speedily, he fell into a deep sleep that lasted many sunsets before his breath gave out completely. The elder had been so distraught at what had occurred that he set about finding a method that would ensure the same mistake would not be repeated. Drafos went onto explain that now each potion had its own symbol and these symbols were known between the elders who were responsible for medicines. Oracle was amazed at the inventiveness of the symbol creator and asked Drafos who the elder in question was. Drafos hung his head shamefully and replied, "It was I who gave the wrong potion; I. It is my duty to protect the village from harm by the wisdom that has been passed down for generations and I neglected my duty."

Oracle embraced the doleful elder and said, "I am astounded by your invention and will use the same symbols as you on my potions. When one sees another's hand get burned by fire, there is no need to put one's own hand into the fire to experience the burn; it's far easier to learn the lesson without pain. Now, be happy Drafos," he said clapping the elder on the back, "We have much to learn from each other, without getting burnt."

A thought began to steal through his mind.

Symbols hold power.

He could use this idea in his own village, so instead of all his followers *knowing* what concoctions were needed in each remedy, he could use the symbols. Then when a particular medicine was needed his followers could be told what symbol to bring, rather than the individual ingredients. He could then choose which of his followers he imparted that specific information to and almost instantly knew that his children would be the only ones who fully understood the symbolic codes.

At noon, Oracle made his excuses to Drafos and went to meet his followers as agreed, most of who were already assembled and talking amongst themselves. Oracle stood in the centre of the seated circle of followers and asked them how they had got on with their tasks with the villagers and there were rumbled affirmations of enjoying the morning's activities. Many of the group commented on how happy and content the elders appeared, and how they went about their undertakings joyfully and without complaint. Oracle had also noticed this and had found it strangely reminiscent of how their own elders had once been, maybe not so obviously, but similar all the same.

Oracle then focused the discussion on the earlier conversations and the questions he had directed his followers to consider. The first to speak was Shelpie, "I have reflected on what I have seen since arriving in this settlement and observed how I *feel* different," she paused, as if trying to find words to convey something she herself did not fully understand and then continued, "I noticed that when I was observing the villagers during the welcome and celebration, I was astounded by their indifference to 'God.' I was shocked by their ignorance of their benefactor."

Brekno interrupted her excitedly agreeing and speaking eagerly said, "Me too Shelpie, I mean look at the food that was served last night, meat, fruit, leaves, honey and berries, and all of it stored to provide for so many, yet not one of them even mentions 'God.'" Shelpie animatedly agreed with his comments and soon others were offering their suggestions and findings. Oracle allowed the discussion to continue for a moment or two, before holding up his hands and seating himself on the ground. "So", he posed, "If I were to ask any of you if you would be happy to remain in this settlement, rather than continue on with me in search of greater knowledge and wisdom, which of you would decide to remain?"

Oracle's eyes scanned the faces of his followers who looked bemused at the suggestion, before Brekno raised himself to his knees and said, "Who amongst us could remain here, where there is no mention of 'God' and the villagers afford no respect to the forest's magnificence. There is no offering of sacrifice or sharing of bounty with the very creator of the abundance."

Another young man, still pubescent, rose to his feet and looked to Oracle, who indicated that he should speak. Festo cleared his throat and acknowledged Brekno's words before speaking himself; "Friends,

I agree with all that has been said and I, for one, would not choose to remain in this settlement to the detriment of knowledge given by 'God' to us through Oracle. If I were to stay here what would become of me if I fell ill? Who would offer a sacrifice for my recovery?"

Festo looked about him and Oracle rose to his feet, beckoning Festo to sit and then responded to the query; "Festo poses a question for each of us to consider. Today, while I was communicating with the forest it informed me of the ignorance of this group of settlers. The forest spoke of their greed for its bounty without thought of *who* was providing the abundance. To emphasise the villagers lack of respect for the wisdom of the forest I was told of an event that had taken place a few seasons ago, where an elder gave an incorrect potion to another. This was due to a lack of respect for the power of the bounty that the forest provides; remember 'God' holds the power of life and death. The elder who was ill, fell into a sleep that lasted for many sunsets and then he died!"

Oracle looked about at the group and suggested, "In our village that mistake would never happen because we respect the forest and understand its power and 'All Seeing Eye.'"

The followers nodded their heads in agreement and Festo cleared his throat once more to speak. "Friends", he began, "I cannot remember as clearly as some, about the time before we knew 'God'. I cannot remember seeing people parading naked, proud, as if their bodies are more magnificent than the gifts and wonders that the forest provides; it embarrasses me to see such disrespect and vanity. So I have contemplated on what it is that makes me feel different and the only answer can be that I have 'God' and the settlers here do not." And with that he sat down.

Oracle touched Festo's shoulder in appreciation for his words and then said, "We have 'God' and they don't and that is what makes us different but what is it that 'God' gives us that makes us unique?" He looked about the faces until Brekno answered his enquiry.

"The forest gives us everything and without it we have nothing," he pondered at his own words and then encouraged by Oracle continued,

"So even though it appears that these settlers live in abundance, it is only an illusion, because the abundance belongs to the forest and not to them. The forest has the power of life over death." At this point Oracle interjected a reminder of the elder who had died here, before ushering Brekno to continue, which he did excitedly, "Exactly! The elder should not have died, but the one who administered the potion believed that he held the life of his friend in his hands and instead of seeking guidance from the forest as we would always do, he persisted in his belief with tragic and unnecessary results."

Oracle held out his arms and turned to spin in every direction saying, "This is what makes us different. We understand that there is a greater power, a power that deserves respect and devotion. Look about you at the treasures that have been created and the knowledge that this profusion of nature provides for us, and understand that to ignore the magnificence of the forest is to also ignore the power that such magnificence can wield. You are different because you are devoted to magnificence, bathed in its brilliance and protected by its 'All Seeing Eye.' You respect this power by adornment, humility, celibacy and devotion and the power that sees everything *acknowledges* your attentiveness by protecting you against all harm. Remember how our children were saved; they were saved because we respected the words and demands of the forest." And with that he began to stamp his feet encouraging the others to join him.

Oracle spent much of his time learning from Drafos about the symbols that identified the various potions and shared some of his own concoctions in return. Oracle, through the diligence of his followers, had developed many remedies that were effective against a variety of ailments and Drafos was content with the reciprocal nature of their meetings. When he was not with Drafos or any of the other elders he would spend time alone, deep in turbulent thought about how to exert his dogma in the settlement. He asked one of his followers, Selenie, to find out, as innocently as possible, about the incident that the forest had related to him with regard to the elder who had died and also urged the others to ensure that they discussed the events in their own settlement with regard to their children. Festo was especially articulate in this subject as he himself had been one of the afflicted youngsters, so Oracle implored him to tell the tale to as many villagers as he could.

Soon Selenie returned and Oracle took her to a private location where they sat together and talked. Selenie enthusiastically reported that everything 'God' had communicated to Oracle was true; the events had happened exactly as had been told. Oracle made no comment and encouraged Selenie to continue. The woman repeated her account and when she had finished Oracle asked her if she was aware of what type of serpent had poisoned the elder, to which she replied, "Yes Oracle, it was the serpent with the bands of yellow. Apparently the elder had been seeking out a certain seed head that grew by the marshy ground where those serpents lay their eggs, hidden under the foliage; he just disturbed a nest and paid the price, although with the correct medication he should have recovered to full health within two sunsets!"

Oracle praised Selenie's attentiveness and told her to gather the other followers together before the evening's entertainment began.

When they were all gathered he asked them about their discussions with their hosts and each, in turn, informed Oracle of their dialogues. Festo related that he had worked with the foragers and that when they sat and relaxed for refreshment, he had told them his story and watched their amazement. Oracle was pleased with what he had heard and informed the assembled group that any follower who was proving their devotion by remaining celibate, was now free of this incumbent and should enjoy the pleasures of the settlement while they could, as they would soon be leaving to return to their own village.

The followers were all exuberant and Brados lingered behind after the others had left. He sat down beside Oracle and spoke apologetically, "Oracle, I am honoured to be in this group and each day I give sacrifice to the forest for the wondrous gifts it bestows." Oracle went to speak, but Brados raised his hand and continued, "I am ashamed to admit that I didn't believe in the forest, or in the words that were spoken by you, yet the forest never gave up on me and invited me to learn what it is to believe. When Relta was away from me, I missed her so much, and one night I went to the sacred stump and challenged the forest. I called out that if it wanted me to believe in its power it should return Relta to the village so that I could share in her company. I told the forest that if it did this one thing, that I would serve it for life."

He hung his head low and nodded slowly before raising it again and continuing. "The forest proved more powerful than I had ever imagined; not only did I see Relta again, the forest gave her for me alone, and I, for her. For this I am the most dedicated and devoted of followers. I apologise for my conduct and my doubt." Oracle faced his old adversary and embraced him, and as his head rested briefly on Brados's shoulder he smiled to himself, thinking, "Yes Brados I know. I listened to your challenge", before releasing his embrace and urging him to continue with his devotion because "as the forest gives, so can it take away."

Oracle had work to do, alone, before the evening festivities, so he excused himself, saying that he needed to reflect, and went about his secretive task unbeknown to the others.

That evening Oracle prepared himself for the events that only he knew lay ahead and, while all the villagers were preparing the festivities, he covertly made his way to the hollowed out tree and searched for the symbol carved into the mud stoppers. Once found, he threaded the vessel carefully onto one of his leaf garlands, so that it remained hidden amongst the foliage and then joined in the feasting, particularly enjoying the company of Rispie who had adorned her body with flowers and fruits.

After the food was eaten Oracle asked if he might speak to the throng, and his followers, who were dispersed among the settlers, began to 'whoop' their approval and before long everyone was seated encircling Oracle and waiting for him to speak. Oracle felt magnificent and stood tall above the seated mass of faces and then he spoke, "Friends we have relished your company and have delighted in passion, discourse and the sharing of knowledge." He paused while the crowd banged their hands on the ground in appreciative approval, "Soon we will leave your settlement and return to our own village some six sunsets from here. We came here to share something of greater importance than just potions and remedies and I feel that this sunset is a perfect moment to impart this knowledge to you."

He gazed about the group and caught Festo's eye and indicated that he join him in the centre of the circle, he put his arm about his shoulders, "Festo here, is testament to the knowledge I am about to share with you and I will let him speak, but first I want to explain about 'God.'" And with that Oracle told his tale of communication and sacrifice, before handing over to Festo, who with great animation enthralled the gathering with his near death experience; once he had completed his tale, the villagers beat the ground and 'whooped' in celebration of his saving.

Oracle once again took centre stage before calling his next witnesses to join him, Brados and Relta. Brados recounted his anecdote of challenging 'God' and, once again, the settlers applauded his account. Oracle thanked both of his followers and asked them to be seated and then, taking on an air of authority, said, "We have shared our truths with you and want to share 'God' with you as well. We will teach you everything we have learnt from the forest and soon you will be enjoying the wonderful benefits that come with devotion."

He opened his arms expectantly but only one person spoke; it was Drafos, "Oracle", he said, extending his open hands in friendship, "we have enjoyed and benefited from your company and wisdom, but the bounty you speak of is *already* ours for the taking. We have no need to waste our time weaving garlands, or hunting for extra meat to sacrifice. No man would want to be joined to one woman, nor man; we are free to enjoy each other. We have no need for your 'God' but neither do we say it is wrong for you to believe. We enjoy our settlement, our way of life and our traditions, traditions I might remind you, which are shared through all tribes across the land. Any one of us could choose to leave this settlement now and would be welcomed anywhere because we share traditions, language and medicinal knowledge, but Oracle, if I were to visit *your* village would I be able to blend in so easily? I think not. So, let's hear no more of 'God' and sacrifice and let's enjoy the festivities before the sun spoils our pleasures." And with that he clapped Oracle on the back and waved his hands for the crowd to disperse.

Oracle looped his arm through Drafos' and they walked to where some villagers were already beating out a rhythm to encourage the mood for dance. Oracle appeared congenial and chatted about the delights of the meal they had been served and other such uncontroversial topics. They sat on the ground and began to clap their hands to the drumming until Rispie appeared naked, all garlands gone, and pulled Oracle to his feet and wrapped herself about his body to the pulsating beat; he told himself that for a short while he could forget his plans and enjoy the frivolities as he pulled her body close into his own and caught the subtle scent in her hair.

A short time later he informed Rispie that he needed to take a walk into the forest; he felt as if 'God' was calling him. He began to move away, when she caught his arm and asked if she could go with him. At first he shook his head and refused her request, but then he thought better of it and relented, much to her delight. They excused themselves and walked entwined in each other's arms, away from the clearing. Once they were away from the perimeter Oracle explained to Rispie that he had to perform a sacrifice and gathered together a variety of flowers, fungi and herbs and laid them out in front of himself, before lying prostrate on the floor, with his face buried in fallen leaves.

After a few moments he began to mutter and moan, twisting his still horizontal body in feigned anguish. Rispie tried to comfort him, unsure of what to do, when suddenly Oracle began to turn until his face was looking up into hers, his eyes almost looking through her and spoke, pleadingly, "I have tried, please you have to believe me, but they have no interest." He continued to writhe on the ground and Rispie fell to her knees beside him, attempting to calm his brow, but he twisted his head away and continued his begging, "Magnificent forest, please do not do that, be merciful I beg you, please." And with that he dropped his head to the side as if in a faint, causing Rispie to cry out his name, pleading with him to awaken.

Oracle waited a few moments and then struggled to open his eyes, shielding them from the setting rays of the sun. He feigned exhaustion and forced his apparently weary body to its knees before dropping his hands to his sides and shaking his head back and forth repeating the words 'no' again and again. Rispie did not know what to do, desperately trying to find the words to stop Oracle's torment until finally, with great exertion, he rose to his feet and encouraged her to follow his lead, then he embraced her and recounted to her, his experience.

He told her that 'god' was not happy with the words spoken by Drafos and was intent on vengeance, the manner of which was not revealed to Oracle, but what was made known to him was that 'God's' reprisal would only cease when Drafos begged the mighty forest and pleaded with his own life for forgiveness and the settlement's deliverance from retribution. Rispie did not understand the concept of 'God' so struggled to understand *how and why* such a threat to her settlement could even exist and Oracle, sensing her perplexity, decided to confuse her even more by implying that she was a witness to all that was said; had she not seen his torment and heard the words that were spoken?

Oracle began to mystify Rispie by insisting that the forest had been encouraged to see her wearing her respect for its magnificence, in the form of garlands, and was prepared to spare Rispie if she offered sacrifice to 'God' right now and bear testament to all that had happened. Oracle was extremely animate when speaking and Rispie felt a twisting sensation of fear weaving its way through her body; she was a young woman, fit, strong and healthy and had no desire for any form of suffering. Oracle became insistent, advising Rispie to grab this opportunity with both hands before the forest relented and sealed her fate along with the remainder of the settlers. Oracle kept repeating the events, with subtle changes to give power to the experience, until Rispie, bewildered and frightened began to believe Oracle's inflated version of the tale. Oracle, sensing her vulnerability, quickly took her hand, pulling her towards some vines, which he began to frantically pull from their support and twist about her body. Rispie herself participated in her adornment, until she was wrapped in the leaves of the vine. Oracle then told her to go and gather fruits and bring them to him and he would show her how to offer sacrifice and plead forgiveness for her distrust of the forest's magnificence.

Rispie did as instructed and soon returned with an abundance of berries that she carried securely in a large leaf. Oracle told her to lay the sacrifice on the ground and to lie, face down, on the forest floor and plead for 'God's' protection and forgiveness. Rispie did as she was told and, as she did, Oracle stood above her desperate body and felt the familiar surge of power run through his veins. After a while he pulled her to her feet and told her that the forest was happy with her sacrifice and that she would have nothing to fear from the forest as long as she never denounced its power and continued to afford 'god' respect and obedience. Oracle then, satisfied and empowered, urged that she should not speak of what she had witnessed, unless he gave her permission to do so and told her that he could now love her completely. Before returning to the throng, Oracle and Rispie spent time together in passionate pursuits, Oracle's arousal enflamed by the feeling of power that 'converting' Rispie afforded him.

The evenings festivities were enjoyed by everyone and Oracle and his followers spent what were to be their last hours, before they returned to their own settlement, in the enjoyment of people they had spent many sunsets with and Oracle himself spent much of his time with the elders, gleaning as many last fragments of knowledge as he could before the evening was over, until at last people began to move away from the centre of the clearing and all were sleeping.

Oracle had no intention of sleeping and, as the moon started to decline in the night sky before making way for the brightness of day, he made his way to the edge of the marsh, where he stooped in a squat listening and watching the ground for movement. In his hand he held a small branch with a fork at the end, which he used to trap two serpents before milking them of their venom. Returning back to the settlement he felt a wave of excitement run through his body making him throw back his head in silent triumph; he would show them *who* held the power of life and death.

As the sun rose in the morning sky Oracle felt the caress of Rispie's hand on his brow and he opened his eyes to meet her smile. In his mind he knew that he would not be leaving her behind and unbeknown to her, his smile in return, reflected this. Rispie said that she should help to prepare the morning's fruit, honey and nuts and kissed him on the cheek before attending to her task. Oracle stretched and then fumbled in his discarded garlands for the waxed, rolled leaf that cosseted the venom, feeling relieved by its detection. After adorning himself he made his way to where the elders had gathered to share food and conversation and, after friendly acknowledgements, sat amongst them and listened to their talk, joining in where appropriate.

He told his companions that his group would be leaving before the sun rose too high in the sky as they wished to make a swift return to their own settlement and share their new knowledge and wisdom. Oracle rose to collect some fruit from the woven platter in the centre of the group, plucking a large leaf from his garland to place them in. He then furtively placed this leaf on top of an identical leaf which, on its underside, he had carefully spread the venom. Others were also picking at the platter, selecting particular berries and eating them, before returning for another. No one noticed as Oracle, once his own fruit was selected, covertly rubbed the venom on the underside of the hidden leaf over the remaining fruit.

He then casually made his way around the large gathering to sit next to Drafos, discarding the hidden leaf as he walked. Drafos welcomed him in friendship, and when Drafos leaned forward to reach for some fruit, Oracle extended his fruit-filled leafy platter to share, which, of course, Drafos accepted with thanks. Soon the settlers began to go about their daily tasks and Oracle called his group of followers together and made ready to leave. Before their final farewells Oracle and his followers gave a final sacrifice to the forest asking for a safe and speedy return and their hosts 'whooped' in celebration and enjoyment at their visitor's final display of unnecessary obedience. As Oracle and his group left the settlement he wondered what lay ahead, laughing out loud and his followers, believing he was joyful, joined him.

They had been journeying for a couple of hours when they decided to have a rest beside a small clearing and feast on some of the nuts and seeds that their hosts had so generously provided them with. Oracle relaxed with his companions seemingly enjoying their conversation when suddenly he began to tilt his head first to one side and then the next, as if trying to 'overhear' some distant sounds, then he slowly rose to his feet and turned to look in the direction from which the sounds had come. Others did the same and when Selenie went to speak, Oracle raised a finger to quieten her, indicating that they all remain silent. Oracle then began to shake his head from side to side, turning to look at the bewilderment on the faces of his followers before asking, "Did any of you hear that?" Without waiting for any response he continued, "The forest is telling us to go back, something is wrong, we have to return…do any of you *feel* that?"

The followers looked at each other, concern and puzzlement generating a sensation of quiet alarm and then Festo began to nod his head in agreement and soon others were following suit until finally Brados announced, "Yes I can feel it, there is something wrong we have to return Oracle, I can feel it."

Soon the rest of the group were urging Oracle to heed Brados and to depart as quickly as possible, so he turned to Brados and enquired, "Why is it important for us to return Brados, what do you know?"

Brados shrugged his shoulders in frustration and said, "There is just something inside, and it makes me feel uneasy." Brados turned to the others asked excitedly, nodding his head as he did so, "Don't any of you feel it?" Others began to get caught up in his anxious questioning, nodding their heads, until all of them were imploring Oracle to return to the settlement. Oracle conceded to their pressure but not before remarking to Brados, "My friend, I hope that your *feeling* proves right otherwise we have lost a sunset and I long to be with our own kind."

They reached the edge of the settlement as the sun began to set and the villagers were grouped at the far side where the elders would normally gather. A silence hung in the air, which was only disturbed by the crying of babies. They had almost entered the clearing before anyone even noticed their return and when they did the settlers ran to greet the returning guests, crying and lamenting their situation. Oracle and a few of his followers made their way to the centre of the gathering, where the bodies of the elders were laid out in a row, almost lifeless, each covered in beads of sweat disturbed by the quick shallow breaths that sustained life. Oracle scanned the elders before asking anxiously, "Where is Drafos?"

Rispie answered, rushing forward to stand close to Oracle, "He is not harmed Oracle, he is not harmed. He has gone in search of a remedy, he and some others, but we have no understanding of what the cause of the fever is. Please Oracle, you must help him. He is the only one left who understands how to make the remedies. The rest are struggling to breathe. Please let me take you to him." And with that she pulled at his arm. Before he followed her one of the villagers asked, "Why did you return?" to which Oracle replied, "Ask Brados, it was his notion that we should return!"

As he was led away by Rispie he heard Brados recounting how 'he had somehow *known* that they should return' to the astonishment of the listeners.

Drafos could not believe his ears when he heard Oracle's voice calling out to him in the forest and he made his way towards his voice calling out his name as he did so. Once the pair came face to face they embraced hurriedly before Oracle asked what had occurred. Drafos told the perplexed Oracle that not long after he and his followers had departed, some of the elders complained of head pain and then began to show signs of fever, but there did not appear to be any cause. He said that there were no marks on the bodies, abnormal insect bites, or swellings or bruising; he could not understand what could have caused the illness.

Oracle pondered for a moment and then asked, "What about the food they shared this morning?" Drafos replied with a deep sigh, "No, we considered that. The food was shared out on platters from a central store, if it was contaminated then there would be others, not just the elders, and anyway, both you and I shared food from that platter. No, it cannot be the food; it has to be something else. I just have no idea what." Oracle patted his back and said that he would call his followers to assist Drafos before beckoning to Rispie to escort him back.

Once they were alone he took her by the shoulders, looked into her eyes and said in hushed tones, "This is it Rispie, this is what the forest told us would happen." Rispie became agitated by the awareness asking, "What should we do, we have to tell Drafos what happened." Oracle nodded his head, "You are right Rispie, look, I know my return from here, you need to go back to Drafos and tell him what you witnessed the forest telling us, he might listen to you." And with that he turned and gently pushed her, encouraging her to be quick. Meanwhile Oracle returned to the clearing and ordered that some juice be squeezed into a large empty shell and brought to him. Once he had his request he distracted the group by asking them to cool the bodies of the feverish elders and, while they went about their task, he covertly emptied the contents of the potion he had removed earlier from the hollowed out tree and poured it into the fresh juice. He then instructed the villagers to make the mouths of their patients moist with the juice and, if they could, try to encourage each to drink as they were losing so much fluid through perspiration.

Eager to assist, the villagers went about their duty, passing the large shell from one to another, pleading with the elders to drink at least a little. As Oracle watched the contaminated fluid drip into each elder's mouth he felt a rising in his groin; he held the power of life and death and it made him feel glorious. Oracle was still attending the sick when Rispie returned with Drafos, who grasped Oracle by the shoulders, begging, "Is it true what Rispie has told me?" Oracle looked in the man's frantic face and slowly nodded his head, "Yes, it is, Rispie was there she saw it all," and Rispie acknowledged his words by anxiously nodding her head and then recounting the tale to the assembled settlers.

People began to clamour around Oracle and Drafos asking them what they were to do and Oracle shook his head, before Rispie suggested that Drafos should do what the forest had requested and beg for forgiveness. Oracle and some of his followers took up her words and soon the whole settlement was ordering Drafos to address the matter. Oracle whispered to Rispie, "It is, after all, his fault. He was the one who challenged the forest." And Rispie repeated his words aloud, "It is Drafos's fault, he challenged the forest," and soon everyone was accusing Drafos and telling him to do something before any others became afflicted.

Drafos was confused, intimidated even, by the accusations of blame but feared that unless he did something the villagers would continue to implicate him, so he turned to Oracle and asked frantically, "What should I do?" Oracle felt conquest and decided to enjoy its spectacle, while at the same time making everyone else aware of the humiliation of disbelief. He told Drafos that he should adorn himself in garlands in respect of the forest and then return to the gathering, which he hastily did. Oracle then told him that he should stand at the edge of the forest and plead for the lives of the villagers, in the same way he himself had done so many seasons ago.

The villagers were reminded of the tale Festo had told them and encouraged Drafos to do his utmost to stop the spread of the illness to the rest of the village, so he called out to the forest, begging and pleading for the lives of the villagers until in guilt ridden anguish, he fell to his knees and began to weep. Other villagers also began to cry, joining Drafos in his pitiful lamentations, some of them pulled leaves from nearby trees and held them in their hands in an attempt to emulate Oracle and his followers while others kept themselves busy watching the children, who had been removed to the furthest side of the clearing, for any signs of contagion. Oracle was in no rush to stop the drama and, even though he knew that all of the affected elders would surely die, enjoyed the expression of remorse, grief and guilt that was being played out before his eyes. He noticed that some of his own followers had become affected by the mood and walked amongst them, occasionally embracing a tearful companion or offering words of compassion and encouraging them to offer their own sacrifices to show solidarity with the settlers and guide them in doing the same.

Oracle felt strangely aroused by the actuality of the situation, knowing that he was the only person who understood the reality of the punishment sent by 'God.' He walked about the settlement watching the various groups of mourning individuals and listening to them desperately searching for solutions to a problem that they did not understand. Oracle was pleased with his achievement and sought out Rispie leading her secretively into the forest where he satisfied his ardour to the drifting laments of the villagers.

The elders all appeared to be in a sleep of death, neither responding nor stirring to any kind of stimulus as Drafos continued his guilt ridden lament throughout the night, while others attended to the elders watching for any sign of release from the desperate malady. Oracle slept for a while and then, without observance, contaminated a vessel containing drinking water with a potion that would bring about a headache, nothing more, to anyone who drank it. He placed the polluted vessel close to where the children had been safely removed, in the knowledge that this water would be offered to them before any other and, satisfied, returned to the other side of the clearing where the vigil for the return to health of the elders was still continuing.

Drafos was a broken man, lying on the ground almost covered in leaves, fruits and blossoms that other villagers had surrounded him with by way of sacrifice, belief or purely out of desperation. His voice was hoarse from his pleading and his eyes swollen with the relentless outpouring of grief and as Oracle watched the desperate individual he felt the delicious surge of power move through his body almost making him want to laugh out loud at the pathetic individual who lay almost buried from view. Oracle feigned camaraderie with the wretched Drafos and pleaded for him to join him in some sustenance before continuing his vigil, but Drafos refused saying, "How can I eat while they lie in deathly sleep? It is of my doing, not theirs; I challenged the forest, not them. I have to continue until my last breath, until all are saved and then, and only then, will I enjoy food and drink."

Oracle patted the man on his back and nodded his agreement before ordering his followers to join him and, once gathered, they all made their way into the forest. Once they were alone Oracle addressed the group, "Friends, I fear that the lives of the elders will not be spared." He looked about his followers as they heard his words, "The forest is not happy with the pleading of Drafos and has told me that others will die, maybe the whole settlement will pay the price of disobedience to the power that sees everything." His followers murmured and shook their heads in disbelief of such an absolute punishment and some pleaded with Oracle to beg the forest to spare the settlement.

Oracle held up a hand to silence the group before continuing, "What can I do? The forest knows that we respect and display our devotion to its magnificence. This settlement was warned of what would happen and still chose disbelief. This is not our fault. We have to remain strong in our belief that, regardless of the contagion of the sickness, that we, who believe, will not suffer. We need to leave the settlers to nurse the sick and we have to ensure that enough food is provided for the villagers' needs. I want you, Brados, to organise a hunting party with some of the settlers." Brados affirmed the request with a short nod. Oracle then looked at Selenie, "Selenie, you must gather together a group and go foraging for fruits, nuts and seeds." Oracle watched as Selenie and Brados selected followers to join them in their task and as Festo was about to join Selenie's group he called out to him, telling Festo that he wanted him to remain.

Once the followers had departed he embraced Festo and then took his hand, walking him to a fallen tree where he encouraged him to sit. Both men sat silently for a while before Festo hesitantly questioned, "Will they be saved?" Oracle looked up through the trees then shrugged his shoulders saying, "I have no answer to that. Do you think that the power lies in these hands?" He held out his hands dramatically before letting them drop lethargically to his sides, "Festo we are so small in comparison to the forest, we sustain one life while the forest supports every single living thing, including us. I have asked the forest to accept their sacrifice and acknowledge their belief in its absolute power, but I have received no reply. I have to await the outcome like everyone else."

Festo hung his head briefly and then turned to Oracle and asked, "How is it, Oracle, that the forest speaks with you? Why can only you hear, even though we all believe equally?" Oracle pondered the question for a while before realising that he could use this to his advantage. "I hear the forest in my head, Festo. At first it was difficult, maybe I would just hear a word or two, but then I began to understand more clearly so that now, when I ask a question, or the forest wants to converse with me, I am clear about the communication." Oracle paused for a while before continuing excitedly, "Festo, you should try it."

Festo shrugged his shoulders asking, "Try what?"

"Communicating with the forest!" He turned to face Festo and then held him gently by the shoulders; "I can show you, stand up and ask a question of the forest, any question, but ask in a strong voice so that it may be heard." He pulled Festo to his feet and then continued his instructions, "What question do you want to ask?" Festo shook his head from side to side before offering feebly, "Are the elders going to die?" Oracle nodded his head slowly and then said, "That is a good question to ask, so what you have to do is to speak your question aloud and then quieten your mind and see if you hear the reply 'yes.' Do you understand; just listen for the word 'yes'. If you do not hear the word 'yes' then we know that the elders will not die, so remember, be observant and listen just for the word 'yes'."

Festo nodded and reminded himself, under his breath, to listen for the word 'yes'. "Good," Oracle smiled, "Now Festo ask your question." Festo raised his head to the treetops above and called out passionately, "Oh, mighty forest who sees everything please answer my question." He paused and then raised his hands skyward and continued, "Will the elders die?" He closed his eyes and remained still, his hands projected to the distant heights of the sky far above, and listened for the word 'yes' and as he focused his thoughts in search of the word, it exploded into his mind again and again; yes, yes, yes. He shuddered and dropped his hands to his sides before falling into Oracle's outstretched arms and in gasping breaths said, "It said 'yes', Oracle, the elders are going to die!" And with that he fell exhausted to the floor.

Oracle knelt by the side of Festo and then gently lifted his head and supported it on his own knee. He stroked his young face, beaded with sweat and gazing into his own face, reflected in the eyes of Festo he smiled, "So Festo, you have spoken with 'God.'" He leant and kissed Festo's brow, "How does it feel Festo to know that 'God' communicates with you?" Festo slowly moved his head from side to side, "I felt so afraid; scared that I might have angered the forest with my question, but I continued to listen and focus my attention on 'God's' response until I heard the word 'yes' repeated inside my head again and again." Festo began to get excited, struggling to his knees and taking hold of Oracle by the shoulders, "I spoke with 'God' and 'God' answered me!" He laughed excitedly then got to his feet and began to dance around.

Oracle began to dance beside him until both fell to the ground and, in the heat of the midday sun exhausted their exhilaration in passionate pursuit of each other. Finally they lay fatigued by lustful pleasure, naked in a tussle of leaves that carpeted the ground. Oracle stroked his own body idly and said, "Festo, you are very special to me as you obviously are to the forest. We should not share our knowledge with any other as the forest has told me that you and I are the 'chosen ones' and that 'God' wishes only to communicate with us." He turned his head to look at Festo, "You understand that we are special and that we must not abuse 'God's' trust in us. You know that we have to spread the forest power and wisdom across the land?" Festo raised himself into a sitting position and turned to Oracle, "It is hard to explain how I feel, or to say what I understand. I feel exhilarated and honoured yet also sad at the word that was communicated to me. I also know that exchanging passion with you was the most enjoyable union I have ever had and I feel guilty to have felt such pleasure when everyone else feels such pain."

He let his head fall onto his chest and Oracle raised it with a finger so that their eyes met and said, "You will stay with me forever Festo. You will enjoy the pleasures that I bring to you, women, men, however many, as long as *I* bring them to you. You and I are chosen and I am here to guide you. If you take pleasure with any other they may be jealous of your status with 'God' and may try to steer you in the wrong direction. Many have tried with me." He paused and added weight to his statement with a strong nod, "I have never spoken of it, but some have tried, like Drafos to ridicule 'God' and implore me to think no more of sacrifice, even tempting me with lustful pleasure, and I have never wavered, but you Festo are young and do not have the years of experience that I have."

Festo nodded in agreement as Oracle continued, "So, to make sure that your belief in the power of the forest does not falter, you will remain faithful only to me and what I offer you which, I hasten to add, will be bountiful." Oracle took Festo's hands in his own and said, "You must swear your devotion to me and know that once sworn, only death can remove." Festo slowly nodded his agreement and Oracle smiled, "Good, then I want you to call out your agreement so that the forest hears your words and understands the penalty that will await you if you break your oath." Festo offered his hands up to the sky and called out, "I am devoted to Oracle and the magnificence of the forest and remain faithful in my devotion to death." Oracle felt the surge of power pump through his body, making his heart pound, and fell to his knees in awe and wonder at his own brilliance.

That evening there was no change in the status of the elders and there was some concern about the children, many of whom were complaining of head pains, much like the elders had the previous day. Oracle decided to call a meeting to talk to the villagers so assembled everyone available and began to speak, "Friends, I know that you are concerned about the elders, but there is nothing that I can do about that situation; that lies with Drafos. I also know that you are worried about the children who have begun to exhibit the same symptoms as the elders." He looked about at the anxious faces nodding their heads and continued, "I believe that the forest may respond to our strong devotion, so I am asking you to leave the care of the children to my followers who will offer sacrifice to the forest for their return to health, but I do not want their commitment to be disrupted by displays of disbelief, so ask that any of you who doubt the power of the all seeing forest should remove yourself from that part of the settlement and tend to other tasks."

A buzz reverberated through the group, which Oracle silenced with his hand, "Listen to me friends. You walk around naked showing no respect for the fruitfulness of the forest. You use its bounty for your every need but never offer anything in return; this is ignorance. Leave the task of returning the children to health to those who are not uninformed and maybe your settlement will survive." Oracle then organised his followers, putting Festo in charge of the sacrificial offerings and adornment of the children's naked bodies. Oracle then took Festo into the forest and told him to ask the forest whether the children would live, following the same process that he had before and Festo fell to his knees proclaiming that the forest had once more replied to him with a resounding 'yes'. Oracle feigned great joy and then said to Festo, "I have a special task for you Festo. You must take Brados, Relta and Selenie and set up a special place for sacrifice. Adorn it with blossoms and fruits and you must offer sacrifice for the health and safety of the remainder of us who have not yet been afflicted. As you know, disease affects the old and the young first, so we need to show our dedication and devotion to the forest in the hope of preventing further contagion." Festo agreed and set about his task while Oracle quietly secured himself in the branches of a tree and observed the clearing.

For two sunsets the clearing was split into two very separate camps and as the children began to recover from their head pain the first elder died. Slowly over the next two sunsets all of the afflicted elders died while all the children recovered. Drafos had not eaten during the duration of his vigil and lay in a crumpled heap amongst the mass of flowers and leaves that had been offered in support of his repentance. Oracle approached the fragile man and sat down next to him, sinking into the foliage that surrounded him, "Drafos, can you hear me?" Drafos squinted through his bleary eyes and nodded his head slightly. Oracle continued, "You can lay here no longer my friend, you must eat and regain your strength. I am going to help you to your feet and then take you for some fruit."

And with that he requested the assistance of two villagers to drag the almost lifeless body to the centre of the clearing where food was being shared. Oracle told the villagers to take care of Drafos and, as he was about to leave, he felt a hand grip his ankle and turned to see that it was Drafos who was holding it. Oracle asked Drafos what he wanted and Drafos indicated for Oracle to come closer so that he could hear his words. Oracle stooped so that his head was close to Drafos' and then strained to hear the hoarse soft words that left his lips, "I believe," before he smiled and strode away.

Now, I could continue with the story for another couple of centuries, telling of how the settlers in different villages began to hear of the events that occurred. Maybe nomadic tribes spread the tales, or maybe the children, who in later years decided to move to other villages. Maybe Oracle came up with more ridiculous ways of showing devotion, like giving one tenth of everything you own or earn to 'God,' or possibly in some form of physical mutilation so that your allegiance to 'God' was carved into your physical body. However Oracle decided that obedience should be displayed, he could make others do it, even if that meant sexual depravation, mutilation or self flagellation, because he had generated fear in them and he was aware that fear is contagious.

But he had also set another method of gaining devotion and that was through belief; this combination is incredibly powerful. Oracle understood that by controlling the knowledge of medication and medicines that he also controlled the health of the population so to have power over as many people as possible he needed to gain as much knowledge in this field as he could, ensuring that the assimilated wisdom remained with him. He may have shared some of this knowledge with groups of people, but the important remedies and potions would soon become secret from everyone but himself and a select, and trusted, few. Oracle had achieved what many of us spend a lifetime trying to achieve; power. The problem with power is that it brings with it a sense of fear all of its own; fear of the *loss* of power and this can feel almost as shocking and terrifying, as the fear of death. To maintain his position of supremacy it may have served Oracle to raise others to a position of influence or command, as long as their first priority remained to obey *his* creation of 'God.'

Oracle may have ruled until the end of his days, growing fat off the toil and servitude of others, or he may have encountered his nemesis. What if Festo began to tire of always serving under Oracle? What if Festo decided that he wanted to lie with whom he desired, rather than at the dictate of another (A bit like Henry VIII)? What if Festo created his own 'God' or hijacked the forest 'God' for his own? What if there was another Oracle living in a different settlement that had also realised this route to power?

Well eventually, if you followed the story from beginning to end, you might end up where you are today; in a world full of religions and cults, all believing in the same thing, 'God', but expressed in different ways. Imagine the wealth that these religions would possess as they, upholders of the faith, took more and more from the faithful in their devotion and obedience to 'God' and how they would use that wealth to gather more and more followers because with each new follower came a new 'blank cheque' to ward off evil powers, sickness and destitution.

The final outcome of this story would be of a planet controlled by powerful groups that had gained their dominance through fear, and victory over their opponents by death and propaganda. It would be no surprise to find that eventually, only a few groups would remain, gathering strength and membership by offering the ultimate membership reward card; eternal life in paradise. Of course they would have to compete with each other for members to sign up for their 'loyalty cards,' so they could offer bonuses like 10 paradise points if you mutilate your children's bodies before they are old enough to argue against such a barbaric act. In that way the children grow up to believe that it is acceptable, any other kind of reasoning would make them realise that their parents actually agreed to them being physically abused or mutilated in some manner and that would not make any sense in their heads, especially if the parents were otherwise loving and caring.

Or they might deem that no child could be buried with dignity, close to where its family could spend time in quiet reflection, if it had not had a drop of water rubbed on its forehead. One group might also 'demonise' the other groups, degrading their way of life, as lived through their beliefs, insisting it would offer nothing in comparison to their own, stating 'God' belonged to them, any other 'God' was fake and could not provide eternal and everlasting paradise, as it did not posses the power to do so. Even if, as an individual, you did not believe in 'god' full stop, it might be that you supported the religious leaders of your host cult simply because you did not want to be ruled by the religious leaders of some foreign cult. And so it spins on and on until it has to inevitably reach the ultimate battle of 'God' versus 'God.'

Is this not where we have now found ourselves?

Most countries have governments that are filled to overflowing with members who yield to religious pressure – for the religious bodies have the financial power through years of tithing and greedy exploitation – to purchase representation so that their religious interests are maintained. Vast amounts of money, which could be supporting people to achieve, are being spent on weapons to destroy; annihilation given preference over creation.

Have you ever considered how this long story of religion will play out?

Ask yourself some searching questions about your beliefs to find out what it is that you believe. I have listed some of the thoughts I considered when thinking about my belief in a personal 'God' defined as one who exists as a supernatural being, who created and designed everything in the universe.

My thoughts:

1. If this entity is so powerful then why does 'God' not speak to us all? Why would 'God' leave such important matters as 'life eternal' for one specific individual to communicate?

2.   If we are loved so much by 'God' why not stop the destruction, violence and death? Why would 'God' want to destroy that which it had created? And if you answer that 'God' gave us free will, then why try to annihilate the free will bestowed by 'God' on each of us to choose our own path?

3.   If 'God' is 'all seeing' then 'God' must have already seen the end result of its creation, so why bother to 'go through the motions' of something it has already experienced?

4.   Who created 'God'?

5.   Would not a 'God' that designed and created us in perfection (created in the image of its own perfect being) be offended by us mere mortals covering such a creation with our own pathetic manufacture of garments?

6.   Might not 'God' feel a little put out by our insistence of worshipping its brilliance, not in the presence of its magnificent creation, but in buildings constructed by man?

7.   If 'God' created us in its image then why do we mutilate 'God's brilliant representation?

8.   If we are so sure in our belief in 'God' then why do we insist on forcing our views into the minds of our children, not allowing them to reach their own enlightened conclusions for themselves?

9.   And finally if 'God' is all-knowing then 'God' must understand all that is to be understood, so what would be the point of life, even given free will, as being omniparous

'God' would produce all things including the outcome of free will?

Those of us who do not believe in a personal 'God' cannot sit on the fence of religious indifference as the two words are incongruent with each other and, if the battle for religious power continues on its eventual path of devastation, then there will no longer be a fence to sit on. For those of us who do believe in a personal 'God' we have to explore our own beliefs. I am not here to tell you what to believe or even to say that my truth is right and that your belief is wrong, after all, I am a madwoman; I just express my own thoughts and tell you not to believe them. Find your own truth. Explore, enquire and believe whatever you will. Each of us is responsible for the world we inhabit and if we continue to bury our heads in the religious dogma that perpetuates the battles for religious supremacy, then we *are* responsible for the bomb that obliterates a city or the bullet that destroys a life and, in turn, a family.

Throughout history there have been 'free thinkers' who have attempted to enlighten us about religious dogma and the arrogance and stupidity of it all. No matter which part of the world these enlightened individuals originated from, their beliefs run parallel with each other, speaking of a 'God' within, represented by internal wisdom within our own control rather than an eternal power that dominates without our control. Many of these free thinkers did gather followings of people who, for one reason or another, believed that there had to be a different way and, once the powers that be realised that people were actually listening to them, the paranoia set in. The end result would be death and devastation to those who challenged the base of power, or the religious order. And if the crowds continued to listen, knowing somewhere deep inside, they were hearing the 'truth', then the 'free thinker' would be hijacked and made into some kind of religious prophet and so the cycle of dogma, fear and control would begin once more.

When I read the words of Jesus, Mohammad, Tao, Krishna, Buddha and a whole host of others, the thing that strikes me is that they are all essentially teaching the same thing, yet their individual words have been twisted and turned and wrapped in silk robes, incense and ritual until they become lost within dogma, power, fear, political intrigue and hatred.

It is my belief that we are God. I do not need to wear any man-made sign to prove my allegiance or attend gatherings to participate in rituals, or to only eat certain foods at specific times, or deny myself anything. I do not need to prove it to you, or my sister, or any other being on this planet because if you do not believe me, then it is really your problem, not mine. And of course the reverse is also true. You do not need to prove to me that your belief is truth because then, if I didn't believe, it would possibly become my problem, not yours. This is really what it all boils down to, all the hatred, wars, devastation, manipulation, greed and domination and I guess I think there has been enough of that. So if we all just supported our own beliefs and allowed others to do the same then there would be no problem. Why should it really matter to me what you believe? It shouldn't. As we have already discovered, you may believe yourself to be too fat, too ugly, too happy, or too sad and that has no impact on my own life so why should your belief in 'God' affect me any differently?

There has been an individual, in recent history, that I think spoke at the same level as the greatest orators of 'truth', John Lennon. Through his music he conveyed his thoughts on this world that we inhabit and many became enlightened in listening to his songs and like so many before him, he was killed for generating a following. He posed questions that those in power had no answers for and rather than wait for John to threaten the 'world order' as more people questioned their own beliefs, he was 'taken out' of the equation. Those who control the masses with the image of the cross, backed up by the bullet, had learnt from history.

Do you think John Lennon would want to be seen as a 'prophet' and have his beliefs turned into limitations of freedom? Would he want people to hang golden bullets from chains around their necks in memory of his life, sacrificed so unnecessarily? I don't think so. All John Lennon wanted people to do was 'imagine.'

I ask you now to question your own (and I use that word loosely) beliefs and to imagine a world where you could live without limitation, restriction and dominance and allow each and every one of us to do the same. Maybe then you, like me, will imagine a heaven created right here, right now, on Earth.

The Bit Where I Rant About...
Food

I went to visit a friend of mine the other day, one who I have not visited for over a year. We sat in her garden chatting about various things, while her two year-old daughter and five-year old son played with various toys. Her daughter, Ruby, is at the stage of saying single words and looks like a cherub with blonde corkscrew curls, beautiful clear blue eyes and the face of an angel.

As Jo and I talked, Ruby came and started to play with the grass and dry mud close by. I watched her delight at pulling up the grass and crumbling the dry mud into a powder and watching, fascinated, as it dropped through her fingers. I also became spellbound and joined in with her play; breaking the mud and watching it fall through my own fingers. Ruby then stood up and toddled a few feet away where something had caught her eye, so I began to talk with Jo again. Moments later Ruby stood before me and held out her hand in which she was holding a small piece of cardboard, onto which she had placed some stalks of grass. I held out my hand to take her offering and our eyes met. There was such intensity about her that she held me mesmerised, a connection so strong that I felt as if she held the wisdom of the multiverse in her eyes. As I took hold of the small square of brown cardboard, she uttered a single word in a strong clear voice, "Food."

I smiled and replied, "Thank you. Yes it is."

I haven't really touched this book for months. I have thought about it, but somehow, could not express the words that I wanted to say and, during the year that has passed, I realise why. I didn't know the answer. And if I didn't know the answer then, really, what was the

357

point in ranting on about everything without at least offering *myself*
a way forward. A major part of the whole 'control' jigsaw puzzle was
missing and I didn't know what it was. My time over those months has
not been wasted. I have spent hours and hours on research, looking
for answers, answers that appeared so hard to find. But, guess what? I
think I have found them.

At times I thought that I had been wasting my energy. I mean, just
who the hell did I really think I was, to believe that anyone would be
interested in listening to me rant on about our responsibility for our
own lives when I still appeared to be stuck in the whole quagmire of
some form of control myself.

Yes the government stinks, religion keeps our minds focused on
the 'happy ever after in heaven,' preventing us from finding paradise
right here, right now. The education system is the biggest pile of crap
going, but, we still have to send our children there to be indoctrinated
into the same 'hamster wheel' of mind-depleting regurgitated crap that
we, ourselves, never really understood, or more importantly, benefited
or escaped from.

Labels keep us grounded in the worst possible way, limiting our
endless potential of possibilities into some cheap 'tag' that we hang
bravely from our necks, praying that it will bring us some kind of
acceptance, if not from ourselves, then maybe at least from others.
And, hey, you know what, if it doesn't, then we just have to find some
other poor bastard with a bigger 'tag' than us, to either empathise or
sympathise with, or, if all else fails, we can measure our 'tag' against
theirs, and at least feel a little better about ourselves, if only for the
slightest of moments.

I kept thinking to myself; what is the point, Rose? And do you
know what? I kept hearing a voice, somewhere deep inside me,
crying out, silently, "The point is Rose that it doesn't matter who else
understands, the important thing is that *you* understand, and then you
can at least give others the opportunity to have *choices* to take control
of their own lives. The answer, the key to the whole thing, is right in
front of your nose; *you* have to be able to see it, smell it, hear it, taste

it, and feel it."

For months, I kept looking. One question kept pushing itself into the front of my mind. The same question kept surfacing, even when I honestly did *not* want to think about it, trying so hard to put this fucking book out of my head and to give myself some peace.

There it was again.

"What is the key? Why can so many brilliant human beings keep on living this way?"

It tormented me. Drove me on a journey I didn't want to go on. It took me into hours of research, non-stop reading, at the computer, surfing the Internet, waking in the night, praying that the answer would make itself clear to me. My thoughts kept churning; trying to make some sense of the world I existed in. I mean, most vegans that I have known on my journey, have been 'spiritual,' knowledgeable, well read, and informed. How could they, if they are aware, keep themselves tied to, and imprisoned within, the system? Surely these people are our saviours? How come they have not organised themselves into some kind of 'change the world right now' group and have a representative who is ready to take on, and then change it for the better? What was holding them back? Why would they keep on living a life like this, if they could change it?

* * *

For many months I appeared to be going round in circles. I would visit one website and then click on a link and get transported, almost magically, to another. My partner, Mostafa, would come home from work, and ask me if I had got any further with my book, and I would reply, "I didn't touch it today."

* * *

What I didn't realise was that the multiverse was performing its miracles, even though I couldn't see where it was taking me; every single day of the past nine months I have been working on my book, this book, I just *thought* that I 'hadn't touched it.' I was on a journey... destination as yet unknown!

My voyage has taken me to so many places, but I suppose the most important place it has taken me is inside, and beyond, myself. My Fairy Godmother has been communicating with me all along; I just never took the time to really listen. Again and again, I would get taken to sites that talked about food. The question was, "What is the key? Why can so many brilliant human beings keep on living this way?" and the answer was repeated, "The point is Rose, that it doesn't matter who else understands, the important thing is that *you* understand, and then you can at least give others the opportunity to have *choices,* to take control of their own lives. The answer, the key to the whole thing, is right in front of your nose; *you* have to be able to see it, smell it, hear it, taste it, and feel it."

It was like a thorn in my side that wouldn't go away.

I remember once, years ago, having the worst pain in the sole of my foot. I kept looking, trying to locate whatever it might be that was causing me so much pain, but each time I looked, I could see nothing, yet when I put my weight on my feet, it felt as if I was bearing down on a shard of glass. For days I put up with the torture, dreading putting my shoes on to make myself ready to fetch the children from school. Finally I found the culprit. I had to use a magnifying glass to even see it, and to really focus, but once I had, I was determined to rid myself of the cause of so much unnecessary torment. Do you know what it was? It was a fine hair from my own head. I had been for a haircut and for some reason, one of my hairs had found its way into my shoe and become stuck in the sole of my foot. This was the thorn in my side; something that I was doing to me and causing me pain, albeit inadvertently or, more importantly, unknowingly.

When I began writing this book, I did have an idea of where I *thought* it was heading, yet I had no notion that it would lead to where it has. I began to research food and to find out as much as I could about it. I bought books and read them from cover to cover, digesting the most indigestible facts about what we eat. The more I read the more sense it made to me.

Then it hit me. If most people are sad, for whatever reason *they may think,* what is it that really causes their individual sadness, what is the common denominator? At first I'd thought it might be the subliminal messages, or the education system, or the dogma, or even the water. But the problem kept surfacing that for most of the people to be fooled most of the time, it has to be something that *most* of us do *all* of the time. Well, not everyone has a TV set, most people have given up on religious dogma, not everyone drinks tap water and many of us never gave a shepherd's shit about education. So, what the hell is it that virtually each one of us does on a daily basis? The answer, of course, was right in front of my nose. Every time I lifted it to my face, it would be right in front of my nose.

Food was the answer. Food was the thorn in my side. And I guess it might also be the thorn in yours. We are being fed total bullshit, from the cradle to the grave, literally. We are eating bullshit. Food is the answer and I had to 'see it, smell it, hear it, taste it, and feel it.'

We all *need* to eat. We are effectively poisoning, and imprisoning each other with food; even the mighty vegans. How sick is that?

Little bits and pieces of what I was discovering made perfect sense. A seed, in its natural form, if introduced to water, will sprout. It is alive and filled with energy and potential. Inside that small seed is the possibility for growth, given the right environment. It is alive, full of power and, at the point that it sprouts, has extreme potential. If you take that seed and heat it up by roasting, boiling, frying etc and then allow it to cool and introduce it to water, it will not sprout. It is dead and has no capacity for growth. The energy has lost all of its potential.

So what is that we are really putting into our bodies? Is our food vibrant, alive and full of potential? Or is it dead and devoid of any promise or possibility? This made perfect sense to me. If we put life into our bodies, then we live. If we put something dead in our bodies, then what are we actually nurturing our bodies with? Then came the part about fats and, maybe, one answer to the huge obesity issue that we as a race are facing at this point in time. All fats, once heated above 117 degrees, become extremely harmful to our bodies. When we eat heated fat, our bodies do not know what to do with it, as it is recognised as a poison. So, one of three things can happen; either the body flushes it out of our system as quickly as possible, or it seals it off in little pearls and deposits it around the body or, in some cases, it will store it in fatty deposits like lumps. My partner, who looks really slim and fit, has these fatty deposits all over his body, yet people often say, "He's so lucky he can eat what he likes and not put on an ounce!" The thing is he has already been for surgery to have some of these fatty deposits removed and was actually planning to go for some more; this is lucky?

The more I read, the more I understood and the more I understood, the more I wanted to read. How can everyone be controlled? Through the food we eat, that's how! For three months I kept researching and eating my cooked food, telling myself that I ate a fairly healthy diet, 'telling myself' are the optimum words here! It is amazing how we can convince ourselves that we are eating healthily, focusing on the things we *don't* eat, rather than the crap we do. I mean, I would bore people to death with talk of my 'meat free' diet; I could talk forever about the things I *didn't* eat, forgetting easily the garbage that I did.

My favourite types of crap were jelly babies, jelly beans, fruit pastilles, chocolate, Turkish delight, chocolate, roasted peanuts, roasted cashews, liquorice allsorts, chocolate, cheese thins, grilled cheese, chocolate... get the picture? Yet I never seemed to acknowledge that I actually ate these things, at least not to myself. For over 20 years I have been a 'committed' (or should that read self-*labelled*) vegetarian and my last two children were raised as veggies, so surely that must mean that we were healthy.

It was strange at first, making that connection between food and control. I didn't want it to be true. I didn't want to think that for the whole of my kids' lives I had been feeding them poison, food without life, which can only bring dis-ease and death. The thing is that once something has been made aware to you, it is very difficult to just switch it off. I struggled with this potential awful truth for three months and then decided that I could ignore it no longer. I decided to go 100% raw. No meat, no fish, no dairy and nothing cooked above 117 degrees F.

Did it make a difference? You bet your life it has! My life has changed. It has changed so much that I feel alive, really alive. I am experiencing life in a way that I never dreamed possible. For six months I have eaten only raw, healthy, vital food and my body has responded in such a way that it is difficult to explain. I can do everything. I can be anything. I am everything and everything is I. I eat, therefore I am. And what I eat develops what I am. Life begets life. And, of course, the opposite is also true. How can we ever hope to be all that we are, when we are denying the vehicle of experience, to express itself fully?

So how does food, specifically cooked food, control us? The answer to this question has so many levels that it is challenging to know where to begin, so I will start at the beginning of life: birth.

When a child is born, it may already have received 'programming' from the parents, more especially, and importantly, its mother. I have already ranted on about 'labels,' socialisation, and alienation and they all play a major role in keeping us hooked into a system that categorises us, makes us believe we belong to specific groups that are, of course, superior to all other groups, provoke fear, doubt and a whole host of insecurities, but what was missing was 'cooked food programming.'

* * *

Even before a woman decides to conceive a child, her body and that of the future partner, are already overloaded with a variety of processed foodstuffs, which in turn process *us* and affect every single part of our being. As a woman is born with her supply of unfertilised eggs intact, it follows that these eggs need sustenance until the end of their natural life, or the beginning of a new life. Everything that we eat, in some way, touches these potential new lives without us really being aware of it.

The same applies to pregnancy. Women are forever being told

that eating this, or drinking that during pregnancy, can affect our 'unborn' child and many women, wanting the best possible start for their prodigy, listen to the 'experts' and deny themselves whatever the latest government backed advisor may be telling them. In fact, if you now smoke during pregnancy, the world and its dog will be able to accuse you of 'child' abuse yet, it does not seem all that long ago that smoking was a socially acceptable thing to do, and the very 'expert' who is now condemning you, almost probably smoked during her own pregnancies. Whatever the 'rights or wrongs' of smoking during pregnancy, the point is that we are aware that *what we do* when pregnant has a potential affect on our soon to be born child.

I am sure that we have all read stories about heroin addicts giving birth to babies who suffer real withdrawal symptoms from their mother's addiction. Well, I believe the same is true of processed, cooked food, but let's begin by imagining that the baby has been born, and let's put to one side for a moment all of the conditioning it is going to receive during the next few years and focus on how, or more importantly, *what* we feed it during the first five years of life.

I had my first child when I was 17 years old; the year was 1975. It was not really 'hip' to breast-feed a child; after all, women were now 'free' and shouldn't want, or indeed have to have, an alien sucking the lifeblood from their bodies, careers or relationships. The possible misinterpretation of women's liberation (which I became deeply engaged with a few years later) sold many women on bottle feeds. It left women free to continue with their careers, share the total responsibility of child rearing and engage other people to nurture the child, usually 'new men,' during the nightmare of sleepless nights. It somehow made sense!

This new belief was also propagated by the huge infant milk conglomerates and then rammed down our throats, and our children's, even though we may not have been fully aware of it, by the mass marketing around this relatively new, and definitely lucrative, product. Women's magazines would feature the latest celebrity mothers, some single and others with partners, delighting in how easy it was to feed the baby with formula and then we would gaze at pictures of their fantastic bodies and somewhere, deep inside, an image was pasted onto our 'wait till I have a baby' board, pending a future time when it would remind us that we too would bottle feed and get our bodies, and independence back. This was not to be the case for me!

Even though I was old enough to conceive a child, I was not considered old enough to make specific decisions regarding my baby and so I bowed to the pressure of my midwife mother and breast-fed. In those days, having a baby meant a five-day hospital stay. No one got out any sooner; well, not unless you were one of those that didn't really care about your new baby's well being! As my delivery was an assisted breech, it meant that I had to stay in the maternity unit for eight days. Even though the ward was full to bursting point with new mothers, there was only me and one other on the whole of M5 who breastfed.

At first, all the others mothers seemed 'better' than me; they were older and appeared somehow wiser, and virtually all of them had smart partners who brought them flowers and kisses; breastfeeding seemed to alienate me from them even more. During the night, their babies were taken to the nursery and fed by the midwives, whereas me and the other breast-feeder would be gently woken and told that our babies were ready to be fed. Once or twice I was told that if I was tired they could 'give baby a bottle so you can rest,' but I always declined, as somehow, these midnight hours were magical. There was no one around gawking at me, fewer nurses and of course, none of the 'real' mums. I loved to just be there with my little Faye, feeling her suckle from me, stroking her peachy cheek and soothing her with some quiet lullaby. I will always remember those immensely special hours in hospital with her.

On about day four of my confinement one of the midwives came to speak to me; she fondly referred to me as 'her little cow,' even in front of the other mothers, which raised sneers or chuckles. She was a really lovely midwife and I can see her so clearly now as I write, and meant no harm by her 'pet' name for me. She asked me to go with her to the intensive care unit (ICU), as she wanted to ask me something, but felt that I should first *see* the reason for her request.

When we entered the ICU, I was amazed to see it so full of incubators and cots all nestling a tiny baby, some so small I could not imagine how they were even alive. The midwife explained that so many women have no desire to breast-feed and that 'some of these little mites would benefit greatly from some mother's milk.'

*   *   *

She encouraged me to look at the babies and said how so many women these days forget what their breasts are actually for. We then went and sat in a side room and she spoke to me about how important it would be for these babies to have some real milk, explaining that with bottle feeds the babies often become constipated and suffer from colic, which only exacerbates the problem that they were admitted to ICU with initially. Then she showed me a 'milking machine' and explained that I had a healthy milk supply and could come to this room once my own child was satisfied, 'milk' myself and that this would then be given to the babies most in need; she added that it would also increase my own milk supply.

*   *   *

I felt special, for the first time in a long time.

The next morning I agreed to do it and spent the next four days providing extra bottles of breast milk. In return I was given a key to a fridge on the ward that had supplies of gold top milk. There were a couple of conditions to me supplying milk and they were all to do with food. I was not to eat grapes, or more than a single orange, not to take any medication other than what was prescribed and to make sure that I ate plenty of vegetables. If you have never breast-fed then you may not be aware of the effects of what *you* eat can have on your child, but lets just say this, whatever you put into *you* comes out of them, literally! So, it is fair to say that the connection between breast milk and what we eat is well established. Breast milk is the best start you can give any child and I am not going to say anything other, however, just what kind of condition is the breast milk in.

*   *   *

Now, this is where I really had to take the bull by the horns and do some research. If food was the answer then I needed to comprehend what, how and why it was happening. It has taken a lot for me to understand all the confusing terms and 'jargon' found in many of the documents I have read and then there is also the political, as well as commercial, influence to keep the truth hidden from people by not making information *available*. By available I mean in easily understandable language, in places where people are going to see it. Much of the information I came across was more by luck than judgement and most of it I kind of tripped over in the dark.

To read a great deal of what I read required a dictionary and a degree not only in linguistics but also in chemistry, physics, animal husbandry, genetics, biology, statistical research, hieroglyphics and an idiot's guide to bullshit. Having said all of that, what I did read bothered me…enormously.

First of all, I had to understand a term called bioaccumulation, which is 'the process in which industrial waste and toxic chemicals gradually accumulate in living tissues.' The only way I can understand bioaccumulation is that it is a kind of snowball effect, and it is all to do with the food chain.

If we look at our intake of say, fish, for example (and yes fish fingers *do* contain *some* real fish) we are at the top of that food chain. So, what happens to the fish that end up on our plates and, more importantly, in our bodies? Well, we start at the beginning of the food chain with phytoplankton, which are incredibly small and they survive on nutrients that are found in very low concentrations in the water. Along with the nutrients they require for existence, they also take in a lot of 'man-made' crap, which we are going to call 'endocrine disruptors' (ED's). So, phytoplankton are happily sifting for nutrients in the sea and along comes a zooplankton, which eats the phytoplankton along with all its ED's. This then concentrates the ED's (the first roll of the snowball). Then some small fish come and eat the zooplankton, further concentrating the ED's and so on until a huge tuna fish, which now has effectively all the others ED's concentrated in its body, is caught and served up to you on a plate.

*   *   *

Now, that tuna steak that you just ate can have ED's, accumulated in the lipid tissues, *millions* of times higher than the concentration in the water it first came to be in. Of course, once *you* eat it, the bioaccumulation continues, so we can begin to imagine the levels it can reach in humans (one huge snowball of ED's).

*   *   *

Researchers have been attempting to measure the amount of 'man-made' crap that is floating out there on our seemingly beautiful oceans and the Algalita Marine Research Foundation even skimmed a 100-kilometre area of the North Pacific and found six times more plastic by weight, than naturally occurring zooplankton. Now, the thing with these plastics is that they concentrate and absorb toxins and then fish and birds, mistaking the bits of plastic for food, ingest them.

*   *   *

So, when you have your tuna steak it may say on the packet 100% pure tuna, but what it doesn't state is a whole long list of ED's that you are consuming in the form of *food additives* from all of the man made crap that has been ingested throughout the course of the food chain. Now, interestingly enough, the FDA calls these ED's that move from man-made crap into food, "indirect food additives" and, of course, they do not have to be listed on any packaging. The woman who eats the tuna and then breast-feeds her child, is, effectively, adding that child to the next level of the food chain where bioaccumulation continues its growth. And before anyone says that they don't eat fish, well, the same process occurs in *any* food chain, so the beefburger you might enjoy is also part of the food chain, and bioaccumulation continues, more so if the cow has been fed sheep!

* * *

Having said that, breast milk is still the most beneficial gift a mother can give her child to support it during its first months of life. Every mother, who is physically able, *should* opt to breastfeed her child. Her child is entitled to that. And what every mother is entitled to, is the truth about exactly *what* her food contains, so that she can make an *informed choice* about exactly what she is feeding her baby, especially if that food is coming from her own breast.

So now I need to talk about ED's so that we have an understanding about their role in our bodies.

All multicellular animals control and coordinate their internal bodily processes through two main systems. One is electrical and works via a network of nerves connected to the organs and tissues; this is the nervous system and it is very quick to respond. The other is made up of chemical 'messengers,' called hormones, which can access all points of the body; this system is much slower than the nervous approach. This is called the 'endocrine' system.

* * *

These two systems work together in harmony to control all of our bodily processes and functions. There are also receptors, molecular structures within, and on the surface of the cells, which bind with hormones and a feedback system between the glands and organs controls the level of hormones that are circulated to maintain the body at its optimum.

* * *

The endocrine system deals with most bodily functions and is a vital system controlling the thyroid, pineal, adrenal, pancreas and gonads. So, when we talk about an endocrine disruptor (ED), it does exactly what it says it is; it disrupts the natural instructions of the hormones. R.J. Kavlock et al say it this way: "An exogenous agent that interferes with the synthesis, secretion, transport, binding, action, or elimination of natural hormones in the body which are responsible for the maintenance of homeostasis, reproduction, development and/ or behaviour."

* * *

Exogenous basically means something which is introduced from, or produced, outside the organism or system. So, in essence an ED goes into the body and fucks up the system. A couple of other things to mention here about these wonderful little ED's. They happen to be attracted to fat and they can leach into liquid. Wow, clever little so-and-so's, aren't they? Now, there is another point to mention here. There are at least 85,000 existing chemicals and every year thousands of new chemicals are added to the list, each of them a potential ED *in its own right.*

* * *

Let's add a little synergy. What happens when two or more of these 'babies' get together? Well, I don't know about you, but even just looking at the number of chemicals that we know *already* exist and then beginning to add individual combinations and then triple ones, it looks like it might be a huge number of possible synergistic outcomes! Now, if you add to that potential number of combinations synergy with our *own* chemical hormones, well!

* * *

The thing that we *do know* is that some of the chemical combinations are totally lethal. We also know that many of these chemicals are attracted to fat and can accumulate in the body at a much greater rate than our bodies can clear them. The other cause for concern is that some of these chemicals can access our growing, unborn child, by crossing through the placenta; a dioxin is just one that can achieve this with ease.

* * *

So, what is a dioxin? Well, there are a few differing opinions on this so I will not limit your choices, rather I will offer basic positions for and against.

* * *

Position 1- For Dioxins:
A dioxin is a man made chemical, such as weed killer that virtually everyone uses and it kills plants by enzyme inhibition. This makes the plant unable to function properly, so it turns yellow and dies. As so many people use dioxins in weed killers and we are not all turning yellow and dying, it follows that it is probably not toxic to humans. To play safe, never touch it, breathe it in or eat any food that has been sprayed with a dioxin, until it has been washed thoroughly. Sounds safe, eh!

*   *   *

Position 2- Against Dioxins:

Dioxin is the name generally given to a class of super-toxic chemicals. It is formed as a by-product of the manufacture, moulding or burning of organic chemicals and plastics that contain chlorine. It is the nastiest, most toxic man-made organic chemical; its toxicity is second only to radioactive waste. It is a powerful hormone-disrupting chemical, binding itself to the cell's hormone receptor, literally *modifying* the function and genetic mechanism of the cell. There is no 'threshold' dose and the effects can be very obvious or very subtle. Do not come into contact with it.

*   *   *

So we have two differing tales on old dioxin. How about researching a particular dioxin to see if we can assess a little more clearly whether we should 'just avoid it' and, 'not eat any food that has come into contact with it until it has been washed thoroughly,' or, avoid it at all costs. Well, as luck would have it, there is a dioxin that I had heard about and maybe you have too: Agent Orange.

*   *   *

Agent Orange had its beginnings in the University of Chicago during WWII. Basically, a clever, enlightened guy called Professor Kraus realised that he could create certain infusions of hormones (yes, those things that your own body is full of) that would regulate the growth of the plant. He also discovered a way to get this chemical mix just right so that it gave the plants (broadleaf vegetation) cancer, and some within as little time as 24-48 hours, would be dead.

*   *   *

Kraus realised that heavy does of his magical mix (2,4-dichlorophenoxyacetic acid (2,4-D)) could generate the cancer growth spurt and clear vegetation. He decided, in his wisdom, that this *discovery* might be useful for the war effort but thankfully, especially for Europe, Russia, Asia and huge sections of Africa, the war finished before army scientists found any *use* for 2,4-D. Not so lucky for Vietnam.

* * *

Once the army scientists had got hold of the 2,4-D they began to experiment and discovered that by mixing 2,4-D with 2,4,5-trichlorophenoxyacetic acid (2,4,5-T) this combination had a *devastating* affect on foliage and dioxin was nothing more than a *useless by-product* of herbicide production. Now, I don't really want to go into Agent Orange, or Vietnam, in any major way, so will just give a brief overview of what took place.

* * *

Operation Hades (they choose the most adorable names for these missions), later renamed Operation Ranch Hand, began on January 13th 1962 and by September of the same year Ranch Hand had managed to defoliate 95% of 9,000 acres of mangrove forests.

* * *

By 1971 an estimated 12 million gallons of Agent Orange was dropped by the ever-obliging Ranch Hands across Vietnam. In fact, just to make sure the job got done properly the Ranch Hands sprayed with a herbicide mix that varied from 6 to 25 times the suggested dosage.

* * *

By 1965 the government were aware of the toxicity of Orange and that it was in fact 'exceptionally toxic' and that the dioxin produced could travel, not only in wind-drift, but through vaporisation. In fact it was determined that Orange could drift for more than six miles (10K).

* * *

Orders were given that "helicopter spray operations (Agent Orange) will not be conducted when ground temperature is greater than 85F degrees and wind speed in excess of 10mph." (Gen AR Brownfield Army Chief of Staff).

* * *

Then came Project Pink Rose where at Chu Pong Mountain 15 B-52s dropped incendiaries on an already 'Oranged' area. They called this operation 'Hot Tip,' ironically sweet, don't you think? Whether the government were aware or not, what they had now done was to increase the toxicity, as burning dioxins significantly raises their toxicity levels.

* * *

Wow!

* * *

Diamond Alkali was one of the companies involved in producing Agent Orange and, in the mid-60's, found that a fairly high number of the employees at the plant were complaining of 'painful and disfiguring' skin diseases. State Health Officials visited the plant, looked around, said nothing and left.

* * *

In 1969 Bionetics Research Laboratories completed a study that showed that dioxin caused deaths and stillbirths in laboratory animals. The Joint Chiefs of Staff sent out a message to the Commander in Chief Pacific on November 4th 1969:

* * *

"A report prepared for the National Institute of Health presents evidence that 2,4,5-T can cause malformation of offspring and still births in mice, when given in relatively high doses. This material is present in the defoliant (Agent) Orange. Pending decision by the appropriate department on whether this herbicide can remain on the domestic market, defoliation missions in South Vietnam using Orange should be targeted only for areas remote from population. Normal use of (Agents) White and Blue can continue, but large scale substitution of Blue for Orange will not be permitted."

* * *

This may have been due to the fact that one of the components of Agent Blue was arsenic!

Over the nine year period of defoliation the soldiers on the ground were often doused in the mist of Ranch Hands spraying and when they returned to life back home, some began developing unusual health problems, such as skin and liver diseases, abnormal numbers of cancers to soft tissue organs, such as lungs and stomach, high numbers of birth defects among children born to the Vietnam Veterans, wild mood swings and painful skin rashes known as chloacne.

* * *

I guess that kind of speaks for itself, but I will give one last verdict on dioxins and this is from the World Health Organisation:

*   *   *

"Dioxins are environmental pollutants. They have the dubious distinction of belonging to the 'dirty dozen' – a group of dangerous chemicals known as persistent organic pollutants. Dioxins are of concern because of their highly toxic potential. Experiments have shown they affect a number of organs and systems. Once dioxins have entered the body, they endure a long time because of their chemical stability and their ability to be absorbed by fat tissue, where they are then stored in the body. Their half-life in the body is estimated to be seven to eleven years. In the environment, dioxins tend to accumulate in the food chain. The higher in the animal food chain one goes, the higher is the concentration of dioxins."

Nov 2007.

*   *   *

Let's remind ourselves of the role of the World Health Organisation (WHO):
"WHO is the directing and coordinating authority for health within the United Nations system. It is responsible for providing leadership on global health matters, shaping the health research agenda, setting norms and standards, articulating evidence-based policy options, providing technical support to countries and monitoring and assessing health trends.

*   *   *

In the 21st century, health is a shared responsibility, involving equitable access to essential care and collective defence against transnational threats."

*   *   *

So, now we have a bit more information about what we are actually dealing with when we talk about dioxins.

*   *   *

There are some important points to remember about dioxins, which we will refer to again later, however for now, just remember 'vapourisation' and 'burning increases the toxicity of dioxins.'

So, if breast milk has the potential to contain dioxins, wouldn't feeding our baby 'infant formula' be preferable? Well, actually the answer to this question is a resounding 'no'. There is so much information out there on the web about cow's milk that it would take a whole book to write about it so, again, I will just give some pertinent facts:

*   *   *

Infant formula was designed to be a medical nutritional tool for babies who are unable to breastfeed. Formula does not fully meet the nutritional and immunity needs of infants, leaving their immune systems flailing. An infant's immune system has three aspects: her own immature, developing immune system; the small component of immunities that passes through the placenta during natural childbirth (and to a lesser degree with premature births and caesarean sections); and the most valuable, living portion that is passed on through mother's milk on an ongoing basis. Remove any of these components and you take away a vital support structure.

•   No concocted formula will ever contain everything a baby requires
•   They are thinking of adding fish oils to infant formula, in fact, they already have in Europe (think food chain and snowball)
•   Breast milk contains leptin, which has an effect on the baby's ability to recognise when it is full, formulas do not have this.
•   Researchers are trying to find a replacement 'leptin' to

'hardwire' the infant's brain against obesity, regardless of how fat laden its diet may grow to be.

• Throughout the world a baby dies every *second* from unsafe bottle-feeding.

• There have been issues regarding the safety of the plastics used in packaging, bottles and teats (remember dioxins are found in plastics).

* * *

The whole point is that you need to take a real good look at what is happening with our milk production, 'cos that infant formula most likely comes from cows that have fed on Bovine Growth Hormone and antibiotics. I am not here to advocate how anyone chooses to feed their child, it's just a pity that it can't be the child who makes the choice, rather than fashion, convenience, pressure to earn money to have 'things,' vanity, lack of knowledge, money-making corporations, media influence and subliminal messaging.

* * *

So what about soy infant formula?

* * *

On this one I will voice my opinion loud and clear…

* * *

NO WAY, JOSE!

* * *

Soy infant formula really is the last resort. There have been so many incidents concerning soy formula that it would take the next 10 pages to list them all, so, once more, here are just a few:

- Thyroid issues
- Levels of aluminium 1000 times higher than non-soy formula
- Manganese levels 200 times that of breast milk
- High concentrations of manganese can pose a threat to the immature metabolic systems of babies
- High manganese levels increase the likelihood of hyperactivity
- A spoonful of soy formula may be deficient in linoleic and oleic fatty acids. DHA- brain growth factor, epidermal growth factor, lactoferm, casomorphin and immune factors such as IgA, neutrophils. Macrophages, T-cells, B-cells and interferon – are all provided by a mother in breast milk to her baby
- A soy fed baby ingests the equivalent of 5 birth control pills worth of oestrogen a day
- Soy babies' isoflavone levels, in comparison to non-soy fed babies, increased between 13,000 – 22,000 times
- Isoflavones increase incidence of epitheral incidence, goitre and hyperthyroidism
- The whole sordid soy story (check it out on the web)

* * *

From what we discussed earlier there are some other important issues to consider when we think about the first foods our babies will ingest. We are already aware that plastic can contain ED's and we are also aware that ED's love fat and there is plenty of that in baby formula. We also know that ED's bioaccummulate as they progress through the food chain. There is also the effect of dioxins in the food chain through the use of pesticides on grass and animal feed and, let's face it, in the cold light of day, who really knows what the fuck they are feeding cows. The last remaining image I have of cows on UK television is seeing hundreds of carcases being burnt in pits due to the threat of 'mad cow disease.' And what was the cause of this horrendous slaughter of the innocents? Why, feeding them infected sheep of course. Cows eating sheep… I still can't quite get my head around that one!

There is something else you should know about cows. Most of us are informed regularly about the almost perfect food that is 'milk', well, hey; this may not be the case. In fact, you would be better never to touch the stuff again.

*   *   *

In 1959 each cow had an annual milk yield of 2,000llbs. That has now increased to 50,000llbs per cow. Just read that once more. From 2,000 to 50,000llbs. That one sentence should be enough to make you sniff a fat rat.

*   *   *

What is going on?
How can that be?

*   *   *

Bovine Growth Hormone, that's what (could that be a chemical?). Not only do they add this totally unnecessary chemical to the milk, by giving it to the cows, they then pasteurise it! (Chemicals love fat and heat). Pasteurisation then kills off all of the enzymes in the milk that would possibly assist our bodies in digesting it, if it was in fact a food that our bodies were designed to eat, but you know what, it isn't.

*   *   *

Here's an interesting fact regarding Mr Louis Pasteur. He and one Claude Bernard, a physiologist, had a disagreement about pasteurisation. Although Bernard did agree that microbes existed he said, "Terrain is everything." Bernard contended that even though microbes were everywhere, that it was not they that determined if you got sick, rather it was determined by the health of the body the microbes assaulted, which was the crucial fact. It is said that to prove his point, Bernard drank a glass containing cholera and, as he professed, suffered no illness. Louis Pasteur finally, on his deathbed, admitted that his own theory might be flawed.

* * *

Hey, too right, Louis.

* * *

But for most children, cow's milk is something that they will be given once they are weaned from either breast milk or formula. It happened to mine as I tried to get as much 'nutritious' milk into my own kids as possible. For them, and I am sure many others too, one of the first foods they will eat in the morning will contain milk products and we will send them to bed with the same. In some countries the government is so convinced (yeah, right) of the health giving benefits of milk products that they actually give them away, free to kids in school.

* * *

When Richard Nixon was in power, members of his staff team (staffers) were indicted for accepting $300,000 from the dairy lobby for making milk part of the school lunch programme. Has it benefited the children? Well, Robert Cohen of the Dairy Education Board, a non-profit making organisation, commented that since New York pumped in surplus milk, cheese and butter into the free school lunch and breakfast giveaway programmes under the USDA, it has coincided with a 52% rise in asthma deaths among minority children. In fact 90% of African Americans and most Latino, Asian and Southern Europeans lack the genes necessary to digest lactose, which is, would you believe it, the primary sugar in milk. So I don't suppose those particular children have benefited from the giveaways. And, the American Association of Paediatrics state that milk consumption is the number one cause of iron deficiency in infants and is also responsible for 60% of ear infections in children under the age of 6 years.

Ever had an ear infection? Oh, not nice. Not nice on two levels really. The first being that the child is experiencing pain and the second that the 'cure' will probably be antibiotics and painkillers (more chemicals).

* * *

My own daughter Faye lives with the result of receiving antibiotics at a very early age. As I have mentioned I had Faye when I was a teenager and, when she was three months old she became a little 'tetchy.' Being very insecure in the position of mother, I decided to take her to our GP, who informed me that she had an ear infection. Even though I was breastfeeding, I had just begun to introduce baby rusk as the 'experts' advised at that time. My GP prescribed antibiotics, which I dutifully attempted to spoon into her more than reluctant mouth (do you think that maybe she was more aware at this tender age than me?).

* * *

Some months later, when I had begun to introduce whole cow's milk diluted with boiled water, she again got an infection and once more was prescribed antibiotics. About 18 months later Faye had another infection, in her kidney this time, and no matter what was prescribed the infection would not leave her body. In the space of a few months Faye received around four different antibiotics. Finally the infection appeared to have been defeated.

* * *

When she was around three years of age the infection returned and Faye had to visit outpatients for a series of rather intrusive and intimate x-rays using dyes as well as a wide variety of tests. The results were that Faye had a reflux on one of her kidneys and that the infection was resistant to a wide array of antibiotics. The prognosis was that Faye would basically have to live with the recurring, rather virulent infection until she was old enough to have an operation to repair the reflux and stitch up some pockets in her bladder that were a result of damage through the infections.

* * *

As we evolve, so do infections.

* * *

So, lets move on to baby foods. Let's be honest. How many of us actually buy fresh produce, blend it and feed it to our children? I can remember feeling so tired that I didn't even have the energy to feed myself what I considered proper food so it was easy to rid myself of any maternal guilt and purchase a jar of ready made food, after all, the advertisements stated it was made 'for baby, just as nature intended' and the babies on the adverts looked so healthy and happy. It never occurred to me to question the food I was giving my child; I only ever questioned my own parenting skills.

* * *

Being a mother is very competitive, even if you don't want it to be. You kind of get caught up in this constant fight for pole position and if other mothers are ahead of you with their child then you at least try to be ahead of someone else and theirs. I have heard mothers comment on the age that their child was weaned: "Oh, my little Georgie was eating solids at three months, no problem, and look at him now, only eight months old and eating a Chicken Drummer meal, with fries and a side order of garlic bread" pride beaming from her face with a kind of "beat that bitch" tone in her voice.

* * *

We are encouraged by the mass media marketing scandal, to feed our kids absolute shite because it is *normal* to do so and absolutely unmoral not. Big business makes big bucks from marketing to our fears and our kids supposed needs, and they play us off against each other; mother against mother, child against child and worst of all mother against child.

* * *

I remember going to birthday parties when I was a child and they were always in the home, with home-made food and home made entertainment, like pass the parcel, pin the tail on the donkey and musical chairs. The fun part of the party was playing the games and generally running around expending lots of energy. The food was something that kind of got in the way of the fun. There were no party bags, just a wrapped up slice of home-made birthday cake that you would eat later, if you didn't fall asleep first. Today the party is all about location and food; no musical chairs in case a child gets hurt, but hey, we can poison them, no problem. And as an additional bonus we will give them a bag full of the stuff to take home.

* * *

Around 18 years ago a neighbour of mine had a daughter who

developed terminal cancer; she was four years old. Another neighbour and I decided to do a fundraiser to try to get enough money for the little girl to have a special treat, anything she liked.

* * *

Do you know what she asked for?

* * *

A visit from Ronald McDonald! Not her fault, not her parents, just fucking brilliant marketing at a child's level; we are not at fault here because we are unaware that there is a fault! How corrupt is that really? And another pause for thought... whatever happened to picnics? They use to be fun. Going out to a park or into the countryside and spreading out a cloth. Now it's all theme parks where of course it is easier to buy the family lunch at a takeaway on site rather than lug a heavy icebox from a far distant car park and then carry it all the way back. I mean you have paid an enormous amount of money for a wristband so that your child can go on as many rides as possible. They won't want to waste time eating a picnic and, let's face it; everywhere you go at theme parks there are kiosks and stalls, restaurants and takeaways. Parents struggle with screaming kids who are 'hungry, Mummy, pleassse!' two minutes after leaving 'Happy Henry's Hamburger Hut.' So, then they have ice cream or candyfloss, or doughnuts, or slush or, sometimes, all of it. And what do they say when you finally get home?

* * *

"Can I have something to eat now?"

* * *

The thing is that you are probably eating a similar diet to your kids, so by now you are more than a little tetchy, tired and also in need of something further to eat so, when you finally arrive home, open the front door and trip over the small stack of fast food leaflets that have been posted while you have been out, it seems like a good idea to order a pizza.

* * *

Finally the mega pizza, plus side orders arrives complete with a free tub of ice cream and everyone tucks in and do you know what, because you are sharing the food from the same box, everyone seems to have the urge to eat more than they really want. It's that 'eating chips syndrome', the one where your own chips from the chippy always appear to be lacking, or over greasy, or cold, yet if you pinch a chip from someone else's bag, they taste lovely and really more-ish and you try to eat as many as possible without totally pissing off the purchaser who, thankfully, is usually a friend or family member. It's like when we have to share we are worried that there won't be enough.

* * *

You are, by now, totally exhausted and really need to stretch out so decide to rest for a while. The pizza deal came with diet soda so you open a can and guzzle down the gassy, pin-prick fizzy liquid and begin to feel the first signs of indigestion. Your kids are still hyper, but you put that down to a day at the theme park and just hope that bedtime is easy tonight. You flick on the TV so you don't even have to think. That's when the advertising giants have their pick of your hard-earned cash, like some huge vulture just hanging around waiting for their victim to run out of energy. Without even realising it's happening, you decide that once the kids are in bed you will indulge in some chocolate, because you deserve a glass and a half of pure cream goodness. And later that night as you get ready for bed, you will look at your body and begin to despair at one of a whole long list of 'what's wrong' with it and wonder what it is that you are doing to deserve all this!

* * *

I thought that food was energy. So why does it make you tired? I thought food was good for our bodies. So why do we get indigestion, heartburn, colic, flatulence, diabetes and cancer? I thought food enables you to work, rest and play. So why do we have problems with all three? I thought that food was satisfying and filling. So why can we eat and eat and eat and never feel satisfied for more than a couple of hours?

* * *

What is going on? Why don't we feel full any more, especially when sharing food? I have been to weddings where people's meals are served to them plated by waiters and generally people just manage to clear their plate and I have also been to weddings where a buffet is provided and been totally shocked at the behaviour of guests. I am amazed that some of them don't bring shopping trolleys to just cart the food back to their tables. I detested attending any kind of buffet when I was veggie because unless you were the first in the queue, the food, complete with its 'vegetarian' label would be devoured, or buried under a mountain of sausage rolls, luminous white triangles of bread filled with tuna, egg and slithers of something resembling ham and a couple of lamb bhajis by someone who comments, "Might as well give the veggie stuff a try." Then, when you look around at the tables afterwards, there is so much food with just one bite taken from it, usually the food reserved (ha, ha) for the vegetarians. As to the sweet section of the buffet, well I have seen people load up *dinner* plates with a wide variety of tarts, cakes, trifles and flans without as much as a guilty backward glance.

*   *   *

What is this all about?

*   *   *

There has been a real trend over the past couple of years for 'eat as much as you like' restaurants, where you pay a set price and can eat the whole buffet, as long as you can do it in two hours. I often used to go to a Chinese restaurant that opted for this kind of dining and I honestly have no idea why I kept going back.

*   *   *

The tables are packed so tightly together that you cannot help but be distracted by your neighbour's conversation. There is also little room to pass between tables and you can actually see people trying to map out in their minds the easiest way to get back to their own seat. Highchairs are lined up against one wall waiting for children to be strapped in, conveniently blocking a nifty route to the buffet. Then there is the queue. People watch impatiently as others before them spoon the most appealing portions and morsels on to their plates. Some diners queue-jump, realising that if they don't get to the king prawn and crab meat first, it might be all gone, leaving them with oriental veggies and mushroom curry. Some people annoy others by deigning to talk to their dining companions while at the servery, and voices become raised along with blood pressures.

*   *   *

The sad thing is that it is not just adults who are queuing up and behaving like this, it is children, too. What are we teaching them? There is nothing social about these places. And what are we leaving them? Are we providing them with a future food supply that is beneficial and sustainable?

* * *

We kind of come full circle really to the story of chemicals, hormones and synergy. According to the National Union of French Apiculture, Albert Einstein spoke of an apocalyptic vision "If the bee disappeared off the surface of the globe then man would have four years of life left. No more bees, no more pollination, no more plants, no more animals, no more man."

* * *

I guess that kind of 'vision' should maybe concern most of us but would only prompt us into action if it appeared that there was any likelihood of it happening. Well, hold on to your hats, 'cos it looks like its happening and once again, it is difficult to find available information about the real cause of the alarming decimation of bee populations without there being some kind of 'hidden agenda' or commercial/ financial incentive to whoever is putting out the findings. What we do know is that the bee populations are suffering from something called Colony Collapse Disorder (CCD) and beekeepers in USA report that in the East Coast they have lost 70% of their stock of bees and 60% on the West Coast.

* * *

Many theories have been espoused to explain why CCD is happening and an awful lot of them come from government agencies and/or the makers of herbicide/pesticides or genetically modified organism (GMO) producers. However, research has been carried out independently and Professor Hans Hinrich Kaatz discovered that the gene from GM rapeseed has been transferred in the bee gut to microbes thus depleting their immune systems. This same professor is a little concerned about going public with the findings as when Dr Arpad Pustzal claimed that GM potatoes damaged the stomach linings of rats, he was sacked and had his work discredited. And another bee expert found that the sting and intestinal tracts of the dying bees were cancerous!

*   *   *

So what is the story with the bees?

*   *   *

Well around 40 years ago bee populations use to fall foul of an infection known as American Foulbrood (AFB) and a chemical called tetracycline had effectively combated AFB over those years until 1996. Then, out of the blue, a tetracycline resistant strain was confirmed in bee populations in both Wisconsin and Minnesota in the USA and Argentina. So as those countries are miles apart, and at that time CCD only affected specific states in the USA, was there a common denominator? Well actually it appears that there might be!

*   *   *

During the 1990's millions of GM crops were planted in both areas and these crops were called Round-Up Ready. This means that the seeds were genetically modified so that when they were sprayed with Round-Up (weed killer that gives the plants cancer) they would not wither and die along with everything else. The seeds of these GM crops were also sterile so that the farmers could not use them, therefore making them reliant on the GM producers for future seeds. The interesting fact here is that the antibiotic resistant gene used in the creation of Round-Up Ready seed was resistant to tetracycline.

*   *   *

How strange is that?

* * *

They actually create infertile GM seeds using a gene that is resistant to the very antibiotic that has stabilised the bee population for over 40 years. Do they not realise that bees pollinate plants and that they feed this pollen to the young bees?

* * *

Why on earth would they want to do that?

* * *

Well, the whole GMO story is another long and sordid one but basically the words 'total food control' spring to mind. So why would they want to control the food? Well maybe because the next step is GMO prescription plants, which are already being produced. These are plants, usually sunflowers and maize (pharma plants) that are producing six major drugs:

1. Vaccines
2. Industrial enzymes
3. Blood thinners
4. Blood clotting hormones
5. Growth hormones
6. Contraceptive drugs

Could there be a link between pharmaceutical companies and the makers of Round-Up, like there is a link between food and illness? As it turns out there is.

* * *

In April 2000, Pharmacia & Upjohn merged with Monsanto Company. These are two massive companies employing thousands of people across many countries. Now when I try to get my head around that, it sounds very much like one is producing the 'food' to create the illness and the other producing the 'food' to create the medication, but maybe I have got it totally wrong, after all I am totally mad!

* * *

So let's go back to GMO's and the benefit of producing our food from these modified seeds. In my research I came across the most incredible story of Percy Schmeiser who took on the might of Monsanto at the age of 73 years. His story is amazingly unbelievable, and then instantly, horrifically believable. Basically this guy and his wife are third generation farmers who have acres of granola fields in Canada and they have been producing organic seed banks for around 50 years. Well, Percy bought some Round-up, not to use on his crops but to use in the ditches around his fields and was kind of amazed that even though most of the other weeds died, that there remained some granola looking apparently live and healthy. At first he thought that he had produced his own 'Frankenstein' variety of granola. He mentioned it to a few of the other farmers and then, without any notice or warning, he received a summons that Monsanto were taking him to court for 'growing' their patented GM granola.

* * *

What this guy uncovered is amazing and worrying. Basically the courts sided with Monsanto saying that Percy had infringed patent law and thus:
- It does not matter how GMO plants get into a field, even if this is via direct seed movement or cross-pollination, it is the property of Monsanto.
- All his seed stocks must go to Monsanto.

- He was not allowed to use his seeds again for anything, not even research.

* * *

His organic land was no longer organic, his research of over 50 years he could no longer use and basically Monsanto owned his farm.

* * *

Percy decided to fight and refused to give up and soon other farmers were coming and saying that the same had happened to them. Monsanto had their own police force, who it was alleged would intimidate farmers, and some of those who had bought into the Monsanto GMO dream showed him contracts that tied them into so many knots that a sea scout would be unable to undo them all.

* * *

The farmers said that Monsanto had made four claims about the massive benefits of producing crops from GMO's:
1. Bigger yield
2. More nutritious
3. Less chemicals
4. Feed a hungry world

* * *

The major reason that most of the farmers who did sign contracts did so was for point three. Farmers were concerned over the amount of chemicals that were being used on their lands, not to mention the costs of the same, and believed that GMO crops would reduce the amounts used.

So what did the farmers find?

1. Yield of granola down 6.4% and soya 15%
2. The quality of GM food is 50% inferior to conventionally grown food
3. More chemicals were actually used, including super chemicals
4. It is their belief that the introduction of GMO's will actually lead to world hunger on a huge scale.

* * *

What Percy also found out was that the Government, who give regulatory approval of GMO's, actually get money in return for each bushel produced, and so it follows that it is in the government's best interests to support GMO production. Percy also found out that GMO's are extremely dominant and through cross-pollination, infiltrate conventional seed, thus rendering it useless. In fact he goes as far to say that the granola and soy crops in North America are all now genetically altered. Just as an aside, Monsanto also produces 87% of all US Soya beans (2005) maybe that is why the vegans are stuck in the system!

* * *

So we still need to find a connection to understand why the pharmaceutical companies joined forces with the GMO and herbicide producer Monsanto and why the bees are dying.

* * *

I guess the first question must be what is the basic ingredient of Round-up herbicide and the answer is 'glyphosate' which is the world's best selling herbicide and represents an astounding 60% of global 'broad spectrum' sales. So does glyphosate pose any threat to humans as it is a chemical and, as we are already aware, one of our major bodily systems is also chemical?

The Institute of Science in Society states: "They have now shown that glyphosate is toxic to human placental cells, killing of a large proportion of them after 18 hours of exposure at concentrations below that in agricultural use. Moreover, Round-up is always more toxic than its active ingredient glyphosate; at least by two-fold. The effect increased with time and was obtained with concentrations of Round-up ten times lower than agricultural use."

* * *

So, now that Monsanto has produced an herbicide that kills 'weeds', what does it do next? It produces dominant strains of GM seeds that can infiltrate organic varieties, which are actually called Round-up Ready, as they are not affected by Round-up herbicide meaning that when fields are sprayed everything but the GM crops are wiped out. It makes these GM crops resistant to tetracycline, which is threatening the bee population and then joins forces with a pharmaceutical giant to produce GM pharma plants to produce medication. Yes, I am mad!

* * *

So are GMO's used anywhere else in the food chain?

* * *

Of course they are! German National TV interviewed a farmer who had got hold of some GMO, grew it illegally and fed it to his cows and as a result, they all died! I wonder if the deaths of the cows had anything to do with their stomach lining, like the bees and the rats, where it appears that they become cancerous.

* * *

The next question therefore has to be is there an increase in cancers of the digestive tract in humans? For the answer I visited our friends at the World Health Organisation where it states that:

"Colon and rectum cancers are rare in developing countries but are the second most frequent malignancy in affluent societies. More than 940,000 cases occur annually worldwide, nearly 500,000 die each year. Migrant populations rapidly reach the higher level of risk of the adopted country, a sign that environmental factors play a major role."

* * *

Surely Monsanto and companies like them should be made to prove that the foods that they are producing are safe for human and animal consumption (food chain, fats, heat and snowball) but according to Phil Angell, Monsanto Director of Corporate Communications, when he spoke on the subject to the New York Times (October 25th 1998),

"Monsanto should not have to vouchsafe the safety of biotech food, our interest is in selling as much of it as possible. Assuring safety if the FDA's job."

* * *

But the FDA is the government and they get paid by the bushel, so the words 'blurred' and 'boundaries' kind of spring to mind here. So what is the master plan behind all of this apart from the obvious one of making as much money as possible?

* * *

Maybe they understand that many people want to take control of their own health and are actually beginning to question the whole food production industry. I, like many other vegetarians, thought I was doing the right thing by eating soya products, blissfully unaware that I was probably eating GMO food. Others are choosing to purchase organically grown produce, but as Percy said earlier the GMO food infiltrates the fields rendering them useless for organic production and field tests conducted in England found that it was theoretically possible for small quantities of GM pollen (the stuff that possibly kills the bees and then when the hives are no longer active, not even a scavenger will invade them to eat the larva or honey) can be transported up to nine km. This is termed 'horizontal gene transfer'. Meanwhile, a whole host of GM pharma plants are being grown for medicinal purposes in a joint venture with Monsanto and are Round-up Ready (resistant to tetracycline, which means the bees die).

* * *

The GM crops are also being used to feed animals, which we then eat, usually after cooking (food chain, heat, fat, snowball). Do you think that someone somewhere is genetically modifying bees so that they are able to produce Round-up Ready bees that could dominate the already decimated bee populations of the world? This would mean that millions of us would be reliant on GMO's whether we liked it or not and they could basically tinker around with genetics so that we could fall foul of whatever disease they wished to inflict upon us, and then they would have the medication already produced to 'cure' us.

* * *

No...too farfetched. It could never happen. Remember, don't believe what I am writing as I am a madwoman, do the research yourself and find out if you are mad too!

* * *

But, keep heart...human*kind* will win out against human*greed*. The day after I wrote this section both my mother and Anne contacted me informing me about an article in our local newspaper, The Coventry

Evening Telegraph. Both were aware that I had been researching the whole 'bee' story and magically, not to mention, synchronistically, this is what I read:

Headline. Dave's invention is just bee-rilliant!

Apparently a scientist from Coventry, Dr Dave Chandler has come up with a marvellous invention to rid bees of varrola mite, which is the cause of the viral diseases that are the source of the horrendous 50% loss of bee populations in the US alone.

* * *

Does his invention rely on ED and dioxin producing chemicals? No. He uses the equivalent of a fungus footbath. Dr Chandler is quoted as saying, "We can't rely on chemical pesticides to control pests because they develop resistance. That's why we're focusing on biological methods, using one organism to control another."

* * *

Now doesn't that make sense to you?

* * *

Fungi are so totally amazing and it is believed that they were the first organisms to 'arrive' on this planet. If you get a chance check out 'Six Ways Mushrooms Can Save The Earth' on the Internet website 'Ted Talks.'

* * *

The most amazing thing is that when one person realises that something is amiss and decides to do something about it, we all reap the rewards.

* * *

One person!

* * *

Percy Schmeiser took on Monsanto and guess what? He recently won his case at the Supreme Court! He may have lost years of work and a viable farm but his determination at the age of 73 has meant that Monsanto's stranglehold on North American farmers has at least loosened. Dave Chandler has not just sat back and thought 'so the bees are dying, never mind.' He has absorbed the whole enormity of what could happen if bees continue to die at the rate they are and has done something about it. The selflessness of these two guys alone will mean that you and I, our children and their children may one day get to eat real food.

* * *

Food is meant to be nourishing, enjoyable, pleasurable, and satisfying and health giving. I think it was Shakespeare who wrote, "If music be the food of love, play on." Well, I would like to turn that around a bit and say, "If food be the music of love, bring it on."

* * *

There is so much that I could write about the negative side of our food industry but I think it is best to just focus on the magical and inspirational side of food instead. This whole planet is so miraculous and I do it a dis-service by continuing to rant about all that is wrong with it. If I continue to do that then all I will manifest is more of the same. There is so much that is right about the food that is available and maybe if we focus our attention on the positives then the beneficial foods will appear in abundance.

*   *   *

When I began my own raw food journey I did not do it for reasons of weight; I did it because what I was reading made sense to me. I watched youtube.com videos of people who had already begun their journey and I had been amazed at how *they* had changed. It was really that, actually seeing outlooks transform rather than bodies, which convinced me and they continue to inspire me.

*   *   *

There is one guy who set himself a raw food challenge of seven days and when he set out on his journey he appeared to be a stereotypical 'red neck' type. All bravado and bullshit really! Then, as he progressed through the days, some kind of attitude change began to shimmer through. By day seven of his challenge he was talking about the spiritual side of being and, in fact, decided that his next challenge would be to meditate on a daily basis! This is how totally amazing raw food is; it transforms you from the outside in and the inside out.

*   *   *

When I began my journey, I was in no way prepared for the changes that raw food would bring about in my own life; changes that will stay with me for my lifetime. At first I was concerned about what I was going to eat and about how I would get rid of cravings for foods that have internal programmes linked into them, such as snuggling down with a bar of chocolate wrapped in a quilt and watching a DVD. The connection between the DVD, chocolate and quilt equalled 'you deserve to pamper yourself,' so how would I pamper myself now?

*   *   *

Then there was the social aspect to it all; especially 'family days' like Sundays when my mum always comes to my house for a home cooked 'roast' dinner. I kept thinking what would happen then; I mean should I continue to make her dinner and then eat some raw food myself, and if I did, how would I cope with the aroma of Sunday dinner?

* * *

It slowly began to dawn on me that my physical being, the 'bot', liked things the way they were, after all, the way things had always been done had got us this far in life, why jeopardise it now. I would find myself having major conversations with myself, and the 'bot' (Rosebot as she is affectionately known) would haul up all kinds of excuses not to even begin the journey and, once I did embark, would constantly prod and poke at me with lame excuses to stop. Was it easy in the first week? The answer is no, it wasn't easy, but then again, it wasn't exactly hard either.

* * *

The hard bit was shutting up Rosebot and all her other 'bot' friends who deigned to visit the mad woman who has now totally lost the plot. Prior to me going raw, friends and family would visit and we would chat about 'stuff', mainly safe stuff that wouldn't rock the boat; very surface calm. We would venture into my world of perceived madness, but only briefly, and the slight ripples would peter out and we would be on safe ground once more. In fact, once I got on my soapbox about any particular subject the other 'bots' would find a way to change the focus to something a little less provocative. Raw food was something else though! It was as if the 'bots' perceived that they could be a target for this 'food fad' and rather than just uttering, "Well, it's your choice. I think you are mad but at the end of the day it's up to you!" they went into panic stations. I was examined, explored, pleaded with, argued with and finally called names. Basically I had lost the plot. At the time I had no understanding why people felt such a need to defend their own stance and to ridicule mine; now I do.

* * *

So much has happened over the past seven months that I have been raw that it is difficult to see the different stages of awareness, as I am now living so completely in the present. Being in the present means totally letting go of the past and allowing the future to be just that. It is about being right here, right now and embracing each and every moment as entirely as you are able. It is being aware that in each moment you have a choice and, that if you are not in the moment, that choice is something that maybe you are not aware of. In this way life kind of drives itself and you are just a passenger taking up a seat.

At the beginning I was more focused on what I was eating, and by that I mean I was concentrating on what foods I could put into my body to keep Rosebot happy. I was also very interested in the effect the food was having on my urine, my faeces, my skin and my general well being. The first week was really a running battle with myself. Like, every now and then, my mind would wander to any number of different cooked foods and at times it didn't just wander, it became fixated on a particular food. I would 'hear' a voice mentioning the words 'Hagan Daas Strawberry Cheesecake ice-cream' and then I would get images of the tub and then another little voice would say, "All you have to do is get in the car and drive to the supermarket and you can have it, taste it, mmm... yummy."

* * *

This little voice reminded me somewhat of a child who is asking for sweets in a supermarket and when they are told 'no' the first time the child just becomes more insistent, and on and on, even though they have been told quite forcefully, "You are not having any sweets do you understand?" The child may become quiet and sullen for a while but then begins the whole cycle again until the parent, exhausted from the burden of shopping and the constant, embarrassing pleading of the child, finally gives in and the child gets the sweet.

* * *

Once I had made this connection in my mind I decided to talk to myself 'like an adult,' so when the voice spoke I would respond by thinking, "I can eat whatever I choose to eat and in this moment I choose to eat raw foods!" In doing this it felt like I was not depriving myself of anything, after all, I could eat anything I chose. The next step would be to find, make, order or create the raw food equivalent of whatever food it might be that my inner child, AKA Rosebot, desired and then it was easy.

* * *

I trawled the Internet seeking out exciting raw food recipes and began to recreate these new meals for myself. Then, almost without my being aware, I realised something sensational; I was never hungry. It was incredible! As I went through each day I found that the smoothie that I made for my breakfast actually kept me going until lunchtime. I had no hunger 'pangs' so to speak, just an awareness that I should now go and make myself something else to eat. For me this was a revelation, I mean, I used to have my breakfast of cereal and milk, maybe a slice of toast with butter and jam and a cup of tea and by mid morning I was ready for a chocolate bar, or a packet of crisps. And, even then, I would be thinking of what I was going to eat for lunch!

* * *

This was something else again... no hunger. It was a great revelation and, from then on, it just got easier and easier. I would fill the fridge with the most luscious fruit and my kitchen shelving was lined with Kilna jars full of nuts, seeds and berries and, anytime I felt like it, I could grab a handful of something nice to nibble on.

* * *

The thing I did notice was that raw food has a strength to it that, at first, kind of threw my palate a bit. It was as if the distinctive taste of each particular food was amplified, to the level that with some food I had a kind of 'whoa, so that's what that *really* tastes like' moment. So, in the beginning I chose to mellow flavours by adding slightly less of some particular ingredients or, in other cases, omitting them altogether. An example of this might be raw chilli.

* * *

By the end of the first week I had come across a website that actually sold raw chocolate and, if the truth be told, I was kind of missing the odd bar of 'happypamperness'. I didn't even know that chocolate could be eaten raw and so set out on the journey to chocolate heaven by ordering a single bar.

* * *

I can vividly remember the anticipation of its arrival and, when a few days later it was delivered, the magical moment of holding something so precious in my hands. I had thought that being raw meant no chocolate, yet here I was actually holding some. I really savoured that first bar of chocolate. I smelt it through the wrapper and undressed it from the same, like I would a lover. I marvelled at its form and stroked its silky smooth darkness. It was almost as if I didn't dare break off the first piece in case the magic of the moment was broken with it.

* * *

I sat at the table and just looked at it before finally snapping off a single chunk and then splitting that in half again. I held it between my fingers, closed my eyes, took a deep breath allowing the aroma to fill my being and then placed it in my mouth. The flavour of the chocolate was incomparable to any 'cooked' version I have ever tasted, at first almost too powerful yet, dancing in my mouth, my taste buds gave a fluttering Mexican wave of approval. It was so amazingly distinct that I did not need to eat any more at that moment; I was able to just enjoy the very essence of it. If this had been a box of 'Dairy Whatever', I would have consumed the whole top tray without much more than an 'mmm...that was okay, now I'll eat the orange cream.'

*   *   *

That first bar of chocolate was shared with friends and lasted a whole, blissful week! Prior to going raw, I would have eaten a couple of kilos of 'whole nut' in the same time period.

*   *   *

Then I discovered raw cacao, made my own chocolate and, not only did I make trays of the stuff, I could also eat as much of it as I liked. This inspired me to look at cacao-based recipes on the Internet and I came across David Wolfe's site, www.thebestdayever.com and learnt so much about other raw foods, not to mention raw lifestyles that I began to create some power-packed delights.

*   *   *

I was extremely lucky to have my friend Anne to support me and, during the first week of my journey, she would often come and question me about raw food and share meals with me. After one week of inner questioning, Anne declared that she too was going to change her diet. This was fantastic for me as it meant I had someone to 'share' food with, who could understand what the highs and lows really were.

*   *   *

At this point there had not really been that many lows, which continued for a couple of weeks, until I got really fed up of continually explaining to all and sundry *what* I was eating every time anyone saw me putting anything in my mouth. At first I was more than happy to discuss the reasons for wanting a raw food lifestyle, however after a couple of weeks I was getting tired of saying the same things or hearing the same negative comments about *my* choice. I felt as if I just needed to have some time by myself and became less tolerant of having visitors. This lasted for two weeks during which time I had purchased a dehydrator and was experimenting with crackers and cookies in between what was basically 'going on a bit of an emotional roller coaster'.

*   *   *

I spent much of my time alone in the house, not really wanting to be with people, preferring instead to be on my own. I began to feel almost disconnected from the human part of the world; twice a day I would take my two dogs on long walks and just look at the trees, or flowers, or sunsets. I would listen to the birds, or be aware of the wind musically awakening the leaves in trees or the crunch of the ground beneath my footfalls. Everything just appeared in every way to be more beautiful than it ever had before. Time lost its meaning and I found my own; just to experience this very moment.

*   *   *

The 'downs' were not so good and made me feel cheated on many levels and I questioned myself about so many beliefs that I had never been aware that I had before. I also researched like never before and found out so much about food I could literally have written a book just about the total crap that I have eaten for most of my life and the whole corrupt system of feeding us poison so we purchase the medication to put our devastated bodies into some kind of half-hearted working order; all done to remove our focus from control, to health and survival. I felt very gullible, used and hooked into the corrupt system by generations of lies and deceit.

* * *

I believe now that I had to go through this as "the truth shall set you free" and knowing the truth, I could now totally disengage from that system. And, at the end of two weeks of contrasting total bliss and confronting my own lack of awareness, I felt able to invite friends round once more.

* * *

For those interested in the weight loss side of the equation, in the first four weeks I cleared from my body 14lbs! At Christmas 2007 I weighed 11stones 4lbs (158lbs) and managed to squeeze myself in to a size 14 outfit for the staff 'do.' In February 2008, just four weeks into raw food, my partner bought me some new jeans for Valentine's and they were size 12. I have to say that even though weight loss was not anywhere near the top of my agenda for doing this, I was amazed by the ease of losing this weight, while eating so much food and never feeling hungry!

* * *

The other fantastic thing about eating this way is that after about 30 days, your taste buds change and suddenly raw chilli tastes just great. You begin to understand how to blend flavours together, which deliver just the eating experience you are looking for. I also realised that when I was in the kitchen preparing food, it was as if a 'spirit chef' was guiding me, so much so that Anne and I named this 'feeling' Cyril! If we were concocting something new and were unclear as to what to use to sweeten, enhance or moisten a particular dish we would pass it to Cyril and 'voila,' whatever it was would be perfect. It was as if there wasn't any doubt about anything we prepared, it all just happened magically and the results were always 'our favourites.' At first Anne would follow me around with a pencil and pad attempting to scrawl down recipes as they were being created but, after a short while, we gave up on this because each meal was always completely individual no matter how we may have tried to replicate the original and each of them was perfect in their sameness and diversity.

*　*　*

I began to notice some other changes too. I had decided that if I was to 'go raw' I wanted to do it completely, so, even though I took some supplements previously, I stopped taking all of them on the day I went 100% raw. One of the supplements I took was Cranberry Extract (Triple Concentrate) as I was prone to cystitis. I would drive to London every week and have to make at least two stops along the route to go for a 'pee' and every time I sneezed, coughed or laughed too much, I would 'leak' – quite embarrassing really, but all the advertisements 'programmed' me into believing that this is usual for a woman of my age! This on its own was bad enough, but cystitis makes life a misery and at least once a month I would be going for a pee every 10 minutes and sometimes would pass small amounts of blood.

*　*　*

It is amazing that when you 'have' something like cystitis you are so aware of it because of the awful affect it can have on your day-to-day life, yet, when it is not there, we forget that we are affected by it. So, over the weeks I had kind of forgotten that I had these issues and it was only when we were on a journey to London and got caught up in a two hour traffic jam that I realised that I had not had any problems whatsoever with my bladder. In that moment I also realised that I had laughed so much that my jaw had ached and had coughed for England during the first few weeks of raw food and not had a single drop of urine leave my body uncontrollably. In the middle of the M1 I wanted to shout and scream my news to all and sundry, but instead I just sat giggling to myself with the utter amazement and joy at it all!

* * *

I was also a migraine sufferer. Whenever I felt a migraine coming on – it would start with a dull kind of pain above my right eye – I instinctively knew that I had to get home as quickly as possible. Once there, I would take a bucket and a glass of water upstairs, seal out any kind of light and hide myself in the depths of darkness. Most times I would vomit until my body was aching with the peristaltic movement that was beyond my control and the flashing lights would burn my eyes until I felt as if I wanted to pull them out. I am not a lover, or believer, in medication but if I knew a migraine was coming I would take anything! Normally, you get a kind of warning with migraines and those who have never suffered them do not understand how you know exactly what has to be done to 'ride them out.' Once, on an NLP course I was attending, I received migraine-warning signs loud and clear, and knew that I had to leave immediately. I was about 40 minutes drive from home and didn't quite reach the front door before I vomited everywhere. Migraines are monsters!

* * *

Well, guess what? No more migraines. The freedom is wonderful. I also noticed the disappearance of a couple of 'moles' I had, one on my neck and the other on my leg and scar tissue seemed to be almost vanishing before my eyes.

*   *   *

The other amazing revelations were more 'spiritual,' emotional and an awakening that is hard to explain. Events became synchronised ahead of time; traffic lights would turn green, parking spaces would appear, enough money was always in my purse, relevant websites appeared by magic, people contacted me at the same time I was in the process of contacting them and parks would be empty when I wanted solitude. The moment always seemed to be perfect!

*   *   *

I also became so aware of the two very definite 'parts' to me. I really began to understand the 'bot' part of me; the one covered in all the labels and I began to be able to separate my 'bot' from my 'being.' I didn't have to behave like Rose any more; Rose was just a label given to the 'bot' that was, in reality, the vehicle of physical experience. You don't have to wear any labels at all. Wow! That is also so totally liberating; you don't have to do what you have always done, you can just be. How fantastic is that! There doesn't have to be a reaction. You don't have to live up to the labels that have adorned you for so many years. If once the reaction to another driver, who tried to 'sneak in' to my lane, would have been to absolutely make sure he didn't get in, now there was a realisation that I had choices in my reaction and increasingly it would be to smile and wave them in. And eating a raw food diet made it all effortless. Life just becomes so easy!

*   *   *

After eight weeks on raw food, my weight loss was 28Ibs and my dress size was now a 10. I found this incredible as I was eating such good food and never felt hungry, no bloating, no full belly, no indigestion, just total eating bliss.

* * *

During the first two months I created all kinds of delicious meals. I made ice-cream, spaghetti Bolognese, crackers and dips, lasagne, nori rolls, chilli, curry, stir-fry and noodles, cookies, energy bars, shepherds pie, rhubarb crumble, Iranian fesenjan, cheesecake, apple pie, carrot cake, burgers, crisps, chocolate bars ago-go and smoothies from Heaven. It appeared that just about anything could be created raw.

* * *

My partner is Iranian and one of the things we loved to do together was cook! He is an amazing chef and in fact, after being vegetarian for 20 years, two years before turning raw, I went back to eating meat and dairy. With hindsight, I am glad that I did, as I have the memories of so many wonderful moments cooking and eating with Mostafa. Although he did support me on my raw food journey, he had made his own choice regarding food and, while at work he would cook for himself; he would then eat whatever I prepared when at home. The Iranian New Year is celebrated on April 21st and, like most celebrations, food plays an important part in the festivities. I decided, as he would be working on that day, that I would cook him a meal and share it with him (I had been advised by a friend that this would be a lovely thing to do, and I agreed). Selfishly, to some extent, I decided to prepare the food that had always been my total favourite and the one that I had missed most during my years of vegetarianism; blue fillet steak, mushrooms, tomatoes, onions, chips, salad and a huge hunk of white bread spread thickly with butter. Now, even though this is not a traditional Iranian dish in any way, shape or form, Mostafa was totally delighted by my efforts to celebrate with cooked food.

* * *

The table had been decorated and set, a bottle of red wine (Shiraz, of course) had been opened and left to breathe and the steaks were ready to hit the pan. Proudly, I carried through an amazing platter of sizzling food and we toasted the Iranian year of 1387, before beginning to eat. One of the things I love about sharing food with Mostafa is that we eat from the same plate. It makes it so very intimate.

* * *

The first thing I did was to cut myself a piece of steak and I placed it in my mouth and then promptly tipped it right back out into my hand; it was burning hot, so hot that I couldn't keep it in my mouth. So I blew it and tried again. All I could taste was blood. I swallowed it almost without chewing and decided to give the rest of it a miss! Have some mushroom, I thought to myself, so I put a chunk of it into my mouth and bit down. Mistake! The hot oil actually burnt my tongue, leaving those annoying little heat spots on it for the duration of the evening. Next came the tomato, which was like a slimy hot sponge of mushy pulp… yeuk! I didn't even bother with the chips or onions.

* * *

There was one item there that I had totally missed… bread! Bread is still an issue with me even to this day. I love bread in all its shapes and forms. So, I pulled off a chunk, spread it with butter, took a bite, realised the butter was a mistake, scraped it off and devoured the whole chunk along with some salad. It was really nice (if there are any raw food chefs out there who know how to make raw bread please let me know).

* * *

We had a really enjoyable evening and I decided to finish our celebration meal off with coffee and chocolate but I realised that I had no raw chocolate anywhere. Mostafa disappeared and returned moments later with a huge bar of my old favourite which he had been keeping in reserve for me 'just in case,' since I began the raw journey. At first I didn't want to have any, and then I thought, 'well why not?', so I broke off a chunk and put it into my mouth. I had anticipated the taste but... it was awful, fake, an impostor. It felt grainy and had no taste that I would ever discern as being of 'chocolate.' It really quite shocked me and then totally released me.

* * *

After 12 weeks my dress size was 8 and I had lost a total of three stones (42Ibs). My body shape was shifting in a way it had not changed before and sometimes I did not recognise the body to be mine. I have always had a 'bit of a belly'; even when I was 21 years old and was a fitness instructor, my tummy was one of those that was always far too rounded and endless sit-ups did little to flatten it. For fat, it was without a doubt the most stubborn area of my body. Yet, the body that stood naked in front of the mirror appeared to have a flatter tummy than it had ever had. My breasts seemed to change as well, both becoming balanced in size and shape and I became aware that the little pearls of fat that had once made their presence known just beneath my skin, were also disappearing.

* * *

I realised, almost accidentally, that I didn't really have to wash my hair, and that on the odd occasion I did, the comb would glide through rather than becoming enmeshed in a mass of tangles. There are probably so many more changes that have, or are, taking place, yet it is almost as if you don't notice that they are have happened until you are reminded by past memories.

* * *

The most amazing change has been in my awareness. Every day is special. Every moment is filled with potential. Time does not exist. There are no boundaries. I am free and limitless. The veneer of the illusion has cracked, like a veil being lifted from my eyes; I now fully understand all that I have written about in this book and all that I have experienced on my incredible journey through life.

*   *   *

My body communicates directly with me in a way that it never has before and in a manner that is beyond words to describe; it can only be experienced. What it does do however is to 'tell' me what food it needs, which is amazing. For a while I kept getting the 'message' 'fruit.' So I ate mostly fruit. Honey comes up quite a lot, as does Chia seed. And when it 'speaks,' I listen.

*   *   *

At the beginning of June 2008 my body kept 'telling' me not to add salt to anything, which kind of goes against the grain (excuse the pun), as most raw recipes do add either Celtic sea salt or rock salt to their ingredient lists. So, I did some research and found that everywhere I looked salt was seen as a given. The thing was that I had really begun to act on my instincts and I kept getting this knowing feeling to stop adding salt, of any kind, to any food. I talked it over with Anne who said that she had never added salt when she ate cooked food, but, we both understood that any processed food, such as bread, butter, cereal, soup, etc. all had added salt, so thought that maybe her body had made up its quota from those kinds of foods.

*   *   *

No matter where I looked on the Internet, it appeared that salt was not only a necessary addition to raw food but a necessity. It rattled around my head for days and then finally I came across a web page, which mentioned that David Woolfe was adamantly against salt being added to raw foods. Finally, I had the connection I needed, so I searched his videos to find the one referred to in the article I had read, only to discover that he not only advocated salt (Celtic and rock) but that he personally drinks an infusion of salts and pure water on a regular basis. I was stumped. I thought that maybe he'd had a change of heart since posting the videos, so decided to check out his online shop; surely if he knew that salt was not beneficial he wouldn't sell it... but it was there, Celtic Sea Salt!

* * *

Feeling confused, I went back to the website with the original article and actually posted a comment, asking for a link to David Woolfe's video on salt. Amazingly, a day later, I got a response which said that the post was 18 months old now and that the website had made a mistake and accidentally put down David Woolfe's name in place of the 'genuine' David (David Klein PhD) who had made the claim that additional salt was actually non-beneficial. I was also informed that the article had now been corrected. The amazing thing about the whole episode to me was that as I had scanned down the article I had been attracted to David Woolfe's name, knowing him as a guru in the raw food world, so had read the whole thing rather than ignoring it. This is what I mean about magic happening!

* * *

There is no such thing as an accident and it was no accident that I read that article, so I resolved to be my own guinea pig and eliminate added salt from my diet totally. This I did on 12th June 2008. I decided that I would book an appointment with my General Practitioner (GP) a month later, discuss with her what I had been doing and request a full blood analysis. This I did and I have to say that she was very supportive and helpful.

* * *

The blood analysis was completed four weeks later and the results were totally amazing! My blood is perfect, totally perfect! For over a month I had eaten no additional salt, in any form. The only salt introduced into my body came from the natural fruits, seeds and vegetables that I was eating. During this same month I ate mainly fruit and salad. And here were the results of four weeks salt-free... perfect blood. I even checked out all the levels given in the data printout of my blood analysis against official statistics and mine was always perfect. Wow!

* * *

I also began to meditate and was blown away by the whole experience! Now, I have never really meditated before, well, I did go to a group a few times, where we all sat in a circle in a village hall, and were talked through a 'visionary' journey and then left to sort of drift off to 'wherever' on our own. Afterwards, we could share our experiences and it appeared that it worked for most of the others as they would talk of the wonderful 'visions' that they had, yet for me it just seemed to start a whole load of inane head chatter that wouldn't cease and I didn't really want to share it with anyone, not even myself.

* * *

Mostafa and I cleared out my daughter's old room and I found the frame of a garden recliner that my mother had given me years ago. Anne provided me with a spare duvet and cushion, which I laid over the plastic straps of the old frame, facing the window. I gathered together a few bits and pieces to make it more 'chilled,' along with a portable CD player left by my daughter. This room became Tibet and I loved it! The first time I decided to meditate was on my own and I didn't know what to expect. I thought, as I prepared suitable music, that I should try to remember the gist of the 'tale' from the group so long ago yet, as I tried to recall it, I got a clear 'knowing' that I should just relax and all would become clear to me.

* * *

It is quite difficult to express in words so much that happened that did not involve any actual words. I felt guided, knowing what to do rather than feeling, or hearing it said. I began to breathe, in a way I had never done before and, as I did so, I experienced tingles all over my body as if the breath was touching every single cell. My 'bot' mind began to have a conversation with 'they,' except that 'they' did not use words; it was just an amazing knowing that my 'bot' understood.

* * *

That first meditation was magical for me. After that it became a daily pleasure to go to Tibet and connect through meditation and I learnt so much about both individual parts of me, and my amazing connection to 'they', or the whole. At first, when I knew to breathe out and enter the stillness, I would worry that I might forget to breathe in again and one day in particular I learnt a valuable lesson about myself through this.

* * *

As I went through the deep breathing, I would feel a sense of trusting that the breath would come and, if I thought, 'it's been a while now, take a breath please' I would feel an overwhelming sense of reliance and belief and sure enough the breath would come. I also kept feeling a sense of letting go; that it was OK to trust this experience… that 'they' were guiding me and taking care of me.

* * *

At one point, on this particular day, it was as if I was operating a video camera, taking footage of familiar experiences from my past. At first the video seemed to move fairly fast and then it would slow down and fix on a particular event and I would experience again specific moments. These events spanned my life back to a time when I lived in Liverpool as a young child. At first none of it really made any sense. Then came an overwhelming feeling of never having trusted. This was followed by a sense of "not even trusting us to breathe for you, yet we do it all the time." The rest of the meditation was warm, relaxed and blissful. Anne was in Tibet with me on this day and we shared our experiences, during which it became blatantly obvious what was being conveyed. Anne and I share books and she had just given me a wonderful book to read called 'The Divine Matrix' (Greg Braden).

* * *

After we had finished discussing various things, I decided to read a couple of pages of this book and the first line I read was about mirroring and trust. I read out the passage to Anne and said, "For all these years I thought I trusted people, but I now realise that I haven't. All those images I saw were times when I have said that I have trusted, but you know what, I really didn't. I put that 'mirror' up and it was reflected back to me; I was actually attracting distrust. 'They' made me aware that in reality I didn't even trust myself to breathe so, if I didn't trust myself to do that, how could I possibly trust anyone else?"

* * *

My meditations are so enlightening and I learn so much, not just during them but also often in synchronistic moments that would occur afterwards. I became aware of all the 'labels' that I still adorn my body with and, in one very visual meditation, it was as if my body was just covered in them, so many in fact that some obscured the words of others. I can remember thinking, "Surely that cannot be me" and before I had even really had the thought, I had a knowing sense that it was. I realised that in some kind of perverse way that I really didn't know myself too well at all. I would find myself asking, "Who am I?" and would look at my reflection in the mirror and say, "Hello Rose," as if greeting a long lost friend. Sometimes, I did not recognise the face looking back at me. I had changed and you could see it in my smile, hair, shape, skin, and eyes! Then, due to my new body shape, my clothes were also quite different, so all in all it was quite a bizarre period for me.

* * *

In a strange way, the world had changed, too. So many once important things seemed incredibly unimportant and so many other things, that previously I had barely noticed, came to the forefront of my awareness. Everything seemed to make sense, yet nothing made sense at all! By that I mean that once government's, double yellow lines, global warming, soya, fitness centres, car boot markets, money and a whole list of other things that had once made some kind of sense to me, now seemed rather irrelevant, yet, sunsets, energy, the sound of silence, a smile from a stranger and synchronicity made total sense.

* * *

My life was, and continues to be perfect in every moment and in every moment I can find perfection. My meditations were also changing and I began to go to a place that was yellow and once the yellow filled my mind's eye, it would begin to sway into a field of corn. From there the colours would change, like the merging colourful bands of a rainbow and while this was happening I would feel a presence and a knowing to 'come with us.' As I entered the world of physical stillness, I felt complete trust; trust in my body to breathe, in my heart to beat and in my blood to flow. No other world was of any importance. And I was free to go with them.

Through the colours I would catch glimpses of things, though what these were was of no importance, the experience was the essential thing; I had no labels to attach. Then 'clouds' would appear in a pale blue infinite sky and I was part of everything.

*   *   *

On a few occasions I would experience the formation of something, something 'hidden' yet revealing itself, like the structure of a place totally unknown to me. As soon as I attempted to identify what it was, it would disappear. In just accepting and experiencing, I could see, yet the moment I attempted to 'understand' I became blind. I am experience.

*   *   *

Processed and cooked food is preventing our unlimited potential to be. We are feeding it to our children and limiting them from being. It is a programme of conformity, where every single burger will taste exactly like the rest, no matter where you eat it in the world; that in itself is limiting. And as each burger corresponds to some exact 'standard,' when you eat it you too conform. We are limiting our child's amazing capacity for taste and restricting their experience of it to sameness. We are unknowingly putting their bodies into a constant battle with the food that they are eating; in the 1930s an experiment proved that when cooked food was eaten, the body released thousands of white blood cells into the digestive system, yet when raw food was consumed the white blood cells did not arrive in their masses. What are white blood cells for? They are our protectors, they keep us free of dis-ease and illness, they attack poisons before they jeopardise our systems. If these white blood cells are constantly protecting us from cooked and processed foods, it follows that they cannot also be taking care of other bodily assaults. Could this be the reason that so many of us are falling foul to infections, illness, skin complaints, headaches, and a whole long list of other ailments?

* * *

Raw food is amazing. In each food there are unique enzymes that aid its digestion, yet once the food is cooked, these are destroyed and our bodies have to divert our own naturally occurring enzymes to aid digestion. These are often taken from the liver, leaving it depleted. Our own enzymes do not match those of the food, so even proper digestion does not occur, leaving us with feelings of indigestion, stomach ache, heartburn, acid, constipation, colic and many other angsts.

Is this really what we want for ourselves and, more importantly, for our children?

* * *

We have the right to choose and we have the right to know and our children deserve nothing less than our full knowledge of what we are doing on their behalf. This coming generation will be the ones who carve the next and so on. We will be the ones on the receiving end of their care one day and if the world is full of young adults who are full of dis-ease, how on earth are they going to care for us? It is no good to sit back and opt out of responsibility for our lives, the lives of our children and our future. We owe it to ourselves at the very least, to throw off the labels and heal ourselves; it is our responsibility.

* * *

All of us are connected like individual drops of the same ocean and even the smallest ripple affects us all. We have to understand that we are letting the 'bots' run the show. Imagine it this way; if a robot is sent to Mars to gather samples, for our investigation here on earth, 'we' the people of earth are in control of how the robot behaves, even though it is so many miles away from us. We instruct it to pick up this rock or that particle and secure it for our perusal and knowledge. Now imagine that something 'gets into' the robot's system, so that instead of performing our requests, it just kind of spins round in circles or picks up bits that we don't require, we would say that the robot has malfunctioned and either we would attempt to track down what had occurred and repair it, or it would be left to carry out its pointless spinning until it eventually either crashed into something and smashed itself, or, it ran out of energy, or, we disconnected it from the main source. Our 'bots' are no different. We are here to be the physical experience of our greater self; we are the individual drops that make up the experience of the collective ocean.

* * *

Generations ago, something got into our systems and corrupted them. To my mind this something was added salt compounded by the cooking and processing of food. It is my belief that there never was a 'missing link.' It has been reported and scientifically proven by a dentist that the human face shape is evolving rapidly due to the food we now eat. Our faces are becoming more pointed and our jaws are no longer able to support the teeth that we once all produced. Many people are born without wisdom teeth ever appearing, children are undergoing dental surgery to have overcrowded mouths realigned by the removal of teeth and braces are part and parcel of growing up.

* * *

This is evolution occurring right in front of our eyes and it is taking place within a couple of generations. What if, once upon a time, we did all live as nature intended, in our own Garden of Eden? What if something cataclysmic occurred that changed our habitat and closed off huge sections of our environment through floods and droughts?

What if we had once lived in harmony with all the other plant-eating animals, sharing living space and food and then suddenly the whole surface of the planet altered so that not only did we have to migrate to other areas but, due to the event, the availability of food became scarce? Suddenly our companions would become our competitors and survival of the fittest would become the order of the day. Maybe humankind decided to take a leaf out of the book of nature itself; after all, we would be aware that some animals actually killed others from just existing alongside them. It may be possible that in the beginning we just 'killed off' some of the competition to ensure our own survival but what if we decided to mimic the carnivores that were not reliant on the ever-competitive supplies of fruit, leaves, seeds and roots?

*   *   *

The 'problem' with meat is that it has to be consumed rapidly before it becomes rancid or infested with all the other scavengers who rely upon it, such as flies, bacteria, etc. Also the carnivores are built to digest meat and have powerful jaws and digestive tracts that match the food they are preying upon. They can break through the largest bones and dissolve them internally. Maybe it was noticed that when the meat had been pulled off the carcass and left to dry out in the sun that it became easier to digest and possibly someone had the bright idea of actually speeding up that process by heating it artificially, especially if there had been a change in climate and winter had become an extremely competitive time for the plant eaters. Why not supplement our natural diets with some cooked meats? This would also be quite 'social' with groups gathering together around warm fires to await the spit roasted wild boar as it cooked.

*   *   *

It is also possible that during the catastrophic event that seas and lakes dried up, leaving huge salt deposits and maybe our ancestors came upon animals that were preserved in these salt basins and were still edible, bringing about the introduction of salt as a preservative. This could have introduced salt into our feeding system as an added component rather than a naturally occurring part of the food. The thing with salt is that we cannot store it in our bodies so we have to excrete the excess. Could this be the reason why we began to lose our bodily hair and to sweat?

* * *

We are the only animal that sweats, apart from horses, and they only do so when humans push them to absolute extremes and what do we give the horses that we push beyond their natural limits? Why, a salt lick. Maybe the salt overwhelmed our system and so we evolved to accommodate it for our very survival. Interestingly, the brow is the only part of our body that excretes sweat for all reasons, thermal, mental and emotional.

* * *

What if we once made full use of both sides of our brain and in fact, rather than being reliant on our five senses and language as a means of communication, we used other senses located in the right hemisphere to exist with each other and nature?

* * *

We already have proof that when cooked food enters our body there are no enzymes left in the food to process it, so we have to divert our own away from the task they are instinctively there to do. We also know that white blood cells are redirected from their normal protective opus to aid the digestion process. So let's take this one step further; imagine that you are walking to the North Pole and you do not have adequate protection from the cold. The body needs to survive, that is its purpose, and it is aware that the major internal organs need the most protection to ensure continued existence. The body would divert all its energy into protecting these organs, even if it meant sacrificing a toe here or a finger there or maybe even a bit of nose or ear. In doing so it safeguards its existence, even if its continuation is more limited. It would naturally know that to lose a finger is not life-threatening but to lose the liver or heart means death.

*   *   *

So, in cooking food maybe we began the process of deactivating the right hemisphere of the brain and became more reliant on the left hemisphere's more linear capabilities. Then came the adding of salt, which we should remember my blood tests proved is not necessary – for my survival, at least.

*   *   *

What if salt actually prevents the pineal or thyroid gland from operating effectively and in doing so has made the 'bot' malfunction? The pineal gland is right in the centre of our brains and has the resemblance of a pinecone. The pineal gland also contains rods and cones, exactly the same as in the eye, so why are they there? Interestingly, the pinecone is reflected is so many religions and cultures, including Egyptian, and the Pope even has one on his staff. Hieroglyphics also show pinecones and it was the Egyptians who first made bread (cooked and prepared with salt). Hieroglyphics were pictorial; they were not labels, rather images recorded for all to view. This evolved into the written letters of labels, so maybe it is at this point in evolution that the complete malfunction of the 'bot' occurred and existence took a more linear swing. Or more probably, the eating of cooked food brought with it a different kind of existence, socialisation, where people no longer foraged in small groups, eating as they went about their individual search for sustenance, relying more on instincts than language. Seasons would also have become of much greater importance as the preserving of food ensured survival during winters when competition was at its height. People would group together to eat and language, rather than instincts impaired by cooking and adding of salt, would have developed the beginnings of a linear existence. The 'bot' actually believes that it is in control, as it no longer has to bow to the connection of 'all that is' – the right hemisphere, as it has been 'switched off', a bit like the robot on Mars; Houston we have lost contact!

* * *

I do have my ideas on this subject and believe that it is possible for us as a race to reclaim our very reason for being here, to experience physical life and comprehend just how magnificent this ocean is that each one of us is part of. Our 'bots' *belief* that they are in control may have begun slowly but now, many generations later, we have invented and totally believe in a linear, left hemisphere model of reality. Could this have been the time referred to in the bible when it speaks of Babel and of Lot's wife turning to a pillar of salt!

* * *

Our 'bots' have relied on language and created 'time' to survive and each believes he or she is a human being. Yet being is the last thing we actually do! We create separateness, an individual, each defined by labels and we essentially believe that these labels are who we are. It is only when the 'bots' go to sleep, or are not present (through day dreaming, mediation etc) that our being can actually express itself.

* * *

This book did not begin as a journey; it began to raise awareness of limitations and as a way of understanding the controls that exist in our societies. I have decided to leave it as an unfolding journey of awareness, even if only my own. For generations now we have let the 'bots' make a total mess of this incredible universe; a universe that is a physical expression of our collective brilliance, or in other words we have let the lunatics take over the asylum that we have created from Eden. Our brilliance has been side tracked into manifesting the most devastating separations whether they are labels, limitations, religions, education, war, deforestation and potential for nuclear annihilation. The 'bots' that we believe are acting in our best interests, our leaders, are no different from that crazy robot on Mars spinning round in circles until ultimately it ceases to exist. And rather than accept that maybe there is a problem with the robot, we just replace it with something exactly the same.

* * *

We do not have to live like this. This life is, primarily, your responsibility yet each of us has a greater joint duty to the whole. In being separate, we focus on the 'I, me, mine'; we cannot see what we are, nor even begin to understand the vastness of our collective magnificence. The wonderful reality is this; the snowball effect that we talked about at the beginning of this rant is a universal consequence and as one of us begins to embark on the road to enlightenment and being, the effect is accumulative.

* * *

It is my belief that the food we eat is programming us; depleting our bodies by forcing our systems to do tasks they were never meant to perform. We are all time bombs waiting for the body to become devastated by one disease or another, heart disease, cancer, depression, Alzheimer's, diabetes, obesity and a whole long list of others; take your pick, or should I say, let the food do it for you! Would any parent knowingly limit their child's potential? Would any parent want to cause their child suffering and pain? Would you ever inject someone you love with poison? Well, that is exactly what we are doing.

* * *

Apathy follows ignorance around like a faithful hound and sometimes it is easier to just blank out the truth, yet "the truth shall set you free," and not just you. We are all connected. We can free ourselves and in doing so we liberate others until, like the ocean, we once again become whole.

The Bit Where I...
Cease Ranting

Writing this book has been an incredible journey for me personally. As I re-read it I can see how, within the space of a single year, I have grown. My whole voyage through *this* life has been the most astonishing, miraculous and precious of all expeditions, for it has brought me to where I am now and there is nowhere else on earth that I would rather be than living my life right here, right now.

* * *

My life has been full of the greatest *teachers* on earth and possibly even, off earth. For most of my life I did not even know them to be teachers, as teachers to me were graduates awarded a certificate to instruct others; a label dangled from the necks of only specifically qualified individuals. How wrong could I be? Every single person I have encountered along the way has been my teacher. Every human, animal, plant, seed, insect, cloud, sound, taste, sight, smell and, most importantly, feeling has been my tutor and this magnificent planet, labelled Earth, is both the greatest teacher of all and the most wondrous classroom that any student could ever wish for.

* * *

Life is the greatest 'game show' ever and each of us *is* both a member of the team and a contestant in our own right. To win, and win we shall, is to work together to solve the puzzle and the quandary is, how to create heaven here on earth. Does that appear to be an impossible task? How can it be impossible? We have all the answers right here, right now. We have access to the greatest books written, all full of clues to direct us on our quest. We have admittance to the greatest minds containing unimaginable wisdom that can find solutions for what we might *believe* is the impossible. We are surrounded by nature that combined with astounding technologies, guides us to new methods of *seeing the infinite possibilities* of re-creating Eden.

* * *

Like any game there has to be an element of chance, to receive the 'get out of jail free,' pay a 'parking fine' or even a 'visit the dentist, pay £20' cards. But when we engage in the game, every time we pick up those dice and roll them, we are enabling ourselves to move forward *even if* some of the dice rolls *appear* to be moving us backward.

* * *

Allow me let you into a little secret! There is no such thing as backward; everything is moving you towards the winning post. I have realised two of the most important 'keys' to winning this game and creating heaven on earth. These keys do not open chests that are full of gold coins, diamonds and endless precious gems, nor do they open chests full of status, false power and ego. These keys appear to be invisible, yet they are presented to us at every given opportunity, in the form of a thought. This thought is the combined wisdom of all that has ever been and whether we choose to *listen* to it, or not, will always be a personal choice.

* * *

Any team is made up of individual players and the fate of the whole, lies within each one. We are the drops of water that experience ourselves as the collective ocean, the most powerful force on the planet. The ocean is the life force of earth and each of us a single drop within. The ocean is affected by everything that touches it and can generate itself into a tsunami with the ability to destroy all in its path, it can form itself into ice-bergs and rip through steel as if it was a mere piece of tissue or, it can provide tranquilities and safe passage to our destination.

* * *

When you play a team game you participate, whether on the field or off. Imagine life to be a game of football. Do you just think 22 players play the game on the pitch? No, that would be an insult to 'the beautiful game.' Imagine if just 22 people walked out into the stadium to play, with no referees, no linesmen, no managers, coaches or substitutes. I am sure that the players might enjoy the game but if you were to ask them, "What would be the perfect game for you?" I am sure that most would answer, "To be on the winning side in a World Cup Final!"

* * *

Why would that game be any different to being on the winning side of a game played with friends in the local park? Because most of the people on the planet are in some way involved and contribute to the whole atmosphere of triumph, of being on the winning side of the World Cup final. And if you were on that team and fouled another player and were shown a yellow card, would it dissolve the sweet taste of triumph, when the final whistle was blown? No, you would still share the glory of winning. And if you were a spectator, one of the crowds, would you feel any less triumphant than the players themselves? No, you would be jubilant that your team won and might even be aware that your belief in them charged them with the energy to win and defeat the opponent.

*   *   *

Whether you believe it or not, every single one of us contributes to the winning. Even the guy in the crowd who shouts the abuse at the player on the pitch, eliciting a reaction from that player and getting him 'sent off' enables the team to change tactic whilst still holding on to hope. And that change in tactic may be the gift that wrong foots the opponents to enable us to score. As they say in many of the commentaries, "It ain't over till the final whistle blows."

*   *   *

There are two important keys to being on the winning team. The first key is forgiveness. Each of us really has to have an understanding of exactly what forgiveness means. It does not denote feelings of superiority over those we deem to have 'hurt' us. It does not mean saying, "It's OK" when someone comes to confess his or her perceived guilt at any action that they believe caused us pain. It is an understanding that we can only ever really hurt our self; it is the action of forgiving ourselves and in so doing we forgive others.

*   *   *

Something that happens in a moment does not have to last a lifetime. We were born to evolve, to grow. How can that happen if we try to remain the same by holding onto our pain and dragging it like a huge suitcase behind us on our journey? How can we climb a mountain or swim to the depths of the ocean when we are lugging a trunk full of weighty misery on our backs? Every single step of your journey has brought you to this place right now and in this moment you have the choice to let go of the baggage and run free. You have the choice… isn't that amazing!

*   *   *

In not forgiving ourselves, we become stagnant. We live in dark water where we can hardly see through the murk at the potential that lies close by, offering with it the chance for the flow of life to become charged. Who are we to forgive others? Are we so perfect that we are free of any blame? I think not. And as it is an impossibility to give and receive love when you do not love yourself, it is also impossible to forgive until you have forgiven yourself.

*   *   *

Each and every day should begin with forgiveness of the self. I have forgiven myself for being the little girl in the field with secret 'uncle'. I have forgiven myself for being the child who never learnt, the teenager who got pregnant, the mother who wasn't quite good enough, the partner who saw only her own side of the story, the person covered in labels that identified with each, the friend who got it wrong and the one who thought they were always right.

*   *   *

We can only ever truly forgive someone if we truly know what it is that we are forgiving. Life is not something that happens to us. We are all participating in our individual existence and contribute to everything. An argument takes two people and sometimes even when we know we are right, in the same instant we should also know that we are wrong. In blaming others we give our power of choice away and become engaged in nothing more than a battle of egos. This game of life is so much more than that. Will it matter in a hundred years time whether they were right and you were wrong? No. Will it matter in a hundred years whether we create Eden here on earth? I think so.

*   *   *

Jesus was right when he said, "Father forgive them for they know not what they do."

For most of us don't really know what we are doing. We chase the unimportant, haul the unworthy, covet the insignificant and miss the most important gift of all, the moment. In each moment you have infinite possibility. You don't have to argue, you don't have to shout, cry, despair, fear or hate. You don't have to wear the label. You choose these feelings and emotions, no one else. If that is so, then forgiveness begins and ends with the self.

* * *

The second key is awareness and through this door you will realise just how absolutely certain victory is. You hold the power right inside you to create the perfect pass, score the winning goal and join in with the victorious cheer. You need to raise your own awareness of exactly what you are putting into your body as well as how you are labelling it and then absolve yourself. You have been programmed to behave in this way over generations; it was not your fault. Let it go. Once you begin to forgive yourself you suddenly become free. The stagnant pool becomes part of the ocean once more and adds its energy to increase the overwhelming might of life force.

* * *

Freedom means not having to drag those trunks full of trauma behind you, using vital energy to pull them along. Freedom brings you awareness, as your thoughts no longer remain trapped inside a case of 'hurts,' as through self-forgiveness all hurt is removed and the self can become aware of the real purpose of life. Clues are noticed and synchronicities abound that make magic appear before your very eyes. At first, you may confuse these with the labels known as 'coincidence', or 'accidents', until the awareness arouses within and you realise that there are no accidents, you are in fact the magician. It is like having an endless rainbow full of wishes and as awareness increases, you know that for heaven to be on earth it needs to reside within you. It is not for me, or anyone else for that matter, to tell you what to believe, as we have already discussed truth is a personal thing. I have spent time, for my own benefit and understanding of what I believe to be truth, in researching and questioning in order to gain insight, but in doing so I realise that everyone's truth is their own, therefore what I have sought answers to is somebody else's truth; it is an opinion of what truth is. However, in listening to the truth as others perceive it we have choice and that offers at least awareness that there are other possibilities and explanations; we don't have to keep doing the same old, same old just because we believe we have to. I am a madwoman who has realised that awareness is the path to heaven and self-forgiveness the chariot to carry you there.

*   *   *   *   *

Lightning Source UK Ltd.
Milton Keynes UK
09 November 2010

162606UK00002B/21/P